# BEST SERMONS

*EDITED BY GEORGE PAUL BUTLER*

# BEST
# SERMONS

## 1947-1948 EDITION

*Essay Index Reprint Series*

BOOKS FOR LIBRARIES PRESS
FREEPORT, NEW YORK

INTERNATIONAL STANDARD BOOK NUMBER:
0-8369-2487-8


LIBRARY OF CONGRESS CATALOG CARD NUMBER:
74-134065


PRINTED IN THE UNITED STATES OF AMERICA
BY
NEW WORLD BOOK MANUFACTURING CO., INC.
HALLANDALE, FLORIDA 33009

To
JEREMIAH MILBANK
who quietly helps
to bring in
the Kingdom of God

The 52 sermons in this volume have been selected from 6447 submitted to the editor for consideration.

A sincere attempt has been made to choose the sermons that represent the best sermonic efforts of the great churchmen of our day, as well as to discover and recognize unusual excellence in the sermons submitted by younger men who may be the great preachers of tomorrow.

All sermons have been selected for their homiletic value and their spiritual message for our time.

THE INCLUSION OF ANY SERMON IN THE VOLUME DOES NOT MEAN THAT THE AUTHOR OF THAT SERMON APPROVES OR AGREES WITH THE CONTENTS OF THE OTHER SERMONS OR WITH ANY SERMONS IN THE VOLUME. Each has been allowed to speak his own words in accordance with the faith of his own church or denomination. No sermon criticizing any other religion by word or inference has been included.

*Best Sermons* is intended as an anthology, not a book of theology.

# CONTENTS

[ ix ]

[x]

[ xi ]

# FOREWORD

## PREACHING IN AN AGE OF DISILLUSIONMENT

*by*

HENRY SLOANE COFFIN, D.D.

*President Emeritus, Union Theological Seminary, New York
and a Minister of the Presbyterian Church*[1]

IN A TIME when the minds and hearts of men everywhere are constantly faced with frustration and disappointment the Gospel is the good news of God's loving purpose for mankind. It is this Gospel that the preacher brings to a disillusioned world in our day, and it is his task to make possible communion between God and man. The Spirit may speak to men through their own thought and feeling, but the preacher is the instrument under God to impart His mind to them. The most momentous event in human relations is "that the living God should speak to and have fellowship with a company of his people."

The Gospel is good news of what God has done for us, and of what he gives us. Worship is adoration, offering and communion. A sermon must help men to understand the mystery of God and His love, must help them to adore Him, to offer themselves to Him, and to commune with Him. Sermons must provide a meeting place for God with men. Some do not. They may be instructive; they may be enlightening diagnoses of the times and of men's current moods; they may give good counsel on the conduct of life; they may be moving appeals to personal and social righteousness. But they stop short of supplying means for God's personal fellowship with men.

The truth with which a sermon deals is never impersonal. It is not a proposition or a principle: Christian preaching is "truth as it is in Jesus." No sermon fulfills its purpose unless it supplies a personal encounter with God in Christ. It may start with an Old Testament text; it may have applications to such psychological problems as handling one's worries and mastering one's fears, or to such social questions as decent housing or race relations; but it must bring these questions at length into the presence of

[1] Parts of this Foreword are from *The Public Worship of God* by Henry Sloane Coffin, published by The Westminster Press, 1946, and used by their kind permission.

God as He is fully revealed in Jesus, and let His listeners confront Him, the Wisdom and Power for life, without whom problems personal and social remain insoluble.

In both sermon and sacrament God is personally present and giving Himself to those who will receive Him in faith. In a sermon He is suffused with the personality of the preacher and brought home with the force of His conviction. Its message comes from God in that it rises out of His historic self-revelation recorded in the Scriptures. It comes from Him more immediately in that it has laid hold of and is spoken through the mind, soul and voice of a living ambassador. And in preacher and message God himself faces a congregation and speaks. "As though God did beseech you by us: we pray you in Christ's stead, be ye reconciled to God." We believe in the real presence of God in Christ in the ministry of the Word.

A sermon claims the offering of the whole selves of its hearers to God. It is truth appealing to and enlisting their intelligence. True, some preaching is too exclusively an appeal to reason, but much more, particularly in our contemporary church services, is intellectually negligible. It neither stimulates nor satisfies the intelligence of its listeners. Men listen to a speaker on the discoveries of science because they are confident that he is trying to be accurate and is communicating truth. Middleton Murry justly complains of preachers who are a combination of "unction and woolliness." We have all suffered from some, like Dickens' Mr. Plornish, "a little obscure but conscientiously emphatic." A primary duty of a preacher is to think thoroughly and clearly the message he is bringing.

Horace Bushnell insisted that "there cannot be much preaching worthy of the name where there is no thinking. Preaching is nothing but the bursting out of light, which has first burst in or up from where God is, among the soul's foundations." The sermon ought to be an opportunity for the offering of minds to God.

But a sermon, as has been said, is never the presentation of abstract truth, but of truth personalized in Christ, and again personalized in the message and presence of his ambassador. Phillips Brooks, who defined preaching as "truth through personality," spoke with admiration of a sermon to which he had listened from the British novelist and poet George MacDonald. In one of his novels, *The Marquis of Lossie*, MacDonald describes the preaching of a schoolmaster,

> To those who understood, it was as if he would force his way through every stockade of prejudice, ditch of habit, rampart of indifference, moat of sin, wall of stupidity, and curtain of ignorance, until he stood face to face with the conscience of his hearers.

Preaching is the appeal of a man's entire self—mind, imagination, heart, conscience—to the entire selves of his listeners. Browning's Canon Caponsacchi had a preacher's spirit when he spoke of himself as prepared to "burn my soul out in showing you the truth." Only so could he become a transmitter, and as Pompilia found, "flash the word God gave him back to men."

A sermon has to kindle the imagination. Men feel intensely only what they *see* as well as hear. Preachers have to turn ears into eyes. A sermon has to get down deeper into the mind than thought. Someone described preaching as "truth carried into the heart by passion." Above all it has to grip the conscience. The difference between a sermon and other public speeches lies in its aim at an immediate commitment of hearers to God. Preaching does not achieve its goal until, with conscience penetrated, listeners say to themselves, "I must."

We must win individual souls, but we must also win men and women of every race and land until all the world and every realm is brought under God. There is a consecration of the soil so that agriculture assumes its sanctity as the supply of daily bread for the whole family of our Father, of the sources of power for industry and its machines that "holiness unto the Lord" may be upon our vast organization for production, of our schools and colleges that the curse of secularism may be taken from our education and gains of knowledge be dedicated to the service of a spiritual commonwealth. Preachers must develop in congregations the imagination and conscience to attempt to make actual what they sing in Ellerton's hymn:

> Thine is the loom, the forge, the mart,
> The wealth of land and sea,
> The worlds of science and of art,
> Revealed and ruled by Thee.

Such sermons are most potent means of worship, moving men to offer themselves, with the all-embracing community to which they belong, a living sacrifice unto God.

Far too much current preaching is moralistic. It is exhortation to *do* or to *be* something. The Good News is not primarily a summons to effort. That way lies despair. The Gospel is the announcement of an unspeakable Gift whom men are to receive: "Behold, I stand at the door, and knock." Preaching is the means—God comes in the spoken word, and the response desired is not agreement with the preacher's ideas, but an opening of the soul to Him, who, however faultily, is presented. The Gospel is always an invitation to comradeship: "Come unto me." "I will come in to him, and will sup with him, and he with me." Through sacrament and through sermon it is Christ himself who comes to us.

After a rich experience in his own life, Thomas Chalmers preached the free offer of salvation through Christ. W. Hanna reports in his *Memoirs of the Life and Writings of Dr. Chalmers*, one of his hearers saying:

> He would bend over the pulpit, and press us to take the gift as if he held it at that very moment in his hand, and would not be satisfied till every one of us had got possession of it.

[ *xv* ]

So to offer God in Christ in a sermon is akin to showing forth His grace in the broken bread and the outpoured wine, and to minister Him, the living and present Saviour and Lord. Such preaching brings God to men, and men to God.

# INTRODUCTION

## PREACHING: AN EXPERIENCE OF THE SPIRIT

"Go thou and preach the Kingdom of God."  LUKE 9:60

PREACHING has justified itself over the centuries as the most effective means of reaching great groups of people with the Gospel. In the hands— or more exactly—in the minds and hearts and mouths of the Augustines, Pauls, Peters, Wesleys, and Jonathan Edwardses, men have been drawn to church or mission or revival and have been soundly converted and have consecrated or reconsecrated themselves to God and His Kingdom on earth.

It is the preacher who molds the spiritual life of the nation and it is to the preacher the world today looks for leadership in faith and the brotherhood of man. The last six years have afforded me the privilege of reading 18,327 sermons for these first three volumes of *Best Sermons* to select 52 for each volume, 156 in all, from over thirty countries in twelve foreign languages. As I read these sermons I was encouraged to see the quality and strength of the preaching being done in the Church in our day. One could see clearly and firmly that the clergy believe what they preach and preach with deep conviction.

There is hope and faith in current preaching. Pessimism and cynicism stalk men in some quarters, but not in the sermons sent for consideration for this volume. Truly, prophecy is not dead! Conservative preachers, liberals, and men who take a middle position in theology have all presented their messages with great sincerity and all have been given the opportunity to have their sermon included in this volume as they delivered it. The clergy are not mere dabblers, but men of force and courage and insight—and the Church still has the capacity for leadership both in crises and in normal times. The drama of God and man and good and evil is still the greatest theme in all the world. How often ministers turn to Phillips Brooks for their own personal inspiration!

Most of the preachers whose sermons are included are in the active pastorate where they preach week after week to their own congregations. A few are theological professors whose own preaching and work in training young men to preach have won them wide recognition; and there are sermons by several relatively unknown men, one by a man in his first parish. It has been good to find confirmation of the fact that our ministers, priests, and rabbis are not afraid to talk of sin, selfishness, and salvation, to see that they point out specific sins as well as general sinning and show the way to a redeemed self and a new world under God.

In the sermons, poetry, history, philosophy, literature, and sociology are all laid under tribute to the cause of homiletics. The sermons themselves are on the Church, prayer, God, Christ, immortality—and other similar topics to inspire men to greater faith. It is encouraging to discover how much most men use the Bible itself in preparing, writing, and delivering their sermons. The city of God is brought nearer to man by such sermons.

Words are the means of conveying the minister's message, the tools of the well-trained mind, and the use of the right word at the right time can greatly increase preaching ability. Much of a sermon is directly connected with the minister's delivery—his personality, his voice, his gestures—and consequently something is lost in writing, yet sermons by many pulpit masters are in such an excellent combination of the oral and written style that *the sermon is basically preserved* as it was given. Therefore, ministers in small churches who wish to improve their preaching have always studied the sermons of the great preachers and work to enlarge their preaching vocabulary and to develop their own style.

The preacher, Father Murphy says in his book for the Catholic clergy, is an "agent of Christian thought," and "an instrument of God."[1] while Dr. Coffin says "worshipful preaching . . . confronts men with the living God . . . to 'bring' man to fellowship with God."[2] In discussing the improvement of preaching, Gerald Kennedy, one of the growing young preachers of our day, recently wrote, "As a part of the preacher's discipline, it is a good thing to write . . . not for manuscript preaching" but "to save us from carelessness" and for "a more careful choice of expression."[3]

If the Church is ever to grasp its opportunity for spiritual leadership in the world, now is the time. The spiritual and materialistic forces are engaged in a more far reaching struggle than ever before in the history of the world. All too often the forces of evil seem to rout the timid forces within a man or a nation when temptation comes in public or private life. If men are to win in the lifelong struggle for their souls, they must have a rebirth of the spiritual elements in their lives so that they have the power to rise above evil. War, crime, prostitution, stealing are all the results, not the causes, of sin in millions of hearts everywhere; sin destroys—divine love creates and recreates. Men everywhere must find their souls if peace is to come or endure in individual hearts. The spiritual leaders of the world must lead the way in personal religious living, in education, in business, in politics, and in international affairs. While the Church is not a specialist in international law, it is a specialist in the interpretation of the spiritual life and it must point the way to eternal principles for the guidance of people everywhere.

[1] *A Priest Must Preach*, Rev. Thomas Regis Murphy, pp. xi, 1.
[2] *The Public Worship of God*, Henry Sloane Coffin, p. 135.
[3] *His Word Through Preaching*, Gerald Kennedy, p. 15.

And if any "power" in the world is to bring peace in our time it must be religion with its doctrine of brotherly love and the Fatherhood of God for all mankind. Millions of people want peace. Even Germany and Japan are ready to cry out *"Nie wieder Krieg."* Men who have recently returned from Russia are convinced that the Russian people do not want another war. Yet we still fear and distrust Russia—probably because of the distrustful diplomacy she has manifested through her representatives at the United Nations and in Washington. Pope Pius XII has worked indefatigably for the cause of peace. The Church Peace Mission, composed of great leaders of the Protestant church, has given much time and effort to winning the peace for everyone. But so far power politics seems to have made real peace almost as nebulous as it was during the war. Yet to read Pere Riquet's sermon on the ruin wrought by war is enough to make us leave off killing and destruction generation after generation.

It is my fervent hope and prayer that reading, studying, and meditating on these sermons will bring new light to laymen and clergy alike, but more especially that it will inspire a new, fresh stream of thought that will find its way into sermons of such power and conviction that a new day for the world may dawn. No minister should ever do less than his best in the pulpit. "Preaching exists, not for the propagating of views, opinions and ideals, but for the proclamation of the mighty acts of God, . . . and it is this that will always give preaching a basic and essential place."[4]

For the next volume, I should like all clergymen everywhere to feel that their sermons are welcome for consideration. Manuscripts may be submitted in care of the publisher, or sent directly to me. I am especially anxious to give new men a chance to be represented and urge such men to send me their very best sermonic work. Basically, of course, I am seeking the *best preaching by anyone anywhere.* I hope to find several more excellent evangelistic sermons and one or two on religious education, two highly important subjects today if we are to bring men to God and to train our children in the way of faith.

The miracle of God's unfailing love is still above human comprehension!

G. PAUL BUTLER

*New York and Fairlee Haven*
September 1, 1947

[4] *Heralds of God*, James S. Stewart, p. 5.

# ACKNOWLEDGMENTS

TO THE thousands of clergymen who so kindly sent me their sermons for consideration for inclusion in this third collection of *Best Sermons* I am happy to express my appreciation. To each of the 6,447 clergymen who gave me the privilege of reading their sermons I would like to say that I personally read every sermon manuscript myself, although the final selections were made with the advice of the members of my Advisory Committee.

It is impossible to praise too highly the wisdom, fairness, and judgment of the individual members of this Committee, Dr. Ralph W. Sockman, Dr. Paul E. Scherer, Dr. Joseph R. Sizoo, Dr. Adolph Keller, the Very Reverend Ignatius Smith, O.P., the Reverend Gerald G. Walsh, S.J., Dr. David DeSola Pool, Dr. Israel Bettan and Dr. Israel Goldstein. Each of these distinguished clergymen is himself a preacher of great ability. Without their help, the book would not have been possible in its broad scope and in its representative and ecumenical character.

Publishers have been most gracious in permitting quotations from their copyrighted volumes and I am glad to acknowledge such permissions from the following:

Abingdon-Cokesbury Press for the quotations from "When the Sun Was Risen," by James Allen Kestle, and *Take a Look at Yourself*, by John Homer Miller.

*Christian Century Pulpit* for the sermon by Elmer S. Freeman.

*Current Religious Thought* for the several sermons originally printed by them.

Harper & Brothers for "Christ Himself is Christianity," reprinted from *On Being Fit To Live With*, by Harry Emerson Fosdick; for the quotations from *Introduction to the New Testament*, by Robert H. Pfeiffer, and from *The Christian Faith*, by Nels F. S. Ferre.

Bruce Humphries, Inc. for "I Give Thee Thanks," from *Holy Flame*, by Georgia Harkness.

The Macmillan Company, New York, for the quotations from "The Trial of Jesus," by John Masefield, and "The Leaden Eyed," from *Collected Poems* by Vachel Lindsay.

Sheed & Ward, Inc., *Thought Magazine,* and Father R. F. Grady, S.J. for the translation of the sermon by Pere Riquet.

Simon & Schuster, Inc. for the quotation from *The Life of Greece*, by Will Durant.

The Westminster Press for the quotations from *The Age of Orthodoxy* and *The Divine Human Encounter*, by Emil Brunner, and *The Public Worship of God*, by Henry Sloane Coffin.

To Miss Elinor Inman of the Columbia Broadcasting System for her co-operation in helping me to find several excellent sermons given on the Church of the Air programs by Dr. David DeSola Pool and Dr. Oscar Blackwelder.

To His Eminence Francis Cardinal Spellman for special permission to use the poem quoted in my introductory note at the head of his sermon.

To Erwin Mueller, George W. Forell, and Erica Butler for special co-operation in translating sermons from the German by Dr. Martin Niemoeller, Dr. Karl Barth, and Dr. Emil Brunner; and for Father Grady's special permission to use his translation of Pere Riquet's sermon from the French in which it was preached.

To the many bookstores that helped by sending sermons or by recommending ministers, pastors and rabbis who should be invited to submit a sermon, I am anxious to express my gratitude.

To William Smith and the National Council of Catholic Men a special word of thanks is due.

I am especially grateful to the 158 important religious leaders in the nine European countries (where I went in my wide search for sermons) who so graciously received me and gave me their advice and co-operation in securing sermons or needed information about the Church and religious conditions in Europe today. His Holiness, Pope Pius XII, gave me one of the most unusual audiences on my entire European tour. It was also a rare privilege to confer with His Excellency The Most Reverend Monsignor G. B. Montini, Acting Secretary of State at the Vatican; Karl Barth took the time in the midst of his busy life to discuss the religious situation in Switzerland and in Germany; Clayton Williams' co-operation in France was of invaluable assistance in interpreting and in arranging conferences with French religious leaders; Dr. Adolph Keller took nearly a week in the midst of his busy life to arrange appointments in advance and to go with me to meet some of the important preachers of Switzerland; and to the many bishops, church officials, several cardinals, and a number of government officials who helped me in my wide search for sermons in England, Scotland, France, Switzerland, Holland, Luxembourg, Belgium, Italy, and Germany I wish to record my appreciation, even though they are too numerous to all be listed here.

# BEST SERMONS

# Christ Himself Is Christianity

REVEREND HARRY EMERSON FOSDICK, D.D., LL.D.

*Minister Emeritus, the Riverside Church, New York*

Dr. Fosdick is one of the great preachers of our time. Whenever he speaks churches are filled on Sundays or week nights. Born in Buffalo in 1878, his ancestry is typically American, a family of hard working people engaged in various trades and professions.

He was educated at Colgate University, Colgate Divinity School, Union Theological Seminary and Columbia University. In recognition of his achievements in the church and in education, Colgate, New York, Brown, Yale, Glasgow, Princeton, Boston, Ohio, Columbia, Michigan, Rochester and Harvard universities have conferred the honorary doctorate upon him.

Upon graduation from Union Theological Seminary in 1904, he was pastor of First Baptist Church in Montclair, New Jersey, for eleven years. During part of that time he was instructor in the Department of Practical Theology in Union Theological Seminary, and in 1915 became Morris K. Jesup Professor of Practical Theology, giving his major time to the Seminary and preaching each Sunday in one of the universities.

During the first World War he spoke throughout Great Britain under the British Ministry of Information and among American troops under the Y.M.C.A. in France. After the war his professorship in the Seminary was resumed and he became stated preacher at First Presbyterian Church, New York, January, 1919, which latter connection was severed on March 1, 1925. He has traveled widely in Egypt, Palestine, China, Japan, England and Scotland, speaking for important conferences in most of these countries.

In October, 1926, he assumed the pastorate of Park Avenue Baptist Church, New York, and some time afterward entered upon the building of the Riverside Church, now one of the most magnificent churches of the entire United States.

His twenty-two books have reached a vast audience and many of them have been translated into French, Danish, Norwegian, Swedish, Spanish, Portuguese, Chinese, Japanese, Hindustani, Arabic and Bulgarian. The Second Mile, The Manhood of the Master, The Meaning of Prayer, Twelve Tests of Character, The Modern Use of the Bible, On Being a Real Person, A Great Time To Be Alive, and On Being Fit To Live With, mark him as one of the great voices of our day.

"Christ Himself Is Christianity," is one of the greatest sermons in Dr.

*Fosdick's long and brilliant career. His emphasis upon Christ himself as Christianity strikes a note ministers and laymen will welcome and shows his grasp of the meaning of Christ in our world. His preaching has probably affected more men in American churches than any other preacher of our day.*

## Sermon One

### *Christ Himself Is Christianity*[1]

THIS Christmas season finds us a rather bewildered human race, facing a confused world, man's wild behavior dangerously out of control. No neat formula from anywhere can solve our problems or allay our anxiety, but today we turn to one man in the New Testament who lived in an age not unlike our own, and who carried on with hope and confidence. He wrote the letter to the Hebrews. In his time, too, the world was shaken. Within the confines of the Roman Empire nations, races, religions, economies had been poured into the artificial unity of one world before men were ready for one world. Confusion reigned, and as for his own people, only a few years before he wrote Jerusalem had been laid waste, the Holy Land desolate, its population slain or scattered. Over his world, too, man had not been able to establish intelligent, ethical control, and in that situation, as Dr. Moffatt translates it, he wrote in his second chapter: "As it is, we do not yet see all things controlled by man; what we do see is Jesus."

That text seems made for us this Christmas season. The writer was thinking of an old psalm—

> What is man, that thou art mindful of him?
> or the son of man, that thou carest for him?—

a psalm which describes God's purpose, crowning man at last with glory and honor and putting all things in subjection under his feet, establishing, that is, man's intelligent, ethical control over the world. Well, says this writer, we are a long way from that; we do not yet see all things controlled by man; but with that negative statement he does not stop. He adds the affirmative factor that for him changes the whole perspective of his outlook: "What we do see is Jesus."

In saying this the writer was not turning from realistic facts to a beautiful ideal; he was turning from one set of facts to another fact. Jesus, too, was a fact. He had actually come. That life had been lived. If we are to base

[1] A Christmas sermon. Reprinted from *On Being Fit to Live With*, by Harry Emerson Fosdick. Copyright, 1946, by Harper & Brothers. Used by special permission.

our lives on facts, must we not take that fact in too? As this writer saw him, Christ was a towering, challenging, revealing fact, and to see him changed his whole outlook on life. On the threshold of our Christmas season we try today to share that experience.

Let us start by saying that Jesus' coming was a prophetic fact. Once on all this planet there was just one form of life, one-celled creatures in the slime along the ocean's edge, but looking back on that so small beginning we see it now as a prophetic fact. Once there was the first emergence of what could be called a human mind, putting two and two together and drawing conclusions from premises, but dim as that dawning intelligence was, it was a prophetic fact. Once, about five thousand years before Christ, there first appeared on earth what could be called a social conscience, its earliest expressions still readable in Egypt's ancient literature, but hesitant and uncertain as that social conscience was, who can measure the significance of that prophetic fact? Once everybody thought the sun revolved about the earth, and then Copernicus came, and in one mind and those it influenced there dawned a new way of thinking, and that was a prophetic fact.

This is the way the world runs. Always the new beginnings to which the future belongs are born, as it were, in a manger, their prophetic import seen by none save three wise men, it may be, and a few shepherds. So in every generation, in some realm or other, there is always some Bethlehem in which amid the world's darkness a new light shines, with few to notice and fewer yet to believe, and yet there is the great prophetic fact of that generation and, it may be, of all future time.

Thus the writer to the Hebrews saw Jesus—not chiefly as a beautiful ideal. In Christ's coming he saw something tremendous happening in the world, the emergence of a prophetic fact that would outlast all the mighty things that withstood it. In this very paragraph where our text is found, the writer calls Jesus "the Pioneer" of our salvation. So to him too the world was wild, uncivilized, uncontrolled, but at least this much had happened—the trail blazer had come. Is not that the way everything worth while starts? Once there was no scientific medicine—but then Pasteur; once there was no competent nursing for the sick—but then, Florence Nightingale; once there was no religious liberty free from the State's regimentation—but then, Roger Williams. To all such cases at the start our text applied: we do not yet see all things brought under control. Far from it! But we do see the pioneer. At least he has come; the movement he represents has begun; that much has happened. Such confidence about Christ this Chrismas chiefly means to me.

In this congregation today there must be much hidden pessimism concerning the possibility of man's intelligent, ethical control over this world, and when the lovely stories of the Christ child are retold, in all the sentimental beauty with which Christmas clothes them, that may only make the stark realities seem starker yet. It takes more faith than I have, a man may say, to believe in the triumph of Christ's way of life in such a world. To which I answer: in all these cases we have just rehearsed, the crux of the matter was not simply faith, but intelligence and insight. It takes intelligence and insight to recognize, at first, Copernicus and Pasteur and Florence Nightingale and Roger Williams and all the rest for what they really are—prophetic facts to which the future belongs. For that I plead today in our thought of Christ. He is the Pioneer; he has begun a new way of life. All things brought under man's control we do not yet see but this much has happened—the trail blazer has arrived. That is something. "What we do see is Jesus."

Moreover the coming of Jesus was not only a prophetic but a momentously influential fact. We have been living through a generation when the determining influences in human history have been more and more defined in impersonal terms. Heredity, that settles everything; economic determinism, that settles everything—such has been the strong trend in our generation's thinking. You students at the University know how far this has gone, some saying that geography and climate account for almost all our human story; some, like the Marxians, that economic determinism is the explanation; some, like Veblen, that technical developments, such as machine industry, are the really determinative factors; and always the exponents of heredity saying that it is our genes that predestinate us all to be what we are. So, in a world discouraging enough already, this powerful emphasis on the impersonal factors predetermining our destiny has made personality seem a helpless by-product and mere victim of the impersonal.

And now Christmas comes again with its ringing announcement of a personality who splits history into B.C. and A.D. That message we critically need. There have been times when Christmas could be merely sweet.

> "The Christ Child stood at Mary's knee
> His hair was like a crown;
> And all the flowers looked up at him
> And all the stars looked down."

God grant us all a taste of that poetic, lovely side of Christmas in our homes this year! But the full meaning of Christ's coming goes far, far deeper. Into a world where all the deterministic factors men enlarge upon today were in full force and effect, a child was born under the humblest of conditions in a conquered province of the Roman Empire, and in some thirty years only, of which only a few months were spent in public ministry, had his chance to say his say and reveal his quality. And to multitudes he has changed the whole complexion of the world. There must be something to be said for the proposition that it is personality, too, that shapes the course of history. We cannot tell the story of music, or art, or science, or ethics, or philosophy, or religion, and leave creative personality out. The coming of a great person is the most influential event in history.

[4]

So, once more, our text comes true: "As it is, we do not yet see all things controlled by man; what we do see is Jesus." To be able to say that today, nearly two thousand years after Jesus' birth, is astounding. What chance had he to survive? Were not all the impersonal factors against him? And as for man, man tried hard enough to get rid of him. Herod tried it, slaughtering the innocents in Bethlehem. Pilate thought he had done it, on Calvary. And ever since, by every device that disbelief and wickedness can use, men have endeavored to be rid of him. But here he is still. This changing, shifting, wayward, brutal world can get rid of a lot of things—but not of a personality like that.

Early in this last war a member of the British Parliament in public debate exclaimed, "God help the British Empire if it must be defended by the ethics of the Sermon on the Mount!" One can easily understand his feeling that. But now the war has been fought, and modern war's true nature has been lighted up with such lurid horror as leaves the whole world stunned, and the atomic bomb has come, and today everyone with any sense is saying, God help the British Empire and all the rest of us if we go on with this process generation after generation! Ah, Christ of God, we cannot get rid of you. Whenever we seriously seek the world's salvation, we come back to you. You are not just a beautiful ideal; you are the most persistent, inescapable, and in the long run influential figure that ever entered human history.

Now let us bring what we have been saying closer home to our private lives. The coming of Jesus, more than a prophetic and influential fact in history, is a profoundly moving fact in personal experience. It is not abstractions but persons who most deeply influence us.

The organ in this church is dedicated to William Newton Clarke. When I was an undergraduate in college he was a professor in the graduate department in the university. I was having a perplexing time with my religion then. I had thrown almost all of it overboard. During my sophomore year wild horses could hardly have dragged me inside a church. I started out for my junior year telling my family that I was going to clear God out of the universe and begin all over to see what I could find. But there, walking across the campus, was William Newton Clarke. He knew more about modern thinking than I began to know; yet there he was, a Christian, an intelligent, forward-looking, intellectually honest Christian. His very presence seemed to say: Essential Christianity is not irreconcilable with modern knowledge; he who is afraid to face facts does not really believe in God; come, the truth shall make you free. I have had a grand time in the ministry these forty years and more, but I am sure it was not geography or climate, economic determinism or technological industry that put me there. It was a person— William Newton Clarke—who opened the door.

What is the most moving force in our experience as we sit here? People —some of them still with us, some of them passed into the unseen. What most helps us to keep straight when we dreadfully want to go crooked, or steady when we are tempted to crack up? The love, the example, the persuasiveness of some people. What is it that most of all would utterly wreck our lives? To have some people let us down. Not abstractions but persons most deeply determine our lives.

To be sure, this is more apparent in some realms than in others. Someone here may already have been thinking, Why cannot religion do in this regard what science does? Science makes no such fuss as religion does over its pioneering personalities; science abstracts the ideas of Darwin, uses the valid, discards the residue and moves on; but the pioneers themselves, while honored, play no such part in the thought of science as Christ plays in the adoration of Christianity. To which I answer, You are quite right; in this regard, there is a difference between science on one side, and, on the other, such realms as art, music, morals, love, religion. We can abstract the ideas of Darwin and forget Darwin himself. But, friends, we never can abstract the art of Toscanini from Toscanini; Toscanini's art *is* Toscanini. We never can abstract the lover's love from the lover, keeping it and forgetting him; the lover's love is the lover. We never can abstract the quality of Jesus from Jesus, and forget him; Jesus' quality is Jesus. Science may be made a realm of abstract propositions, but religion is a realm of personal, spiritual values which always must be incarnate to be seen and understood. If it is to be real, the word must become flesh and dwell among us. So William James when asked to define what he meant by the word "spirituality" hesitated, and then said he was not sure he could put into words what he thought spirituality meant, but he could point to a person who was it—Phillips Brooks.

Thus to the writer of the letter to the Hebrews Christ himself is Christianity. Ask him what the persistent, eternal factor in Christianity is, and he will offer no abstract theology in answer; he knows that theology is changeable; he says, "Jesus Christ . . . the same, yesterday, to-day, and for ever." Ask him what it means ethically to live a Christian life and he gives no abstract code of moral laws; he knows that moral customs alter; he says, "Consider the Apostle and High Priest of our confession, even Jesus; who was faithful to him that appointed him." Ask him where he finds the stimulus and power to carry on when the road is rough and his answer is, "Consider him that hath endured such gainsaying of sinners against himself, that ye wax not weary, fainting in your souls." Say to him that the world is going to the dogs, that mankind is stupid, brutal, uncivilized, incorrigible, and he says, True enough! "We do not yet see all things controlled by man; what we do see is Jesus."

Some kinds of Christianity I can get on very well without. What relevance have they to a man's problems, trying to live a strong and decent life in a time like this? But Christ himself—my soul! if he could get at us, live in us, shape our thought and our behavior by his spirit, that would make all the difference in the world.

[6]

The upshot of this matter comes close home to our present need. The coming of Jesus, prophetic, historically influential, personally moving, is a very reassuring fact too. Heaven knows we need reassurance! Reviewing this last war, we are appalled at the physical destructiveness involved. The hideous facts brought out in the Nuremberg trial, the hideous fact that even before the atomic bomb a hundred thousand civilians were burned to death in one night's raid on Tokyo, the fact that civilians killed by raids on Hamburg outnumber those slain in Hiroshima or Nagasaki—such facts are fearful in their prophecy of physical ruin, unless man changes his ways. But to those, too, who care about man's character quite as much as they care about man's body, the facts are frightening. Dr. Urey, one of our foremost atomic scientists, said this last week: "The morals of the human race have degenerated in an unbelievable way in the last five years. It is not to be expected that they would not further degenerate in a future war."

In all confused eras such as this, what does human nature do? It always looks, not so much for some thing as for some one to believe in. So Germany believed in Hitler and said, He is the answer! So Italy believed in Mussolini and said, He is the answer! We say that people believe in imperialism, nationalism, democracy, communism, and all the rest. Granted! We need not belittle the importance of these abstract beliefs. But we never get to the bottom of the matter until we see how inevitably we humans believe at last, not in isms but in incarnations. It is they who make abstractions real and powerful. Remember Marshal Foch's saying, "It was not an army that crossed the Alps; it was Hannibal."

Christmas means this at least: a personality has come into the world concerning whom millions believe that he is the answer. Even Paul never said, I know what I have believed. The mystery of life so deep, the confusion of the world so great, he sometimes did not know what he believed. What Paul said went deeper: "I know him whom I have believed." That is Christianity! I wish I could persuade someone here who never has accepted it, to accept it now. I am not inviting you to sign a theological creed on the dotted line. I am not inviting you to join a sectarian denomination, and subscribe to its peculiarities. I am inviting you to see Christ, his revelation of God, his basic principles, his way of life, his spirit and quality, and so seeing him, to say, He is the answer! Cannot we see whither the contrary answers are plunging the whole world now? He is the answer! That is the everlasting truth!

[7]

# A New Christendom

REVEREND GERALD GROVELAND WALSH, S.J., PH.D., S.T.D.

*Editor,* Thought Magazine, *Fordham University, New York*

*Although Father Gerald Walsh is less known as a preacher than as a scholar, teacher, editor and author, his diction, voice and personality will be remembered by all who have listened to his public lectures in New York, Boston, Buffalo, Rochester, Cincinnati, Baltimore and many other cities and by those who have heard him on such radio programs as* Invitation to Learning.

*Born in South Norwalk, Connecticut, he was sent for his primary education to Canada and for his secondary education to England. At the University of London he came out first in the B.A. examinations in Latin and Greek; at Oxford he won the Gibbs scholarship, the Marquis of Lothian prize and first class honors in the final examinations in the School of Modern History. After eight years devoted to the study of philosophy and theology he secured the double doctorate of the Gregorian University in Rome.*

*His teaching experience includes four years in England, five years at Woodstock College in Maryland, three years at the Gregorian University and ten years at Fordham University Graduate School. He has contributed many articles to scholarly reviews in England, Italy and America, and is the author of* The Emperor Charles IV, A Study in Holy Roman Imperialism, Medieval Humanism *and* Dante Alighieri, Citizen of Christendom. *He contributed the chapters on "Roman Catholicism" in* Faith for Today *and in* Great Religions of the Modern World. *He is a founding member of the conference on Science, Philosophy and Religion, and one of the editors of the projected seventy-two-volume translation of the Fathers of the Church. He took a large share in translating the first volume* The Apostolic Fathers.

*The sermon printed here was preached to an almost exclusively Protestant audience at the Woman's College of the University of North Carolina on December 9, 1946. It shows his understanding of youth today, faith, education and life and dramatically presents Christ as the key to life and faith and salvation.*

# Sermon Two

Text: And so the child grew and came to his strength, full of wisdom; and the grace of God rested upon him. . . . And after going up to Jerusalem, as the custom was . . . he went down . . . to Nazareth and lived there in subjection. . . . And so Jesus advanced in wisdom with the years, and in favor both with God and with men.   St. Luke 2:40-52 (Knox version)

THERE is a story in the Gospel of St. Luke so simple as to seem naïve. A boy was twelve. He lived in Nazareth. He went up to Jerusalem, according to an old tradition. He returned home. He lived in subjection to his parents; yet he advanced, he made progress in both wisdom and experience, and in favor with both God and men.

That is all. Yet notice the time and place. It was in the reign of Caesar Octavian Augustus, the founder of the Roman Empire; and in a province bounded on the one side by Mesopotamia and on the other by the Mediterranean. Four worlds met in this child of Nazareth: East and West; Antiquity and the Modern Age.

Notice, too, the key words of the story. They fit into pairs: tradition and progress; wisdom and experience; God and man. Notice, above all, that the young Christ holds these things together. He does not put them asunder. He stands, as we say today, for integration, not for disintegration. He does not divorce tomorrow from yesterday, the future from the past. He builds no wall between wisdom and experience, philosophy and science. He digs no chasm between God and men, between grace and charm, between religion and social relations.

Unlike certain of our contemporary social theorists, Jesus Christ did not think that the liquidation of the lessons of history is the condition for a better world. He did not hold—with some of our educators and men of affairs—that experimentalism and realism must take the place of ideals and human values. Least of all, did he think that religion is jealous of life, that the grace of God is an enemy of gracious living, that the "separation of Church and State" means the elimination of revelation and redemption and the silencing of prayer in our schools, our markets and our legislative halls.

It begins to look as though the child in the village in the ancient world has a message for the modern age. Perhaps he has a medicine that can heal the sores of our economic, political and cultural life. Let us see.

Three views of life and history have struggled in our generation for supremacy and universal acceptance. We have labeled them with names that deserved a better fortune. We call them "communism," "fascism" and "liberalism."

To what excellent uses the word "communism" might have been turned! It might have been used for the noble experiment of the first followers of Jesus Christ when "none of them called any of his possessions his own, everything was shared in common" (Acts 4:32). Or it might have been used for that miracle of community living we call monasticism. Or, at least, it might have been reserved for that ideal of the common good or general welfare that we like to link with our own democracy. It was not to be. "Communism," in the concrete, is the communism of Marxist ideologists. Communism has come to mean the ruthless plan of the Russian revolutionaries. It means the liquidation of the past in the interest of the future, the repudiation of tradition in the name of progress, the building of Utopia on the ruins of history.

The word "fascism" has fared no better. The *fasces*, the rods and ax that symbolize public order are proudly stamped on the coins of our American democracy. "Fascism" might have meant no more than loyalty to public law; but it means, in fact, the repudiation of principles, the scorn for wisdom, the elimination of philosophy. Particularly in its Prussian form, in the nazism of junkers and militarists, it has stood for economic experimentation and political efficiency at the price of human and moral values. It has meant the trampling on men in the name of machines. It has meant the denial of personal rights in the name of the omnipotent state. It has meant the sacrifice of both the common good and personal freedom to the moloch of a brutal "public order."

So it is with "liberalism." The word belongs, by right, to those among us who believe in the importance of personal liberty because we believe in the dignity and destiny of man. It belongs to those of us who have a philosophy of human free will and a religious hope in the reality of immortal life. But "liberalism," in the muddle and confusion of contemporary slogans, is a label for the rejection of religion. It means polite contempt for the divine graces of revelation and redemption. "Liberalism" has come to mean a veto on God, much as "communism" is a veto on property, and "fascism" on personality. Just as "fascism" has torn down the wall between law and tyranny, so "liberalism" has effaced the frontier between liberty and license. In the name of "self-expression" it has dignified degradation. In the name of "life" it has glorified lust. It has gilded sin and called it sanity.

These three views of life and history do not dwell in ivory towers. They had their roots, indeed, in the brains of professors. In a way you can find all three in Hegel. But as we meet these things today, the seeds of speculative materialism, positivism and atheism have taken on the monstrous size of historical realities. Marx has been swallowed up in the sprawling leviathan dominated by Moscow; Nietzsche, in the far-flung frontiers of a now (happily) defunct Grosz Deutschland; and Comte, in that world of opinion that takes its cue from French free thought.

And so it is that out of the heads of the philosophers and then out of the concrete policies and plans of Moscow, Berlin and Paris has come a deification of disintegration. The world is rapidly forgetting the child of Nazareth and his integration of history with progress, philosophy with efficiency, religion with social relations.

In this moment of crisis, more than ever before, there is a call on all Christians to come to the rescue of culture and civilization. We must tell the world of Christ's lesson in integration. We must steep our souls in the deep mysteries of our faith—the mystery of the union of two natures in the person of the Incarnate Word; the even deeper mystery of the Oneness of God in the Persons of Father, Son and Holy Spirit. To a world distraught by disunity yet seeking for some basis of world community we must recall the cry of St. Paul: "One Lord, one faith, one baptism, One God and Father of all, who is above all and through all and in us all." We must keep repeating Our Lord's gospel of integration: "What God has put together, let no man put asunder."

It is true that the full impact of Christian thought on a divided world will only be fully felt when Our Lord's prayer shall have been answered and there will be "one fold and one shepherd." But in the meantime, the moral, intellectual, political and economic disintegration of the world cannot wait. All Christians, all men who believe in God, all men who accept the unchanging values of truth and justice can find a program for common action. They can find in the imperishable traditions of Athens, Rome and Jerusalem a wisdom, experience and grace which they have sought in vain in the shifting plans and baseless propaganda of Moscow, Berlin and Paris.

Ancient Athens taught our Western world that there can be no veto on wisdom, truth, logic, first principles—except at the price of intellectual confusion. From the thousand years of Roman history we have learned that there can be no veto on the lessons of the years, on the tradition of law and justice—except at the price of political and economic chaos. From Jerusalem, from the revelation of divine law in the Old Testament and from the gospel of grace in the New, we should surely have learned that there can be no veto on God, on His Will for truth and justice and human dignity—except at the price of moral corruption and social sickness.

It is not as though our Western world had never tried to hold together the triple tradition of Athens, Rome and Jerusalem. Christendom, in fact, is the name given by historians to that noble experiment. It was an all too fleeting period. Nor did the temple of the medieval synthesis ever reach the roof or pinnacles. But the foundations were laid. The plans were prepared. There was a map of peace in all men's minds. There was the will for peace in most men's hearts. From Ireland to Italy and from Poland to Portugal, one world of Christendom wanted a reign of truth and justice, and was willing to pay the price of subjection to the sovereignty of God.

Christendom died, it may be, of a broken heart. In the sober language of history, it died of the disease of disintegration. Not that the ideal of Christendom is too good to be true; but the load of integrated living seems too heavy for unaided human shoulders. The modern centuries have preferred this or that part to the whole. The fourteenth bequeathed to us the initial heresies of the modern world—nominalism, or the notion that we can know reality without bothering about ideas; and nationalism, or the notion that we cannot love our country without hating the rest of the world. The fifteenth century gave us aestheticism and individualism—the vain hopes of finding beauty in isolation from goodness and truth and of defending individual rights in isolation from social duties. Even the splendid century of Luther and Loyola, Shakespeare and Cervantes was filled with the clashing ideals of humanism and puritanism, as though man could do without God, or religion renounce all human values. The seventeenth century strove for the conflicting extremes of legalism and libertinism, so that kings no longer drew the line between law and tyranny and commoners were content to forget the difference between liberty and license. The century of Voltaire and Rousseau began in rationalism and ended in romanticism. It turned restlessly from reason without revelation to emotion without reason, and failed to reconcile the claims of the head and the heart. The following century rallied to the slogans of scientism and socialism. On the one hand, it wanted its material facts in a spiritual vacuum; and, on the other, it drowned the rights of individuals in an ocean of social duties. Our own century has given us communism, fascism and liberalism.

No wonder that men are turning wistfully to the integration of a vanished Christendom. They want, of course, a New Christendom—not the old one. That belongs to the past; and the past, like fallen leaves, is meant to nourish new life, not to renew its own.

In this New Christendom, men will try to hold together those ideals of common good, public order, personal liberty which communism, fascism and liberalism have torn asunder. Men will stop pottering about with plans—however seemingly "efficient"—until they have defined the human purpose of a world society and have accepted the principles that alone can make this purpose valid.

In this task of building a New Christendom we shall need the lesson in integration taught us by Jesus of Nazareth. We shall need to remember his wholeness and holiness, his synthesis of tradition and progress, wisdom and experience, grace and charm. We shall need to recall that he "grew," made progress, changed. No one wants to foist on the modern world the dead pattern of the Middle Ages. For example, a New Christendom without modern science is as unthinkable as the medieval synthesis without the logic of Athens and the law of Rome. Nevertheless, a New Christendom cannot be built on science alone—on jet planes and atomic energy. It cannot be built on philosophy alone—on a purely human conception of truth and justice. It will need the favor, the grace, the communication from God of faith and hope and charity.

[ 12 ]

The New Christendom will learn from the Prince of Peace. It will have the right to hope for a world at peace. It will not put asunder what God has joined together—wisdom and prudence and grace; philosophy, science and religion. It will learn from Athens and Rome and Jerusalem the condition for world order—an integrated conception of the dignity, duty and destiny of man.

## THE CHRISTIAN LIFE

# The Radiant Heart

REVEREND EMIL BRUNNER, PH.D., D.D.

*Professor of Systematic and Practical Theology and Rector of the University of Zurich, Switzerland, and a Minister of the Swiss Reformed Church*

*One of the foremost theologians of the Protestant world, Dr. Brunner has been intimately associated with Karl Barth in the most vigorous religious movement of our day. Because of his social interests, he has tended lately to diverge from Barth. Emil Brunner was born in Switzerland December 23, 1889, and was educated at the universities of Zurich and Berlin. At the age of thirty-three he was made Privatdozent at the University of Zurich, and in 1924 was made professor of systematic and practical theology. He was appointed rector of the University in 1942. He was ordained in the Swiss Reformed Church in 1922. He is the recipient of the honorary D.D., Münster, 1925; Edinburgh, 1931; Utrecht, 1936; Oxford, 1937; Oslo, 1946; Princeton, 1946.*

*He held distinguished pastorates in Switzerland and has lectured at many universities in Europe, Great Britain and America. At the invitation of Princeton Theological Seminary he was guest professor of systematic theology for the academic year 1938-39. When World War II became imminent, he returned to Switzerland because he felt he could not remain in a safe place when his native land was in possible danger. Since returning to Switzerland he has been lecturing in Zurich and other universities.*

*He is the author of* The Divine-Human Encounter, The Divine Imperative, Our Faith, The Theology of Crisis, Justice and the Social Order, Revelation and Reason, Man in Revolt.

*This sermon, preached in Zurich during the war, reveals Dr. Brunner's grasp of the world situation, of man's need of God, and of the living truth of Christmas.*

## Sermon Three

TEXT: And the angel said unto them, Fear not: for, behold, I bring you good tidings of great joy, which shall be to all people. For unto you is born this day in the city of David a Saviour, which is Christ the Lord. LUKE 2:10, 11.

ONE who preaches today is in danger of attempting, at any cost, to say something that will bring joy. Christmas is a time for joy. And it is also bitter wartime when it is necessary to light a candle of happiness for people in their fear and sorrow. One is in such need of joy, and especially today. That is true; but then we are treating the Christmas message just like the rest of the Christmas magic: On December 26 everything is over and it is gray and dull again. However, God did not become man so that we might celebrate a beautiful Christmas. And our unhappiness and darkness will not vanish just because we indulge in a little Christmas poesy. All this Christmas-tree poetry cannot help us. We are living in very realistic times and, therefore, need a very realistic Christmas message, a message that will stand up under the dreadful reality.

And the true, the Biblical Christmas message is realistic too. It begins with a very appropriate word: "Fear not!" Yes, it is just this that is at stake, and it is just this that is so difficult today, not to fear what is and what is to come. We are afraid of darkness, and who can deny that it is dark today, darker than ever before? And it is well to remember that Jesus Christ too came into a dark world. A very un-Christmaslike world. He was born into a people and a land that was crying out under the heels of the soldiers of an army of occupation.

And this occupation ended with the destruction of the city of Jerusalem in one of the worst blood baths known in history, in which the Jewish nation was destroyed and the remaining Jews scattered to all parts of the world. And Jesus Christ was born in poverty. Does he not say of himself: "The birds have their nests and the foxes their holes, but the Son of Man has no place to lay his head." He came into a world so dark that it could not bear him who was Light, but hanged him, the Son of God, to a criminal's cross.

Truly, the coming of the Saviour is not a poetic and idyllic Christmas story which the poet and the artist would have us wrongly believe time after time, but from a purely human point of view it is a dreadful tragedy. It is an uncanny darkness which the Light of Jesus Christ illumines, a darkness as weird as our time, with the horrors of a world war, starvation, the

[14]

shooting and annihilation of the Jews; a darkness, then and now, in which one may have every reason to be afraid. He came into just such a world where times were hard and became even harder after his coming, just as in our time we too must be prepared for the worst which is yet to come. Therefore, the angel's message of "Fear not" must not be confused with a cheap optimism which believes everything will end all right.

And yet the darkness which first comes to our minds is not the real darkness into which Jesus came and to which the "Fear not" applies. All that we read in the newspaper and all the similar sorrow in our midst is not the greatest darkness, but only the prelude to darkness.

There is only one thing which can be totally dark, and there is only one thing which can be wholly radiant, and that is the heart. Everything else, the things we call world history, social conditions, political relationships, etc., in short, all the things about which we talk most of the time and which fill the newspapers and history books—these things are only environment, not the center itself. The heart is the center. If there is darkness in your heart, you might be placed in a paradise and yet remain in darkness; for the darkness of the heart is much stronger than all the radiance of nature and one's social surroundings. And if there is radiance in your heart, men can place you in a hell and you will still remain radiant, for the radiance of the heart is much stronger than all the darkness of nature and of the social environment. A short time ago I read letters from people who are living in a veritable hell, yet such a light radiates from them that one realizes that the very darkness of hell can't put out the radiance in their hearts. The Christmas message of Jesus Christ deals primarily with this darkness and radiance of the heart. Only here can one understand the significance of the Christmas message, not from the so-called great world, not from historical things and events. Looking at the outside world, at political and social circumstances, the lot of the early Christians was difficult enough; there was far more darkness than light. In spite of that they were able to say, "God put a radiance into our hearts so that we were illuminated on the face of Christ through the knowledge of the glory of God." The center of mankind is the heart; the Gospel of the coming of the Lord Jesus Christ deals primarily with the darkness of the heart and the radiance of the heart.

For it is not, as most of us think and all of us are time after time tempted to believe, that our hearts receive their light from the outside, that first the political and social environment must be changed so that we can be happy, so that there can be radiance in us; but it is the other way around. First there must be radiance inside the hearts, then there can also be radiance in the outside world. Darkness and radiance go from the inside out, and not from the outside in.

Why do we celebrate Christmas, something which happened nineteen hundred years ago in a far corner of the world? One does not live off the past. What does this, which is so far removed in time and space, matter to us?

We are, after all, people of the present and need help for the present. What has the thing we fear today to do with what happened then? How can it be the remedy and the salvation for our present needs and sorrows? What does it mean: "Fear not, for I bring you good tidings of great joy, which shall be for all people; for today in the city of David is born the Saviour which is Christ." Are we really these people, does it really mean our fear and our joy? Is he, who was born then in the city of David, truly our saviour, for our needs?

Some say it has proven untrue. For nineteen hundred years this message has been made known throughout the world, and yet the world is no better, living in the same fear, in the same horrors, in the same unhappiness as then. What is a saviour who does not save, what is joy which does not cheer, a redemption which does not redeem? Our first answer is this: A doctor moves into a quarter where a certain disease rages. He possesses the remedy for this disease and wants to help the people with it. After a while they say, He has not helped us, the disease is still here just as before. Then it is found that they did not even go to the doctor nor use his medicines. Is not, then, the complaint, He has not helped us, foolish? When Jesus Christ says, "I am the light of the world: he that followeth me shall not walk in darkness, but shall have the light of life," and now people say, "You lie, we are still in darkness," and then it becomes known that they did not follow him—is not then their complaint foolish? How can a doctor help when one does not take his medicine? How can Jesus Christ help when one does not accept him? But perhaps there are those who did "accept him," and so from these let us hear if he spoke the truth, if they, since following him, no longer "walk in darkness, but have the light of life." See, that is the difference between surroundings and the heart: my house, my garden, my social and political circumstances can be changed without my presence and without my knowledge, but not my heart.

Jesus Christ, however, goes directly to the heart because the heart is the center of mankind, the center of darkness as well as the center of light. Only from there on can we understand what Christmas is, who Jesus Christ is and what his coming means to us. The outside world—the social and political, the historical outside world—does not concern him for the present; for he knows that its change—useful and necessary as it may be—is not decisive. The dark heart remains dark even in the most radiant surroundings, whereas a change of heart means everything, for the radiant heart brightens its surroundings and remains radiant even in the darkest surroundings. Just as a good doctor does not waste time on outside symptom treatment, but goes directly to the source of the disease once he has diagnosed it, so Jesus goes to the center of the sickness of mankind, to the heart. What is its sickness? Just this darkness. And from where does this darkness come? Like any darkness it comes from there being no light. And why is the light which could illumine the heart not there? Because something is blocking its way. But what is this light which illumines the heart? That everyone knows. There is only one thing which really illumines the heart, and that is love. If the heart is filled with love, it is radiant; if it is devoid of love because something is blocking the way of love, it is dark.

That we are lacking in love wise men have always known. But the fact that they have never really known what love is, is evident in the commandment they gave mankind: "Thou shalt love!" It was correct, of course, but did not help. For here is the need: the loveless heart cannot love. The command, therefore, accomplishes nothing, at least nothing definite. For the heart cannot love of its own accord, it can only love if it is in love (*"wenn es in der Liebe* ist"). But we are not in love because we are not in God. For God is love; only the heart that is in God can truly love. Only if we are in God, can we be in love with our neighbor. But we are not in God because we want something other than God, something beyond God and beyond our neighbor, ourselves.

We do not believe that God's love is our life: we think we know better than that. As a stubborn child that runs away from his parents because he assumes he knows better than they what is good for him, and then finds himself in difficulties, so we run away from God in the assumption that we can find our own happiness and so get into unhappiness and darkness. And once we are in this predicament, we cannot get out; the road back to God is blocked, we are in our own way. Our guilty conscience hides the love of God from us; our guilt separates us from Him. Perhaps that is why we yearn for love—there is no man who does not yearn for love!—but we cannot find the way to it because we cannot find our way back to God. Eventually, we do not even believe that there is a God; and if we do still believe in Him, we do not believe that He is love, that He loves us. Were we not disobedient and unfaithful, how can He love us! It is thus that our own heart, which was created for God's love, imprisons us in lovelessness and separates us from God. That is our predicament, that is the real darkness of mankind from which comes all other darkness, even today's world war.

And into this situation came Jesus Christ, to reinstate us, the loveless, into God's love. That is the secret of the person of Jesus Christ: he is the only human being who can do that (*"Er ist der einzige Mensch, der das kann"*). And he can do it because he himself is the personification of God's love, the love of God become man. No human being can get us out of the darkness of the heart with his love. Of course, it is good for us to have someone like us; but it can't really help us. For there still remains the separation from God and with it the darkness in our hearts. A person who loves us cannot say to us: In my love is God's love for you. An ever so loving person cannot promise us God, cannot forgive us our sins, cannot take away from us our fear of death, cannot promise us eternal love. And without eternal love, a love that never ceases, our hearts cannot escape fear, worry and darkness. Jesus, however, is the man who can say to us: In my love is God's love. It is he who

[ 17 ]

may say that because he himself is the love of God, his love is God's love, his word is God's word, his deed is God's deed. That is the secret of the man who is God, and of God who is man, the God-man, and that is the miracle of Christmas. "God became man for the good of man." The love of God from which we became separated through our own guilt came to us as man, so that we might again live in the love of God.

So it is in the Christian faith. Probably all want love. But they want love without God. They do not believe that God alone is love, and so they try it themselves. Up to a certain point they are quite successful. But they cannot banish darkness from the heart; it remains as a dread of life, as fear of death. Or it remains as selective love; some, one loves; others, one hates. It remains as a resignation toward a dark world where cruelty and meaninglessness seem to have the last word. So it is: for man's heart was created for the love of God because it was created through the love of God. That is why man's heart is sick, dark, perverted, while it does not live in the love of God. Just as a fish perishes when out of water, so the heart of man perishes outside the love of God. It becomes dark; it is poor in light and life. The spirit of man can still accomplish powerful deeds, but these deeds cannot bring real joy, cannot bring him or others real blessing if they do not come out of love. But they can only come out of love if the heart is filled with the love of God.

But how may we obtain this love of God which comes to us in Jesus Christ? Quite simply in that we accept it. Nothing else but that is meant by the often misunderstood word "faith." Faith means to accept the love of God offered us in Jesus Christ. And now we understand why that doctor, who two thousand years ago came into this sick world of man, healed so few, and left so many unhealed. Because so few believed in him. For everywhere in the New Testament it is written: "For God so loved the world, that he gave his only begotten Son, *that whosoever believeth in him* should not perish." Faith or unbelief decides everything. But faith means to accept the love of God which Jesus Christ offers us, permit God to love us, believe it: yes, God, my Father, my Creator, I believe that you love me.

This is so simple and yet it comes so hard. It is so simple that every child *can* and so difficult that the most intelligent and the most highly educated *cannot*. (*"Es ist so leicht, dass jedes Kind es kann und ist so schwer, dass die Klügsten und Gebildesten es nicht können"*). It is difficult because we continue to suppose that we ourselves can change the heart in darkness; or because we suppose that God cannot love us who have been so unfaithful. Or because we doubt: Is God really love? Is Jesus Christ really God? Is the forgiveness of sins really for us? Or it might be difficult because we are so obsessed with our self-love and love of the world that we never seriously reach out for God's love. That is why there are always so many whose hearts remain in darkness, even though outwardly they might be Christians or at least live in Christian surroundings. And yet it is also so simple that nothing more is necessary than to listen to that which God says to you in Jesus Christ: Man, you, whom I created and whom I know by name, you, man, whom I know a thousand times better than you know yourself, whose many evil intentions I know, those no other man knows, yes, even those you yourself do not know, you, benighted, deceitful child of man, I say unto you: I love you to all eternity, and nothing can separate you from this love of mine, if you will but accept it.

And that, my friends, is celebrating Christmas. This Christmas joy, then, is not confined to the 25th of December; this radiance, then, is not extinguished with the Christmas-tree candles; God's love, then, embodies what the Lord expresses: "He who followeth me shall not walk in darkness, but shall have the light of life." This radiance is prepared for all of us; let us receive it especially in the Holy Communion. For the Lord's Supper has exactly the same significance as the Christmas message: "Fear not, for I bring you tidings of great joy." "Christ the Saviour has come." "Behold, I stand at the door and knock: if any man hear my voice, and open the door, I will come in to him, and will sup with him, and he with me." Amen.

## THE CHRISTIAN LIFE

# It Is Hard to Be a Christian

REVEREND ROBERT JAMES McCRACKEN, D.D.
*Minister, The Riverside Church, New York*

*Dr. McCracken has had a very busy life. Born on March 28, 1904, in Motherwell, Scotland, in a home that had inherited the great traditions of Scotch Presbyterianism, he attended school in Motherwell, and having been spiritually awakened in the Motherwell Baptist Church, became a member of it in 1918. He attended Glasgow University, from which he graduated in arts with an M.A. degree in 1925 and with a B.D. in theology in 1928. Soon after he became minister of the Marshall Street Baptist Church in Edinburgh.*

*After four years in Edinburgh, Dr. McCracken was called to be minister of the Dennistoun Baptist Church in Glasgow, and in 1933 was appointed lecturer in systematic theology in the Baptist Theological College of Scotland. For the next four years he carried responsibilities both as preacher and teacher. In 1937 McMaster University at Hamilton, Ontario, invited him to become associate professor of Christian theology and philosophy of religion. Then followed a year of special study at Cambridge University, after which Dr. McCracken returned to Canada. From the outset he associated himself with ecumenical interests and activities. All the Protestant communions in Canada have sought his spiritual leadership. During the past three years he was on one occasion or another daily preacher at the Toronto*

Conference of the United Church, daily preacher at the General Council of the United Church of Canada, lecturer on the Pitcairn-Crabbe Foundation at Western Theological Seminary in Pittsburgh, lecturer before the McGill Theological Alumni in Montreal and before the Knox College Alumni in Toronto. For the last five years he has been the guest preacher during the summer at Yorkminster Church in Toronto. He has just completed a term of notable service as president of the Baptist Convention of Ontario and Quebec.

As preacher, pastor, teacher and administrator, he has had a wide and useful experience before becoming successor to Dr. Harry Emerson Fosdick. In May, 1946, McMaster University awarded the honorary doctorate to Dr. McCracken. On October 2, 1946, he was installed as minister of the Riverside Church, New York City.

Dr. McCracken presents the challenge of the Christian life, shows the need for self-discipline and self-denial, urges subjugation of the flesh in the interests of the spirit. Originally Christianity meant to live adventurously and dangerously. He sets a worthy preaching standard in keeping with the traditions of the great Riverside Church.

## Sermon Four

TEXT: Enter ye in at the strait gate: for wide is the gate, and broad is the way, that leadeth to destruction, and many there be which go in thereat: Because strait is the gate, and narrow is the way, which leadeth unto life, and few there be that find it.

MATTHEW 7:13-14

IN THE light of such an injunction no one need suggest that Jesus got his disciples on false pretenses. He painted no glowing picture. He told people bluntly what they would be in for if they elected to go after him. He made them count the cost at the start. With a love of reality that would brook no evasion, he first faced the facts for himself and then insisted that candidates for discipleship should do the same.

There are in the main two ways by which to secure the support and allegiance of men. You may bribe them or you may challenge them. You may appeal to the selfish instinct in the heart of every man or you may appeal to the heroic instinct; and the nature of the appeal will do much to determine the quality of the response. Bribe, and you will get lip-service, eye-service, time-service and, when the storm breaks, many a defaulter. Challenge, and at once you sift the wheat from the chaff. Challenge, and those who respond will proffer the utmost love and loyalty of their hearts. Jesus, who knew what was in man, knew that. With him it was never a bribe, but always and everywhere a challenge.

That is what we find here. There is nothing in this passage to indicate that the way to heaven is easy. You are making a colossal mistake if you think you can saunter along it with your hands in your pockets. Christian discipleship is not—what great numbers of people suppose it to be—a sort of pastime which one happens to be keen about, just as others are keen about games or music or literature, something that can be taken up and set down at will or according to inclination. "You will not yawn yourself into heaven with an idle wish," said Richard Cecil. Or as Samuel Rutherford put it, "You will not be carried there lying at ease upon a feather bed." I know, and you know, where those men learned that language. It was from the lips of him who said: "Enter ye in at the strait gate: for wide is the gate, and broad is the way, that leadeth to destruction, and many there be which go in thereat: Because strait is the gate, and narrow is the way, which leadeth unto life, and few there be that find it."

How little that note is sounded today! There is an impression abroad that religion first and last is a comforting and comfortable affair, a device to preserve the status quo and to create patience and passivity in the midst of conditions as they are. Not infrequently one hears it said that Christianity is so much "dope," that Christians use their faith in God as a couch on which to recline, that they have taken the crosses out of their churches and put in cushions instead. Dr. Inge has proposed a new last line for the verse of a very familiar hymn, so well does he think it describes the average twentieth-century Christian:

> They climbed the steep ascent of heaven
> Through peril, toil and pain,
> O God to us may grace be given
> To travel by the train.

We laugh at that, but I wonder whether we can afford to, or whether we have any moral right so to do. Are we not laughing at ourselves? One thing is beyond dispute. Twentieth-century Christianity, by and large, has lost the stringent note. For most of us there is no cross in it, no abstinence, no self-denial, no subjugation of the flesh in the interests of the spirit. I put it to you that the common notion is that a Christian is a person who goes to church on average once a week, and tries in a mild and quiet way to live a decent life. I put it to you that young people, when they look at the church and its program, are not made to feel that Christianity is a creed for heroes or that to embrace it means, in Nietzsche's phrase, "living dangerously." If I may use a slang phrase to make my meaning sharp and clear, I would say that religion in these days has very little "kick" in it. It scarcely gives any offense. As a rule, it is much too timid to make its influence felt outside its own immediate sphere. On most public occasions it shows itself overanxious to placate and accommodate the state and the world at large. It is not organized as a fighting force in national and international life, nor is it attacking with high-hearted confidence in its own superior powers the battalions of evil. The drink trade can flourish right under its eye. So can the armaments industry. So can all kinds of injustice and oppression. The man on the street has little reason to think that Christianity is a straining and strenuous enterprise, or that Christians are a company of people committed to the turning of the world upside down with a view to setting it right side up.

But that was the general impression of Christianity and of Christians in the first century. It meant something then to be a Christian, and it cost something. No one from A.D. 30 to A.D. 313 thought of Christianity as a comfortable religion or of dismissing it as so much "dope." In the general mind, it was associated with effort and enterprise, with persecution and tribulation. It was a creed for heroes; it put men on their mettle; it tested all their powers of endurance. It set them hard tasks, confronted them with perplexing problems, matched them against apparently superior odds. The first Christians, however, were persuaded that their faith was absolutely indispensable to the welfare and salvation of mankind. It was something to live for, to fight for, and, if need be, to die for. Its enemy was not a power to be circumvented, outwitted or ignored, but a power to be ceaselessly and relentlessly attacked, and attacked right out in the open. In a book which he wrote some years ago, Dr. Foakes Jackson drew attention to this feature of the life of the early Church. Civil life in those days, he says, was comparatively secure and tranquil; those who wanted quietness and safety could have it; but there was one danger spot—the Christian Church. Join that and you took the risk of being thrown to the lions. To that circumstance, thinks Dr. Jackson, may be traced in no small measure the phenomenal growth of the Church in those centuries. It became a center of attraction for heroic souls, and as such conquered the world of that day.

It should never have ceased to be that. What the armed services have been in recent years for countless young men and women the Church, the army of the living God, should be in every generation. Some time ago, a well-known surgeon in Britain, discussing the whole problem of work and wages, had this to say: "What is happening today is that nobody works for the sake of getting the thing done. The result of the work is a by-product; the aim of the work is to make money to do something else. Doctors practice medicine, not primarily to relieve suffering, but to make a living—the cure of the patient is something that happens on the way. Lawyers accept briefs, not because they have a passion for justice, but because the law is the profession which enables them to live. The reason," he added, "why men often find themselves happy and satisfied in the army is that for the first time in their lives they find themselves doing something, not for the sake of the pay, which is miserable, but for the sake of getting the thing done."

In itself, that is an interesting judgment. I should like, amending the last sentence, to make it read thus: The reason why men often found themselves happy and satisfied in the Church of the first century was because for the first time in their lives they found themselves doing something, not for the sake of the pay, which if you are thinking in terms of earthly rewards was scandalous, but for the sake of getting a great task done. When the Church becomes militant again, when its strategies are less timid and stereotyped and more venturesome and courageous, when its social conscience is keener, when church membership costs something, not only in cash but in time and labor and, possibly, in reputation, it will once again become a center of attraction for heroic souls. Of late across the Atlantic it had become that. There is the story told about the wife of a young Norwegian pastor who was permitted to visit Bishop Berggrav on his birthday, where he was held at the time in a concentration camp. Into his captivity she smuggled a cake of her own baking, on which she had inscribed the words: ECCLESIA MILITANS, ECCLESIA TRIUMPHANS ("A militant Church is a triumphant Church"). If we had forgotten it, the war served to remind us that there is something in human nature which responds to the challenge to live adventurously and dangerously.

I have been insisting that twentieth-century Christianity, by and large, has lost the stringent note. Why is this? Is it not because it has lost the note of stringency in the person and teaching of Jesus? Great numbers of people think of the Master as a meek and gentle soul who went about everywhere breathing mild benedictions, yet that comes near to being a caricature of all the true facts of the case. There were two sides to the ministry of Jesus. On the one hand, he went about doing good—healing the sick, giving sight to the blind, relieving those who were in mental distress. On the other hand, he went about giving the most violent offense to all sorts of folk—his relatives, the disciples, the scribes and the Pharisees, the people with vested interests like the money-changers in the temple. He was so outspoken and inflammatory in his language, so uncompromising and unconventional in his behavior, that he was excommunicated, stoned, hunted from place to place in Palestine, and finally nailed to a gibbet as Public Enemy Number One. He said once that he had come to cast fire on the earth. He said on another occasion that he brought not peace but a sword. No one can read the Gospels and not perceive how sensitive he was to the fact that men were likely to be offended by him and his message. "Blessed is he whosoever shall not be offended in me" was the word he sent to John the Baptist who lay in prison, baffled and bewildered by the line Jesus was taking; while to his disciples he said, as he faced his greatest ordeal, "All ye shall be offended because of me this night." Read the Gospels, and if you have never noticed the fact before, it will surprise you to discover how often and how deeply Jesus gave offense.

But, someone may say, What was there about Jesus to give offense? Of all characters is not his the most winsome and gracious? True, but dare you overlook the sterner elements in his character and message? How stringent he was, for example, in the matter of enlisting disciples! He never made it easy for a man to be his follower. "Strait is the gate"—that was what he said. "Lord," cried one man, "I will follow thee withersoever thou goest." It was an enthusiastic offer, and another type of leader would have closed with it at once, but not Jesus. He knew that enthusiasm is sometimes fitful and shallow, which accounts for the sobering reply, "Foxes have holes, and the birds of the air have nests; but the Son of man hath not where to lay his head." "Lord," cried another man to whom had been addressed the call to discipleship, "I will follow thee, but suffer me first to go and bury my father." And swift as a rapier thrust came the response, "Let the dead bury their dead, but go thou and preach the kingdom of God." "Lord," cried still another candidate for discipleship, "I will follow thee; but let me first go bid them farewell, which are at home at my house." It was for all the world like a man asking for embarkation leave, yet to that man Jesus addressed one of the sternest words the world has ever heard: "No man, having put his hand to the plough, and looking back, is fit for the kingdom of God."

There was the case, too, of Nicodemus—intrigued by Jesus, coming to him under cover of darkness, making a cautious, tentative, you might almost say patronizing, approach: "Rabbi, we know that thou art a teacher come from God: for no man can do these miracles that thou doest, except God be with him." And Jesus breaks in on what was promising to be a pretty little speech with a sledge-hammer sentence, out of all apparent relation to what Nicodemus had been saying, "Verily, verily, I say unto you, Except a man be born again, he cannot see the kingdom of God." And when Nicodemus, completely taken aback, mumbles and fumbles and stumbles, Jesus as it were completes his overthrow: "Art thou a master of Israel, and knowest not these things?" How this Man among men challenged men, dared them, made life stern and demanding and awesome! He would have no headlong followers, no impulsive converts. It was not that he did not want disciples; it was rather that he wanted dependable, expendable disciples.

In the church nowadays we are so pathetically anxious about numbers. Can he draw a crowd? is almost the first question pulpit committees ask. Can he fill the collection plates? is commonly enough the second. Jesus was anxious not about quantity but about quality. That is why his winnowing fan was in such constant use. He told us that the big battalions would never be found assembling before the strait gate or crowding on to the narrow way. "Few there be that find it," was what he said. It is an easy matter in these days to become a member of the company of Christ. Indicate the slightest desire in that direction and a minister is on your doorstep and at your service, arranging for a comfortable pew and a friendly reception and, of course, a set of freewill offering envelopes. In the Galilean days it was a terrible thing to be a member of the company of Christ. It meant the strait gate, the narrow way, the denial of self, the shouldering of a cross. "Are you able," said Christ to the handful of men round about him, for the crowds had gone, "to drink the cup that I drink of?" Are *we* able?

Consider one other matter. How stringent Jesus was in his moral standards! The marriage bond is indissoluble; fornication is not even to be thought of; covetousness is idolatry. We are to love our enemies, to bless them that curse us, to do good to them that hate us and to pray for those who despitefully use and persecute us. It is the inwardness of the ethic of Jesus that is the really exacting thing about it. Other moral teachers condemn the sinful act—he goes deeper and condemns the motive that prompts the act. The Commandments, he says, are broken in thought before the sinner proceeds to the act, and the sin remains, even if no open offense is committed. It is so characteristic of Jesus to attack the disease when others are tinkering with the symptoms. So he rebukes acquisitiveness rather than wealth and gets the poor man as well as the rich one. He rebukes hatred rather than war and gets the pacifist as well as the nonpacifist. He rebukes lust rather than adultery and gets the respectable churchgoer as well as the woman of the streets. "Ye have heard that it was said by them of olden time, Thou shalt not commit adultery: But I say unto you, That whosoever looketh on a woman to lust after her hath committed adultery with her already in his heart." Wherefore, "if thy right eye offend thee, pluck it out . . . if thy right hand offend thee, cut it off . . . for it is profitable for thee that one of thy members should perish, and not that thy whole body should be cast into hell." We have heard those words so often that they have well-nigh lost their edge and meaning; those who heard them for the first time were aghast at their severity.

Here without doubt is one reason why Jesus gives offense to many today. It has to be remembered that while some people reject Christ because they cannot understand him, others reject him because they understand him only too well. They know that his demands are stringent and exacting, that they involve a cleaning-up of the inner life, the substitution of self-denial for self-interest, the subordination of the material to the spiritual, and they are not prepared to toe the line or pay the price. They prefer the wide to the strait gate and the broad to the narrow way.

"Madam," wrote Samuel Rutherford to Lady Kenmure, "I persuade you that the greatest part but play with Christianity; they put it byhand easily. I thought it had been an easy thing to be a Christian, and that to seek God had been at the next door; but oh, the windings, the turnings, the ups and downs that He hath led me through, and I see yet much way to the ford." That is the authentic note. No one yet ever entered into the kingdom of Heaven without tribulation; not perhaps the tribulation of fire and persecution, but the tribulation of a humble and contrite heart, of the flesh subjugated in the interest of the spirit, of a life poured forth like spilled wine in the service of others. If our religion is of such a pliable and elastic

[ 25 ]

sort that it has cost us no pains to acquire, no self-denial to preserve, no effort to advance, no struggle to maintain holy and undefiled, whatever else it is, it is not the religion of him who said, "Enter ye in at the strait gate: . . . Because strait is the gate, and narrow is the way, which leadeth unto life, and few there be that find it."

## The Song of the Exiled

REVEREND EDWIN LEWIS, D.D., TH.D.
*Professor of Systematic Theology, Drew Theological Seminary, Madison, New Jersey and a Minister of the Methodist Church*

*One of the great thinkers of the Christian world today, Dr. Lewis preaches on a dramatic situation that occurred by the canals of ancient Babylon, where the Israelites had been taken in captivity. From his two texts he draws a message for hearts today that face exile, lost hopes, a ruined world. The power of God working through a man of God makes Ezekiel an inspiration as Dr. Lewis develops this fine sermon.*

*Born at Newbury, Berks, England, in early life he engaged in mission work in Newfoundland. He entered the United States in 1904 and graduated from New York State College at Albany and from Drew Theological Seminary. He was Drew Fellow at Free Church College, Glasgow and took his Th.D. from Drew in 1918, with specialized study in Erasmus and Luther. Dickinson College conferred the D.D. (causa honoris) in recognition of his accomplishments.*

*In 1916 he joined the faculty of Drew as instructor in New Testament Greek and systematic theology; since 1920, professor of systematic theology and philosophy of religion. During 1936-37 he traveled in the Orient, lecturing at Aoyama Gakuin, Tokyo; Peking Union Seminary and Nanking Union Seminary, China; Union Seminary, Seoule, Korea; and Leonard Theological Seminary, Jubbulpore, India. He has been special lecturer in theology at Pine Hill Divinity Hall, Halifax; Southern Methodist University; New Brunswick Reformed Seminary; Candler School of Theology; Union Theological Seminary, Richmond; Gammon Theological Seminary; University of Chicago Divinity School; Southern Baptist Seminary.*

*He was joint editor of the Abingdon Bible Commentary. Among his books are* Jesus Christ and the Human Quest, Manual of Christian Beliefs, Great Christian Teachings, God and Ourselves, A Christian Manifesto, The Faith

We Declare, A New Heaven and a New Earth, A Philosophy of the Christian Revelation, The Practice of the Christian Life *and* The Creator and the Adversary.

*Who after all can put chains on a man's spirit? The answer is beautifully given in "The Song of the Exiled." What puts the song in man's heart? That also is answered here.*

## Sermon Five

TEXT: By the canals of Babylon, there we sat down, yea, we wept, when we remembered Zion. Upon the willows in the midst thereof we hanged up our harps. For there they that led us captives required of us songs, saying, Sing us one of the songs of Zion! How shall we sing the Lord's song in a strange land?

PSALM 137:1-4

Now it came to pass . . . as I was among the captives by the Chebar canal, that the heavens were opened, and I saw visions of God. EZEKIEL 1:1

THE verses just quoted set the stage for a dramatic contrast. The verses from the psalm, and the verse from Ezekiel, presuppose the same situation. The priest-prophet Ezekiel is one of the captives of Israel now forcibly settled in the irrigated areas of Babylon. These people have been uprooted from their native land: they are henceforward to be included in the ranks of "the dispossessed." The things they most passionately love are far away. Great stretches of sandy desert are between them and their hearts' desire. The very expression, "by the canals of Babylon," and the very expression, "the captives by the Chebar canal," are charged with a dark significance. They appear to carry a flat denial of the great purpose for which Israel had been ostensibly raised up. Those who are captives should, by all the evidence, have been the most free men in all the world. Yet their distant Zion is in ruins; their once magnificent Temple is a stoneheap; they have become virtually slaves; and the life of their state has ceased to exist.

What did these unwilling exiles do? Much of the answer, although not all of it, is contained in Psalm 137. They gave up. They lost hope. They wept as they labored by the irrigation ditches. They unstrung their harps. The strains of music were too painful to be endured in the memories they evoked. They refused any longer to sing the Lord's song. And they were frank to say why. The Lord's song did not belong in such incongruous surroundings.

All these monstrous images which bespoke the bestialities of an alien faith, these flat unbroken expanses of land, so different from the rolling hills of Galilee or the rugged terrain of Judea, these harsh unfeeling overlords who treated an elect people as though they were menials—what place had the Lord's song here, where its every declaration was denied, and its every harmony transformed into a grating discord! Only where it was written could the Lord's song be properly sung, only where circumstance and sentiment agreed. But in captivity—no; in a strange land—no; among sneering tormentors—no; when life was tottering to its foundations—no. Come the day—the promised and therefore certain day of the return to Zion—and harp and voice would again mingle in the glad acclaim. But not now. They could weep, but they could not rejoice. They could lament bitterly, but they could not sing.

So said many, and perhaps so said most. But not all. There were unconquerable souls even among the irrigation ditches of Babylon. Many an immortal psalm, immortal by reason of the resolute faith it expresses, came out of those dark days. Psalm 71 is the courageous utterance of an old man of the exile—and what can be sadder than aged men and women dispossessed, and no time left to rebuild the ruins? He remembered, not without deep yearning, the days of his freedom and prosperity in Jerusalem, the respectful salutations of his neighbors, the honor duly given to a man of probity, the solemn sacrifices in the Temple, the rejoicing throngs on the great festal days. And what now? The taunts of the tormenters. The mockeries of strangers. Affliction for his daily bread. The certainty of burial far from the tombs of his fathers. Does he keep a resentful silence? Far from it. "Thou art my hope, O Lord God: thou art my trust from my youth. . . . Hitherto have I declared thy wondrous works. Now also when I am old and gray-headed, O God, forsake me not: until I have showed thy strength unto this generation, and thy power to every one that is to come."

Whence came the glowing utterances of the man we call the second Isaiah? They came out of that same time and place which had rendered so many others dumb. The inextinguishable confidence that breathes through the amazing fortieth chapter was the confidence of an exile! "The everlasting God, the Lord, fainteth not, neither is weary. He giveth power to the faint, and to them that have no might he increaseth strength. Even the youths shall faint and be weary, and the young men shall utterly fall. But they that wait upon the Lord shall renew their strength: they shall mount up with wings as eagles; they shall run and not be weary; and they shall walk and not faint."

Ezekiel was one of these unconquerable souls. Indeed, it is not impossible that but for Ezekiel there had been no second Isaiah. More than any other one man, Ezekiel assured the continuance of the faith of Israel in the alien land, and for that matter for centuries afterwards, since he is rightly called "the Father of Judaism." Where is there anywhere a book that begins more dramatically than his book? "And it came to pass, as I was among the captives by the Chebar canal, that the heavens were opened, and I saw visions of

God." Read the words against the background of Psalm 137, and their significance is inescapable. Here is a man who compelled denial to become affirmation. He and his companions were plunged into an abyss so deep that most of them could see nothing but the darkness and the restricting walls. But Ezekiel looked in a different direction: *he looked up*, and he saw the otherwise invisible stars.

This declaration of Ezekiel has about it a dramatic quality more arresting even than that with which the first Isaiah begins his sixth chapter: "In the year that king Uzziah died"—which is to say, in a time of dark uncertainty for Judah— "I saw the Lord sitting upon a throne, high and lifted up." Threatening political confusion only served to throw Isaiah back more securely on the stabilities of the divine. Over Ezekiel the exile, too, the heavens opened; but they did not open of themselves. They opened because Ezekiel audaciously reached up and thrust them apart, the better to see what they concealed from fearful and earth-bound souls. And because it was thereupon granted to him to see the invisible, he also, like Moses before him, endured. The visions that he describes have in them something of the baffling character of the visions of William Blake. For this reason, there are those who would call him psychopathic. Perhaps he was. Perhaps the contradiction of faith and circumstance set up a tension which made it difficult at times for him to hold the center. It would not be surprising if this were the case. But it were better to be taunted as a psychopathic, and be aware of the ineffable mystery of God in suchwise that the soul found fitting staith, than to be so coldly rational, so impeccably logical, so rigidly intellectual, that God could no more be seen and felt than a rose could bloom and shed its fragrance at the heart of an iceberg!

In actual fact, it is not circumstances that determine whether or not one shall sing the Lord's song. If the song is already in the heart, it will manage to get itself sung. That song has been heard in many an unexpected place, and often enough has been listened for in vain where silence was least justified. If ever a man sang the Lord's song in a strange land, that is to say, in conditions that seemed to deny all that the song affirmed, it was Jeremiah buying the field at Anathoth. When he bought the field he was in prison; Jerusalem was on the eve of destruction; Jeremiah himself had declared that there would be wide and long-standing desolation. Yet he, a prisoner, bought for cash a piece of land of which he never expected to take actual possession, in order to dramatize before unbelieving men his faith that there were some things that could not be destroyed. A song of triumph went up that day from the guardhouse in which Jeremiah was a prisoner!

Condemned to drink the hemlock, Socrates faced his judges unafraid, and reaffirmed before them his faith that no evil could befall a good man, either in life or after death. Thrown into the jail in Philippi, Paul and Silas did not lament in the fashion of the exiles of Psalm 137: instead, they prayed and sang, and the testimony of their song reached into the heart of the jailer himself. Years later, in another prison, this time in Rome, Paul wrote a letter to this same city of Philippi, to those who in turn had received the jailer's testimony, and there is in all the New Testament a letter in which the note of joy is sounded as it is in this letter to the Philippians: "Rejoice, and again I say rejoice!" The fear and jealousy of the aging Gothic ruler led him to throw into prison his loyal and high-minded official Boethius. In hourly expectation of a brutal death, Boethius wrote in the prison one of the great classics of our race, *The Consolations of Philosophy*. John Bunyan might still have written *Pilgrim's Progress* had he never been thrown into Bedford jail; and Dante might still have written *The Divine Comedy* had he never been banished from his beloved Florence. All we are certain of is that it *was* in Bedford jail and that it *was* in alien Ravenna respectively that these two valiant souls sang what was veritably the Lord's song, and those who know the secret of St. Cecilia may hear it still. Men can put chains on other men's limbs: only the man himself can put chains on his own spirit.

It was the thought of Plato, and many have followed him in it, that every man is an exile. He is an exile of eternity. Earth is not his true home. He has wandered from his native land, and a deep nostalgia is upon him. This may be only a philosophical conceit, but there is a truth at the heart of it. The truth may not be recognized by the man who sees himself as nothing but one more animated clod. But it is given to some men to "fetch their eye up to God's style, and to manners of the sky." They do not think so ignobly of themselves as to suppose that the little day of their life is bounded with a sleep. They are the men who, while in the world because they must be, are yet not of the world because they have so chosen. They know the tears that wait on all human affairs, but they also know Wordsworth's "obstinate questionings of sense and outward things."

There are such men, and for them every land is a strange land. The dearest and most familiar place is not wholly their home. They are as eagles that must wear a hood. Children of earth indeed, but children of starry heaven as well. Their predicament is the issue of their vision, but in their predicament lies their challenge. They hear the mocking voice: "Sing us one of the Lord's songs." They could make the ancient reply, and declare that the Lord's song may not be sung save in the Lord's land. But not if the heavens have opened above them in their captivity, and disclosed visions of God. For then they know that there is no place to sing the Lord's song except where they are. The Lord's land is always a distant land: it is never the here and now. The here and now is the place of exile. The clank of the chain is never still for long. The signs of bondage are on every hand. Never a day goes by but the lash of the whip is felt.

What then? Acquiescence? A black vault for a sky? A mutter of despair? A neglected harp? A forgotten song?

It need not be so, and for many it has not been so. Just because the land is a strange land is the reason why the Lord's song should roll across it in ever-increasing power. To wait for a more favorable time and place in which to sound forth that song is simply to confess that there is no song in the heart. If the song is there, it will make itself heard. An unsung song is a nonexistent song.

The exiles in Babylon gave proof of that: at least, many of them did. Often they declared that they would keep silent in the alien land, but once back in Zion they would send a burst of song to heaven itself. And did they? They did not! In the course of time, a group of them were allowed to return. One wonders if they crossed the desert with the glowing words of the second Isaiah still ringing in their ears. "Ye shall go out with joy, and be led forth with peace: the mountains and the hills shall break forth before you into singing; and all the trees of the field shall clap their hands." At last they reached the land where they fain would be, the land in which it would be so easy to sing the Lord's song.

And a deep silence fell upon them. There was no sound of rejoicing. What voices were heard were voices of lamentation. The longed-for deliverance turned out to be no deliverance after all. Loads were just as heavy in Jerusalem as they had been on the banks of the Babylonian canals. More than twenty years passed before even a little field-stone house of prayer was built, and that was done only because of the insistence of two resolute prophets. The song that could not be sung in one place could not be sung in another, because what makes the song is not the place but the singer. If he has no song in his heart, he will sing nowhere, because he has nothing to sing.

It is a subtle temptation—this temptation to wait for a more desirable time and place. That more desirable time and place will never come. One who cannot sing the Lord's song where he is will hardly sing it where he is not! He may think he will, but the motives that restrain him in the one place will restrain him in the other. The exile is permanent: all that changes is the location.

And how the world needs that song! It needs it if only to be reminded of its own exile. If men are not to accept the low, they must be shown the high, and only those can show the high who already know it. The low is so clamant, so insidious, so far-ranging. Men find it so easy to be content with their chains. And that is the one thing that must not be allowed to happen. The only hope of the captives is in men like Ezekiel, that is to say, in men who, in an identical situation with the earth-bound, keep open a highway to heaven.

> Better it were, thou sayest, to consent;
> Feast while we may, and live ere life be spent;
> Close up clear eyes, and call the unstable sure,
> The unlovely lovely, and the filthy pure;
> In self-belyings, self-deceivings roll,
> And lose in Action, Passion, Talk, the soul.

> Nay, better far to mark off thus much air,
> And call it Heaven: place bliss and glory there;
> Fix perfect homes in the unsubstantial skies,
> And say, what is not, will be by-and-by.[1]

This does not involve blindness to actual situations. Ezekiel never called the exile by any other name than what it was. He did not justify want of bread on the earth by assurances of future pie in the sky. He was fully aware of his people's tragedy. He sought to show them visions of God not to induce in them a fatalistic spirit respecting their present lot, but to destroy that spirit. He never said to them, "We are not exiles." What he rather said was, "Exiles though we be, we may still be men of faith as well, and by our faith rise above the exile."

Only in such a spirit is there any hope for our world. To acquiesce in the confusions and superficialities and gross materialisms of these times is to be exiles indeed. Such acquiescence only serves to accelerate the world's progress toward destruction. Exile is only hopeless when it is accepted as permanent, and permanent it need not be while there remains in human hearts some power of "the visions splendid" by which a light shines into the "shades of the prison-house." One Ezekiel may suffice to lift up the hearts of a multitude. Song has a strange power of infection, and especially when it is a song in the night. But he who sings the Lord's song will not sing it to any good effect if he sing it from some distant pinnacle, untouched by the grim actualities and the harsh severities of the strange land. We are called to sing our song

> Not in Utopia, subterranean fields,
> Or some secreted island, Heaven knows where!
> But in the very world, which is the world
> Of all of us,—the place where in the end
> We find our happiness, or not at all![2]

The singer who would keep hope and faith and high purpose alive in the hearts of exiles must himself share the exile. In him the Word must be made flesh.

Salvation is never achieved from the outside: one must belong to what one would help save. Participation in the world's life—this *must* be; detachment from the world's spirit—this *may* be. Many a Frenchman deplored the unspeakable horrors of Devil's Island, but he deplored them from the safety of distant France, and the convicts continued to die like flies. It was by a man who knew that he must participate in what he would redeem, while yet maintaining a detachment of spirit from its nameless sins, that the colony was at last transformed. Charles Péan sang the Lord's song in a strange land, as Devil's Island must have been to him, and at last it made itself heard—*but that was why.* Men who had long since forgotten that there

[1] Arthur Hugh Clough.
[2] Wordsworth.

could even be such a song became the subjects of its transforming power—but only because Charles Péan *sang it where they were.*

And for the Christian, this is God's own way. The doctrine of the Incarnation may be regarded as just one more abstract idea. Or it may be regarded as the deepest truth of life, since it means that even God came into the strange land, Himself an exile of eternity, to sing in the strange land His own song. The path God trod is the ultimate path. By no other path than this can man's necessary exile prove to be the vestibule to a holy of holies.

# Claim Everything

RUFUS M. JONES, LL.D., D.D., LITT.D., D.TH.
*Professor Emeritus of Philosophy, Haverford College, Haverford, Pennsylvania and a Minister of the Society of Friends*

*As teacher, preacher, writer and thinker Rufus M. Jones has left his impression upon many minds among the Society of Friends as well as upon his students and upon the public where his many addresses have won a friendly hearing. Born in South China, Maine, in 1863, he graduated from Haverford College in 1885, studied at Heidelberg University, the University of Pennsylvania, Oxford and Marburg, and has received the doctorate from Harvard, Swarthmore, Marburg, Earlham, Columbia University, Yale, Williams, Colgate and Colby.*

*He began his long career as principal of Oak Grove Seminary, Vassalboro, Maine, 1889-93, when he joined the faculty of Haverford College as an instructor and was professor of philosophy from 1901 until he became emeritus in 1934. He was college preacher in many colleges and universities and is a minister of the Society of Friends. His messages over the years have been thoughtful, helpful, devotional. He has planned much of the work of the American Friends Service Committee for European Relief and has been one of the active leaders among American Friends, popularly called Quakers.*

*He has written fifty-one volumes, most of them in the religious field, among which are the following:* Practical Christianity (*1899*); A Boy's Religion from Memory (*1902*); Quakerism: a Religion of Life (*1908*); Studies in Mystical Religion; Clement of Alexandria; The Quakers in the American Colonies; Stories of Hebrew Heroes; Spiritual Reformers in the Sixteenth and Seventeenth Centuries (*1914*); The Story of George Fox; Nature and Authority of Conscience; The Boy Jesus and His Companions;

Fundamental Ends of Life; The Church's Debt to Heretics; Flowering of Mysticism; A Small Town Boy.

*"Claim Everything" was preached at the Five Years Meeting in Richmond, Indiana. Dr. Jones' interpretation of Paul's famous passage in I Corinthians brings the possibilities of the life with Christ into epic perspective and lights up the meaning of life. This sermon illustrates Dr. Jones' ability to interpret "Quakerism as a way of life"; "to him all life is religious and there is no division between practicing religious forms and being good members of families and of society."*

## Sermon Six

TEXT: All things are yours; whether Paul, or Apollos, or Cephas, or the world, or life, or death, or things present, or things to come; all are yours; and ye are Christ's; and Christ is God's.

I CORINTHIANS 3:21-23

I T WOULD be difficult to match this passage in grandeur of sweep or in the inclusiveness of its claim of what belongs to the person who is in Christ.

I wish we could think of it not as words in a Book written nineteen hundred years ago, but as words fresh and new, said by the living Spirit of Christ for this hour. The ancient words must come to life and thrill us again as they must have thrilled that group in Corinth who heard them for the first time. If what is said here is a fact, it is a tremendous fact.

"All things are yours." This great triumphant assertion of St. Paul began originally in an effort to bring together the several parts of the Church in Corinth. Each tiny fragment was losing its joy and power by missing all that the other fragments might have contributed, if only they had discovered that they could join their spiritual forces in a higher unity in which all co-operated to the enlarged power of each. That higher unity is expressed in the great words: "You are Christ's Body"—the new Body here on earth in which He lives and through which He expresses Himself. What an amazing thing it would be if we had a church which literally and truly were Christ's Body! The Church exists so that Christ may continue to be vitally operative in the world.

I said once, in friendly conversation with a distinguished Roman Catholic canon: "I should like to know what you would say if you met a person who plainly possessed grace in his life and yet had never used what your church calls *the means of grace*." Without a moment's hesitation he said, "I should say that that person belonged to the invisible Church, and that that is even more important than belonging to the visible Church." What this broad

[34]

spiritually-minded Roman Catholic meant by the invisible Church is what I mean by the higher universal Church of the living Christ, the life-imparting Spirit of Christ, that is above and inclusive of all that is true and pure and beautiful and lovely and genuinely real in the now divided denominations or sects of Christendom. It is the living God our souls want—not some substitute for Him. We must say "Thou" and not "it."

During World War I a Roman Catholic went out under fire to minister to a boy who lay dying in No Man's Land. "Padre," the boy said, "I do not belong to your Church." "No," said the chaplain, as he knelt by the dying boy, "but you belong to my God and I have come to bring you comfort."

A short time ago in World War II, a ship was torpedoed and was sinking rapidly when it was discovered that there were not life belts enough to go round. The chaplains of the different communions at once took off their life belts and gave them to the men, and with their arms around one another they went to their death together—all in that dread moment members of the same Church! Perhaps someday we shall discover as St. Paul had discovered, that religious life is an expansive, an inclusive affair. Of two alternatives, instead of choosing either-or, you take both. When you get back to the springs and sources they are close together, though the rivers which issue from them may, like the Rhone and the Rhine and the Danube, be separated by a continent. When you get back to the headwater you have all the rivers that spring from it. In the spiritual sphere truth is inclusive; it transcends all its interpreters. They are apt to be temporal and partial.

In the tales of *The Arabian Nights* one of the heroes had a magic tent of silk which could be folded up and held in the hollow of the hand, and it could be spread out to cover an imperial army. The overtopping truth of our Christian faith is like that tent. The humblest believer can squeeze it down to fit his inmost need and it can expand like the sky and cover all Christ's flock of followers. We need to come back to St. Paul's inventory and stock-taking, and lose our partial littleness and exclusiveness in the breadth of the holy universal Church of the living God. All of a sudden, in this stock-taking of St. Paul, there comes an unexpected "Unearned increment." St. Paul's primary purpose was to take his readers beyond the partial view of a single interpreter, to show the danger of sectarian fences. If he had been an ordinary man he would have stopped there, but he throws in an extraordinary "unearned increment." The canvas stretches out and takes in the world and life and death and things present and things to come—a curious list of assets. We can claim everything for the complete Christian life.

It has usually been supposed that you cannot be a true Christian and at the same time love and possess "the world." They are generally considered exclusive alternatives. But it is possible to view the world from a level above it and to make it minister to all the higher issues of life. An ancient prophet declared that it is possible to have holiness unto the Lord on the bells of the horses, and the common pots and pans shall be as sacred as the bowls before the altar. One can possess and enjoy the world without owning it, to have and to hold.

I think perhaps our greatest single task now is to bring this huge world, with its atomic energies within our grasp, under the dominion of Christ. We cannot go on halting between two opinions, either of reverting to a stark barbarism of destruction *or* a world organized and controlled by moral and spiritual insight. We must make our decision and enter our vote for the conquest of the world by the Spirit. The highest moment in man's history will be the moment when we can say *the world is ours, for we have won it for Christ*. This will be the date of the new creation of man.

There is an immortal story of a man who turned his back on life because he was tied to the multitude of things he owned. The moment the kingdom of God comes in a person's soul the world becomes his because now he can enjoy and appreciate it.

Science has been thought to be antithetic to religion. Just the opposite is the case. Every truth which science discovers and verifies ought to enlarge the scope and range of life. How much larger our Father's house is than men used to think. There are more stories to it than we supposed, and we are more sure than ever that the visible part has come out of an invisible world which is ours.

And *life* is ours. This means much more than existence. Life is not measured by length. It is measured by interests, by sympathies, by width and height and depth. Not long ago a social worker knocked on the door of a house in the slums. A woman opened the door a crack and said: "You needn't come in here. Me and my husband we don't take no interest in nothin'." That isn't life. A man given to exaggeration was describing a factory he had seen. "It was," he said, "five thousand feet long, two hundred feet high." His wife stepped on his foot under the table and he added— "and four inches wide." Some lives have little width. Life involves the subsoil wealth, the aims and aspirations of the soul. Religion is life to the full, fresh initiation into life.

And *death* is ours. St. Paul, strangely enough, puts death among our assets. It comes at last, when Christ opens the door—not as defeat, but as gain and liberation. It is divinely right to put death among the assets of the soul. Without this beneficent provision we should go on endlessly growing old. The days would grow to years, and years would add themselves and make the centuries, and we should go on accumulating habits, getting more fixed and set, blocking the new generation with its fresh ways and new ideas—a dead weight against experiment, change and advance. Yes, death is a necessity for freshness of life, for creative living and for progress. I was walking along a great highway one day, filled with grief over the loss of my only son, when suddenly I saw a little child come out of a great gate which swung to and fastened behind her. She wanted to go to her home behind the gate but it wouldn't open. She pounded in vain with her little fist. Then she wailed as though her heart would break. The cry brought the mother. She caught the child in her arms and kissed away the tears. "Didn't you know I would come? It is all right now." Yes, there is love behind our closed gate, too.

> Death is but a covered way
> That leadeth into light
> Wherein no blinded child can stray
> Beyond the Father's sight.

Things present and things to come are ours. We can spoil life by being near-sighted (myopia) and we can spoil it by being far-sighted (presbyopia). Some persons are weak in futurity and some fail to see the significance of *now*. Most of us hated grammar in our youth, with its dull tenses—present, future, perfect, pluperfect—was, has been, will be, and now. Well, all these tenses are ours. "Now is the accepted time." The fine art of living is the cult of the present moment. If this hour is sordid, how or why do you expect eternity to be a blaze of glory? If God is not love now He never will be. But the cult of the present may spoil our lives, if we have none of the glory of going on. It was St. Augustine who said: "I saw God and I sought Him; I had Him and I wanted Him." If your religion is true, it makes your present moment sublime. If it is an abounding religion, it glorifies the future with sunset splendor, for things present and things to come are ours.

## THE CHRISTIAN LIFE

# God's Unashamed

REVEREND RAY FREEMAN JENNEY, D.D., LL.D.
*Minister, Bryn Mawr Community Church
and President, Church Federation of Greater Chicago*

*Dr. Jenney is a very able preacher, a good pastor, and a splendid church executive. The qualities of a fine mind, a friendly nature, a sympathetic spirit, and driving power plus wide experience enable him to proclaim with clarity, conviction and prophetic insight the great truths of a complete gospel of individual and social redemption.*

*He was born in Meriden, New Hampshire, in 1891. He took his theological training at Union Theological Seminary and did graduate study at Columbia University, receiving his B.D. and M.A. from these institutions. He was ordained in the Presbyterian ministry in 1917. Following a pastorate in Faith Church, New York City, from 1919-22, he was called to the pulpit of the*

First Presbyterian Church, Galesburg, Illinois, where he served for four years—and at the same time helped coach the football team at Knox College. Then he went to the University of Pennsylvania as head minister and general director of the United Religious Work. In 1929 he was called to the Park Central Presbyterian Church of Syracuse, New York; during his ministry that church increased in membership from seven hundred to over fourteen hundred. Late in 1942 he became the minister of Bryn Mawr Community Church, Chicago, Illinois, which was composed of thirty-eight different denominations and had a membership of over two thousand. In the last five years, Dr. Jenney has received nearly eleven hundred people into the fellowship of this church, has doubled his current budget and increased the benevolence giving 800 per cent.

During World War I he served as chaplain with the 59th Infantry, A.E.F., was wounded in action and has received the Purple Heart. In 1933 he spent three months in Europe and Russia, studying social, religious, economic and political conditions. In 1936 he spent the summer in England as an exchange preacher. Knox College recognized his ability with an honorary D.D., and James Millikin University honored him with an LL.D. He has done much radio work, has written numerous sermons and articles for magazines. He is the author of Speaking Boldly. In 1946 he was elected to the presidency of the Church Federation of Greater Chicago and is a member of the Mayor's Emergency Housing Committee for the City of Chicago.

"God's Unashamed" was preached in Bryn Mawr Church and was given over radio station WMAQ of the National Broadcasting Company on Sunday, December 8, 1946.

## Sermon Seven

TEXTS: They desire a better country . . . wherefore God is not ashamed to be called their God. HEBREWS 11:16

I do set my bow in the cloud, and it shall be for a token of a covenant between me and the earth. GENESIS 9:13

SCRIPTURE: GENESIS 9:11-16
HEBREWS 11:8-16

IS GOD ashamed of us? Is it because God is ashamed of us that we find ourselves prisoners of despair in these troubled times? Who are the unashamed of God? Those are pertinent questions. "God's unashamed" are mentioned but once in the Bible. In the eleventh chapter of Hebrews, that great chapter which contains the roster of the heroes of the Hebrew faith, are

[38]

written these often neglected words: "They desire a better country . . . where-fore God is not ashamed to be called their God." Desirers of a better country, they are the "unashamed of God"—they are those who are awake to the possibilities of a better tomorrow. In more poetic words, God's unashamed are the ones who see "a rainbow in the sky."

In Genesis we read these words recorded as those spoken by the Eternal One: "I do set my bow in the cloud, and it shall be for a token of a covenant between me and the earth." These great texts from Genesis and Hebrews merit our earnest consideration in these demanding days. The ancient writer of Genesis gave his reason for the creation of the rainbow. To his naïve though reverent Hebrew mind, the rainbow was a picture painted with the sky as a canvas, the vast sky shouldering out the mountains of the earth. With every color of the spectrum—red, orange, yellow, green, blue, indigo and violet—the rainbow was painted by God and hung high in the heaven so that all men could see that God has established a perpetual covenant with all mankind.

What is a rainbow? It is the result of sunlight shining on drops of falling water. Yes, that is the physical explanation of it—but it is more! The rain-bow is a shining arc of promise hung high in the sky to inspire God's unashamed to become comrades of the quest for a better country. Aye! It is God's banner, *not of defeat, but of victory*.

The rainbow, thus rightly interpreted, symbolizes the true nature of God and His right relationship to man. Too often as we witness the forces of nature and of human nature we are led to believe that God is primarily a God of wrath. When we think of volcanoes, earthquakes and pestilence it is no wonder that so many often believe that in some of nature's great mani-festations God *is* angry. When we look upon the hardness of the human heart and see the things in human nature that are dark, when we see the results of uncontrolled passions and appetites, and when we witness the evil in man as it destroys the gardens of God and wounds and kills our fellow men by the millions through all the earth, we come to the conclusion that God is angry with man.

In the past we have revolted against the theology which places "sinners in the hands of an angry God," but it has recently been stated with spiritual insight that we have now put "a good God in the hands of angry sinners." We have sought God's approval of our sins in the exploitation of the weak in both peace and war. We live in a world of mass starvation. Lincoln's well-known words, "This nation cannot endure half slave and half free," have been charged with new meaning— "this world cannot endure half starved and half fed." Granted, "man does not live by bread alone" but man must have bread and so must man have shelter and that shelter fit for the habita-tion of man. The bitter words of an Englishman remain unanswered. He said, "What is the use of belonging to an Empire on which the sun never sets if one has to live in an alley on which the sun never rises?" The provocative words of Pascal rebuke and plague us— "Because we would not fortify justice now we justify force." Yes, we must admit that we have sought, in both our personal and group life, God's approval of our sins of omission and commission. But is that the final word? No! For it is not the beast in man but the best in man that reconciles man to God and enables man to reflect God's glory. "Beholding as in a mirror the glory of the Lord, we are transformed into the same image from glory to glory." This is the saving message that "God was in Christ, reconciling the world unto Himself . . . and hath committed unto us the word of reconciliation."

Although we may have lost our way in the storm, the rainbow speaks to us in terms of assurance, even in the midst of our sins, of a God of justice, a justice that is tempered with mercy. Then, we know with Frederick W. Faber that:

> There's a wideness in God's mercy,
> Like the wideness of the sea;
> There's a kindness in his justice,
> Which is more than liberty.

That's it! Amid the storm and after it, God's mercy shines. It is the faith by which men live. Our hearts would break if it were not true. Aye! As I look deeply into my own heart I know that even the judgment of God will not break my pride, if the mercy of God does not touch my heart. In truth

> I trace the rainbow through the rain,
> And feel the promise is not vain,
> That morn shall tearless be.

Human beings are like rainbows. Coleridge was one of the first to point this out. "We are like rainbows," he said, "made up of reflected splendor and our own tears." Life is a series of alternating storms and calms. We are "up" today and "down" tomorrow; "chinning the curb or riding the clouds." Today, the sky is blue; tomorrow, it is overcast. The mind of man is a world, and storms are driven across its sky. Sometimes it is the storm of sorrow, sometimes the storm of doubt, sometimes the storm of disappointment, sometimes the storm of despondency and despair. Is not this true in all our experiences—that after the storm comes the rainbow? Thus we see the need of true and constant companionship. "She was the rainbow to my dripping years," Carlyle said of his wife. Every true mother, father, wife, husband, child and friend is like a rainbow—a rainbow of promise.

Furthermore, the covenant God proclaims, through His bow in the sky, reveals that in every disaster He, the God of justice and redemptive love, stands ready to help us to desire and to achieve a new earth "in which dwelleth righteousness." Yet, what tragedy often results! We have looked upon *death* as man's last *enemy* but it does not follow that *death* is man's greatest *tragedy*. Men are willing to die for the objects of their devotion, both worthy and unworthy. Death can be faced and taken and defeated. Then, what is man's greatest tragedy? *It is the betrayal of life.*

The personal betrayal of a sacred trust and responsibility by young people and by mature men and women is a tragedy. When one fails to look upon life as an entrustment from God and does not render back to life a full, true and honest account—that is tragedy; when one refuses to make the most out of life, with all its matchless opportunities for growth and development— that is tragedy; when one fails to see and serve the highest and the best in glad loyalty, that is personal tragedy. "And to whomsoever is given, of him shall much be required." Here, Jesus enunciated a ruling principle of life.

The social betrayal of life is an even worse tragedy. The story of one who was born in 1918 in Canada illustrates this point. It is the oft-repeated story of our social disregard for individual life. A baby was born into a desperately poor Welsh family. He was named George Woodrow Jones after Lloyd George and Woodrow Wilson. His name was filled with the prophetic hope of a new day. When he was quite young, we are informed, his family moved to this country and here they met with one misfortune after another and sank from poverty to deeper poverty. George was sent to school only a little while. He learned to read but not to write very well. In the unemployed thirties, he could not get work. In 1940, he was drafted into the service. Here, for the first time in his life, he had food enough, decent clothing and adequate shelter. Of these things he wrote his mother through his chaplain. In 1945, he was killed in Iwo Jima. Was that the tragedy? No!—*George Woodrow Jones never lived*—that was the tragedy! His was the tragedy of hunger, the tragedy of unemployment, the tragedy of poor education. His country was interested enough to feed and clothe and equip him for death but his country was not interested enough to equip him for life. That was the tragedy of it all.

> Let not young lives be smothered out before
> They do great deeds or fully flaunt their pride,
> It is the world's one crime—
> It's young grow ox-like, limp, and leaden-eyed.
>
> Not that they starve, but starve so dreamlessly,
> Not that they sow, but that they seldom reap,
> Not that they serve, but have no gods to serve,
> Not that they die, but that they die like sheep.[1]

The truth is, the Christian religion goes beyond tragedy to redeem life and save it from betrayal. This is the faith of God's unashamed. If we are indifferent to this great fact, then we will surely stand before the open doorway of destruction, and as a result of our sins of omission and commission, we will lose our chance to stand on the threshold of the greatest era of all mankind and rightly use the dynamics entrusted to us.

[1] "The Leaden-Eyed" from *Collected Poems*, by Vachel Lindsay. By permission of the Macmillan Company, publishers.

There are two great dynamics in the world today—the dynamic of the atomic bomb and the dynamic of the Christian faith. At precisely the time when we thought flight and communication would bind the world together we have in our hands the power to blast it all to bits. The question of questions is this: Will the fear that the atomic bomb can be used to blow cities apart be the power which will coerce the nations to live together? If this is true, then it is the first time in the history of mankind that we have the paradox of mechanical explosives assisting in social integration. We must reflect on Bruce Bliven's sobering statement: "History offers no justification for the hope that atomic power will be used for good (constructively) and not for evil." We are already worshiping at the shrine of the false gods of physical power. The question is: Are we good enough to harness cosmic energy to the purposes of God? In this confused and tragic period we must seek not only for physical, economic and political power, but if we are to survive, we must seek and find a moral and spiritual dynamic for all of life. This we have in the Christian faith: the ability under God to discover what is primary, the intelligence to put first things first, and make Him sovereign over life. This must be the major concern of Christians in this critical period of revolution, reconversion, redirection and rehabilitation.

The truth still holds that the smaller we become geographically, the larger we must become economically, politically, morally and spiritually. It was said of the first-century Christians: "These are they that hold the world together." Can we twentieth-century Christians do this? *We can!* In the end, the destiny of man need not be at the mercy of power; it is at the mercy of those who control the sources of power. That is the central message of the Christian religion.

Why do men keep on working after the earth has been shaken and shattered? we ask. What faith is there left in a world that has had a scorched earth policy; in a world where men have bombed babies; in a world where God's fertile gardens of beauty and fruitfulness have become barren and arid deserts of waste in a war-weary world; where animosity, greed and fear are increasing at an alarming rate? Can we help hold the world together? We can if we are God's unashamed!

We know the destructive results of the violent explosion of two atomic bombs. We also should be keenly aware that the explosive power of one Christ-filled life can do more good in the world than any atomic bomb that any scientist has or will ever create. It is not just a period of physical, economic and political revolution in which we are engaged. Something else is required if we survive and that is a moral and spiritual revolution.

"They died that the desert might bloom." This is the significant sentence that describes the building of Boulder Dam, in which eighty-nine people lost their lives. Three basic qualities were needed to complete that dam— intelligent planning, hard work and worthy sacrifice. Here, in part, is found our answer for today. The need for men and women of creative faith is imperative in these reconstruction days. Dr. Arthur Compton recently said: "Science has created a world in which Christianity is an imperative. We will either have to learn to live together with the common objective of the well-being of all or we will not live. It is one world or none." Amid our contemporary perplexities, disillusionments and problems, if we are humble-minded, we shall surely find help. Only as we are redeemed by God, plan, work and sacrifice for those things that are "unshaken in a shaken world," will we be able to help God in the building of a new earth. For "only those can really transform the world whose vision has already transcended it." Then, and only then, can we say with Wordsworth:

> My heart leaps up and I behold
> A rainbow in the sky.

In our childhood we saw the rainbow and were told that a pot of gold was at its end. Many a weary, wet mile I traveled as a child only to come back home to my mother perplexed and discouraged. It was then that she told me that the rainbow of God's promise was a bow that had no end but in the sky of God's dream. She counseled me: "Gold is not the end of life, but God." William Blake caught this thought nearly one hundred and fifty years ago:

> Bring me my bow of burning gold!
> Bring me my arrows of desire!
> Bring me my spear! O clouds, unfold!
> Bring me my chariot of fire!

What gets our attention, gets us! That is a demonstrated fact! Therefore, a high sense of responsibility to life is clear and commanding. It is only as we come to the heart of the Christian message as it culminates in the cross that the deeper meaning of the rainbow is found. Not alone in the rainbow in the sky is told "the wondrous story," but more clearly is it written in the "rainbow 'round about the throne of God" and most clearly of all, in Christ is God's full promise and sovereign power, mercy and redeeming love revealed. Then, the truth of those great words about Calvary have compelling power:

> In the Cross of Christ I glory,
> Towering O'er the wrecks of time;
> All the light of sacred story,
> Gathers 'round its head sublime.

Martin Niemoeller, in his recent visit to the United States, emphasized this truth again and again. In his many sermons given here he stressed the fact that the final ground for our faith is found in the redemptive love of God through Jesus Christ; "We live," said he, "by the forgiveness of God in Jesus Christ and that is the only basis for our peace and our hope."

"We are saved by hope." Aye! but such a faith is born out of the open-eyed, realistic facing of all the dark, dreary and ugly facts of life. But it must be the complete realism that sees also the prophecy of hope. It has been the task of Christianity, as of all great religions, to restore men's faith in the view of fear. In Jesus is revealed infinite faith in God and man in what God is, and what man may become through the power of God unto salvation. "This is the victory that overcometh the world, even our faith."

Belief in a Christlike God will save us from betrayal. Then we, "God's unashamed," will seek a better country with a faith that is born of "courage plus valor." The God of hope will give us a new heart and adequate power, both to desire and to achieve a better country—yes, and more—a better world for all the needy sons of men. This is the good news of God to the unashamed of this and every generation.

> Ye that have faith to look with fearless eyes
> Beyond the tragedy of a world at strife,
> And know that out of death and night shall rise
> The dawn of ampler life;
> Rejoice, whatever anguish rend the heart,
> That God has given you the priceless dower
> To live in these great times and have your part
> In Freedom's crowning hour,
> That ye may tell your sons who see the light
> High in the heavens—their heritage to take—
> "I saw the powers of darkness take their flight;
> I saw the morning break."

## THE CHRISTIAN LIFE

## God in Everyday Living

REVEREND ROBERT LESSING
*Vicar, St. Mark's Episcopal Church, Downey, California*

*Robert Lessing is in his first church as vicar.*

*His sermon was aimed at a most important need in these times—to get people to think in terms of practicing the presence of God.*

*For seven years he served as municipal judge in Torrance, California, before entering the ministry, was active in civic organizations designed to combat juvenile delinquency, is on the executive board of the Boy Scouts of America in Los Angeles County and on the executive board of Los Angeles County Coordinating Councils. While attending the seminary, he was employed as assistant minister at St. Luke's, San Francisco, and had charge of Holy Innocent's Mission in Corte Madera, California. He studied at the University of California at Los Angeles, Southwestern University Law*

School, the University of Southern California, did graduate work in religion, then attended the Church Divinity School of the Pacific, an Episcopal seminary.

He was called in 1946 to be vicar of St. Mark's Episcopal Church, Downey, California, his first regular cure, and is happy in his work there. He is interested in church history, plans to write a history of the Church of England with particular emphasis on the relationship between the Church in England and the Papacy and a reinterpretation of the English Reformation.

## Sermon Eight

TEXT: Doth the plowman plow all day to sow? doth he open and break the clods of his ground? . . . For his God doth instruct him to discretion, and doth teach him.  ISAIAH 28:24, 26

IN ALL of Israel no task was more prosaic, no life more routined than that of the plowman who, day after day, followed his trudging oxen, scratching the surface of the rock-filled earth in the scorching sun. What man of modern times can find his life more simple—more dull than that?

And yet the prophet Isaiah could say of the plowman, "His God doth instruct him to discretion, and doth teach him."

Most of us are startled at this sudden discovery of God walking by the side of the simple plowman, guiding, teaching, inspiring him in a dull task that seems to us to have so insignificant a place in a complex universe.

But why should this be so much of a surprise? What is so incongruous in the companionship between the plowman and the Creator of Heaven and earth? There are several answers to these questions.

In the first place, we have become accustomed to distinguishing between the *intellectual* and the *common* life and excluding God from the latter. We could read of God guiding the eyes of Newton as he watched the falling apple, and inspiring him to work out the theory of gravity, and such a statement would not startle us a bit.

We believe, without difficulty, that Beethoven was the recipient of supernatural gifts; that the poet is inspired; that Michelangelo dipped his brush in celestial colors. But to recognize as supernatural inspiration in the furrow of a plow is somehow difficult. What mystical illumination can the peasant need to break his clods, or bind his sheaves? What need is there for a divine hand in the work of the machinist, the bank clerk, or the housewife?

And yet, when we stop to think about it, we find that our distinction between the intellectual and the common worlds is purely arbitrary. Why should we expect to find God only in the art galleries, the libraries and the concert halls? Why should He guide the hand of the artist and not that of the peasant who is also His child?

When we realize that there is no common world but only *common people*, we see how God can be beside the lowliest toiler in the land, inspiring him to be the best of whatever he is.

Another false distinction that we make is that between the *influential* and the *insignificant* life. It was this fault that drove the writer of the book of Ecclesiastes to distraction. He sought to find God in power and wealth and influence, and then died frustrated—crying out that all life is vanity. His life, indeed, was vanity, for he had built about himself a wall of power and influence which God would not penetrate.

Why should we believe that princes share a divine fellowship that is denied the plowman? Is the king more indispensable than he who tills the soil? Nay. Each task must have its doer. There are nations to govern and fields to plow—music to be written and streets to be cleaned—stars to be measured and buttons to be sewed—and who can say which task is the least?

The superficial distinctions about which men make such ado have no meaning for the God who sees the sparrow fall. He created no kings nor artists nor men of science but only man. And when He comes to judge them all, it will not be by the achievements of pen or brush but by how well they have done His Will.

There is still a third error that we make when we divide the sacred life from the secular. We naturally suppose that the divine voice is heard by priest and prophet, descending upon them with the fire of inspiration. They are dealing with sacred things—the very medium in which God treads. The plowman only digs in dirt—a secular and mundane world so far removed from heaven. And yet, what is the Sanctuary of the Church if it is not the symbol of *all* things Holy? Is not the workbench a sanctuary to him who finds God while he works. That simple man, Brother Lawrence, knew the presence of God while he washed the dishes in a monastery. In the midst of the desert, Jacob was able to say, "Surely God was in this place and I knew it not." The ground where Moses stood was Holy ground—not because of Moses' presence, but because he had found God beside him.

Great men of God have found Him wherever they might be. Isaiah saw Him in the Temple; Ezekiel, beside a stream. We hear Him speak to us in some great choral masterpiece, and yet the man who toiled to make the music paper may have heard Him just as well.

When Isaiah found God walking with the plowman, he saw what we have failed to see—that we, too, can know Him in our everyday living if only we will.

But how, you say? First of all we must look *inward* to examine the condition of our hearts. For God will not visit a heart diseased with greed and avarice—selfishness and false pride—hate and bitterness. Jesus said that if we have aught against our brother, we must not come with our gift to the

Altar, but rather, go and be reconciled with our brother, and then come to the Altar with our gift.

If we have wronged someone or disputed with him and are kept back from making peace because of pride, we shall not hear the voice of God. Of course, this calls for a certain humility that modern man is reluctant to assume. But God who sent His Son to give his life in Palestine will find our humility small sacrifice.

Next, we must look *outward*. Have we built a little wall about ourselves—a little world all our own into which we would have no one but God to enter? Do we think entirely of ourselves while, all around us, others less fortunate suffer for the want of what we could supply? Remember the story that Jesus told, how he said, "For I was an hungered, and ye gave me meat: I was thirsty, and ye gave me drink: I was a stranger, and ye took me in." And the people asked him when they had done all these things for him and he answered, "Verily I say unto you, Inasmuch as ye have done it unto the least of these my brethren, ye have done it unto me."

We may protest, saying that we have done all that could be expected of us by our fellow man. We have endowed hospitals, given to the community chest, and bought pencils from the blind. But Jesus said, "When ye have done all that is required of you, then say, we are unprofitable servants."

True fellowship with our brethren is not manifested in philanthropy. St. Paul said, "Though I bestow all my goods to feed the poor, and though I give my body to be burned, and have not love, it profiteth me nothing." Though we give life itself, it is nothing if we do not give it for the love of God.

Now, by looking *inward* to search our hearts, and *outward* to examine the condition of our relations with our fellow men, we have established a *basis* for uninterrupted communion with God. If we are honest in our self-examination we will discover the imperfections, the human weaknesses that abound in each of us. This discovery should humble us, and our humility should force us to lay these weaknesses and imperfections at the feet of the Loving Father, praying that He will overcome our weakness with His strength, and our imperfections by His perfection.

But this is not some magical formula for knowing God whereby when we have done these things we can expect Him to come and stand beside us. These things are only preparation. We look *inward* and then *outward* in order that we may know something about *ourselves*. To know God, we must look *upward*. The whole center of our universe must be changed. No longer may we submit to the human tendency to make ourself the center of the universe. We must turn from a self-centered life to the kind of life in which God becomes the focal point. We seek that state which St. Paul described when he said, "It is no longer I that live but Christ that liveth in me."

Man could search a lifetime in vain for such a perfect state. He, of himself, is impotent to achieve it. Our whole dependence in life is on God without whom we cannot live or breathe. Only when we make each thought, each deed, each word a prayer can we hope to live in fellowship with Him whose service is most perfect freedom.

If we are ever to know the love of God and to see that love manifested in our everyday living, we must take our eyes from the ground—not the eyes with which we see the plow, but the eyes of faith with which we see God.

There is a scene in *Pilgrim's Progress* where the visitors are taken into a room where "there was a man who could look no way but downwards, with a muckrake in his hand. There stood also one over his head, with a celestial crown in his hand, and he proffered him that crown for his muckrake; but the man did neither look up nor regard, but raked to himself the straws, the small sticks, and the dust of the floor."

He who has his eyes fixed on the straw, the small sticks, and the dust of the earth rather than on the celestial crown—he who puts his faith in the temporal things of the world rather than in the eternal things beyond the stars, can never know the companionship of God in daily life.

Yes, God will walk with the prince, the plumber and the plowman, but they will never know it unless their hearts, and minds, and souls, and bodies are so completely responsive to the symphony of His love that all other sounds are but the tinkling of cymbals.

This is no easy task, but I suppose that its difficulties are not worthy to be compared with the glory of His love which we *may* know. And once we find that love we will cry out with St. Paul, "For I am persuaded, that neither death, nor life, nor angels, nor principalities, nor powers, nor things present, nor things to come, nor height, nor depth, nor any other creature, shall be able to separate us from the love of God, which is in Christ Jesus, our Lord."

## THE CHRISTIAN LIFE

# Reopening Old Wells

REVEREND WILLIAM A. KEITH, D.D.

*Minister, First Congregational Church, Kalamazoo, Michigan*

*Dr. Keith entered the Congregational ministry in 1929, serving as minister of education, First Congregational Church of Oak Park, Illinois, held pastorates at First Congregational Church, Batavia, Illinois, and at Collegeside Church, Nashville, Tennessee. He became pastor of First Congregational Church of Kalamazoo, Michigan, in 1939. Piedmont College granted him the honorary degree of Doctor of Divinity in 1938. Born in Illinois in 1904, he is a graduate of the University of Chicago and the Chicago Theological Seminary.*

*He has served his denomination as moderator of the Tennessee Conference and on various boards and committees. The Michigan congregational Conference named him the preacher for the annual meeting in May of 1947.*

*His wide community interests have included the presidency of the Kalamazoo Ministerial Alliance, the vice-presidency of the Tuberculosis Association, membership on the boards of the Salvation Army, the Society for Pastoral Care, and the Council of Churches.*

*In "Reopening Old Wells," he pleads with men to have faith and vision to go forward in national and personal life trusting in the providence of God.*

## Sermon Nine

OUR thinking begins not with ourselves in the United States but with another people in a faraway land and long ago. In the twenty-sixth chapter of Genesis, the eighteenth verse, this incident is reported: "And Isaac digged again the wells of water, which they had digged in the days of Abraham his father; for the Philistines had stopped them after the death of Abraham: and he called their names after the names by which his father had called them."

Isaac, as head of a nomadic tribe, was moving through the arid lands on the edge of the southern deserts in Canaan pitching his tents wherever he could find sustenance for his people and his flocks. The water supply in that dry land was even more critical than the food supply. Isaac remembered having been in the same country with his father, Abraham. He remembered the wells they had dug and the refreshing waters they had drawn from them. Since those earlier years the Philistines had filled them in and his own people had neglected them. So he set to work to reopen the old wells—to repair the damage done by a foe and by long neglect. He drank again at the wells from which his father had drunk. "And Isaac digged again the wells of water, which they had digged in the days of Abraham his father. . . ."

In the recent past we were with Abraham and his generation of whom it was said, "He went out not knowing whither he went." We, too, went out into expanding frontiers. The first World War made us conscious of the planet as a whole as we took our first ventures into internationalism. Within the year our young men have returned from roaming over the whole earth. We were also recently with Abraham on the expanding frontiers of the machine age. Even those of us yet in middle life can remember our first motion picture, first radio, first automobile and first airplane. Not even the possibility of power from atomic energy startles us in this startling age! Our thinking, also, was recently with Abraham out on new frontiers. I can recall the consternation of some members of the older generation that college age young people should be exposed to the thought of George Bernard Shaw's socialism and Karl Marx's communism. Those were the years in which the most characteristic word in our vocabulary was "adventurous." We were exploring new territory, willing to take the risk of finding new ways of living, new forms of thought.

Just at present, however, our generation is with Isaac instead of Abraham. We have turned back from the far frontiers to colonize our exploration, make it a fit human habitation and discover the faith from which our fathers drew strength and purpose in their time. Meanwhile, the Philistines have stopped and we have neglected these life-giving springs. Now, like Isaac, we would reopen the wells of our fathers.

If there is any word we cherish in this nation out of its past, that word is "liberty." Did not Patrick Henry cry, "Give me liberty or give me death"? More recently we have broadened the term to mean freedom. Have we not had the four freedoms? Surely our fathers drank from the wells of liberty and freedom.

Yet we had all but forgotten that when our fathers drank from those wells they took it for granted that liberty and freedom were in solution with something else. With them it was liberty *and* loyalty, freedom *and* responsibility. Washington and the founding fathers chose not only liberty and freedom but also loyalty and responsibility. They saw clearly that you have freedom only as you choose responsibility. They chose liberty by way of loyalty. So Washington not only led the Revolution as a thrust of liberty but became the first president as an act of responsibility.

Now democracy again has to make that dual choice. We have reached the end of the road when democracy means liberty without responsibility. Too many among us have interpreted democracy as license, the right of every person to do as he pleases, get out of it whatever he can for himself. At the end of that road lies national chaos and finally the loss of liberty. It creates classes of individuals driven only by self-interest and pressure groups whose only thought is to serve themselves. Though three or more fascist powers have been put out of operation we have not thereby saved democracy. We saved the chance to save it now from within by the freely given loyalty of our people to "the general welfare." That means we not only have the right to get but also to give, not only to reap but to plant.

We are nearer fascism today than ever before. We would get it not because some foreign ideology claimed us but because we betrayed our own best heritage. Nor will we avoid it by being led off by an ideological war with Russia or even into atomic war as a way of avoiding our internal crisis. We would get fascism by way of a breakdown of our own life and choose it as a means of establishing order in an utterly chaotic state. Societies exist by both law and loyalty. Public order is the first business of the state. Loyalty is the first business of the citizen. Law is restraint from without. Loyalty is restraint from within. The democratic heritage rests more on loyalty than on law. Now we are at that point in our journey when we need to reopen the wells of our fathers and choose both freedom and responsibility. Edmund Burke, who examined the history of nations, saw this choice when he wrote:

> Men are qualified for civil liberty in exact proportion to their disposition to put moral chains upon their own appetites; in proportion as their love of justice is above their rapacity; in proportion as they are disposed to listen to the counsels of the wise and good, in preference to the flattery of knaves. Society cannot exist unless a controlling power upon will and appetite be placed somewhere, and the less of it there is within, the more there must be without. It is ordained in the eternal constitution of things, that men of intemperate minds cannot be free. Their passions forge their fetters.

These are serious days in the life of our nation. Just when we need a united people not so much to stand up to the world as to be sure of our direction and leadership in the world; just when we need to get our domestic economy running in high gear, then too many of us choose liberty without loyalty.

Democracy has given us a heritage of privilege and opportunity. We want to keep that. The other half of our heritage is freely given loyalty to justice, brotherhood and concern for the common good. These are the justification of freedom. From that deep well of our national faith we need to drink as did our fathers.

This truth which is illustrated by our public life is also illustrated in our private life. That also has often had too much liberty and not enough loyalty.

Perhaps the pendulum swings, we say, thereby choosing a bad figure of speech. When the pendulum swings you get an age of puritans followed by an age of libertines. The figure of the old philosophers of a man driving two horses, one black and the other white, is much better. Take them both in hand with the same rein, let them check each other, but both together be driven down a chosen course.

When personal freedom is given full rein we recklessly plunge ahead. Yet life would be intolerable for most of us if we could not team up with that heady steed. The saying that a man's home is his castle is a recognition that in certain areas of our life we want no public law to tell us what we must do or what we must think. We want the right to draw the blinds even on public opinion. But with that saying went the assumption that every man having chosen personal freedom would choose also good sense and be master in his own house. It was assumed that in home and castle inner restraint would make gentle men and gentle women. Liberty and freedom were teamed with loyalty and responsibility.

However, having made no such working agreement with life we have had an irresponsible generation saying, "I'm free, white and twenty-one." We even gave freedom the name of "self-expression" and under the sanction of popular psychology warned ourselves against the fearful results of repression. Well, see what did happen to us. We had self-expression, with multitudes of people living loose, uncontrolled lives, intemperate in their speech, their drinking and in their sex life. People did silly things and even tragic things, wrecked their own lives and the lives of other people because they chose liberty without loyalty.

No people yet in the history of life on this planet has ever been great nor perpetuated themselves on drunkenness and adultery. These things are wrong because life just will not hold together on that basis. They wreck the lives of individuals. They wreck homes. Finally they wreck a society. Liberty without loyalty ends in ruin.

Here again loyalty is a prior principle to freedom. Recognizing that "public decency" and even "public good" must be protected, we pass laws to hold the outlaw in partial restraint. But the law can go only so far. It finally fails unless there is in the hearts of the people an inner loyalty, a freely chosen allegiance to some ideal for themselves, their mates, their children and finally to the common good.

The moral law is still operating just as in the time of our fathers. We had better drink deeply now of the waters of honor, sobriety, integrity, and good will. They are the only principles worthy of men who carry the light of the moral law within them and who will be forever unhappy and unfulfilled until they bring their innermost lives into conformity with the moral law established from the foundation of the world.

These wells from which men drink for refreshment and renewal have their source in the depths of religious faith. The founding fathers who avowed these two principles of liberty *and* loyalty, freedom *and* responsibility, acknowledged they were from a single source. Both men and states, they maintained, drew their freedom and their responsibility from God.

In the Declaration of Independence they wrote of "the Laws of Nature and of Nature's God" and "that all men are endowed by their Creator with certain unalienable Rights. . . ." Such rights were not conferred by the state but must be guaranteed by the state. That was its responsibility before God. No state or individual group within a society could take away those rights since they had not conferred them in the first place. They were given by God. That faith has given dignity to men. It has lifted them up and fortified them with courage. It has made them confident of the possibility of democracy. In that conviction men have asserted their freedom against tyrants and oppressors. Throughout the history of the West, even to our own time (witness the Confessional Church of Germany), the last citadel of freedom has been in men who took their stand for freedom on something which was beyond man.

Such men were free but they were also bound. Something beyond man had hold upon them. Sir William Blackstone, living at the same time that Jefferson penned the Declaration, wrote in his "Commentaries" on the civil law: "Man considered as a creature, must necessarily be subject to the laws of his Creator. . . . This law of nature, being co-eval with mankind, and dictated by God himself, is of course superior in obligation to any other. . . ." Thus, public law itself is subject to a higher law. Men themselves are responsible to the moral law which they did not make nor do they break with impunity. Liberty is derived from responsibility.

Back of this faith men put into political documents are ideas as old as the Hebrew prophets. They taught that men were endowed with the knowledge of good and evil and were given free will to choose either. Yet God would hold them to strict accountability. His judgment was always over them. "And the Lord said unto me, Amos, what seest thou? And I said, A plumbline. Then said the Lord, Behold I will set a plumbline in the midst of my people Israel." That eternal perpendicular, the demands of moral righteousness, runs through every deed, among every people and in every century. Their conception of one God carried with it the corollary of one people in all the earth. We must respect our fellows and be accountable to God for them since we are of one human family. These are the disciplines of faith.

It makes all the difference in the world just now whether or not we keep open these wells. We may ruin them by neglect or stop them by studied intent. If that happens we will be a generation that cannot guarantee its own freedom and will not accept its responsibility.

In the culture of the West our churches have been like wells men dig in the earth to get at these life-giving springs. More than any other institution they have a conscious purpose to help get at the sources of life by way of worship and instruction. In a nation like our own, with a long tradition of separation of Church and state, it is the responsibility of the Church to be the conscience of the state. The time may be nearer at hand than we think when we will need the Church as the last defense of our liberty. Men will worship something. If they do not worship God then they will worship the state, themselves, some other man or an ideology. Always the first commandment is. "Thou shalt have no other gods before me." From generation to generation we must teach the young and remind the mature of the claim of God and His moral law upon us. Civilization must have a civilizing faith to bring us to high standards of public duty and private conduct.

Despite many valued differences in our three great religious traditions, Protestant, Roman Catholic and Jewish, all of them share the common springs. All of them have the Ten Commandments and two of them share the teachings of Christ. All of them are concerned with the ethical direction of life and call men to worship and serve "one God and Father of us all."

The course of history as we make it in our time will depend upon whether or not our churches are able, by the loyalty of our people, to provide a channel whereby we may draw and drink from these old and proven wells. "A church," says Lewis Mumford, "that taught one part of mankind to walk upright and unafraid through one Dark Age may yet summon up the power that will enable us to avert another Dark Age or to face it, if it begins to descend upon us, with unyielding courage." The Church is not the water. It is the well opening to deeper convictions which come from the free-flowing sources of our faith.

"And Isaac digged again the wells of water, which they had digged in the days of Abraham his father. . . ." Let us also reopen old wells!

THE CHRISTIAN LIFE

# Raggedy Man's Religion

REVEREND GASTON FOOTE, TH. D.

*Minister, Grace Methodist Church, Dayton, Ohio*

*Gaston Foote is rapidly becoming known as a preacher of great spiritual power. Born on a farm in Texas in 1902, he received his academic and divinity degrees at Southern Methodist University, Dallas, and the Doctorate in Theology at Illif School of Theology, Denver. He has traveled extensively, having spent four summers in Europe and one in the Orient. His sermon illustrations are richer for his travel. In 1937 he was one of the representatives of the former Southern Methodist Church at the World Council of Faith and Order at Edinburgh, Scotland. In 1946 he represented the Board of Missions of the Methodist Church at the West African Regional Missionary Conference, Leopoldville, Belgian Congo.*

*His early pastorates were in northwest Texas; he was appointed to Winfield Church, Little Rock, Arkansas, in 1936, went to First Church, Montgomery, Alabama, in 1941, and came to Grace Church, Dayton, Ohio, in 1945. Because of the large crowds that come to hear him two identical morning worship services are held each Sunday. He speaks to numerous high schools, colleges and universities and has been the summer preacher at Central Church, Detroit, Michigan, Foundry Church, Washington, D. C., Trinity Church, Springfield, Massachusetts, and the American Church in Paris.*

*In 1940-41 he was editor of the Arkansas Methodist and is the author of three books, Keys to Conquest (1933), Just Plain Bread (1938) and Lamps without Oil (1944.)*

*"Raggedy Man's Religion" shows Dr. Foote's use of simple, homely illustrations, his faith for today, his insistence that man owes God the best things—his best time, his best talents, his best gifts. The element of surprise is of great value in his sermons.*

# Sermon Ten

Text: And the residue thereof he maketh a god . . . Isaiah 44:17

WHEN I was a boy my mother began quite early to teach me to keep my face and hands clean and my clothes neat. I can well imagine it was a difficult job, particularly in my case, since I remember her having said in desperation, "If you don't wash your face and hands and put on clean clothing, I'm going to give you to the raggedy man." All of us knew the raggedy man. He came at rather regular intervals through the neighborhood yelling, "Rags-rags-raggedy-raggedy-raggedy man." We ransacked the closets for every old rag, old shoe and ancient piece of clothing and gave them to the raggedy man. He seemed quite pleased, though I could not understand why since we never gave him anything we could use for ourselves.

I have had the feeling that many of us treat God, though perhaps unconsciously, just as we used to treat the raggedy man. That is to say, we give God only the rags of life, the things that are left over, the things we cannot possibly use for ourselves. Under such circumstances our religion becomes simply a religion of remnants. Of course, this is no mere modern sin, something new in the field of transgression. Since the days of Adam man has been trying either to ignore God or to make Him so little and insignificant as to be of no consequence in life. Isaiah refers to a man who cut from the forest a beautiful piece of cedar, used part of it to warm himself, part of it to cook his food and with "the residue thereof he maketh a god . . . he falleth down and worshippeth it and saith, deliver me, for thou art my God."

How perfectly this illustrates many current, contemporary attitudes toward religion. We take life for granted—a gift from God perhaps, but a gift with no strings attached. We squander time as though we created it. We cash in our own talents as though God had nothing to do with them. We think of our money as being exclusively our own with no thought of God's part in the production. Just as we loaded the raggedy man down with materials entirely useless to us so we give God, if we give Him anything at all, the spare moments of our time, the ragged edge of our talents, the superfluous of our money.

Consider how we give God the remnant of our time. Not long ago I called on a man who had three sons in our Sunday school and sought to interest him in regular church attendance. His excuse was typical of thousands of others. He worked hard to provide a living for himself and his family; he believed in religion, particularly for his wife and children, but Sunday was his only free day and he preferred to use it as he saw fit. Then he added a statement that was calculated to send my blood pressure up fifty points, "Someday when I get a little time I'm going to surprise you by coming to church." Perhaps he didn't realize that God had given him all the time that he had, for time comes from God, that God had given him just as many hours in the day and days in the year as had been given to the saints. His wrong sense of values had ruled the stewardship of time out of his thinking and he planned to give God such spare moments as would not interfere with his own private schedule of life.

No time for God?
What fools we are
To clutter up our lives
With common things, and
Leave without the Lord of Life,
And life itself.

No time for God?
As soon to say no time
To eat, to sleep, to live, to die.
Take time for God
Or a poor misshapen thing you'll be
To step into eternity
And say, "I had no time for Thee."

Consider how we, perhaps unconsciously, give our children a false idea of the stewardship of time. We want them to do well in school and we insist upon their regularity and punctuality in attendance. They must be quite ill if we give them permission to remain at home. But when Sunday comes, if the weather is inclement or if they feel physically indisposed, we readily consent to allowing them to remain at home. It is hardly surprising, under these circumstances, to see how young people quickly get the idea that religion and the public worship of God are purely optional matters, a sort of appendix to the book of life. We Protestants would do well to remember that the paramount fundamental of Catholicism is attendance upon the Mass. Suffice it to say, their record of holding their children throughout life is better than our own and for precisely this reason. We must teach our children the absolute necessity of dedicated time to the worship of God. Samuel Johnson said, "Religion will glide by degrees out of the mind unless it be invigorated by stated calls to worship." Calvin Coolidge said, "It is only when men begin to worship that they begin to grow." Voltaire, by no means a religious enthusiast, said, "If we change the holy day into a holiday the days of religion are numbered."

Obviously, many people give God the remnant of their time from the standpoint of life's calendar. Entirely too much has been said about fox-hole religion; as though religion were merely an emergency exit from life's difficulties. He who never calls upon God until the situation is desperate will have a desperately inadequate religious experience. It seems that the only way

God could deliver a man from a sinking raft would be for the man to take God with him on the raft. To call upon God only in times of great danger is to miss the whole content of religion. John Wesley said, "Our men die well." But the reason they died well was because they had previously lived well. Religion prepares one for life. To take time for God only a few moments before death is not only a cowardly act but a disappointing one. The rich reward of His fellowship throughout our lives has been denied us. The writer of Ecclesiastes was right, "Remember now thy creator in the days of thy youth, while the evil days come not. . . ."

The story is told of a young man who went to a priest and told him of his life's ambitions. He had planned to go to a university and become an architect. "What then?" asked the priest. He expected to become famous by designing magnificent public buildings. "What then?" asked the priest. He expected to marry and have a family. "What then?" asked the priest. He planned to become wealthy and retire. "What then?" asked the priest. "I see what you mean," said the young man, "I will then make peace with my God." "It's all well," said the priest, "but you must reverse the plan. Make peace with God and all these other things shall be added."

Consider how we give only the remnants to God from the standpoint of the dedication of our talents. There are two fundamental philosophies of life that can be expressed in one word each. The first is the *pagan* philosophy which says I own. It is my body and I can do with it as I will. It is my mind, my life, and I am responsible to no one but myself. The second is the *Christian* philosophy which says I owe. I am responsible to God for my body, my health, my mind, my life.

If as Christian people we are keenly sensitive to our stewardship we must recognize the fact that our talents belong to God. If we have ability to make money it is because God gave us minds to think, hands to work and a community in which relatively free enterprise is practiced. If we have strong, virile bodies to perform our daily tasks it is because God sustains within us the perpetual miracle of life. Every heartbeat is but another miracle of God. Every breath we draw is an evidence of God's goodness to us. And if life is a gift from God our talents are special gifts with which God has entrusted us.

Yet how reluctantly we sometimes give our talents to the building of His kingdom. We put forth the best of our energy in the building of our own kingdom. Business men will go to their labors on Monday morning and give the best of their minds and bodies to the tasks before them. But in the service of the Church they suppose any haphazard contribution of talent will be acceptable. Many expect the best possible religious instruction for their children in the church school yet never stop to consider their own responsibility in instructing the children of other parents. They are quite sure even God will be pleased if they drag their tired bodies to a cushioned pew a half dozen times a year when the weather is good and there is nothing else to do.

Many excuse themselves from the investment of their talents in the

Church on the grounds of limited ability. We do well to remember that in the parable of the talents (Matthew 25:14-30) the Lord did not require the same return from the man who had only one talent as from the man who had five talents. He gave the same praise to the man who, with two talents, returned two additional talents as he gave to the man with five talents and who returned five additional talents. In both instances He said, "Well done, good and faithful servant; thou hast been faithful. . . ." His anathema fell upon the man who, having had only one talent (limited ability), refused to invest it. I do not think we reflect upon the character of the disciples of Jesus when we say that practically all of them were men with definitely limited abilities. Having only one talent they gave it completely to God.

Some years ago in the city of New Orleans I was impressed by the preaching of a young man who sat in a wheel chair, for he was a hopeless cripple, and preached to the casual passerby on Canal Street. His clothes were rather dirty for he was poor. His language was uncouth for he evidently had had no educational advantages. But he was urging men to quit the ways of sin and dedicate their lives to God. If that little cripple, impoverished in body and mind, could be used of God, how much more could we be of service to Him if we gave our talents to His work.

We who have responsible positions in the Church surely ought to remember that God demands of us our best. No church-school teacher has a right to appear before his class with a poorly prepared lesson. No steward has a right to take a position of responsibility and refuse to give the best of his talent to the task. No minister has the right to do less than his best in his sermon before his people. Surely God cannot be satisfied if we are content to give the ragged edges of our talents, the remnants of our abilities, to the work of the Church.

Happy Jack was a sort of institution in my home town when I was a twelve-year-old lad. He had a beautiful hamburger wagon with many windows in it and in each window some tempting morsel for a hungry boy. Not only did Happy Jack know all the boys by name but he entered into all their joys and sorrows. Naturally the boys all loved him and I was not the only boy in town who wanted to be a hamburger salesman when he grew up. Happy Jack had a peculiar love for great literature. In the slack hours of the morning he studied Shakespeare. He could quote long passages verbatim for he had a remarkable memory. One day it was reported that Happy Jack stole a melon from a wagon while the owner was not looking. Of course, this was not the right thing to do, for theft by any name is despicable. But I have an idea that when Happy Jack stands before the judgment bar of God his greatest sin will not be that of petty theft but the fact that he had such a remarkable mind and failed to use it for the glory of God.

Consider, finally, how we give God the remnants, the leftovers, the superfluous of our material possessions. The Hebrews were taught to set aside the first tenth of the yield of the harvest for the Lord; the "first fruit of the vineyard" and "the lamb without blemish." We moderns have reversed the process and our gifts to God's work come after we have paid the butcher, the baker and the candlestick maker. God gets part of that which is left if there is anything left. That the tithe is the scriptural plan of financing God's kingdom there can be no doubt. The Old Testament is filled with admonitions to dedicate a tenth of one's income to the Lord's work. "Thou shalt truly tithe all the increase of thy seed, that the field bringeth forth year by year" (Deuteronomy 14:22). "All the tithe of the land, whether of the seed of the land, or the fruit of the tree, is the Lord's" (Leviticus 27:30). "Bring ye all the tithes into the storehouse . . . and prove me . . . if I will not pour you out a blessing, that there shall not be room enough to receive it" (Malachi 3:10). And Jesus confirmed it in the New Testament, "Ye pay tithes . . . and . . . these things ought ye to have done . . ." (Matthew 23:23).

Dedication of the first fruits of our income rather than such money as we might have left over, is good evidence that we are seeking to put God first, not only in our giving but in our living. Putting God first was the fundamental thesis of the teaching of Jesus when he said, "Seek ye first the kingdom of God and these other things shall be added." Yet when we in America spend one billion dollars a year for the support of all churches and spend two billion a year for candy and cosmetics, three billion a year for movies, four billion a year for tobacco and seven billion a year for liquor, it is poor evidence of our desire to take the words of Jesus seriously.

It is surprising to note the per cent of the people in the church who have taken the vow of church membership agreeing to "support the church" yet who refuse to make a definite financial pledge. Not infrequently the excuse is they are afraid of financial obligations wherein there might be difficulty in payment. Of course, they pledge to pay the house rent, the utility bills, the grocery and drug bills, the notes on the new automobile. But they are peculiarly suspicious of pledges to the church, yet I have never known of a church that forced payment. Obviously the real reason is because contributions to the kingdom are considered optional and payment for material values in life are considered necessary. Old "Mose" was asked by his preacher for a contribution to the church, but Mose insisted that he owed a great deal to his grocery man and must pay him first. The preacher said, "But you have an obligation to God just as you have an obligation to the grocery man." "Ah knows dat, parson," said Mose, "but God ain't pressin' me like de grocery man is."

Jesus knew the strong temptation men would have, tugging at them to put material possessions before the kingdom of God. He repeatedly warned the well-to-do against this sin. He taught that property is of secondary consideration and not a worthy primary object of desire. "Lay up for yourselves treasures in heaven where neither moth nor rust doth corrupt. . . ." The rich young ruler was ordered to give up his wealth, not because it was evil, but because it was preventing his full service to the kingdom. The rich man who filled his barns that he might "take life easy" was called a fool. Because Dives put wealth before his social duty to Lazarus who begged at the gate he was sent to hell. Jesus criticized the rich, not because they were rich but because they were misusing their riches. They were putting money before God. The almighty dollar became their almighty god. From your observation, was not Jesus wise in warning us against this danger?

How much should a man give to the kingdom? If the Jews gave the tithe in the first century surely God expects us to give no less. The basis of our giving, however, should never be mechanical. The measure of our gifts should be according to the measure of our love. Jesus denounced the Pharisees who gave that man might admire them, but he praised the widow who gave half a cent—because her heart was in her gift. He praised the woman who broke an alabaster box of ointment on his head because the gift represented love. If we love God and His kingdom surely in this day of desperate human need throughout the world, we will give all we can. Never again should we treat God as a raggedy man, giving Him the superfluous, the remnants of our material resources, but we should give generously and joyfully out of the first fruits of our labors.

After serving five years as a missionary in Korea, a young lady joined her well-to-do American family at the Christmas dinner table. While her younger brother and sister were presenting their expensive gifts to the father and mother this missionary girl was moved to tears. She said, "I have insisted on living on my meager income and have no money to buy expensive gifts for my parents. But I do have a gift for you." And with those words she brought from under the table a little flat package in which was a red flannel heart tied with a yellow ribbon. Attached to the ribbon was a card which read, "To mother and dad—I give all I have—my heart." The measure of our stewardship is determined by our willingness to say, "To my heavenly Father —I give all I have—my heart!"

# Iron Shoes

### REVEREND C. ROY ANGELL, D.D.
*Minister, Central Baptist Church, Miami, Florida*

*This sermon represents contemporary southern preaching at its best and shows how the combination of simplicity and imagination can illumine the Gospel in current preaching. The name of Dr. C. Roy Angell is almost a magical name in the Southern Baptist Convention. He has brought happiness and satisfaction to the hearts of hearers all through the deep South. His life motto is the Second Mile and his humble, gracious spirit has endeared him to thousands who have heard his messages. He drives home a living truth by the use of stories and illustrations.*

*Dr. Angell is a Virginian by birth. He attended the University of Richmond, studied theology at Crozer Seminary at Chester, Pennsylvania, and took a course at the University of Pennsylvania. While studying at Johns Hopkins University he became pastor of the Fulton Avenue Baptist Church in Baltimore. His other pastorates were at Charlottesville, Virginia; First Baptist Church, Baton Rouge; First Baptist Church of San Antonio, Texas; he came to the Central Baptist Church of Miami from San Antonio.*

*He has been pastor of Central Baptist Church for the past ten and a half years; during that time 5486 new members have been received into the membership. The auditorium of the church seats 2500 and there are capacity congregations at all services. On Easter and Mother's Day two identical services are held each year.*

*Dr. Angell is first vice-president of the Southern Baptist Convention and president of the Greater Miami Ministerial Association. He is a trustee of Stetson University, DeLand, Florida, from which he received his D.D. degree several years ago. His preaching is evangelistic and has a large following of young people.*

## Sermon Eleven

THE most beautiful cluster of promises in the Old Testament is found in the Bible's most unread book. In chapter 33 of Deuteronomy these three promises nestle together: "As the day so shall thy strength be; underneath are the everlasting arms; and the eternal God will be thy refuge." But God never puts promises like these in a group without a reason, and that reason

[61]

is stated in the preceding verse. "Thy shoes shall be of iron and brass." God was lifting the veil of the future a little for some of his chosen people to see. He was saying to them, "Your road is going to be so rough that you will need iron shoes." Then He adds the assurance of these three beautiful promises.

As I read them I do not think that they were confined to this tribe of Asher, but rather God was stating the facts about a normal life, for there comes a day in the life of most of us when God hands us a pair of iron shoes and it is of vital importance that we wear them as a Christian should. We can do this only if we have the faith to appropriate these three beautiful promises.

I saw this admirably done not long ago. I had gone to a high school to preach the baccalaureate sermon. As the processional began, I was startled to see how slowly it moved, and I kept wondering about it until into the door at the end of the long aisle there came a wisp of a girl. She was walking with much difficulty; every step jarred her whole body and then I realized that she was braced with iron from her head to her heels; and I realized another thing which gave me a thrill—the speed of the procession was timed to make it easy for her. Halfway down the aisle her cap jarred down over her eyes. I saw her smilingly nudge the big two-hundred-pound boy who was marching with her. With an answering smile he adjusted her cap, because her arms wouldn't go up that high. When the time came the principal conferred all the honors but one—for at the close of the presentations he said, "There is one other medal given by the students. It will be presented by the captain of the football team to a young lady who has been a great inspiration to our entire school." The same big, two-hundred-pound boy came forward leading the little girl in the iron braces. His speech was something like this: "This is the biggest medal I ever saw because everyone in the school wanted to have a part in buying it, but it isn't big enough to express our gratitude to this young lady. On one side of it is inscribed her name, 'Christine,' and on the other, our pet name for her, 'Miss Inspiration.' Through these years of school life she has worn iron braces and suffered continually, but no hardship has been tough enough to wipe off the smile on her face. Sometimes when the going would get rough for us out on the athletic field or elsewhere, someone would invariably mention her name and we would just grin and buckle down." When the commencement exercises were over and I finally got through the crowd to Miss Christine I asked what appeared to her a superfluous question, for I inquired if she were a Christian. Astonishment was written all over her face and her answer was a classic. "No one could be a tenth of what that boy, in his exaggeration, said about me and not be a Christian."

God does not ask us all literally to wear iron shoes such as this little girl wears, but few of us ever walk along life's roadway without finding a pair of iron shoes. God never promised a Christian that there would be no suffering. The grandest little man that ever lived, Paul, wore iron shoes from

[62]

the beginning to the end of his ministry. One day when the load got too heavy he asked God to take them away, but instead God gave him more grace. Even Christ, the only begotten Son of God, walked into the Garden of Gethsemane, on down through Pilate's court, and up the hill of Golgotha wearing iron shoes.

*Quo Vadis* ends with a climactic picture of Simon Peter trying to run away because the iron shoes were hurting his feet, but when he met Christ going to take his place on the firing line he put them back on and returned to his martyrdom.

God knew if we Christians were going to wear our iron shoes like real soldiers of the cross we would need these three beautiful promises to lean upon. There is no repetition here. Look closely at each one of them:

The first one is: "As the day so shall thy strength be." This was Alexander McClaren's favorite text. He said he learned how true this verse was when he accepted his first job in Glasgow. He was just sixteen and his home was about six miles from the big city. Between his home and Glasgow there was a deep ravine that was supposed to be haunted. Some terrible things had really happened there. He was afraid to go through it even in the daytime and at night it was out of the question. So on Monday morning his father walked with him to work and in parting said, "Alec, come home as fast as you can when you get off Saturday night." Thinking of that deep ravine, McClaren said he answered, "Father, I will be awfully tired Saturday night. I will come home early Sunday morning." But his father was adamant, "No, Alec. You have never been away from home before and these five days are going to seem like a year to me. Come home Saturday night." Reluctantly Alec answered, "All right, father. Saturday night." All the week long Alec said he worried about that black ravine. When Saturday night came he was more scared than ever, but he wrapped up his belongings and went out to the end of the gulch. He said, "I whistled to keep my courage up but when I looked down into that inky blackness I knew I couldn't go. The tears came unbidden—then suddenly in the ravine I heard footsteps. I started to run but hesitated for those footsteps were very familiar. Up out of the inky darkness into the pale light, as I watched, came the head and shoulders of the grandest man on earth. He was bound to have known that I was scared, but he only said, 'Alec, I wanted to see you so badly that I came to meet you.' So shoulder to shoulder we went down into the valley and I was not afraid of anything that walked."

How beautifully this illustrates this most essential truth. Essential for every Christian. "As the day so shall thy strength be." When the dark and unknown passages of life come there also comes Christ. Wasn't it Stern, one of the first of the English novelists, who wrote, "God tempers the wind to the lamb that is shorn"? Maybe this was the lesson God was trying to teach us when He sent the manna to His children in the wilderness. There was just enough for each day.

The second promise, "Underneath are the everlasting arms," no doubt had its origin in something the writer of this book had often seen in the mountainous wilderness over which he had traveled. In the chapter before this he refers to it. He had seen an eagle teaching its young to fly. The ceremony began with the destruction of the nest. The old eagle tore up the nest and threw the pieces over the cliff. Then she took the little eaglet on her broad back and circling carried him high into the sun. Then she tilted her wings and slid him off into space. Fluttering, screeching, screaming, he drifted down. The old eagle circled around him. Long before he reached the sharp crags and rocks below, she glided under him and caught him on her broad wings. Two or three times she repeated this as if to say, "See, you cannot fall for underneath are the everlasting wings." The writer changed the picture just a little and made it read that "underneath are the everlasting arms of God." We need this message badly for we do not travel far along life's roadway before we realize that we need God's protection and His help.

When David described God as "The Good Shepherd" he was using the most endearing and realistic words he could find, for the Good Shepherd would do as David had done, fight the beasts of the forest and the birds of the air for his flock. If one of them was wounded or sick it found beneath it the everlasting arms, tender and strong, the arms of the Good Shepherd.

The next one, "The eternal God will be thy refuge," states in beautiful poetry another great promise that we will have to lean upon if we wear iron shoes as a Christian should. We need to know that we have a sanctuary into which we can go so that our strength may be renewed like the eagle's. There are times in life when life is too much for us and we cannot keep our chins up. We are wounded and sick of heart. We need a refuge.

Maybe this is what Jesus was talking about when he said, "Go into thy closet and shut the door and stay alone with God." Certainly this is what Jesus did. He left his disciples and climbed up into the mountain and spent the night alone with his Father. As someone beautifully stated it, "He went into the silence with God."

One of the greatest sermons that Dr. George McDaniel ever preached was not preached from the pulpit, but preached from the saddle one morning at dawn and just to me. We had been enjoying for some time the music of a pack of fine foxhounds as they chased a wily red fox. On this particular occasion we had ridden across ahead of the dogs to the high rock cliff in which this old red fox had taken refuge several times before. "Marse George," as we called him, was eager for a glimpse of the fox that his dogs couldn't catch. We had concealed our horses in the bushes and were sitting very silent and still when around the edge of the high cliff on a shelf of rock the big red fox nonchalantly trotted to the mouth of the dark, deep den. He stopped a moment and lifted his head to listen. The dogs were a great distance away so he casually sat down and began to smooth his fur and lick his paws. At intervals he would prick up his ears and listen intently and then relax. Then finally when the dogs got close he trotted unhurriedly into the dark cavern behind him and, I can imagine, sat relaxed and unafraid as he listened to the furore of the hounds as they surrounded the entrance to his home.

Dr. McDaniel laid his hand over on the pommel of my saddle and with deep emotion said, "There's a great sermon. When you have a safe refuge to which you can go in the time of trouble the hounds of life don't worry you much."

I think God intended, when He put in the hearts of men the idea of a home, that it should be just this. A place to which we can go at the end of a trying and haggard day to renew our strength. I know that in this passage God realized we would need a refuge when the hour came for us to wear our iron shoes, and He had the writer of Deuteronomy to take it down for all the world to read, "The Lord God is a refuge."

## THE CHURCH

# The Church's Role in America's Future[1]

REVEREND OSCAR FISHER BLACKWELDER, D.D., LL.D.
*Pastor, Lutheran Church of the Reformation, Washington, D. C.*

*Dr. Oscar Fisher Blackwelder, known as a speaker at educational, youth, pastoral and religious conferences throughout the country, is pastor of the Lutheran Church of the Reformation in Washington, D. C., to which he came in 1933. Before this appointment, he had been pastor of the Virginia Heights Lutheran Church, Roanoke, Virginia, and Christ Lutheran Church, Baltimore, Maryland. He also served in the National Preaching Mission under the Federal Council of Churches, speaking in about two-thirds of the cities the Mission visited.*

*Dr. Blackwelder was born in Newberry, South Carolina, and was graduated from Roanoke College, Virginia, and Southern Lutheran Theological Seminary, Columbia, South Carolina. For twelve years, he was a member of the Board of Publication of the United Lutheran Church in America, and is now a member of the executive board of the Church. He is at present a member of the Council of Washington Cathedral, a member of the board of trustees of American University, a life member of the Kiwanis Club, and served a term as president of the Washington Federation of Churches. He is the representative of his Church to the Federal Council of Churches.*

[1] Reprinted by permission of Current Religious Thought.

*He has written numerous articles and pamphlets, and is the co-author of* Epistle Messages, A Faith for These Times, The Parable of the Empty Soul, It Was for You, But Christ Did Rise *and* The Reality of Preaching.

*The message has been given several times at important religious functions: it was given before the Chicago Sunday Evening Club on November 17, 1946, at the the laymen's banquet at the biennial meeting of the United Lutheran Church in America in Cleveland, as well as in Washington.*

## Sermon Twelve

TEXT: Render therefore unto Caesar the things which are Caesar's; and unto God the things that are God's. MATTHEW 22:21

SOMETHING of eternal purpose is getting done at the heart of this painful and difficult world. To share to our fullest as churchmen in that process may reveal to our generation the Christian meaning of life.

No institution is taken for granted today. There are many who ask, Should not the Church be required to render an account of its stewardship and show just cause for its continued existence?

The measure of a church's right to live lies not in its distinctive doctrines but in what it does with those doctrines, in the questions and problems those doctrines are made to tackle. Neither is a church's right to live measured by its uniqueness of worship but by what it does with people and communities through that worship. Distinctiveness and uniqueness may mean sectarianism while the Church must be concerned with a total pattern of culture. Thus a part of the Church's right to existence is its preparedness to do Christlike battle with non-Christian cultures, as today with militant atheism, dominant nationalism and pagan secularism. Only a total body of Christian culture can do that. When the Church enables men to out-think, out-love and out-live the world, it demonstrates its right to existence.

Whether the organized Church to which you and I belong has a vital future in this country depends upon what it does in the struggle for freedom.

God has put the desire to be free in the hearts of men. History becomes the story of the search for that freedom. Those who help to set men free are working on the side of God. Those who enslave men are doomed to perish. Freedom comes by building life, society and government on truth, righteousness and love, and so on God. Religious liberty, the chance to do this, is, therefore, the foundation of free government and the Church's place is in the vanguard of the struggle for freedom.

We have heard much about freedom of speech, freedom of press and

[66]

freedom of worship. These and the other freedoms mutually defend one another, but they are defended ultimately by freedom of worship. When that freedom goes or is silent the final bulwark of social liberty has departed, the spirit which creates and sustains a bill of rights.

Because we are equal before the Supreme Judge of the universe, we have the right to equality before the courts, the laws, the judges of men. An oath in court to Someone higher than the man who sits on the bench illustrates the principle. Because we are equal before God we have the right to education so we may move toward equality of opportunity. After we have talked with God, we have the right to talk with men. We have the right to freedom of speech because we are sons of God.

To guide men into the fullest development of this sonship is to make them morally and spiritually free. It is the Church's role to show men how Christ sets them free by providing peace of conscience and inner unity; by making available to them power to do what they ought above what they please; by developing those internal constraints which make external restraints increasingly unnecessary. Such free men belong to that aristocracy upon which democracy rests. Only morally and spiritually free men can bring political and economic freedom to the world.

We churchmen, therefore, must extend our influence so that racial and religious minorities are not oppressed; so that every qualified person no matter what his color has a right to vote in free America; so that mob violence is denounced wherever it lifts its ugly head; so that selfish, brutal, well-paid pressure groups shall not control our government.

We cannot have a free America without a more stable home life. This Church of ours must give itself more intelligently to a type of marriage counseling and ministry which will help reduce the rate of one divorce out of every three marriages now current in this nation.

This Church of ours must so relate the Christian faith to mental health that we do something constructive about the one person out of every twenty-two now living in the United States who, the best authorities estimate, will spend a part of his lifetime in a mental institution.

We of the old-line churches must come down from our sophisticated pedestals and practice Christian brotherhood with the masses on the other side of the railroad tracks or we leave them to the frail ministry of the emotional fringe cults.

We churchmen who count ourselves members of the old-line political parties must help make vocal the hopes of men on both sides of the railroad tracks or they will be driven into the arms of the political radicals.

The way of freedom is in a total ministry like that. So the Church's role in America's future is to be an INSTRUMENT OF FREEDOM.

But there can be no freedom without justice. The Church demonstrates her vitality by being THE PROMOTER OF JUSTICE.

[67]

On Main Street, in the crossroads store, on Capitol Hill, with the AFL and CIO, in the Peace Conferences, in church conventions, the determining question remains: "What doth the Lord require of thee, but to do justly, and to love mercy, and to walk humbly with thy God?" These are the destiny- and history-making words of the world. Justice, love, reverence! They are like ascending steps. Industrial and international good will wait for men who climb those steps.

But we don't do much climbing when the issues of daily bread and world order are tackled by those whose only formula is the primordial clash of self-interests; by those who in the name of collective bargaining count the public out and defy the courts; by those who try to build political parties on group interests; by those whose present strategy is planned confusion; by those whose intellectual ceilings are so low that a public prayer for God's guidance is an offense; by those whose concept of justice is not moral right but a rule book backed up by brute force. This is a ruggedly practical world but the democratic way of life is not limited to such dead-end procedures.

I heard the president of a national patriotic organization assert that there is no such thing as twentieth-century Americanism, that America's dates with destiny are 1776 and 1789. Those of us who hold highest faith in the documents conceived in those immortal years believe they are organic, dynamic instruments which cannot be dated because they embody the living principles of justice, love and reverence, capable of meeting the issues, the blind spots and the dead spots in each generation.

When the God of eternal justice through such principles lays hold on truly competent minds of spirit and skills, a piece of paper on which they write may become a page of history. It may be a Magna Carta. It may be a Declaration of Independence. It may be a Constitution of the United States. It may be an Atlantic Charter. God grant in our day it may be a formula for economic justice that will bring industrial and international peace. Here is where the Christian faith enters the task.

What we call the mind of Christ, I believe, is a combination of justice, love and reverence. And that combination is the world's hope! A man who is only just will soon be less than just. A man who is only square will soon be less than square. A man who only practices the golden rule soon will practice much less. Justice, love and reverence are perfected in Jesus Christ and climax in his cross. His residence in a man's mind brings to that man living guidance, growing insights, a sharpening of his sense of justice. The basic social need of this earth is justice through Jesus, which I want to call evangelical justice. It rises infinitely above the clash of self-interests; it stirs a passion on every side for total justice; it inspires men to struggle for the rights of others and thus ultimately to secure their own. Since a scientific civilization has made the world neighbors, may such evangelical justice make us friends.

There is at least one new fact under the sun which makes this task imperative. That something is high-powered machinery. We have had machinery for a long time but we have not had high-powered machinery until now. And because of high-powered machinery it is now possible to provide the essential physical needs of life for every man, woman and child on the face of the earth for the first time since creation's morning. But that possibility will never be fulfilled except by way of the kind of justice for which I plead.

Such justice means the use of high-powered machinery to produce abundance, dedicated to human need rather than scarcity, dedicated to profit. Higher wages do not guarantee a higher standard of living. A higher standard of living only comes through mass production at prices every man can pay. Not cheap money but cheaply priced goods and plenty of them can bring a higher standard of economic living. And this will mean providing necessities for all before luxuries for any.

Perhaps the sharpest of all our economic needs is housing. America must have thirteen million new homes in the next ten years if we are to sustain the nation's strength in families and children. And these homes must be at prices people can pay. No issue more clearly proves the futility of continued bitter clashes. Private and public housing, as private and public schools, are needed in co-operation and not in competition to provide the homes America requires.

The Church which would be vital in America's future thus must endeavor to lay the mind of Christ, as Luther did, radiantly alongside this distorted earth until men, tortured by the difference, rise up to build the kingdom. The Church must turn the searching light of Christ upon every problem that bruises, crushes or stains human life and thus keep the splendor of God in the souls of man.

The Church in America's future is to be THE INSTRUMENT OF FREEDOM and THE PROMOTER OF JUSTICE. Thus the Church may be also THE BUILDER OF PEACE.

Some churches and some churchmen have been divisive elements in communities and the body politic. They have remained aloof. They have not rendered a corporate community service. Such social isolation in the name of rendering testimony is little more than a method of defense for those who feel an inferiority complex and are ill at ease in the rough and tumble of life. The Christian faith is here for the unity, for the healing and for the peace of the nations.

One little word of five letters describes the current world picture. That word is "s-p-l-i-t." The world is split vertically into nations; nations are split horizontally into races; races are split obliquely into classes; within classes, homes are split as the increasing divorce rate indicates; within homes are what the psychologists call "split personalities." With our modern scientific skills we have left out a "cement," necessary to hold life together. This lack calls for the Church's ministry of reconciliation. In company with other men, I want to champion a six-point platform by which the Church may practice this ministry of reconciliation and perhaps become the world's pioneer builder of the peace.

(1) *The Church must help heal the wounds of war.* Four-fifths of the world is in misery. Even with the increase of our domestic difficulties, America is in the remaining one fifth. The Church must develop more individual workers who will stoop to heal the world's wounds, workers like an American incubator dealer who flew at his own expense 56,800 hatching eggs to Poland.

(2) *The Church must help provide the good will on which the world can rebuild its life.* Every local parish in America should be kept in personal contact with a parish in a devastated country in order to build good will. We churchmen must see that business interests and certain representatives of our government do not undo whatever good will has been achieved. Some missionaries can build more good will with the spirit of Christ and ten dollars than the average ambassador with his cocktail diplomacy and a large entertainment fund.

(3) *The Church must help create a conscience on economic and social injustices.* The earlier burden of this sermon address is upon that text. We must see ourselves in relation to all men through the eyes of Christ. We must lift up our total life and live it to the glory of God.

(4) *The Church must help promote racial appreciation.* The variety of the human race may be the spice of existence in the kingdom of God. There are perhaps ten million Christian Negroes in America. Their leadership is often very inadequate. Is this enormous Christian potential to be regarded as a backdoor accessory to the Christian Church? Does any sensible general undercut any part of his army? Churchmen should deal with human individuals as members of a spiritual community on the basis of individuality and not color. Unless the Church does this, the Christian fellowship will be undercut by political and economic movements already committed to this principle and often with a selfish ethic.

(5) *The Church must exalt the worth of the individual so that in the popular mind souls are regarded worth saving.* Gigantic loss of life in battle, universal cruelty and suffering, have cheapened the value of life in the public mind. Too many men shrug their shoulders instead of shuddering in their hearts when others suffer. The world cannot be rebuilt or saved with such cheap conceptions of life. The Church's world missionary task was never more imperative. Men everywhere are worth saving; men can be saved; that is the Church's mission and message.

(6) *The Church must implement the spirit of forgiveness into the world's life so that international peace becomes a possibility.* In the completest and fullest manner only those know how to forgive who have been forgiven by God. To reconcile man to man and man to himself through the reconciliation

[70]

of man to God is to release into this anxious, bitter and broken world the healing power of God. Such is the way of peace.

"Stand fast therefore in the liberty wherewith Christ hath made us free." That means FREEDOM.

"What doth the Lord require of thee, but to do justly, and to love mercy, and to walk humbly with thy God." That means JUSTICE.

"Blessed are the peacemakers: for they shall be called the children of God." That means PEACE.

This is the work of men of God. This is the role of the Church in America's future.


THE CHURCH

# Love on Pilgrimage: Peter

THE RIGHT REVEREND MONSIGNOR FULTON J. SHEEN, PH.D., D.D.
*Associate Professor of Philosophy, The Catholic University of America, Washington, D. C.*

*Monsignor Sheen's is one of the important living voices of our day. His forceful and convincing preaching makes every listener eager to catch each word. To hear him is to realize that here is a man who believes what he says and who has thought out his message calmly and prayerfully.*

*After graduate work at the Catholic University of America, the University of Louvain, Belgium, and Angelico University, Rome, he was ordained in Peoria, Illinois, in 1919. Step by step he has risen from very modest places in the Church to be one of the most honored Catholic preachers. He taught at St. Edmund's College, Ware, and the Westminster (London) Diocesan Seminary in 1925-26; in 1926 the University of Louvain, recognizing his genius, awarded him the Cardinal Mercier prize for International Philosophy, the first time this honor was ever given an American.*

*Before the war, he was called to preach in Europe nearly every summer from 1925 to 1939, speaking in London at Westminster Cathedral and St. Patrick's Church, Soho Square; at the University of Cambridge Summer School, at Glasgow; in Rome, and elsewhere on the continent. In 1934 he was named a Papal Chamberlain of the late Pontiff, Pope Pius XI, with the title of Very Reverend Monsignor, and the following year, Pius XI made him a Domestic Prelate with the title of Right Reverend Monsignor.*

*During most of the year, he is busy teaching philosophy at the Catholic University of America, but is in such demand as a speaker, that he gives more than one hundred sermons and addresses each year, speaking in almost every major city in the United States to secular and religious groups who throng to hear him. For years he has been the regular Lenten preacher at St. Patrick's Cathedral, New York, and is the special Advent preacher at the Church of the Blessed Sacrament, New York, where his Advent messages are enthusiastically received.*

*He has written some twenty books on philosophy, religion, morals and socio-economic questions, including* Freedom Under God, Whence Come Wars *and* Philosophies at War.

*This sermon is part of Monsignor Sheen's series "Love on Pilgrimage," given at St. Patrick's Cathedral and on the* Catholic Hour *during Lent, 1946. "Peter" was the seventh in his series and was given on March 17, 1946, and is a sermon where the strong emphasis upon prayer and man's neglect of prayer make it a fitting sermon for our day. Monsignor Sheen's beautiful story about the dome of the Basilica of St. Peter's in Rome is one that many will appreciate.*

## Sermon Thirteen

THE most interesting drama in all the world is the drama of the human soul. Were it not endowed with freedom, it might go out to war and enterprise alone and unheeded; but master of its choice, unlike the sun and stones, it can use time and things to decide its destiny, its eternity, and its judgment. Though there are many phases to these dramas, perhaps the most interesting of them all is the psychology of a fall and resurrection.

More concretely, how do some souls lose their faith, and by what steps do they later on recover it? The answer to such questions is to be found in the story of the Apostle Peter, whose name appears first in the Gospel narrative, and who might appropriately be called "The Fisherman Philosopher," for he asked Divine Wisdom more questions than any other of His followers. For example, "To whom shall we go?"; "Whither goest Thou?"; "Why cannot I follow Thee?"; "What shall this man do?" To this searching intellectualist of Galilee, who was born Simon and whose name was changed to Peter, and who out from the bitterness of his spirit cried, "Depart from me, O Lord, for I am a sinful man," we go to study the steps by which he fell and the stages by which he returned. There seem to have been five stages in Peter's fall.

First, neglect of prayer.

Second, substitution of action for prayer.

Third, lukewarmness.

Fourth, the satisfaction of material wants, feelings and emotions.

Fifth, human respect.

*Neglect of prayer.* No soul ever fell away from God without giving up

[72]

prayer. Prayer is that which establishes contact with Divine Power and opens the invisible resources of Heaven. However dark the way, when we pray, temptation can never master us. The first step downward in the average soul is the giving up of the practice of prayer, the breaking of the circuit with Divinity, and the proclamation of one's own self-sufficiency.

That night that our Blessed Lord went out under the light of a full moon into the Garden of Gethsemane to crimson the olive roots with His own blood for the redemption of men, He turned to His disciples and said, "Watch ye, and pray that ye enter not into temptation. The spirit indeed is willing, but the flesh weak" (Matthew 26:41). Withdrawing from these three disciples about as far as a man could throw a stone—how significant a way to measure distance the night one goes to death—He prays to His Heavenly Father, ". . . My Father, if it be possible, let this chalice pass from me. Nevertheless not as I will, but as thou wilt" (Matthew 26:39).

When Our Blessed Lord came back the last time to visit His disciples, He found them asleep. A woman will watch not one hour or one night, but day after day and night after night in the presence of a peril threatening her child. These men slept. If they could sleep on such an occasion, it was due to the fact that they had no adequate conception of the crisis through which Our Saviour was passing, no consciousness of the tragedy that was already upon them. Finding them asleep, Our Blessed Lord spoke to Peter and said, ". . . What? could you not watch one hour with me?" (Matthew 26:40). Peter had given up both watching and praying.

The next stage was:

*The substitution of action for prayer.* Most souls still feeling the necessity of doing something for God and the Church turn to the solace of activity. Instead of going from prayer to action, they neglect the prayer and become busy about many things. It is so easy to think we are doing God's work when we are only in motion or being fussy. Peter was no exception. In the turmoil of the arrest of Our Blessed Lord which followed, Peter, who had already been armed with two swords, allows his usual impetuosity to get the better of him. Slashing out rather recklessly at the armed gang, what he strikes is not a soldier at all, but a slave of the High Priest. As a swordsman Peter was a good fisherman. The slave steps aside, and the blow aimed at the crown of his head merely cuts off his ear. Our Blessed Lord restored the ear by a miracle, and then turned to Peter and said, ". . . Put up again thy sword into its place; for all that take the sword shall perish with the sword" (Matthew 26:52). Divinity has no need of it. He could summon twelve legions of angels to His aid if He wished. The Church must never fight with the weapons of the world.

The father had offered the Son the cup, and no one could hinder His drinking it. But Peter giving up the habit of prayer, substitutes violence toward others, and all tact is lost as devotion to a cause becomes zeal without knowledge. Far better it would be to take a few hours off active life and spend it in communion with God, than to be busy about many things while neglecting the one thing that is necessary for peace and happiness. No such activity is a substitute for watching and praying an hour.

*Lukewarmness.* Experience soon proves that religious activity without prayer soon degenerates into indifference. At this stage souls become indifferent. They believe one can be too religious, too zealous, or "spend too much time in Church." Peter exemplifies this truth.

A few hours later, Our Blessed Lord is led before His judges—and one is almost inclined to say, "May God forgive us for calling them judges." As that sad procession moves on in the unutterable loneliness where the God-man freely subjects Himself to the evil darts of men, the Gospel records, "And Peter followed Him afar off." He had given up prayer, then action, and now he keeps his distance. Only his eyes remained on the Master. How quickly the insincerity of action without prayer proves itself! He who was brave enough to draw a sword a few hours before now strays on behind. Christ, Who once was the dominating passion of our life, now becomes incidental in religion. We still linger as from force of habit—or perhaps even from remorse of conscience—in the footsteps of the Master, but out of the range of both His eyes and His voice. It is in such moments that souls say, "God has forgotten me"—when the truth is that it is not God who leaves us; it is we who stray on behind.

*Satisfaction of material wants, feelings and emotions.* Once the divine fades in life, the material begins to assert itself. The excessive dedication to luxury and refinement is always an indication of the inner poverty of the spirit. When the treasure is within, there is no need of those outer treasures which rust consumes, moths eat, and thieves break through and steal. But when the inner beauty is gone, we need luxuries to clothe our nakedness. It was only natural, therefore, to find that in the next stage of his declension, Peter should be satisfying his body. He did not go into the courtroom; he remained outside with the servants, and in the expressive language of Sacred Scripture, ". . . when they had kindled a fire in the midst of the hall, and were sitting about it, Peter was in the midst of them" (Luke 22:55). There is a process going on in Peter, but it is hardly progress, for it is a downward movement—walking, standing, sitting. That is exactly what Peter did. *Walking:* He "followed Him afar off." *Standing:* He went into the court and stood among the people. *Sitting:* He sat by the fire that the enemies of Christ had built. Luxury had taken the place of fidelity. Never before was any man so cold before a fire!

*Human respect.* The last stage in the fall is human respect when we deny our Faith or are ashamed of it under ridicule or scorn. Worldly religions will get on well with the world, but not a divine. As Our Lord warned: "And when they shall persecute you in this city, flee into another. Amen I say to you, you shall not finish all the cities of Israel, till the Son of man come" (Matthew 10:23). As the blaze of that fire lighted up the face of Peter, it was possible for bystanders and those who came into the court to see his face. And at that very moment when Our Blessed Lord in court was taking an oath proclaiming His Divinity at Caeserea Philippi, Peter was taking an oath, too, but not to reaffirm that Christ was the Son of the Living God, but rather to deny it. There was the clamor of officers: and the saucy laughter of a servant maid, who said, "Thou also wast with Jesus of Nazareth." But Peter denied it. And then another maidservant said that he was one of them, but he denied it again, saying, ". . . Woman, I know him not" (Luke 22:57). Perhaps an hour passed, and then one of the men said to him, ". . . Surely thou art one of them; for thou art also a Galilean" (Mark 14:70). ". . . for even thy speech doth discover thee" (Matthew 26:73). Peter became angry at their repeated affirmations and with an atavistic throwback to his fisherman days when his nets became tangled in Galilean waters, he cursed and swore again saying, ". . . I know not this man" (Mark 14:71). Human respect had gotten the better of him. How often others know what we ought to do, even when we have forgotten. How touchy are those consciences that have abandoned their God; how sensitive they are to even the memory that they once had the Faith. Many a time I have heard such souls say, "Do not talk about it! I want to forget it." But we can never forget—even our speech betrays that we had been with the Galilean.

If there be the steps away from the Faith, what are the steps back to its embrace? They are:

(1) Disillusionment
(2) Response to grace
(3) Amendment
(4) Sorrow

### (1) Disillusionment

Since all sin is pride, it follows that a first condition of conversion is humility; the ego must decrease; God must increase. This humiliation most often comes by a profound realization that sin does not pay; that it never keeps its promises; that just as a violation of the laws of health produce sickness, so the violation of the laws of God produce unhappiness.

This is signified in Peter's case by the fulfillment of a prophecy made by Our Lord to Peter the night of the Last Supper. Having warned His Apostles that they would be scandalized in Him that night, Peter boasted: ". . . I will lay down my life for thee" (John 13:37). And Our Lord answered, ". . . Wilt thou lay down thy life for me? Amen, amen I say to thee, the cock shall not crow, till thou deny me thrice" (John 13:38).

A few hours later, at the very moment that Peter cursed and swore that he knew not Christ, there came through the halls of the outer chambers of Caiphas' court, the clear and unmistakable crowing of a cock. Even *nature is on God's side*. We may abuse it in our sin, but in the end it will abuse us. How right was Thompson when he characterized nature as having a "traitorous trueness, a loyal deceit; in fickleness to me, in loyalty to Him." The crowing of the cock was such a childish thing. But God can use the most insignificant things in the world as the channel of His grace—the vow of a child, a word over the radio, the song of a sparrow. He will even press into the business of conversion the crowing of a cock in the dawning of the morning. A soul can come to God by a series of disgusts.

## (2) *Response to grace*

The next step in the return to God after the awakening of conscience through the disillusionment of sin is on God's part. As soon as we empty ourselves, or are disillusioned, He comes to fill the void. ". . . No man cometh to the Father but by me" (John 14:6). And St. Luke tells us: "And the Lord turning looked on Peter" (Luke 22:61).

As sin is an aversion for God, grace is the conversion to God. Our Lord does not say: "I told you, you would fall." He does not desert us, though we desert Him. He turns, once we know we are sinners. God never gives us up. The very word used here to describe the look of Our Lord is the same word used the first time Our Lord met Peter—the meaning being that "He looked through" Peter. Peter is recalled to the sweet beginnings of His grace and vocation. Judas received the lips to recall him to fellowship; Peter received a look with eyes that see us, not as our neighbors see us, not as we see ourselves, but as we really are. They were the eyes of a wounded friend, the look of a wounded Christ. But the language of those eyes we shall never understand.

## (3) *Amendment*

As sin begins with the abandonment of mortification, so conversion implies return to it. The king in Hamlet asked, "Can one be forgiven and retain the offense?" There are such things as occasions of sin, namely, those persons, places, and circumstances which dry rot the soul. Peter's conversion would not be complete unless he left that arena where maidservants, slaves, and human respect combined to make him deny the Master. No longer will he warm himself by fires, nor sit passively while his Judge is judged. The Scripture records his amendment or purgation in the simple words, "And *going forth.*" All the trappings of sin, the ill-gotten goods, the human respect he won, all these are now trampled under foot, as "he goes out."

## (4) *Sorrow*

But this leaving of the tabernacles of sin would not be enough were there not sorrow. Some leave sin only because they find it disgusting. There is no real conversion until that sin is related to an offense against the Person of God. "Against *Thee* have I sinned," says Scripture, not against "Space-time," or the "Cosmical Universe," or the "Powers Beyond." Given

[76]

a sorrow that regrets offending God because He is all good and deserving of all our love, and you have salvation. Fittingly, therefore, do the Evangelists write, "And Peter going out, wept bitterly" (Luke 22:62). His heart was broken into a thousand pieces, and his eyes that looked into the eyes of Christ, now turn into fountains. Moses struck a rock, and water came forth. Christ looked on a rock, and tears came forth. Tradition has it that Peter wept so much for his sins that his cheeks were furrowed with their penitential streams. Upon those tears the face of the Light of the World rises, and through them comes the rainbow of hope, assuring to all souls that never again will a heart be destroyed by flood of sin so long as it turns to Him Who is Ark of Salvation, the Love of the Universe.

This closes the story of the most human human in the Gospels, who one moment is on the top of a sea wave walking and the next moment beneath it drowning and shrieking, "Lord, save me." One instant he says he will die with Our Lord; an hour later he denies that he knows the one for whom he would die. Who is there who has not within himself those same conflicting elements; willing the good, doing the wrong, and in the language of Ovid: "seeing and approving the better things of life, but following the worse." Peter is the supreme example of the Gospel warning: ". . . he that thinketh himself to stand, let him take heed lest he fall" (I Corinthians 10:12). In no one else is better told the fallacy of humanism, understood as self-sufficiency of man without God, or the utter inadequacy of our own reason and our own strength to get us out of the mess we are in without periodical renewals of Divine Grace that come to us from God.

Because Peter is so much like us in our conflicts, he is, therefore, our greatest hope. The other Apostles wrote less out of their experience than Peter. The Epistle of Paul to Timothy is exhortation; the Epistle of John is a call to brotherhood; the Epistle of James is for a practical religion; but the Epistle of Peter is the summary of his former self and might be called the Epistle of courage. In every line, in every word of that revealed document, we find Peter using his dead former self as the steppingstone by which he mounts to newness of life; to the Peter who was sinking beneath the waves, he the new Peter is courageous: "Who, by the power of God, are kept by faith unto salvation, ready to be revealed in the last time. Wherein you shall greatly rejoice, if now you must be for a little time made sorrowful in divers temptations: That the trial of your faith (much more precious than gold which is tried by fire) may be found unto praise and glory and honor at the appearing of Jesus Christ" (I Peter 1:5,6,7). "And who is he that can hurt you, if you be zealous of good? But if also you suffer anything for justice' sake, blessed are ye. And be not afraid of their fear, and be not troubled. But sanctify the Lord Christ in your hearts, being ready always to satisfy every one that asketh you a reason of that hope which is in you" (I Peter 3:13, 14, 15).

No wonder Our Divine Lord, Who knows all souls in their inner being,

[77]

chose as the head of His Church not John who had never denied, and who alone of all the Apostles was present on the hill of Calvary, but rather chose Peter who fell and then rose again, who sinned and who then was forgiven amidst lifelong penance, in order that His Church might understand something of human weakness and sin and bear to the millions of its souls the Gospel of hope, the assurance of Divine Mercy.

Fittingly, then, when Peter came to the end of his lease on life, he asked not to be crucified as was Our Blessed Lord with head upright, but with head downward in the earth. Our Lord had called him the Rock of His Church, and the rock was laid where it should be: deep in the roots of creation. On that very spot where the man of courage was crucified upside down, with his stumbling feet toward heaven, there now rises the greatest dome that was ever thrown against the vault of heaven's blue, the dome of the Basilica of St. Peter in Rome. Around it in giant letters of gold, we read the words Our Lord spoke to Peter at Caeserea Philippi: ". . . thou art Peter; and upon this rock I will build my church, and the gates of hell shall not prevail against it" (Matthew 16:18).

Many a time I have knelt under that dome and its inscription and looked down below its many altars to the tomb where is buried that Rock who made Rome eternal, because he the fisherman came to live there. No one, I suppose, has ever bent a suppliant knee to that first Vicar of Christ's Church, to whom Our Lord said that a sinner should be forgiven, not seven times, but seventy times seven, without understanding in hope what Peter knew so well: "If you had never sinned, you never could call Christ 'Savior'".

PRAYER: *O God from Whose hands cometh the peace the world cannot give, give us the light to see that peace is the work of Justice, and the concord of all nations the fruit of obedience to Thy Law and Thy Commandments. May we seek not so much to be consoled as to console; to be understood, as to understand; to be loved, as to love, that in pardoning we may be pardoned, and in giving we may receive. We pray for our President, for our Congress, for our homes, our people, our children, our brokenhearted, that we may be reverent in the use of freedom, just in the exercise of power, generous in the protection of weakness, merciful to those who have been our enemies. Not for our worthiness, but because of Thy tender mercy hear our prayer that we may so pass through things temporal as not to lose the things eternal, O Christ Jesus, Our Lord. Amen*

NIHIL OBSTAT: Rev. T. E. Dillon, *Censor Librorum*
IMPRIMATUR: ✠ John Francis Noll, D.D., *Bishop, Fort Wayne*

# Divine Overruling

REVEREND JOHN BAILLIE, D. LITT., D.D., S.T.D.

*Professor of Divinity, New College, Edinburgh, Scotland
and a Minister of the Church of Scotland*

*The Reverend Professor John Baillie is one of the great theologians and preachers of our world today. His teaching and his preaching in Scotland, England, Canada and the United States have a profound influence because he has something important to say and his forthrightness and excellence of thought make his words burn their way into men's souls by their logic and by their sheer truth.*

*He was educated at Inverness Royal Academy, Edinburgh University, M.A., 1908; D.Litt., 1928; honorary D.D., 1930, New College, Edinburgh; Jena; and Marburg. In 1909-10 he was appointed assistant to the professor of moral philosophy at Edinburgh University; assistant to the professor of logic and metaphysics, Edinburgh; examiner in philosophy, Edinburgh University, 1917-19; assistant minister, Broughton Place Church, Edinburgh, 1912-14; served under Y.M.C.A. with British armies in France, 1915-19; professor of Christian theology, Auburn Theological Seminary, Auburn, New York; professor of systematic theology, Emmanuel College, University of Toronto, 1927-30; professor of systematic theology in Union Theological Seminary, New York, 1930-34.*

*His work has been recognized with the honorary doctorate from Victoria University, Toronto; Dickinson College, and Yale University. He was Ely Lecturer, Union Theological Seminary, New York, 1929; Dudleian Lecturer, Harvard University, 1931; Deems Philosophical Lecturer, New York University, 1931-32; Taylor Lecturer at Yale, 1936; and has held many other special lectureships.*

*His books have depth and penetration and include* The Roots of Religion in the Human Soul, *1926;* The Interpretation of Religion, *1929;* The Place of Jesus Christ in Modern Christianity, *1929;* Our Knowledge of God, *1939;* Invitation to Pilgrimage, *1942. He works hard, thinks deeply, writes constructively, rests by fishing and travel.*

*He shows in "Divine Overruling" how God can overrule the evil in man's life and in the world, and uses the old, old story of the sale of Joseph by his own brothers and their lie to their father that Joseph was dead. Professor Baillie's treatment of this theme is done with skill and perception and with the ability to hold an audience. It is a sermon "for the record," and will make the Christian doctrine of divine overruling understandable and may draw many to repentance and faith.*

## Sermon Fourteen

TEXTS: So now it was not you that sent me hither, but God.
GENESIS 45:8

But as for you, ye thought evil against me; but God meant it unto good, to bring to pass, as it is this day, to save much people alive.
GENESIS 50:20

SELDOM has even the troubled land of Palestine witnessed a fouler or more felonious deed than that to which these words refer. All the world knows how it happened. The sons of Jacob had been growing more and more jealous of their brother Joseph. They disliked him first because they thought him a talebearer, carrying from the harem to their father ill reports of the doings of their own mothers, Billah and Zilpah. Their dislike of him increased when their father began to treat him as his favorite and made him a coat of many colors or, as the margin of the Revised Version has it, "a long coat with sleeves," that is, not a coat for working men but a coat for the idle rich. And at last their dislike came to a head when on two successive mornings he came in to breakfast having dreamed a dream, the painfully obvious point of which was that he, a younger son, was destined to lord it over all his brethren.

It chanced that soon afterward Joseph's brothers were far away from home, looking after the flock which their father had established at Shechem on the "parcel of a field" which he had bought from the children of Hamor many years before for a hundred pieces of money. After they had been gone some time, Jacob sent Joseph to see how his brothers were faring. When he arrived at Shechem they were not there, but he met a man who said he had heard them mention that they were going on to Dothan in the next valley; so he trudged on after them to Dothan. As he came over the hill one of his brothers recognized him and called out to the others, "Here comes the dreamer!" and they had a good laugh over that. In a moment their jealousy lapped them like a flame! There and then, as Joseph was stumbling through the boulders to reach them, they hatched a plot to get rid of him forever. The first idea was to kill him and put the blame on a wild beast; "and then," said one of them, "we shall see what will become of his dreams"—and they had another good raucous laugh over that. But Reuben, the eldest, did not quite like this business of shedding blood, so he proposed that instead of killing him they should throw him into a dried-up water hole which happened to be near at hand. By this time Joseph was up with them and, perhaps without deciding as to his final fate, they seized him, they stripped him of the fine coat they hated, and cast him into the pit.

Then they sat down to eat their dinner; but no sooner had they done so than they saw a caravan come over the hill from the north. Dothan was on the trade route from Gilead to Egypt, and there was a good deal of traffic on that road because the famous balm of Gilead was used in Egypt for embalming the mummies. And behold, the story says, "a company of Ishmaelites (or Midianites) came from Gilead with their camels bearing spicery and balm and myrrh, going to carry it down to Egypt." When Judah, the fourth eldest son, saw the caravan approaching, he suggested to the others that they might avoid bloodguiltiness and at the same time make something for their own pockets, if they hoisted Joseph out of the pit again and sold him to the Ishmaelites as a slave. This they did for twenty pieces of silver. And the Ishmaelites, when they reached Egypt, sold Joseph again to Potiphar, the captain of the king's guard.

A foul felonious deed it certainly was, and yet it was in this deed that Joseph long afterward saw the hand of God, saying that it was not really his brothers that sent him into Egypt but very God Himself. But thereby hangs another tale. Joseph's brothers thought they had seen the last of him when the ambling Ishmaelite camel bore him away over the hills to the south; but it was far otherwise ordained. Some years afterward there was a great drought and famine throughout the whole Mediterranean basin. Only in Egypt was there a good supply of grain, because Pharaoh's grand vizier at that time was a most capable and far-sighted civil servant who during the years of plenty had introduced a system of food control according to which one fifth of the produce of the country had to be stored up in great barns against the failure of the harvest in later years. When Jacob heard about this in faraway Palestine, he said to his sons, "Don't stand staring at one another! Do something! Go to Egypt and buy corn!" Well, as you know, when they went to Egypt it turned out that the grand vizier was none other than their brother Joseph who, after some misadventures, had at last risen to this position of high authority in Pharaoh's employ. He recognized them at once, but they quite naturally failed to recognize him in his new dress and setting and grown as he now was to man's estate, nor did he make himself known to them until their second visit when they brought with them the boy Benjamin. Then when the brothers told him of Jacob's pathetic plea for Benjamin's safety, Joseph could contain himself no longer "and cried, Cause every man to go out from me. And there stood no man with him, while Joseph made himself known to his brethren. And he wept aloud: and the Egyptians and the house of Pharaoh heard." Then, having told them who he was, he went on to say, "Now therefore be not grieved, nor angry with yourselves, that ye sold me hither: for God did send me before you to preserve life. For these two years hath the famine been in the land: and yet there are five years, in the which there shall neither be earing nor

[81]

harvest. And God sent me before you to preserve you a posterity in the earth, and to save your lives by a great deliverance. So now it was not you that sent me hither, but God." And then, long afterward, when Jacob was dead, and when the brothers were afraid that Joseph would at last requite them for their evil deed, Joseph said to them again, "Fear not; for am I in the place of God? But as for you, ye thought evil against me; but God meant it unto good, to bring to pass, as it is this day, to save much people alive."

You see, Joseph's reasoning was that if his brothers had not sold him to the Ishmaelites, then he would never have gone to Egypt; and then his brothers would never have gone there, but would have perished in the famine; and then all the children of Israel would have been blotted out from the earth. It was therefore the evil deed of his brothers that led to the preservation of the whole people of Israel. If they had not plotted that foul felony on the hillside at Dothan, God's promise to Abraham could never have been fulfilled. The chosen people would have come to an end, and there would never have been any journey through the wilderness or any Hebrew history or any Old Testament or any Book of Psalms or any royal house of David or any Holy City of Jerusalem or any little town of Bethlehem in whose streets should one day shine the Everlasting Light. For Joseph himself, this going down into Egypt was a means of preserving his family from the famine, but in the eyes of future ages it was much more than that. The Egyptian servitude which followed was in many ways a disguised blessing. Israel went into Egypt a family, and came out a nation. It went in a mere handful of illiterate and semibarbarous shepherds; it came out a people skilled in the arts of civilization. For Egypt was in those days the most advanced civilization in the world. It was there that the Hebrews learned to read and to write, it was there that they learned the principles of law and government and civil order. We cannot easily imagine any other way in which the Israelite nation could have been prepared for the great destiny that awaited it, except this way by which Joseph was sold into Egypt as a slave. Yet all these things were part of God's education of His beloved people. They all entered into His plan for the salvation of mankind. They are all part of the story that leads up to the Incarnation of our blessed Lord who would one day be born from the tribe of Judah, the fourth brother, a rod out of the stem of Jesse. Is it surprising, then, that Joseph should say to his brothers, "So now it was not you that sent me hither, but God"; "As for you, you thought evil against me, but God meant it unto good, to bring to pass, as it is this day, to save much people alive"?

Now that God does work out His sovereign purposes through and by means of the deeds of men, we do certainly believe. When I look back over the way by which God has led me to this hour, when I call to mind His gracious dealings with my soul and life, I see clearly how at every point He was making use of human instruments. God's blessings came to me through the life of my boyhood home, through the influence of my mother, and her self-sacrificing deeds for my sake, through the precept and example of my teachers and of other men of God whom it has been my privilege to know in later years. I know well that if today I am anything better than the very worst that a man could be, or if I have ever *done* anything better than the very worst that a man can do, the honor and the glory and the merit are not mine but theirs. Yet for all this that they did for me I praise God too, and indeed praise Him first and foremost. The honor and the glory and the merit are due in the first place to Him alone. It was He who put it into my mother's heart and into the hearts of my masters to do what they did for me, and to lead me into the ways of righteousness and in the paths of peace. Therefore I can say with Joseph, "So now it was not you that sent me hither, but God."

Yes, but the matter is not quite so simple as that. For these deeds of my mother and of my teachers, which God used as instruments of my salvation, were good deeds. Whereas the deed of Joseph's brethren which God used as an instrument for the salvation of the house of Israel was a foully evil deed. And though we are all ready to believe that God uses the good deeds of men with a view to the furtherance of His own ends, we have perhaps more difficulty in believing that He can and does use their evil deeds, and so overrule them as to make them serve His eternal purpose. And yet we must believe this too. For if God cannot overrule evil as well as good, then I am afraid it is very little that He can do for us at all. If God is able to exercise no control over the dark pages of history, if it is only the bright pages that He can make to fit into His plan, then it is difficult to see how His hand can be present in history to any degree that would really make a difference. For it is of dark pages that history is chiefly made up. "History," said Gibbon—and who should know what history is, if not Gibbon?—"is generally only the record of the crimes, the follies and the mistakes of mankind." What hope do you suppose there is for this generation, if it is only the *good* in the present international situation that God can make to redound to the healing of the nations? And yet, do you think that God is standing aside from it all? Do you think that He has ceased to be gracious? Do you think His right hand has lost its skill and His holy arm forgotten its strength? I tell you, No. I tell you that in the last resort even the Nazi aggressors were instruments in His hand; that even Hitler and Himmler and Julius Streicher were vassals of His ripening purpose. He is going to bring some good out of it all. It is all part of His discipline of the souls of the nations. He who used the crime of Judas Iscariot and the whole murderous intent of men against His holy Son, in order to bring salvation to the world, that at the price of his death you and I should be redeemed to life eternal, think you that He will not likewise turn the deeds of the dictators to His own glory and to the education of our earthly city for the City of God?

God is working His purpose out, as year succeeds to year;
God is working His purpose out, and the time is drawing near
—Nearer and nearer draws the time—the time that shall surely be,
When the earth shall be filled with the glory of God, as the waters cover
the sea.

And if you still say that God cannot overrule evil deeds, then I will only ask you what other kind of deeds you yourself are giving Him to overrule. What kind of material did you offer Him yesterday? Did you provide Him with many good deeds? You don't provide Him with many good deeds, do you? I cannot answer for you. I can only answer for myself.

But now, if God can make use not only of our good deeds but also of our evil ones, why then should we not indulge ourselves in evil deeds as much as in good ones? If God can bring good out of evil, then why should we not do evil that good may come? This, you remember, was the charge that the Romans brought against St. Paul's doctrine of divine overruling. They said that by teaching this doctrine he was as good as encouraging men to sin. If the sin of Judas led to the Crucifixion, and the Crucifixion to the salvation of mankind, then why should not Judas sin again? If you and I had not sinned, we had not known God's forgiveness; should we not therefore sin all the more, that the forgiving love of God be more and more revealed? You remember the words in which St. Paul, in the letter he sent back to the Romans, quotes the charge they made against him: "If the truth of God hath more abounded through my lie unto his glory; why yet am I judged a sinner?" "Where sin abounded, grace did much more abound. . . . What shall we say then? Shall we continue in sin that grace may abound?"

St. Paul, however, has no difficulty in disposing of this reasoning "God forbid." He says, "How shall we, that are dead to sin, live any longer therein?" Let me now in conclusion try to make quite clear what that answer means.

It is quite true that nothing you can ever do can rob God of His glory. He wants you to glorify Him by obedience, but if you chose rather to disobey Him, then by your very disobedience He will still be glorified, making even that to redound to the honor of His name. Think you that God will be the loser, if you refuse the gracious advances He makes to your soul? No, God is never the loser. He remains the sovereign Lord of every situation. It is you who will be the loser. God was able to make use even of the sin of Judas, turning it to account for the salvation of the world. The world was the gainer for the sin of Judas. And God too was the gainer; for in the Cross of Christ His glory was not diminished but rather enhanced. Ah, yes, but the loser was Judas himself. Judas went out and hanged himself. "It must needs be," Christ said, "that offences come; but woe to that man by whom the offence cometh."

And yet, thank God, that need not be the end of the story. It may have been the end for Judas, but it need not be the end for you. In the infinite loving-kindness of God there is hope even for the man by whom the offense cometh. The sin of Joseph's brethren was overruled by God not only for the good of others but also for their own. This is the most mysterious of all God's dealings with us—the most mysterious and the most gracious—that even our own sins may be to us the instruments of grace, because there is a joy for the repentant sinner which is greater than the joy of just persons who need no repentance. Yet St. Paul is once again very anxious that we should not misunderstand it or draw false conclusions from it. Had we not sinned, we had not known grace. Shall we then continue in sin that grace may the more abound? No, that is quite impossible, and precisely for this reason— that grace will *not* abound unless the sin be truly repented of, and if it be truly repented of, then we cannot continue in it. God can only overrule sin in our lives by first making us hate it; and if He makes us hate it, then we shall not even want to repeat it or to continue in it. "God forbid! How shall we, that are dead to sin, live any longer therein?" That is the great Christian doctrine of Divine Overruling.

## DIVINE PROVIDENCE

# Intimations of an Unseen Helper

REVEREND ROBERT B. WHYTE, D.D., L.L.D.
*Minister, The Old Stone Church, Presbyterian, Cleveland, Ohio*

*A native of Toronto, Canada, of Scotch ancestry, Dr. Whyte has been minister of the Old Stone Church in Cleveland since 1935. During his theological course he served as assistant minister in West Presbyterian Church in Toronto and for one year after his ordination in 1915 as associate minister. He then became minister of the historic Knox Church in Ottawa and seven years later minister of the First Presbyterian Church in Philadelphia.*

*He is a former member and Moderator of the Permanent Judicial Commission of the General Assembly of the Presbyterian Church, U. S. A.; a past president of the Cleveland Church Federation, and is now chairman of the Social Work Department; member of the Department of Church Cooperation and Union of the General Assembly of the Presbyterian Church, U. S. A.; member of the Board of Directors of the Presbyterian Ministers Fund; member of the Fenn Distribution Committee of Cleveland. He is a trustee of Washington College, Tennessee, Tusculum College, Tennessee, Bloomfield College and Seminary, Bloomfield, New Jersey.*

*Dr. Whyte is the author of* The Sins That Crucified Him *and* Personalities Behind the Psalms. *He lectures on "Robert Burns" and brings the power of a poetic imagination to much of his preaching. The following sermon shows the transformation in Jacob's life when he knew Joseph was still alive. The Wagons of God roll on . . .*

# Sermon Fifteen

Text: They told him Joseph is yet alive. And Jacob's heart
fainted, for he believed them not. . . . And when he saw the
wagons . . . the spirit of Jacob revived: And he said, It is enough:
Joseph my son is yet alive: I will go and see him before I die.
Genesis 45:26, 27, 28

THE transformation in Jacob's spirit, portrayed in these verses, is ac-
counted for solely by the wagons. Until he saw them and realized their
portent, he was a very tragic figure. Ever since his sons had departed on
their hazardous journey to purchase food in distant Egypt, he had sat alone
in his tent, haunted by bitter memories and tormented by gnawing fears.
Doubt and dread and despair had invaded and dominated his mind. Apart
from the present perils which threatened him—the terrifying possibility of
starvation for himself and his dependents because of widespread famine, and
the dangers to which his sons, especially Benjamin, the darling of his old
age, were exposed in visiting Egypt—Jacob was unutterably lonely and sad.
Rachel, the bride of his youth and the loved and loving companion of the
years with whom marriage had been a beautiful romance, had long since
died in giving birth to their youngest son, and much of Jacob's happiness
in living had been buried in her grave. After her death he had found his
chief joy in their two boys, Joseph and Benjamin. His other, older sons had
brought him little but grief and shame, and they were venomously envious
of the special favors he constantly bestowed upon Rachel's first-born, the
pampered and pompous, but undeniably brilliant Joseph.

Many years before the scene of our text, when Joseph was a lad of seventeen
years, these resentful, vengeful men, inflamed by cruel jealousy, had seized
an opportunity of selling him into slavery in far-off Egypt. With heartless
cunning they had deceived their father into supposing that the boy in whom
his hopes and affections were centered had been killed by a wild beast.
Having soaked his coat in an animal's blood, they brought it to Jacob with
the false but plausible story that they had found it in a lonely spot. The
heartbroken father immediately assumed, as they intended he should, that
Joseph had been devoured by a ferocious brute. Nothing could console him.
His sorrow was beyond the reach of human comfort. In desolation of soul
he cried, "I will go down into the grave mourning for my son."

His one remaining source of solace was Benjamin, the only living tie with
his beloved Rachel, whose cherished memory shone like a radiant star upon
his grief-driven life. And now a mysterious and malignant power in Egypt

seemed bent upon bereaving him of Benjamin also. Often, as the time drew near when he might reasonably expect the return of his sons from Egypt, Jacob had gone to his tent door to scan the horizon for signs of their home-coming, eager to receive them, yet fearful of the tidings they might bring. At length he descried in the distance clouds of dust which betokened the approach of the caravan, the arrival of which he knew was fraught with so much woe or weal. As it slowed to a stop beside his tent door, Jacob discerned in its astonishing length evidence of a plentiful supply of food. He quickly and anxiously examined its human freight, and made the glad discovery that all his living sons, including Benjamin, were there. But what is this strange pronouncement that greets his startled ears? "Joseph is yet alive, and he is governor over all the land of Egypt." We are not surprised at the effect upon Jacob related in our text: "And Jacob's heart fainted, for he believed them not." Small wonder, for Jacob had irrefutable proof of Joseph's death. Behind him in his tent in the box where he kept his most precious possessions was the blood-stained coat of his favorite son, over which his anguished eyes had so often shed bitter and unavailing tears. That sad and solitary memento of Joseph's tragic death testified in mute but eloquent language against the strange and sudden assertion that he was yet alive and occupying an exalted place of power in imperial Egypt. For long years Jacob's heart had been dark with the desolation of the inconsolable bereave-ment of the son on whom he had lavished all the wealth of his love and care. The voices that told him of Joseph's message and gifts were to him voluble but not valuable, clamorous but not convincing. The story of his sons was in-credible until his unbelieving eyes rested upon the wagons, and saw them decorated with Pharaoh's coat of arms, emblazoned with the crest of the monarch of the greatest nation in the world. "And when he saw the wagons . . . the spirit of Jacob revived: And he said, It is enough: Joseph my son is yet alive: I will go and see him before I die."

The wagons were overwhelming evidence of the truth of his sons' recital. Only one occupying a high place in the seats of the mighty in Egypt could have procured the use of the royal wagons. Only such a person, who was also profoundly and personally interested in Jacob's obscure family living in a remote and alien land, would have sent this regal equipage. Jacob knew of no one who combined the necessary influence and interest to explain the presence of the wagons at his tent door. Jacob was aware that his sons had no prestige at the Egyptian court. They had gone to Egypt, in common with a multitude of other pilgrims from famine-cursed areas, as suppliants to beg the privilege of buying bread. In view of these circumstances, Jacob was convinced by the wagons that the wildly improbable tale of his sons must be true. They were incontrovertible proof of the presence and power of someone in Egypt who was personally interested in him. They gave color and credence to the claim that this person was none other than Joseph, whom he had long mourned as dead. The wagons were the visible sign of an invisible authority.

They were the palpable and potent assurance of a love and loyalty in the existence of which he was compelled to believe, even though he could not see. They were intimations of an unseen helper.

Their effect upon Jacob was electric. All his doubts were dispelled. Our text informs us that when they first told him that Joseph was alive and was the governor of all the land of Egypt, his heart fainted, for he believed them not. He cannot be blamed for doubting what sounded like a fantastic tale, but then who but the governor of Egypt could command the use of Pharaoh's royal wagons, and what governor, except he were Joseph, would wield the scepter of authority in the interest of an old and politically inconsequential foreigner, threatened by starvation? The wagons spoke in trumpet tones, banishing his doubts and fears.

They likewise revived his courage. The words of his sons utterly failed to persuade him that their strange story was true, for they seemed like "a tale told by an idiot; full of sound and fury, signifying nothing." Jacob's heart fainted, for he believed them not. But when he saw the wagons with their undeniable intimation of an unseen power and love, the spirit of Jacob revived. Until then he had been only a dejected old man, so very old and broken. But the wagons with their silent witness gave substance to things he had ceased to hope for, thrilled his heart and made his pulse beat high with courage.

But above all, the wagons transformed his sorrow into joy. His blood leaped with joy at the prospect of seeing his beloved Joseph again. The wagons enabled him to believe, even when he could not prove, and he cried, "It is enough: Joseph my son is yet alive: I will go and see him before I die."

It is a bonny story, a lovely parable of unforgettable experiences we have all had, which have banished doubts and fears, revived courage, and brought the light of hope and joy into the darkness of sorrow. The doubts and fears of Jacob, born of bitter knowledge of man's inhumanity to man, his tragic sense of insecurity inspired by widespread calamity, his longing for the touch of a vanished hand, and the sound of a voice that is still, have had their counterpart in the experience of multitudes in every generation. Large numbers of our contemporaries have been forced to endure Jacob's experience of life, from some part of which no one of us is wholly free. If these facts stood alone, our human life would indeed be a tragedy in which individuals were impelled by forces beyond their control to an inescapable fate of utter darkness and misery. But our text brings the glad assurance that these facts do not stand alone. Ever and again there roll up to the door of our life wagons from afar, intimations of an unseen helper.

What then are some of these wagons of God? In the first place, there are the intuitions of the soul. Long ago the apostle Paul reminded the Athenians that the heart of man is incurably religious. There are constant evidences of the incorrigibility of faith in the human heart, furnishing the conviction that in all our voyaging there is something more to be reckoned with than wind and weather and the law of gravitation and the blind forces of nature. No propaganda, no assault however powerful can remove this central conviction from the human mind. Experiences are always happening which make people believe, or at least wish to believe. If the life of the believer is one of faith beset by doubts, the life of the unbeliever is one of doubt beset by faith, for

> Just when we're safest, there's a sunset touch,
> A fancy from a flower-bell, some one's death,
> A chorus-ending from Euripides,—
> And that's enough for fifty hopes and fears
> As old and new at once as Nature's self,
> To rap and knock and enter in our soul,
> Take hands and dance there, a fantastic ring,
> Round the ancient Idol, on his base again,—
> The grand perhaps! We look on helplessly,—
> There the old misgivings, crooked questions are—
> This good God,—what He could do, if He would,
> Would, if He could—then must have done long since!
> If so, when, where, and how? Some way must be,—
> Once feel about, and soon or late you hit —
> Some sense, in which it might be, after all
> Why not, "The Way, the Truth, the Life?"
> "What think ye of Christ, friend? When all's done and said,
> Like you this Christianity or not?
> It may be false, but will you wish it true?
> Has it your vote to be so if it can?"

Every normal person is visited by moods which convince him of the reality of the religious bias in his nature. Every normal person has intuitions which, like Jacob's wagons, are intimations of the unseen.

Supreme above all of our intimations of the unseen is the historic fact of Jesus Christ. When our heart, like Jacob's, is invaded and tormented by doubts and fears, we think of his proffered gift of peace which the world cannot give nor take away. "My peace I give unto you. Let not your heart be troubled, neither let it be afraid." When our spirit is languishing in utter despondency and, like Jacob, we believe not the words of others, we remember him who, with the cross looming large before him, dared to say, "Now is the judgment of this world. Now shall the Prince of this world be cast out, and I, if I be lifted up, will draw all men unto me." And when sorrow fills our hearts because of the awful bereavements and frustrations of separation from loved ones, the thought of him who said, "I am the resurrection and the life," and who established his claims by his victory over death, banishes our sadness and we say, with a meaning Jacob could not know, "It is enough: O thou soul of my soul, I shall clasp Thee again, and with God be the rest." The fact of Jesus is the confirmation of the soul's surmise, the secret of courage, and the source of confidence in the unseen,

[89]

for he is the glorious intimation of the eternal truth of God and victory and eternal life. There was something about him, the way he came, trailing clouds of glory with him, so that he seemed to his friends to be a traveler from another world.

Human language can scarcely bear the strain of men's efforts to express their thoughts and conclusions about Jesus. In him the unseen became visible. In him the life of God was made manifest in human form. In him the Eternal One was presented within the framework of human understanding. What I have just said is simply an attempt to say the unsayable. The reality of which we are sure defies the power of speech to express it in adequate and accurate terms. "Son of God," we call him, for there is no greater name. "My Lord and my God," we say with Thomas, for no less significant and sublime phrase can convey our emotion and conviction concerning him. In the reality of experience he is, as the writer of the Fourth Gospel put, God's other self come down to this world to verify and guarantee the highest faith of the human heart in an unseen helper, an unseen heaven, and the sure realization of our dearest hopes.

Is not the Christian Church also a wagon of God—an intimation of the unseen? History records no more amazing miracle than the sheer persistence of the Church through the ages in spite of the resistance and assaults of its enemies and the perversity and faithlessness of its members. It is the one surviving institution of the Roman Empire. The only explanation of its seemingly infinite capacity for renewal is the statement of the psalmist, "God is in the midst of her, she shall not be moved." Its presence is like Jacob's wagons, giving to the discerning soul an intimation of an unseen helper. Its continuance is a testimony to the indestructibility of religion in the human soul. The New Testament calls it the Body of Christ, the earthly dwelling of his eternal spirit, the instrument of his purpose, the medium through which he expresses and executes his will. Its presence in the world, in spite of persecution from without and apostasies and infidelities within, is recognized by the thoughtful as an intimation of the divine realities to testify to which is the reason for the Church's existence.

We ourselves have the opportunity and the obligation of being wagons of God, intimations of help and salvation. Each of us may be a wagon of God to some troubled, dejected and sorrowing soul. What higher privilege can we have in life than to be an incarnate intimation of the unseen, bringing assurance, victory and hope to others? As the wagons revived the drooping spirits of Jacob with their intimation of love and concern from far away, as the American and British and Canadian armies that liberated the oppressed peoples of Europe brought the guarantee of sympathy and aid, so by our faith and hope and love we may be to sad and bewildered and despairing souls, messengers of comfort and conviction. The very presence of some men is a tonic. In the darkest days of the war there was more reassurance in the brave resolute face of one world leader than in all the statistics ever compiled. When a ship is in danger, or when its human freight fears it is, one radiant word, one spontaneous smile from the captain, is worth more than all the charts and log books that might, with tidings howsoever comforting, be placed in the passengers' trembling hands. A plain-spoken Scot once wrote, "I am a Christian because the Reverend Doctor Marcus Dods is a Christian. Talk about evidences of Christianity, Dods is it." Oh, to be a person like that, to be an incarnate attestation of the doctrines of the Christian faith, of assurance that underneath are the everlasting arms. What greater epitaph could be inscribed on anyone's grave than this: "When men met him, their spirits revived?" Let us use the wagons of God, both as inspiration and as an example, that others may catch the contagion of our unconquerable trust in the unseen, and say with us and because of us:

> When the anchors that faith has cast
> Are dragging in the gale,
> I am quietly holding fast
> To the things that cannot fail.
>
> I know that right is right,
> That it is not good to lie,
> That love is better than spite,
> And a neighbor than a spy;
>
> In the darkest night of the year,
> When the stars have all gone out,
> That courage is better than fear,
> And that faith is truer than doubt.
>
> And fierce though the fiends may fight,
> And long though the angels hide,
> I know that Truth and Right
> Have the universe on their side,
>
> And that somewhere beyond the stars,
> Is a Love that is better than fate;
> When the night unlocks her bars,
> I shall see Him, and I will wait.

# Easter Dawn

REVEREND JOHN SUTHERLAND BONNELL, D.D.

*Minister, Fifth Avenue Presbyterian Church, New York*

When Dr. John Sutherland Bonnell, minister of the historic Fifth Avenue Presbyterian Church, one of the best known Presbyterian churches in the world, took over the program of National Vespers on the first Sunday of February, 1947, he commenced his tenth year of religious broadcasting in New York.

One of the factors that has contributed to his success at his church is his understanding of human problems and his willingness to give his time to counsel with men and women.

Before entering seminary, he had a thorough training as a psychiatric nurse in a mental hospital, and since that time has specialized in psychology.

Up to the beginning of 1947 more than seven thousand men and women have come to him with their problems covering the whole range of human frailties and sins.

During World War II, Dr. Bonnell visited most of the military and naval establishments on the Eastern seaboard, lecturing to chaplains, to combat officers, and to the medical staffs and nurses of the hospitals, as well as addressing mass meetings of soldiers in the chapels and theaters of army camps.

He flew to Great Britain in May, 1941, at the height of the blitz as a good-will ambassador of the Federal Council of the Churches of Christ in America, and of other religious organizations. Before World War II he visited most of the countries of Europe and studied the growth of totalitarianism on that continent.

Born on Prince Edward Island, Canada, he was educated at Prince of Wales College, Charlottetown, and Dalhousie University, Halifax, N. S. His studies were interrupted in the spring of 1916 by World War I. He served in France as acting sergeant major of the Canadian artillery and was twice wounded. After the war he graduated from Pine Hill Divinity Hall, Halifax, in 1922, with a High Honors diploma. He was awarded the George S. Campbell Scholarship which gave him twelve months of travel and postgraduate study overseas. He was ordained by the Presbyterian Church in Canada. He served in three Canadian churches and was called from the well-known Westminster United Church of Winnipeg to his present pastorate. In 1927 he received the B.D. degree and in 1934 the honorary D.D. degree from Pine Hill Divinity Hall. In 1943 he received the honorary degree of LL.D. from Washington and Jefferson College. Among his writings are Fifth Avenue Sermons, Pastoral Psychiatry, and Britons Under Fire.

*This sermon was given at the annual great united Easter Dawn Service in Radio City Music Hall, New York City, on April 21, 1946. His discussion of Easter as the dawn of hope will find a response in many hearts and minds today.*

## Sermon Sixteen

TEXT: Thanks be to God, which giveth us the victory through our Lord Jesus Christ. I CORINTHIANS 15:57

THE dominant note of Easter is hope. It is a festival of rejoicing, as Good Friday is a day of sadness and painful memories. Earth's saddest and gladdest days are but one day apart.

Longfellow says: "The setting of a great hope is like the setting of the sun." It was so with the disciples. It seemed to them that the death of Jesus brought the destruction of all their hopes. For eleven men the world had come to an end. Every star had been blotted out of their sky. Night descended upon their souls. They had expected to see their Master ascend a throne. Instead, they saw him nailed to a cross. Every indignity and cruelty, every act of shame that the twisted brains of cruel men could devise, had been visited upon him.

I never quite felt the full sweep of the tragedy through which the Master and his disciples passed until I sat in the open-air theater at Oberammergau, and witnessed the last showing of the Passion Play before the commencement of the second World War. Six thousand persons were present. The vast audience was gripped by the spell of this unforgettable drama.

For me, the most poignant scene was not the tragedy on Golgotha, but an earlier happening. The mother of Jesus appeared walking down a street, leaning heavily on the arm of John, the Beloved Disciple. She was trembling with fear and dread.

"Oh, my Beloved Disciple, where has my Jesus gone since last you saw him at the house of Caiaphas?"

John strives to reassure her, telling her that she can depend upon Pilate. The Roman procurators have always striven to be just; he will not send an innocent man to his doom, but Mary responds: "I must see him. Where shall I find him? Perhaps even now he languishes in the deepest dungeon."

Cleophas and Mary Magdalene join them as they make for an open square into which several streets converge. Suddenly they are arrested by a tumult. Blasphemy, curses, blows, are borne on the winds, and then these terrible words: "Don't let him rest! On! On! Drive him on! Staggering will do no good. Thou must get on to Golgotha."

With dread foreboding in their hearts, they see a long procession headed by a solitary man bowed beneath a heavy cross.

John turns to Jesus' mother and says: "It appears as if someone is being led to Calvary." There is a sudden thud as the victim's strength gives way and he falls under the weight of the cross. They gaze in horror on the scene. Just as the cross-bearer falls to the ground, he lifts his face, and through the tangled hair and bloody sweat, suddenly they recognize him, and Mary cries out: "It is he! Ah God, it is my Jesus! It is my son!" The swollen lips of the Master utter these words: "My mother!"

In that poignant episode the tragedy and pathos of the Crucifixion is brought to a focus, with all its humiliation and shame. The blasphemy and torture, the nakedness and death of Calvary, can add but little to the heartbreak and agony of this moving scene.

The disciples of Jesus watch from afar the horrors of the Crucifixion. Words cannot describe their despair. Their mood is reflected in the words which John Masefield puts on the lips of Longinus, the Centurion, as he talks with Pilate's wife:

> He was a fine young fellow, my lady, not past the middle age. He was all alone . . . and when we had done with him he was a poor broken-down thing, dead on the cross.[1]

"Here was a tragedy so deep and dark that it seemed to contain no purpose and beyond it there was not even a gleam of hope." Evil had proved stronger than good; hate had defeated love; wrong had vanquished right; injustice had finally triumphed; and the cause to which these men had given themselves with glad devotion was discredited in the eyes of the whole nation.

One of the twelve had hanged himself; another, with oaths and curses, had protested that he had never known the Master. They had all foresaken him and fled.

When the Roman soldiers rolled a huge stone against the mouth of the sepulcher, it seemed to seal up forever, with the body of their dead Master, the hopes of his kingdom.

Their utter disillusionment is revealed in the words: "We trusted that it had been he which should have redeemed Israel."

Against this somber background the Resurrection stood forth in all the glory of an Alpine sunrise. The news spread like fire through Jerusalem. Early on Easter morning before daybreak a little group of women had sought out Joseph's garden, where the lonely stars shone down on a rocky tomb. There the wonderful discovery was made. The stone had been rolled away from the mouth of the sepulcher and the tomb was empty. God's radiant messenger told them that the Lord was risen from the dead!

Then in swift succession came his appearance to Mary—the rendezvous

[1] From *The Trial of Jesus*, by John Masefield. By permission of the Macmillan Company, publishers.

with the penitent Simon Peter—the meeting with the eleven—the realization that their crucified but risen Master was beside them always with divine victorious power.

Little wonder that these disciples so desperate, so empty hearted on the night of the Crucifixion became transformed men. Timid, vacillating, recreant, fearful followers became bold as lions; these pygmies had become giants; these broken reeds became pillars of iron. They swept across the ancient world defying their persecutors, trampling upon difficulties, welcoming stripes and imprisonment, meeting "the tyrants' brandished steel and the lion's gory mane" and rejoicing that they were counted worthy to yield up their lives in service of their Divine Master, until within a little more than three hundred years the cross of the despised Galilean was lifted higher than the proud Roman eagles.

The spirit of these dauntless warriors is symbolized in the defiant words of St. Paul addressed to grim, portentous death:

> O death! Where is thy sting?
> O grave! Where is thy victory?

Thanks be to God who giveth us the victory through our Lord Jesus Christ!

In this atomic age we are in desperate need of hope that is something more than an empty promise. The mood of multitudes of people in our day is similar to that of the disciples following the Crucifixion. They are disillusioned, bewildered, anxious for the future.

Fifty years ago intellectuals were crying out that science should be freed from the domination of religion. Today, every thoughtful individual is living in dread of the results of scientific research. They are now becoming afraid lest the god of science at whose shrine they worshiped so long may turn out to be a Frankenstein who will hurl humanity into the bottomless void.

When an atomic bomb burst over Hiroshima it destroyed, not merely a populous city, but also shattered forever the notion of the inevitability of human progress.

In the nineteenth century Herbert Spencer wrote: "Progress is not an act, not a thing within human control, but a beneficent necessity. This advancement is due to the working of a universal law . . . until the state we call perfection is reached . . . so surely must man become perfect."

According to Spencer's philosophy man would achieve this perfection by his own efforts. What Spencer overlooked is that humanity can as readily evolve toward the worst rather than the best. There is not the slightest support in either science or religion for confidence "in a universal mechanical irresistible movement toward perfection."

In the fifth century of the Christian era, Alaric, with his hordes of Visigoths, swept across Italy and finally captured Rome. The mistress of the world had fallen before the barbarians. Reading the history of the time, one can almost hear the crash of a falling empire and the crackle of leaping flames.

Augustine, who lived through this experience, writes: "Horrible things have been told us. There have been ruins and fires and rapine and murder and torture. This is true. We have heard it many times. We have shuddered at all this disaster. We have wept and we have hardly been able to console ourselves."

These words were penned at the beginning of the fifth century A.D. Fourteen hundred years have passed since that day, and Augustine's words could be reproduced as a description of our own time. Where is the evidence of that automatic evolution that would bring perfection to mankind, that scientific millennium of which Swinburne sings:

> Glory to man in the highest,
> For man is the master of things.

Two world wars in the space of a single generation should have wrecked that false dream and silenced our boastfulness:

> Glory to man in the highest,
> For man is the master of things.

Yes, he is the master of ruin, destruction and death. He is master of everything save his own mad passions.

Did you see that giant plane drop out of the stratosphere not long ago? It spans our continent in seven hours. Isn't science wonderful? That's a long way from the covered wagons in which our forefathers traveled. But what is the meaning of that wailing siren and that strange whistle that becomes a kind of scream? It's a falling bomb! On that corner a cathedral had stood. It took half a century to build it; it was reduced to rubble and dust in half a minute.

> Glory to man in the highest,
> For man is the master of things.

And look what science has done for ocean transportation! The *Mayflower*, having a burden of only 180 tons, took 65 days to cross the Atlantic, but we have left our forefathers far behind. We can cross the Atlantic in an 80,000-ton ship and take less than four days. But what is the meaning of that rending explosion? A liner is blown up. No one had seen the wake of the torpedo and almost every soul on board was lost. It took four years to build her, but she went down in twenty minutes.

> Glory to man in the highest,
> For man is the master of things.

Every gift that science offers to man may be misused if we so choose. Even this radio carrying words on the wings of the wind at 186,000 miles per second, can spread falsehood as easily as truth, can spread hate as readily as love, can spread ill will and suspicion as well as understanding and the spirit of brotherhood.

Professor Julian Huxley tells us that science takes no responsibility for what man chooses to do with its gifts. He adds: "Science has no scale of values. It is morally neutral. Only religion has a scale of values, and the spiritual driving force to realize them."

How impressive are the words of Holy Scripture: "I call heaven and earth to record this day against you, that I have set before you life and death, the blessing and the curse; therefore choose life that thou and thy children may live."

If we find in God's will our peace, these limitless forces placed at man's disposal may be used for combating disease, for eliminating poverty and ignorance, and for lifting the burden off the backs of toilers everywhere. It could mean that the human race is moving forward into its most glorious era. A Godless science and Godless nations may lay waste the earth, but a science that becomes the handmaiden of religion and that lays its trophies at the feet of Christ can make the desert rejoice and blossom as the rose and bring inestimable benefits to mankind.

Two years ago a young American soldier was left dying on the battlefield. As life slowly came back he thirsted for water. There was no one to dress his wounds, and he lay there from Good Friday until Easter morning. When allied planes passed overhead he tried to sit up and wave his arms to attract attention. Constantly he prayed for relief from pain. His prayer was answered, for he slipped off into merciful unconsciousness. When he awoke he was in a hospital bed and a chaplain was bending over him.

"You say, my boy, that you were wounded on Good Friday and that you have been lying on the battlefield ever since? Do you know this is Easter morning?"

"Yes, sir," the lad answered, "for me too it is like a resurrection. Out there, lying on the field, I died a thousand deaths, but somehow we do not mind the Crucifixion when we are sure of the Resurrection."

O Christ, Captain of our salvation, who passed through Crucifixion to Resurrection, triumphing over death and the grave, take this broken, tortured, bleeding world into thy pierced hands and lift it up to the very heart of God.

# Resurrection

REVEREND GEORGE ARTHUR BUTTRICK, D.D., LL.D., LITT. D.

*Minister, Madison Avenue Presbyterian Church, New York*

*Dr. Buttrick is recognized as one of the great preachers of our day. His sermons have a freshness, a Lancashire independence of thought and expression, a vitality, and a sense of the eternal which businessmen, teachers, housewives and people of all walks of life find inspiring. Born in England in 1892, he was educated at Lancaster Independent College in Manchester and took honors in philosophy at Victoria University. His outstanding ability as a preacher and religious thinker has been recognized with the honorary doctorate by Hamilton, Middlebury, Yale, Miami, Princeton, Bethany and Albright.*

*He was ordained to the ministry of the Congregational Church of the United States in 1915 and was pastor of First Union Congregational Church, Quincy, Illinois, from then until 1918. He served First Congregational Church, Rutland, Vermont, from 1918-21, when he was called to First Presbyterian Church, Buffalo, New York, for six years. Since 1927 he has been minister of Madison Avenue Presbyterian Church, New York, and on March 23, 1947 he celebrated his twentieth anniversary as minister of this church. He was president of the Federal Council of the Churches of Christ in America from 1938 to 1940.*

*Six books mark him as a writer of great ability.* The Parables of Jesus, Jesus Came Preaching, The Christian Fact, Modern Doubt *and* Prayer *(almost a classic in the religious field), and his newest book* Christ and Man's Dilemma, *which is an application of the Gospel of Christ to contemporary problems. In the next three or four years he will complete his work as editor in chief of a multivolume commentary,* The Interpreters Bible.

*In this distinguished sermon Dr. Buttrick discusses the Resurrection of Christ and the assurance of faith and man's need of the risen Christ. In a previous sermon included in the second volume of this series, Dr. Buttrick made God's saving mystery full of new meaning. In "Resurrection" he shows with great clarity that man can walk through the open door of Easter, that the bondage of death is broken through God's redemption.*

## Sermon Seventeen

TEXT: And he saith unto them, Be not affrighted: Ye seek Jesus of Nazareth, which was crucified: he is risen . . . MARK 16:6

ON EASTER Eve a strange event occurs at the Church of the Holy Sepulchre in Jerusalem. Hundreds of people sleep on Good Friday night in the church, and thousands more mill for hours in the neighboring streets. They wait for fire to break from the tomb of Christ. They have been told that the fire is symbolic, but they believe it comes from heaven. When the flame leaps, and the priests light their torches, the crowd presses forward —with trampling selfishness, if truth be told—to light their candles from the sacred flame. So people come to church on Easter Day. There are other motives: custom, curiosity, even millinery. But the deep motive, perhaps only half-understood, is to light a lamp at the fire of Christ's triumph.

*The fact of the Resurrection* is a rock fact. The stories about it are not consistent. You would not expect consistency in stories of such breath-taking joy. But the stories gather round the fact to bear their witness: the fact is not at the mercy of the stories. John Erskine, in a recent life of Christ, *The Human Life of Jesus,* is surprised that the Gospels make so much of the Resurrection. He accepts the fact. He says that the disciples rightly felt that their friend, Jesus, was still with them after his death, as we feel that some dear friend we have lost to sight is still with us; but there is no need (he says in effect) to centralize the fact. But Dr. Erskine's description is hardly within hailing distance of the Easter event. The disciples had no such faith as ours by which to believe that Jesus was still with them. Besides, he had been crucified, and a crucified man was accursed, with all his works. Besides, there is no evidence that "they quietly felt" anything. The fact broke on them in shattering surprise of joy. Their Friend, though he was the same, was not the same; for the Crucified had become the Victor, their Friend on earth was now the sovereign Lord of Heaven. A living Flame had burst from the tomb.

Like most people, I went through my skeptic stretch of the road. But even then I could not dismiss the Resurrection fact as "illusion." Whatever our account of Jesus, he clave to the truth and taught his followers a like realism; and they could not easily have woven lies or indulged hysterics about him. Nor do men gladly die for illusions and pray meanwhile for their murderers, nor do illusions fashion the character to redeem a pagan world. I have always been sure that a stupendous disclosure of a Risen Christ took the disciples unawares. Only so could I "explain" (it is a poor word) how a handful of folk, without learning or prestige or rank, could grapple with the seduction of pagan cults and the might of Roman Empire to overcome them. The New Testament has no "in memoriam" mood: it is a sunrise Book, not because of an illusion, but because of a transcendent fact. By that fact the agelong Jewish Sabbath became Sunday—the day on which Jesus rose. History books tell us that the very presence of Napoleon was as victory to his followers: he being with them they could not be defeated. Yet they were defeated, and their leader sent unloved into exile. Jesus was better than victory to his followers: he was triumph though they died and he could not be exiled. The Resurrection rock rises from history more impregnably than any Gibraltar rises from the sea.

*The meaning of the Resurrection* is not hard to trace. Hundreds of sermons are preached each Easter on immortality, but mere immortality is not the Easter message. The disciples themselves probably believed in some kind of immortality even before Jesus came—in Sheol, a pale and shadowy replica of our life on earth. The mere continuance of our tragic life on earth is hardly "Good News." Some religions, Buddhism among them, propose escape from immortality, and see oblivion as salvation from the endless wheel of life. No, the meaning of Resurrection is *resurrection*: not the interminable dragging on of an old life, but a new life springing from death.

*Thus the meaning is that the fetters of evil are broken.* How could Peter live with himself after having lied his way out of danger? How can any man, or any generation, live with perpetrated lies? They are like chains fastened on us. But when Christ rose from the dead, his disciples knew that his whole life and death were held in the life of God. There on Calvary God had dealings with us. What dealings? The word of forgiveness spoken there by Jesus was God's word held in God's power. The sufferings of Jesus there were God's sufferings—the grief of the Holy Father for the sins of His children on earth. The cry of Jesus, "It is finished!" meant that God's war with man's evil had been fought and won in love. There was a Power now available, the presence of the Risen Lord, stronger than all the bondage of our sins. That was the meaning, and *is* the meaning of the Resurrection.

Coningsby Dawson tells of two crucifixes which he saw in France during the first World War. One was fallen and smashed, part of a hand lying there in grotesque irony; the other, further in the wood, was untouched, and weary men had dragged themselves to it to worship and to die. The first crucifix is the one the disciples saw on Good Friday night; the second is the one they *knew* on Easter morning. They also worshiped in penitence, and great awe, and tear-stricken gladness at the foot of the cross.

*The other meaning of the cross is its redemption of our sorrows.* This again implies much more than immortality. Heaven would hardly be heaven if all it offered us was that we still loved only to lose, or found again only to lose. Sorrow in itself has no virtue and no gain. Watch anyone in sorrow, and you can plainly see what sorrow does: it disfigures beauty, and brings on age before its time, and darkens the day. Unredeemed sorrow is slow-creeping death. What would redeem sorrow? Nothing short of the certitude that sorrow is held within a holy Purpose and is gathered up at last in life. The Resurrection meant precisely that certitude. The death of Christ was part of the purpose of God; nay, it was means by which Christ exalted. The seed must be sown, and die, before it can find its springtime. We rightly call a cemetery "God's acre." Perhaps it does not greatly matter whether death comes soon or late, whether life be a day or a hundred years; for death, soon or late, is or can be within the unfolding providence of God. The little girl, who skipped and sang her way across the cemetery, when asked if she was not afraid, said, "No, I just cross it to reach home." That sudden knowledge was the Resurrection joy: the disciples knew that now they would just cross death to reach, not a dreary immortality, but the home of their risen Lord.

Is it surprising that the Resurrection together with Calvary became focal in their faith? They had found deliverance from sin and hopeless sorrow. Christ had appeared. "Peace be with you," he had said. They were old words, but now they had a new meaning. Their old life was new now: it was a journey to eternal life. Nay, it was a journey in eternal life. "Peace be with you," now meant peace to your remorse and peace to your sadness.

Dr. Johnson Ross once told some of us how an old Jewish tailor, who knew the light of Christ, had said to him in the old blessing: "Peace be unto you," using the word "you" in the plural, as if he had said, "Peace to you two." "To me and whom else?" asked Dr. Ross. "To you and the angel looking over your shoulder," said the old man. So Christ spoke on Easter Day, assuring every sad and penitent heart of an angel looking over our shoulder.

*What is the assurance of the Resurrection?* The fact of the Resurrection can still be fact without any assurance in us. The Bible says searchingly, "The devils also believe," leaving us to assume that they were still devils. Any wise preacher preaches about the Resurrection in a strange mingling of joy and fear—joy for the truth, and fear lest he should lead people to presume on the truth. The day has dawned, but the dawning will not save us until we open the windows of life to the day. The bondage of death is broken, but it is not broken for us until we walk boldly in the liberty in which God has made us free. I turned in my *Home Book of Quotations* to the word "Resurrection" to see if others had felt the New Testament joy. What I read was, "See Judgment Day." Of a truth Easter is a Judgment Day!

*"Go and tell my brethren,"* said the Risen Christ. They were his brethren, though one had denied him, and all had fled in fear. So we walk through the open door of Easter when we treat all men as his brethren. They may be potential enemies, but they are first his brethren and ours. They may be recent enemies, but they are first his brethren and ours, and they are now in hunger. They may have a different pigmentation of skin (as if that mattered!), but they are first of all his brethren and ours. The czar in Russia, in the old days when there was a czar, went out on Easter morning, and

saying, "The Lord is risen!" The sentry in turn embraced his king, saying, "He is risen indeed!" All the evidence goes to show that the czar soon forgot the new brotherhood. But the custom had caught the proper meaning of Easter. When we really treat all our neighbors far and near as being with us the brethren of Christ, we walk through the open door of the Resurrection. Otherwise the door is still as good as closed for us—until we use its openness.

"Behold my hands," said Christ in one of the stories of the Resurrection. There were nail prints in the Hands. Any scars in our hands? They can be scarred even though we work with a typewriting machine or a pen. Are we willing to suffer for Christ? We live in a time when selfish nations block world peace, and selfish groups block national welfare, and selfish individuals operate or patronize a black market. In short, we must have our roller-skating rink though world peace never comes. The fact of the Resurrection is still a fact, whether men are selfish or unselfish; but selfishness can never enter into the treasure of the fact. Unselfishness can, and unselfishness always has scarred hands or a scarred heart, and counts the scars all joy—for His sake who died and rose. Livingstone's body was identified by a broken hand: it had been broken by a lion—which never would have touched him had he not gone to Africa in compassion. What will you suffer for Christ? There's the question. If you know Christ you will count the suffering better joy than what the world calls joy. There is no assurance of the Resurrection Fact except such assurance as is given to a hungry man when food is set before him. Who could prove it food except by eating it? How could the man himself be convinced except by eating it? "O taste and see that the Lord is good!"—by trying to live as unto him.

Dr. R. W. Dale, a well-known English preacher, was walking up and down his study struggling with his Easter sermon. Suddenly he stopped and said, "So Christ is now really alive!" He had preached that, and preached it again, and never until that moment had he entered into the assurance. Christ is now in our world, an atomic bomb suspended over us like the sword of Damocles, and he is really alive! We are not alone. We need not trust to our own poor wisdom and our own suicidal power. He is really alive, and we may live and work in the power of His presence.

"Go your way!" said the angel of the Resurrection to His followers. He summoned them to an open grave, and then sent them on a crusade—not alone! Their world was no brighter than ours—not as bright, if we can judge. But they could have said, in words given to the lips of one dedicated long years after to the same Lord, "Through the thick night I hear the trumpet blow." God has not yet finished with His world. Here Christ walked, here Christ died, and here Christ rose from death. His power is our power—if we use it for his sake. "Go your way," said the angel; and added, "He goeth before you."

# The Inner Resurrection

REVEREND ELMER S. FREEMAN

*Minister, First Congregational Church, Menasha, Wisconsin*

*Elmer S. Freeman's preaching is marked by a clear understanding of the New Testament story and an ability to make that old-but-ever-new story fresh and vital to his congregation.*

*He is a native of Connecticut, but spent his boyhood on the banks of the historic Hudson River, at Tarrytown, New York. Most of his high school and all of his college days were spent in California, where he graduated from San Jose High School and the College of the Pacific.*

*After serving for two years in the medical corps, United States Army, during World War I (one year overseas), he returned to California to enter the Church Divinity School of the Pacific, then in San Francisco (now in Berkeley), California. He was graduated and ordained in 1922.*

*He served Episcopal parishes in Santa Clara, California, Honolulu, Hawaii, and Garden City, New York. Resigning orders in the Episcopal Church, he entered the ministry of the Congregational fellowship, and took the B.D. degree of the Chicago Theological Seminary while serving as minister of Essex Community Church in Chicago. In the fall of 1943 he was called to his present pastorate at Menasha. He has also done graduate work at the University of California and at the Sorbonne in Paris. He is the author of* The Lord's Supper in Protestantism *and sermons and articles in the religious press.*

*"The Inner Resurrection" brings a hopeful outlook to the glorious story of Easter and immortality of the soul. He sees the cross as the symbol of Christ's sacrifice, but as a cross that is empty because Christ lives and reigns with God the Father and in men's hearts.*

*The sermon is included here with the kind permission of* The Pulpit, *where it appeared in the Easter, 1946, number.*

# Sermon Eighteen

TEXT: Because I live, ye shall live also.   JOHN 14:19

HUMAN life as we know it swings as it were between two poles, the poles of birth and death. Life is created anew, we say, when a baby is born; life is snuffed out, so far at least as the evidence of the physical senses can tell, when a man dies. All that a man would learn, all that he would like to accomplish, all the impact he in person can make upon the world must be concentrated within the relatively brief space of threescore years and ten. No more than this can either science or philosophy tell us.

Yet deep within the soul of man down through the ages has been an unsatisfied longing, an ineradicable conviction that life here on earth may not be the beginning and is certainly not the end. Wordsworth is but expressing our common universal instinct in his famous lines on "Intimations of Immortality":

> Our birth is but a sleep and a forgetting;
> The Soul that rises with us, our life's Star,
>     Hath had elsewhere its setting
>     And cometh from afar;
> Not in entire forgetfulness,
> And not in utter nakedness,
> But trailing clouds of glory do we come
> From God, who is our home.

And even the stoic Roman philosopher, Seneca, touched by the wand of faith, declared: "This life is only a prelude to eternity. . . . For that which we call death is but a pause, in truth a progress into life."

Let me try by a personal experience to illustrate what I mean. I was in San Francisco, my favorite American city, on one occasion shortly after the two great bridges had been built. It had been some years since my last visit, and I had not seen them. My train arrived after dark one evening, and I had to leave the city about eight the next morning. So in the early morning I went to the one place in the city from which both bridges can be seen. The Bay Bridge, spanning the beautiful harbor to Oakland, was quite clear, but the Golden Gate Bridge was invisible, completely shrouded in the early morning fog. Keenly disappointed, I waited as long as I could, as the sun rose higher, and at last I was partially rewarded. An extraordinary thing happened. The fog lifted, but only between the upright piers of the bridge, leaving the land anchorages still unseen, while the central part of the bridge, the suspension span, became clearer and clearer.

Then it was that I thought: How like our purely human view of life! We see it between the two piers, but the shore anchorages are invisible. Yet we *know* they must be there! I knew the shore anchorages of that suspension bridge must be there, though I could not see them, because I knew that those two tall piers of steel, more than three hundred feet high, fixed though they were in solid rock and concrete, would not for a single hour sustain by themselves the immense weight and pull of the web of steel and cable depending from them. They *must* be anchored; the cables *must* be carried on over the tops of the piers to solid rock on the two shores of the Golden Gate. I could see only what the sunlight and fog chose to reveal, but I knew there was more to the bridge than I could see. I *knew* it did not end at the piers.

Is not that a parable of immortality, a parable fit for telling on Easter Day? So much of life that lies between the piers of birth and death we can see, as the sunlight of our mortal years reveals it. What lies beyond we cannot see, yet we feel with as great certainty as I felt in viewing that bridge that there must be anchorage beyond, to which every girder and every cable is connected, or the bridge of life would quickly collapse into a meaningless tangle.

Instinctively, probably without thinking very carefully about it, even casual Christians recognize this. Our ordinary thinking about life swings, as we said, between the poles of birth and death. But the Christian religion comes to offer a wholesome corrective to so shallow a mode of thought. Our best-loved religious festivals are not Christmas and Good Friday, representing birth and death in Jesus' life, but Christmas and Easter, representing birth and rebirth, life and renewed life; entrance into human, earthly life, and entrance into divine, immortal life. The fog reveals only the central span of the bridge, to be sure, but we are convinced with a certainty which, though it would welcome further or more literal proof, does not depend upon it, that the bridge is a roadway not from birth to death, but from life to life. Christmas, as a Christian festival, is the entrance into that portion of Jesus' life that we can see; Easter is the entrance to that part of his life that we cannot see, but which goes on and on to its secure anchorage in God's eternity.

Again, Easter, as Winfred Rhoades says, is "the Festival of the Forward Look, the Festival of the Great Expectation" in this life as well.

Life that is in any way worth while looks ever forward, with eager aspirations, vivid purposes, beckoning dreams, shining ideals. Childhood looks forward to youth, youth to young manhood and womanhood, young manhood to maturity, maturity to a serene old age. Nobody looks forward to death; almost everybody looks forward beyond death. Even a man as inveterately skeptical as Clarence Darrow could describe himself as "a pessimist with hope." And how many of us thrill to Phillips Brooks' great words, "Death is not the end of life; death is only an incident in the course of life"!

So the instinct of the Church is right when, if our Church year is to be swung like the suspension bridge between the two piers, we make one of them Christmas and the other one, not Good Friday but Easter—not traveling the road from birth to death but from birth to rebirth.

We can easily make a great deal too much of Good Friday. I would not desire to minimize its observance as a day on which to commemorate Jesus' heroic and sacrificial death. But it is a mistake to lay so much emphasis upon the death of Jesus as to make it what Martin Niemoller in an Easter sermon preached before the war, called "a full stop, with nothing to follow." It is a mistake to make so much of the death of Jesus that our whole relationship to him depends upon that death. More and more I am impressed, as I study the mind of Jesus, to find that he never suggests that his death will affect anyone but himself. The theologians have said that because Jesus died, we shall live. But those are not the words of Jesus. What he says, again and again, in substance, is: "Because I live, ye shall live also."

I would not for a moment do away with the cross as a Christian symbol. But I should shout from the housetops that it is an *empty* cross, a cross from which the Lord of life has gone, has risen, a cross which he has transcended and left behind forever.

Men, as Martin Niemoller says in his Easter sermon, thought they had heard the last word about Jesus at the ninth hour on Good Friday. His enemies thought they had said the last word when they saw him laid in the tomb. And they were quite willing to have it so. Jesus had disturbed them when they wanted quiet; he had made them uncomfortable when they desired comfort; he had made men discontented with anything less than the highest when they would have been quite satisfied with second-or-third-best.

Indeed, the enemies of Jesus tried all sorts of material means to destroy him—human courts, a rope scourge, a wooden cross, a rock tomb, a wax seal, the spears of soldiers. They all failed. "He could not be holden of them."

"He's alive!" cries the Roman centurion in Charles Rann Kennedy's play, *The Terrible Meek*. "I can't kill him. All the empires can't kill him."

Christ is ever rising again. Day by day men seek to bury him under the debris of history, or embalm him in creed and phrase and definition, or immure him within the walls of churches and institutions, or smother him under a load of the cares and riches and pleasures of this life, or stab him to death with the daggers of their sins. But always he rises, phoenixlike, from the ashes of the fires of selfishness and carelessness in which we allow his power over our lives to be destroyed. Ever and again he is lifted up out of the common things of life, a vindication of his life and a triumph over the powers that did him to death, and all men are drawn to him as irresistibly as the earth is held in its orbit around the sun. The empty tomb opens before the world, telling us it is God who still has the last word, not ourselves; that on Easter Day life looks forward, onward, upward, God-ward.

"The resurrection sings humanity's dream of fulfillment," says Winfred Rhoades. But there can be no fulfillment except a fulfillment *in persons*. The Resurrection has happened, but has it happened to us? The Resurrection happened to the disciples, and, says Talmadge Johnson, "they themselves went forth, resurrected from despair, to transform the world." As St. Peter says in James Allen Kestle's Easter play *When the Sun Was Risen:*

> His promise he has kept;
> He's shattered grave and death.
> And nevermore shall men
> Want proof of immortality.
>
> My heart grows strong again
> And I shall run—no more
> The vacillating Peter of the past.
> I now go forth,—"The Rock."
> Let men wreak vengeance on me as they will—
> The rack, the irons, yea, even the cross itself—
> The message of the risen Christ is mine.[1]

The Resurrection happened nineteen hundred years ago—and then it happened again to a young man of the Italian village of Assisi whose name was Francis, and he left wealth, position, power and prospects to become *"Il Poverello"*—the little poor one—and by his example of how to live a life with self left out has since put under everlasting obligation to him every man and woman who would learn to put material things in their true places in the scale of values.

The Resurrection happened nineteen hundred years ago—and then it happened again to a young man in Bedford, England, a young man in his own words "the very ringleader in all manner of vice and ungodliness, saying to God, 'Depart from me, for I desire not knowledge of Thy ways,'" and from a certain moment John Bunyan, hearing "three or four poor old women sitting at a door in the sun, talking of the things of God," became the man who could write *Pilgrim's Progress*, a book which has probably influenced more people toward Christian living than any book ever written, save the Bible itself.

The Resurrection happened nineteen hundred years ago—and then it happened again to an eight-year-old girl, blind, deaf and dumb, when a kindly, patient and understanding teacher came into her home, and Helen Keller veritably rose from a grave of silence and uselessness to be a woman "essentially gay, spirited, and sturdy," as Robert Coates describes her.

The Resurrection happened nineteen hundred years ago; has it happened again to any of us? Will it happen? Shall we be different men and women because we have worshiped this morning at the beloved shrine of the risen Lord?

[1] From *When the Sun Was Risen*, by James Allen Kestle. Copyright, 1938. Used by permission of the publisher, Abingdon-Cokesbury Press.

So the message which this Day of Resurrection speaks and sings and prays into our hearts is more than the message of the bridge half revealed by the fog, symbolizing the going on of life beyond what we can see—great as that message is. It is more than the good tidings that the last word in life is always God's word, not man's, that what man would destroy God will rebuild, that he whom man in hate would kill on Good Friday God in love will restore to life again on Easter Day—thrilling as that gospel is.

The Day of Resurrection comes to say to us that God is for all eternity on the side of life, not of death. The Easter gospel peals forth the tidings that wherever there is human sorrow the compassion of God can turn it to joy; wherever there is human pain there is healing to come from the hand of God; wherever there is human frailty the strength of God can undergird it; wherever there is human doubt the grace of God can dispel it.

The resurrection of the human spirit—the inner resurrection—that is our message today. Earth's broken arcs made perfect circles; earth's fogbound bridges revealing their heavenly anchorages; earth's little hopes transformed into great fulfillments—all this telling us that "eternity affirms the concepts of this hour," the hour in which again we hear the voice of Jesus saying "Because I live, ye shall live also."

## EDUCATION

# The Need of Emphasizing Spiritual and Moral Values in Postwar Education

THE MOST REVEREND ROBERT E. LUCEY, D.D., S.T.D.
*Roman Catholic Archbishop of San Antonio, Texas*

*Archbishop Lucey is a fearless preacher, known and respected for the forcefulness of his sermons, especially those on labor and the rights of the workingman. Born in Los Angeles, California, he recognized the call to the priesthood and studied at St. Vincent's College and St. Patrick's Seminary. Then he took a four-year course in theology in the North American College in Rome, where he was graduated with an S.T.D. He was ordained to the priesthood on May 14, 1916.*

*In 1921, after serving as assistant pastor in several churches, he was appointed director of the Catholic Welfare Bureau of Los Angeles. In 1925 he was appointed pastor of St. Kevins Church, Los Angeles, and in 1929 he became pastor of St. Anthony's Church, Long Beach, California. His leadership led to his consecration as Bishop of Amarillo, Texas, on May 1, 1934; and seven years later he became Archbishop of San Antonio where he has won an enviable place in the community.*

*He is vice-president of the Catholic Conference on Industrial Problems, of the Catholic Association for International Peace, and is a member of the Texas State Committee on Postwar Planning.*

*At present he is executive chairman of the Bishops' Committee for the Spanish Speaking. This committee is composed of the archbishops and bishops of the Southwest and was organized for the spiritual and social welfare of our Latin-American people.*

*"The Need of Emphasizing Spiritual and Moral Values in Post-War College Education," was delivered as the baccalaureate sermon at the University of Texas on June 23, 1946. In it, Archbishop Lucey once again shows his mastery of the spiritual and moral sides of life in the modern world. His discussion of materialism, science and education is something to give men pause as we go forward to build a peace and a tomorrow. Economics, international affairs, brotherhood and secularism come under his cauterizing survey, and he pulls no punches when he urges that religion can and should be taught in our colleges and universities if America is to be a Christian nation. The excellence of Archbishop Lucey's preaching makes him one of the few men whose sermons have been in all three volumes of Best Sermons.*

## Sermon Nineteen

ADEQUATE treatment of this subject requires clarification of the words "spiritual" and "moral." There are words and phrases in common use today which have largely lost their meaning, such as "democracy," "liberty" and "the free peoples of the world." A country whose citizens have not the slightest vestige of civil or religious liberties is numbered among the democracies; a totalitarian despot whose people are slaves condemns fascist tyrannies and speaks enthusiastically of the free peoples of the world. A materialist waxes eloquent over the spiritual awakening of submerged peoples and an atheist enters the lists to defend the rights of the human spirit. It is all very confusing. Are spiritual things merely synonymous with culture, education, material progress and human happiness or have those words a deeper meaning?

By the human spirit we mean the soul of man, an invisible, intangible, immortal substance created by God and endowed by Him with the faculties of intelligence and free will. The existence of a spiritual principle of life in man presupposes the existence of God the Creator. The atheist cannot speak of man's spiritual nature and the materialist should never mention the human spirit. To them man has always been and must forever be only an animal.

[109]

It must be obvious to everyone that materialism destroys the foundation of human dignity and human personality. If men are only animals they must be treated like animals. But that is what Hitler did and the conscience of humanity revolted against his atrocities. Hitler's barbarism is a compelling argument for the existence of God and the human soul. He took literally the teaching of those schoolmen who reduced man to the status of an animal. If they were right, he was right. But reason tells us that both were wrong. The mind of man instinctively allows to human beings inalienable rights above the power of the state to destroy.

The rights of man are rooted in his spirit. His origin, his nature and his destiny are not those of an animal. He is a child of God; his fundamental rights are gifts of God; they are a part of his nature; they are not subject to human power.

If a materialist were asked to state the foundation of human rights he would find himself in a difficult position. Perhaps he would say that nature has made man a very high type of animal and therefore his right to life, liberty and happiness must be respected by government and by his fellow men. But the question arises: What do we mean by nature? If we have in mind the God of nature we can speak intelligently of the natural law and the natural rights of man. But if nature is some vague, impersonal abstraction, a blind concurrence of physical forces, then we should not stultify ourselves by attributing to nature intelligence, volition, personality or dignity. And if nature has not these attributes she cannot give them to man. "*Nemo dat quod non habet.*"

But the materialist may claim that the rights of man are recognized by the conventions of society; they have evolved from the mores and traditions of the ages. Man has made so much progress since emerging from the jungle that he has earned the right to be free. This statement serves only to destroy our firm foundation of human rights and liberties. If society merely recognizes the dignity of man we still ask: Where does that dignity come from? And if society is the author of natural rights society can suppress them. That is what Germany did and we know that Germany was wrong.

Thus we are forced to the conclusion that the rights of man can be established and protected only if they are lifted up above society and government and blind nature to the realm of Almighty God. Unless we postulate God and the soul it is useless to speak of human rights as an enduring heritage of man. Granted the existence of a Creator and an immortal soul in every human being, we can also speak intelligently of morality. A moral act is one that is found to be in conformity with the natural law written in the human heart and with the divine law revealed by God. In this philosophy the natural law has God for its author.

At this point we ask: Which of the several sciences teaches clearly and authoritatively the important truths of man's origin, nature and destiny, his rights and obligations, the norms of morality, the essentials of the good life, the laws which bind in conscience under pain of inescapable sanctions. Certainly we do not look to mathematics, geography, biology or any natural science to speak with authority of moral conduct and the human spirit. Only in the science of religion are these truths to be found. The foundations of morality will not be discovered in the shifting sands of public opinion, civil legislation or the conventions of society. Public opinion may be right or wrong but the fundamentals of morality are immutable.

It is greatly to be regretted that the science of religion has been largely shunted out of public and private life. In many departments of human relations secularism is the order of the day. The field of government, for example, is a most important one since the common good is intimately bound with it. Although sovereignty resides in the people, in a certain sense civil government has power from God. It is a necessity of human nature and it therefore functions by the will of God who created that necessity among human beings. Many of the blessings of God are public rather than private, such as domestic peace, world peace, fertile soil, helpful rains and freedom from epidemics. Since, therefore, the power of the government and the blessings of the people are from God, the representatives of the people should offer public honor and thanksgiving to God. But many governments have become secularized. Not only do they fail publicly to worship God but they actually dishonor Him and persecute His people. At best their attitude is one of neutrality and indifference; of them it can be said: "He that is not with Me is against Me."

In the field of education we find the great American tragedy. Being solicitous not to favor any particular religion we have favored the enemies of all religions. A truly religious man cannot be completely satisfied with the present situation in our educational system. Neither our tradition nor our constitution demands that the American school be a godless institution. Certainly the Founding Fathers believed that religion and morality are an essential part of education. That the school should train the mind and not the heart and the will is a disservice to government and the common good, for after all civil government finds the best explanation of its existence and authority in the field of religion and the common good suffers when even the religious foundations of good citizenship are barred from the school curriculum.

Another department of human life which has largely been removed from the influence of religion is economics. Pope Pius XI, of happy memory, declared in *Quadragesimo Anno*: "All of economic life has become hard, cruel and relentless in ghastly measure." In this the richest country in the world, millions of citizens live in economic servitude; they have no voice or vote in determining their wages, hours of labor or conditions of work. In normal times a very large segment of our people are victims of exploitation and injustice. There was a time when the influence of religion was felt in industry and agriculture. The medieval guild established an honest wage and a just price. The economic system functioned for the common good. Today, to a very large extent, greed of gain and lust of power have cast off the controls of religion. Men are debased in industry because their origin, their nature and their destiny have been forgotten.

In that very important department of human life known as international relations the story is the same. The brotherhood of man under the fatherhood of God has been made a mockery and two frightful wars were the consequence. Governments that did not encourage religious principles among their own subjects would certainly not support those principles in the world community. The religious concept of human solidarity was displaced by the blind and selfish heresy of exaggerated nationalism and Western civilization came close to the edge of chaos.

It is not necessary to examine further the history of recent centuries with its abandonment of God and its surrender to secularism. Suffice it to say that human society, struggling to live without God, is in a strained and wretched state. The evil old era now passing away wrought its own destruction.

The foregoing discussion of religious and spiritual values reveals the necessity of moral principles in human conduct. It must be evident that conduct, moral or immoral, is merely the outward expression of inward knowledge, belief and volition. Generally speaking, a man acts as he thinks. He may not always live up to his highest ideals but in general his conduct reflects his thinking. The good life presupposes knowledge of the right and motivation to achieve it. It is to our discredit that several generations of young Americans have been reared with little knowledge of spiritual things and no adequate inspiration to practice virtue. On the contrary, the bad example of their elders has been a stumbling block to youth.

The motivations of religion are many and powerful. Those who are well instructed in religious truth understand their origin from the hand of God, their nature, both physical and spiritual, and their destiny which is a blessed immortality. In a word, religion teaches us what we are, why we are here and whither we are going—which is more than many people know. Religion gives richness and fullness to human life; it adds direction and purpose to our journey; it gives us a reason for living. Moreover, it furnishes the only compelling and enduring motive for living according to law, both human and divine. In simple language this motivation is the love of God or fear of His displeasure. Love is our noblest inspiration; fear of the Lord is a wholesome restraint.

When religious knowledge, faith and love are eliminated there is not much left to control human conduct. Certainly the irreligious masses will not be greatly impressed by civil law and its sanctions because the law is man-made and its sanctions are most uncertain. If we ask the masses of the people to practice justice and sobriety, obedience and purity for the sake of society, they may well answer that they are society and they are a law unto themselves.

[112]

The truth is that human conduct can be controlled only by faith in a power that is more than human; obedience can be demanded only by an authority above the reach of man; morality can be enjoined only by one who has supreme dominion over man in time and eternity. That power, that authority, that omnipotent ruler is God, and religion is the science of God. That is why religion is supremely important.

These are some of the reasons why spiritual and moral values must be emphasized in postwar college education. I have tried.to make it clear that these spiritual values must not be based on vague and nebulous considerations. Young men and women today are a bit sophisticated. We cannot successfully urge upon them the pursuit of the good life without making clear the elements of decent living. Nor can we furnish adequate motivation by appealing to the conventions of society, the honor of their alma mater or their own sense of propriety. These things are not dynamic. There are no compelling moral imperatives outside religion.

But you will answer that religion cannot be taught in a public institution. Let us face this problem realistically and sympathetically for the destiny of our country is at stake. In the first place, let us stipulate that if religion may not be taught in public colleges, neither may irreligion be encouraged. This has happened in the past. A materialistic interpretation of history and life has been given which entirely eliminated God from His universe. There is no conflict between natural science and nature's God. The laws which govern the universe were established by the Creator of the universe. The Almighty cannot contradict Himself. Even the theory of evolution need not disturb the faith of any man. More than a thousand years ago some Catholic theologians favored the theory of the development of the human body from a lower form of animal life but they also believed in God and the human spirit. They knew that a spiritual soul is infused into the human body by the power of God. A college professor who wishes to be fair will not substitute the religion of materialism for traditional Christianity.

Neither should the schoolmen treat religion like a stepchild. Some benevolent persons feel that in a democracy religion must be tolerated even though it makes no contribution to the life of the nation. Schoolmen should know the constructive contribution that religious principles have made to the concept of democracy, to good government and to the progress of our nation. Religion is not a thing apart from life; it is the very foundation of liberty, peace, democracy and morality.

You have all read the *Report of the Harvard Committee on General Education in a Free Society*. Seeking to discover a clear, coherent meaning in liberal education the report declares that "a supreme need of American education is for a unifying purpose and idea. As recently as a century ago no doubt existed about such a purpose: it was to train the Christian citizen: . . . this impulse to mold students to a pattern sanctioned by the past can, in one form or another, never be absent from education." Unfortunately, this distinguished committee sees no way in which religion can be made a part of public education.

A different attitude is shown by the Yale Committee of Ten appointed by President Seymour to study the role which religion should play in a university. This committee has declared that a university which fails to promote a vigorous religious life among its students is shirking one of its major responsibilities. The committee recommends that the present department of religion at Yale which offers only four courses be greatly enlarged and it offers a definite plan for this expansion.

Perhaps such reports as this one by the Yale committee will have a strong influence on the course of religious education in our country. Perhaps the obvious need of religious training will hasten a solution of the problem. Possibly the establishment of departments of religion in our colleges and a larger recognition of religious councils and religious centers on the campus will grant some relief to our present impossible situation.

Finally, it seems to me that there is no law in this land that forbids a theistic interpretation of man, history and human life. Natural theology is a fundamental science. We can discover the existence of God by the light of natural reason. The Ten Commandments reflect the natural law written in the human heart. If we are brave enough to print on our coin "In God we trust," should we not be honest enough to teach in our schools those fundamental imperatives without which we cannot form and fashion the whole man for the good life? There are certain ultimates on which all men of good will can agree—the existence of God, His omnipotence, His wisdom and His mercy; the authority of the natural law, its demands and its sanctions. These are those self-evident truths in which the Founding Fathers gloried and on which they built our American way of life. These are fundamental religious principles which will give some unity and meaning to liberal education as they give purpose and direction to life. These primitive truths are not adequate for Christian living, they cannot be compared to revealed religion, but they are better than nothing and will serve to counteract some of the errors of our day.

This much is clear. There are certain truths found in the science of religion which reveal the dignity of man and the nobility of his spirit. These truths establish also the rights of man, his obligations in society and his sublime destiny. Unless democracy can defend itself by including these truths in general education democracy cannot survive.

# The Virtue of Compassion

REVEREND WILLARD L. SPERRY, D.D.

*Congregational Minister, and Dean of the Chapel, Harvard Divinity School,
Cambridge, Massachusetts*

*Dean Sperry is respected for his insight into the problems of men of our
day, for his spiritual guidance of Harvard students, and for the excellence
of his preaching. As dean of Harvard Divinity School and professor of
practical theology he has exercised a profound influence on the theological
training of hundreds of ministers in important churches all over the
country. As chairman of the board of preachers to the University (college
chaplain) he has drawn to Harvard many of the world's outstanding ministers
for special sermons and courses of religious lectures for the last fifteen years.*

*The distinguished theologian was born in Peabody, Massachusetts, in
1882, was a Rhodes scholar at Oxford (first class honors in theology), studied
at Yale, and has received the doctorate from Yale, Amherst, Brown, Williams,
Harvard, and Boston. He served in the pastorate in Fall River and Boston,
joined the faculty of Andover Theological Seminary, and has been dean
of Harvard Divinity School since 1922. For four years he was also dean
of the National Council on Religion in Higher Education (1927-31), has
given many famous lecture series, including the Upton Lectures at Manchester College, Oxford, the Hibbert Lectures, Essex Hall Lectures, London,
and the Lyman Beecher Lectures at Yale. He is a Fellow of the American
Academy of Arts and Sciences and is known for several significant books,*
The Discipline of Liberty, Reality in Worship, The Paradox of Religion,
What You Owe Your Child, Wordsworth's Anti-Climax, What We Mean
by Religion, Summer Yesterdays in Maine *and* Rebuilding Our World.

*Dean Sperry is accustomed to distinguish between words written to be
read and written to be spoken. His sermons deny themselves the leisure
and literary elaboration which is found in his books. They reveal a certain
bluntness and brevity in sentence style, which he thinks suited to the
spoken word, and to the school and college groups to which he habitually
speaks. This sermon was preached at both Harvard and Yale and created
a profound impression among the students at both universities. His understanding of students, of life and faith and true compassion make this a
sermon to read and reread many times.*

# Sermon Twenty

TEXT: I also could speak as ye do; if your soul were in my soul's stead. JOB 16:4

THE Book of Job is in the main a conversation between Job and three friends known as Eliphaz the Temanite, Bildad the Shuhite, and Zophar the Naamathite.

The contrast between these proper names is striking. Job was "a man in the land of Uz." These clipped monosyllables fit the man himself; he was a person who had been trained down, disciplined by life. Whereas his polysyllabic friends from polysyllabic places had not undergone any such training and self-discipline.

Job was in trouble, real trouble, and his friends were professedly trying to help him. He had had pains of the body, but these were not his worst pain. His worst pain was that in his mind. He reminds us of King Lear out on the blasted heath in the storm, "The tempest in my mind doth make all else seem calm."

The conversation between the four of them goes on for thirty chapters, but it never gets anywhere or proves anything. Job had been hurt; he was puzzled and angry, angry with life, angry with his fellow men, angry with God. His main difficulty was that he could not understand what had happened to him, and why it happened to him in particular. For the moment he made these three men the butt of his anger—"Miserable comforters" he called them. He was never polite to them, nor patient with them, nor even fair to them. It says a good deal for their self-restraint that they kept on listening to him so long.

On the other hand, it must be admitted that they were rather irritating. They were saying the correct thing in a complacent and orthodox way. They were not pharisaical or insincere, but they were thoroughly conventional. The difficulty would seem to have been this: they were trying to help a man in trouble, when they had never had any trouble themselves.

This whole long first part of the Book of Job is like certain conversations in which we have often found ourselves involved. It is not that we are talking at cross-purposes with someone else, but rather that we are talking to *no* purpose. Our minds never really meet, because we have no common ground of experience on which to stand nor premises on which we are agreed.

Thus, in the words of the text, Job put his finger on what is the real difficulty in such a situation, "I also could speak as you do, if your soul were in my soul's stead." In other words, "If you could put yourself in my place and I could put myself in your place, we might understand one another and help one another."

Here and there in the Old Testament we have prophecies of the coming of the Messiah. The greatest of these prophecies are not so much predictions of a specific event in future time as foreshadowings, hints of what was to be the character of Christ. In this sense of the word we might say that our text from Job is a bit of Messianic prophecy. There have been many theories as to the nature of the divinity of Christ, but they all start from a single inference drawn from the life of Jesus; he put himself in our place, and in turn asks us to put ourselves in his place. "He was made in the likeness of man," says St. Paul, "and was found in fashion as a man." "In all things," says the writer to the Hebrews, "he was made like unto his brethren." Whenever the unlikeness of Jesus to us has been so over-emphasized that it has impaired this strong initial sense of his identification with us, the result is what the Church has always called a heresy.

We are living at a time when it is very difficult to see just what the Christian religion may fairly be expected to contribute to our troubled world. But might we say that a Christian ought to be a person who can put himself in the other man's place? This does not mean, necessarily, that he will approve of all that the other man thinks and says and does, but it does mean that he will understand how the other man came to be as he is; as we say in the vernacular, "how he got that way."

There are a vast number of people in the world who seem anxious to do good to others, but who will do good only on their own terms. We meet them on committees, we watch them manage our philanthropies, we find them at work in politics, national and international. They are not bad, but somehow they are imperfectly Christian. They are, if the truth be told in Job's words, "miserable comforters" of our humanity, because they stand aloof from it; they have never identified themselves with it.

Their difficulty may be this: that all their lives they have been able to content themselves with a kind of secondhand life. The platitudes they have inherited from the past have sufficed them. Perhaps they are fortunate. Yet one can only feel that somehow they have missed what being alive at all can mean and ought to mean.

With most of us the difficulty is of another kind. For we suffer today, not from a dearth of experience, but from a surfeit of experience. Mankind, as a whole, has never before had to live through as much as has been the lot of our generation. This surfeit of experience was beginning to be felt even before the first World War. Forty years ago Father George Tyrrell said, "It seems to me that our experience is given us to be the food of our character and spiritual life; but, in point of fact, we spend our whole life storing up food and never have leisure to lie down quietly, with the cows in the field, and ruminate, bit by bit, what we have swallowed so hastily." Of all forms of waste, the waste of experience is the most tragic.

Critics of classical drama have often pointed out that the essence of tragedy is not the conflict of good and evil, that is relatively simple. Nor is it suffering

[117]

and misfortune, painful as these may be. The essence of tragedy is always the presence of what seems to be some needless waste, waste of ideals, waste of affections, waste of sorrow and sacrifice, waste of life itself.

In this sense of the word our time has been, and may yet go on being, a terribly tragic time. The waste of the experience of the years from 1914 to 1918 was vast and terrifying. No immediate personal problem which, one by one, we now face is more grave than this: Is that waste to go on? We are gorged with experiences which we have not yet digested; we have become so habituated to excitement that like the old Romans at their feasts we are half inclined to go out and make ourselves sick in order to come back for more excitement. But that would be a sheer and tragic waste of life, if it be true that experience is given us, not for the sake of the sensation we get from it, but rather that it may be the food of our character and spiritual life. To have learned nothing from these years through which we have been living will be to have lived a merely wasted life. If this be true of those of us who have lived in safety and great comfort here at home, how doubly true it will be of those of you whose experiences have been stern and hard in far-off lands.

So it is that one of your generation, entering the university not long ago, says, "During my three years' duty aboard an aircraft carrier as communications officer, I saw so many men floundering in disordered lives which lacked a central integration: I saw them seek that integration in almost every conceivable form. It was plain to see that only those men with spiritual backbone were the ones who withstood not only the rigors of combat duty, but also—and this was infinitely more difficult—the rigors of moral combat duty which one constantly undergoes in the service. These years in the Navy were a profound experience—spiritually, mentally, morally—and it is my sincere desire to use wisely the lessons learned during them." This man's experience may have been hard—it probably was hard—but there is no tragedy in it. The years that are just ended for him will not be wasted by him.

What he says leads us on to the heart of the matter. Our experience of life may be, in the first instance, the stuff of personal private character. But it is something more than that. It is a passkey into the lives of others. There are three words which describe what ought to be our more generous attitudes toward vast areas of humanity today: the first is "pity," the second is "compassion," the third is "sympathy." There is a difference between the first of these words and the other two. Gilbert Murray in one of his prefaces to the Greek tragedies tells us what the difference is. Pity, he says, is an aristocratic virtue; compassion and sympathy are democratic virtues. Pity condescends; Compassion and sympathy share. The last two words come, one from the Latin and the other from the Greek, but they both mean the same thing; they mean sharing the experiences of others.

You will remember that moving and revealing line of an English novelist who said, "The greatest help we get in time of trouble comes to us from someone who can say to us quite simply, I have endured all that."

We have in those words the secret of the appeal of Jesus to our minds and hearts. He was tempted just as we are. He was hungered and homeless as millions are today. He was misunderstood and rejected and lonely. The greatest thing we know about pain, says a New Testament scholar, is that Jesus felt it. And for the Christian the significance of these facts rests on the conviction that God Himself is not content with a divine and aristocratic pity for his children; but that He has compassion on them and sympathizes with them.

We have here a clew to the Christian use of whatever experiences we may have had over these last years. Some of these experiences were for many of you very hard; others suffered much less. Life has not been easy for any of us. Yet we are here alive, in security and, as the world goes, in great comfort. Our happy circumstance might prompt us to be content with pitying the rest of the world. But that temper will never get us, or the world very far. For there is in our humanity some proper pride, some native dignity, some deep-rooted self-respect which prompts the comeback, "I don't want your pity. I prefer to do without it."

Therefore, we are challenged to fall back on such of our harder experiences as can be translated into the stuff of sympathy and compassion. Your real problem as a Christian is, therefore, this: How far can you honestly put yourself in the place of another whom you would really like to help? How far can you say, "I have endured all that," or if you have not endured it to the full, "I have at least endured enough to understand something of your life and your lot, even though it be from far off?" One can safely assert that from the Christian standpoint the hurts of our time will never be healed by an aristocratic pity. They require the democratic and Christian virtue of sympathy.

There remains, however, one final problem. You may not pretend to experiences you have not had, and all of us know quite well that there are ills in the world that lie beyond our experience. The permutations and combinations of happenings to human beings are infinite in number. No two lives coincide, and, given the totality of man's experience, what any one of us may know and feel is very little. How, then, are we to match a limited life to the limitless occasion for sympathy.

George Duhamel, who began his life as a surgeon in the French army thirty years ago, says in the first of his books written in a military hospital, "Wars go on because there is no way at all by which one man can feel in his own body the pain which another man suffers. For if any man and all men could feel that pain, there would never be another war."

The best we can do is try to cultivate patiently that unselfishness of mind and heart which we know as imagination. When human relationships break down, that breakdown, whatever else may be involved, always implies a failure on someone's part to put himself in the place of another. Thus a student of social affairs says, "The broken link between classes in the modern world is a fundamental defect of imagination." This is the weak link, ending often as a broken link, in homes, in churches, in races, in states. The white Gentile is inclined to talk in a condescending way about the Negro problem and the Jewish problem. But he has never tried to feel what it is like to be relegated to a Jim Crow car in the South, or turned away from an apartment house in the North. It is not the Negro or the Jew who is his initial problem. His first problem is his own unimaginative self. He will never contribute much to the solution of those other problems until he has solved that prior and more intimate problem. He will be, in Job's words, a "miserable comforter" of mankind until he has cultivated the power to put his soul in their soul's stead.

Do you remember the end of Shaw's play *Saint Joan*? The Maid has been burned at the stake in Rouen. Years afterward some of the characters concerned meet again. A bumbling character, the Chaplain de Stogumber, is saying that he has been saved. Saved, says the Bishop of Beauvais, by the sufferings of Christ. Not at all, says de Stogumber—saved by the sight of a very cruel happening he once saw. You have to see it to understand it. It was terrible. But it saved him, though he had been a little astray in his wits ever since. And then the Bishop asks a question which goes very deep and far, "Must then a Christ perish in torment in every age to save those who have no imagination?"


## EDUCATION AND SERMONS FOR STUDENTS

# Scholars Are Human

THE REVEREND CANON BERNARD IDDINGS BELL, S.T.D., D.D., LITT.D., L.L.D.
*Canon of the Cathedral of SS. Peter and Paul, Chicago, Illinois*

*The Reverend Bernard Iddings Bell, canon of the Protestant Episcopal Cathedral of SS. Peter and Paul in Chicago and Consultant to the Bishop of Chicago on Education, was born in Dayton, Ohio, and educated at the University of Chicago and Western Theological Seminary, Chicago. His interests have always been chiefly in religious education and in the relationship between religion and politics.*

*Before the first World War he was dean of the Episcopal Cathedral in Fond du Lac, Wisconsin, and during that war was aide to the senior chaplain at Great Lakes Naval Training Station. The war over, he became warden of St. Stephen's College, a country college of Columbia University, and professor of religion in Columbia University. In 1933 he retired from academic connections and since then has devoted his time to preaching, lecturing, research and writing.*

*A priest of the Episcopal Church, he has written twenty-one books of which the best known are* Beyond Agnosticism; The Church in Disrepute; The Altar and the World. *His most widely sold book is his latest one, published in 1945, entitled* God Is Not Dead. *He has written twenty-two articles for the* Atlantic Monthly *on religious topics and has contributed to* Harper's, *the* Criterion, *the* New York Times Magazine, *to many church papers. He has been in residence and lectured in six of the great English schools, including Rugby and Charterhouse, and has preached in thirteen English cathedrals. He has been Stated Preacher at various times at Harvard, Yale, Princeton, Chicago, Columbia, Williams, Amherst, Wellesley, Vassar, Smith, Mt. Holyoke and many other colleges. He received the honorary doctorate from Western Theological Seminary, Chicago, the University of the South, Columbia University, Colorado College, and the University of the State of New York.*

*His sermon on the humanity of scholars was delivered in Rockefeller Memorial Chapel at the University of Chicago on October 20, 1946. His understanding of the pressures and loneliness of the scholar will make this sermon of tremendous value to those who live the academic life. Dr. Bell sees religion as an art which every man may cultivate for his own soul and for the souls of those whose minds he helps to mold as he searches for the truth of God.*

## Sermon Twenty=one

FOR thirty-five years my work for God has been almost wholly among those who are more than usual in scholarly achievement: critics and historians and research scientists and jurists and educators and physicians and artists and men of affairs. Not all of them have dwelt in universities, for intelligence is not exclusively cabined on collegiate quadrangles; but mostly I have dealt with men and women in academic halls. These, the quick-witted and informed, have certain trials to go through which are peculiar to them, difficulties to overcome which less gifted people rarely meet with; but their distinctive problems are as nothing compared with the problems which they share with the less acutely perceptive. The thing that matters most about a scholarly man is that he remains a man. The thing that matters most about a scholarly woman is that she remains a woman. Life's usual burdens bear down on the scholar as on other people, exhausting, discouraging. What are the pressures felt most crushingly by every man, felt the more as one is gifted with intelligence, trained in scientific method and the careful use of reason? There are three of them.

The first comes from man's realized inability adequately to grasp the meaning of the universe and of himself within it. It is a mark of the maturely intelligent that he is only too cognizant that what he knows, however great a scholar he may be, is inconsiderable when compared with what he does not discern and cannot fathom. Of a few facts and of a few relationships between facts, he can become fairly certain; but what may be the final purport of those facts, of all facts, of himself as he laboriously chisels away at the more manifest edges of Reality? About that he knows, and is aware that he knows, nothing to boast about. There is in every scholar, because he is a human being, a longing to lay hold on something at least of the *why*; but it is a longing coupled with an increasing realization that, by scientific method and by reason, all that can be done is to scratch the surface of the *what*. The intelligent man who relies solely upon empirical techniques and rational deduction becomes necessarily, and most uncomfortably, agnostic. He can hardly deny that there *must be* a *why* to things, a *why* which involves the *what* and which makes the *what* matter, but this *why* seems forever beyond his ken. Here is tragedy indeed; it is no fun to be agnostic, to confess that, of what lies beneath and beyond the obvious, one must remain ignorant. All men experience the pressure of man's cognitive incapacity; the more intelligent they are, the more unendurable this pressure is sure at last to become.

The second of life's major pressures is the pressure of aloneness. Every man seeks to love, to give himself utterly to some being like himself who will as utterly receive, accept, welcome; but everyone becomes aware, after some measure of experience, how impossible an adequate loving is. One may, indeed, without much difficulty find love in terms of the body, in terms of the biological urge; but love so limited does not release one from aloneness. One asks more of a beloved than that he or she be a means toward spasmodic nervous release. The love men long to give is of the whole being; bodily love is nothing much, indeed it becomes enslavement and a bore, unless it is the sacramental expression of a spiritual unity. Spiritual love is hard to come at, difficult to maintain. After a while the intelligent man begins to despair of it. The best of mundane affections fails to release from a dreadful individuality. The relationships of lover and mistress, of husband and wife, of parent and child, are beautiful and to be valued; but, as Francis Thompson once put it,

> Just as eyes grow sudden fair,
> With dawning answers there,
> Their angel plucks them from me by the hair.

What shall one do with one's intolerable aloneness?

The third of life's pressures arises from a realization of man's moral incompetence, his incredible folly, his weakness of will. It would be simple if all that is necessary to insure a living of the good life were the spreading of a clear idea of what the good life is. Alas, it is not so. Down the ages human beings have kept on doing things that they knew were rationally indefensible and have left undone what informed common sense bade them do. So it is today and so, apparently, it will be in the future. Till the end of human history man will be ruinously moved, despite his knowing better, by avarice, conceit, love of power, pride, vainglory, and hypocrisy. The children, not ignorantly but wantonly, will destroy what the fathers painfully have built and in their turn will erect what their descendants will demolish. The more intelligent a man is, the more completely he is aware that there is in him and in his brethren, that there will be in his progeny, this which makes life on earth, despite the various trappings worn in successive generations, come to the same bad end; and he knows that man's ruinous defect is not due to mere ignorance. More and more we learn to master nature, but ourselves we do not, cannot master. Even the learned observer of all this has himself his part to play in the constant tragedy of history; he, too (and he knows it), is, potentially and often overtly, a brute, a coward, a lecher, a liar, and a fool. "Who shall deliver me," cries Paul, "from the body of this death?"

These, then, are the three intolerable pressures: the pressure of the discovered inadequacy of the human mind, the pressure of the hopeless quest to love, and the pressure of that streak of moral cowardice to which is given the name of sin.

It is obvious that the man of intelligence ought to know these pressures for what they are, seek some way in which he may bear them without being destroyed by them or at best narcotized by them into a dulled insensibility; but it is far too characteristic of the contemporary scholar or would-be scholar that for the most part he is unwilling to face up to life's essential pressures. It is no disparagement of scholarship to say this. It indicates no lack of affection for scholars, no want of respect for their attainments, to recognize that the learned man of this moment, with brilliant exceptions, seems anxious not to look at these human deficiencies which he shares with others. Of course they overtake him in the end; but he thrusts them out of his conscious mind as long as he can, as much as he can. I am persuaded that the modern university tends to encourage him in this avoiding of unwelcome necessities. The university of today esteems lightly, indeed hardly notices, those within it whose business it is to remind their fellow scholars, the students, the academic public generally, of what these fundamental problems of human beings are and what they imply. Its major honor is not given in our time to philosophers and teachers of religion. Religion, indeed, is scarcely considered as within the ambit of the modern university except for pedantic and specialized research or for ministerial training, while philosophy increasingly is classed with religion as speculation which, though amusing to some people, is certainly not central and probably not germane at all to the attainment of mature proficiency. In consequence, far too many scholars and aspirants to scholarship attempt, for want of competent and accepted guidance, to deal with the fundamental human problems simply by denying that those problems matter very much.

The scholar is likely to try to hide away from the first pressure, that which comes from man's inability to arrive at meaning, in a pedantic overconcentration on some bit of specialization. The older he grows, however, the more he discovers that, even within that tiny segment of knowledge which he calls "his field," he remains woefully ignorant, ignorant of relationships and integrations, ignorant of what it is all about. At last aware of this, he is tempted to say that nothing has meaning, which logically implies that his investigations and himself the investigator have no meaning. Is the scholar happy in this conclusion? I trow not, for by it he acknowledges that he is less than a man, without significance, utterly moved about by circumstance. Before most scholars will admit that they are of such a low order of being, they revolt—and there they are, back with the rest of us, feeling the pressure of mental incapacity, needing deliverance.

The scholar frequently attempts to avoid the second pressure, to escape aloneness, by vigorous denial of the primary importance of romance. He settles down into a domesticity in which his children and his wife, or perhaps his mistress, are anything but central to thought and action. He becomes a tired and tiresome lover, an apathetic husband, an indifferent father. He is overimmersed in technical labors with books or in laboratories not, as he fondly supposes, because of devotion to the tireless pursuit of truth but rather as one who seeks an anodyne for self-inflicted loneliness. After a while he realizes that he, who now is getting on, no longer young, no longer even middle-aged, has not learned what it means to love, to give and give. He has not learned from human loving the way to love of the more than human. For all his degrees and medals and honors, his monographs and dissertations and high acclaim by his fellows, he is a forlorn and aging man—wistful like other men.

As for the third great pressure, that of human sin, it has become fashionable to deny its existence altogether. The scholar is too likely to shut out those aspects of human conduct that may disturb a calm serenity. Man from his vantage point seems not a creature ruined by weakness of will; man seems only a little ignorant. How simple is the cure, he persuades himself, for all the ills that society is heir to! If all men would only become as scientific, as logical, as dispassionately sagacious as scholars are, earth would be Paradise. How strange that he should think this! Is there in the academic world no willful pride, no base deceit, no conspiracy, no prostitution of high purpose to low device, no compromise with honor? Is a university a veritable Eden? He knows very well that there is sin among scholars, but better not notice it. There is sin in his own heart, but it is more convenient to deny it. It is easier to insist that there is no sin anywhere, only unenlightenment.

And then he is rudely wakened to discover that the wickedness of man—not man's ignorance but man's sinfulness—has taken the product of his scholarly research and used it for diabolic mass murder. It simply will not do to cry *Crescat scientia* and assume that thereby *Vita excolatur*. And so the scholar comes out of his ivory tower, knows himself a victim of sin like other men, knows also (and this is bitter) that by long ignoring of sin he has become less competent to deal with sin than those who have kept right on grappling with it.

It is true of all these pressures that only he can experience them without disaster who is willing to reach out beyond observation, beyond rationality, to apprehension of what neither can reveal. Deliverance lies in the arts and in religion.

The artist denies the validity neither of science nor of reason. He respects them both within their proper sphere, but he knows their limitations. He knows how inevitably one comes to an impasse if all he has to rely on is what they can reveal. He goes on beyond them intuitively, mystically, trustfully, searching for that which is at once too vast and too elusive for comprehension but which may perhaps be apprehended, touched at one point and for an instant only. The artist takes the apprehended meaning and seeks symbolically to embody it in sound or form or color or words. It is these apprehensions which make a work of art significant. The symphony, the poem, the painting, the dance—they have value not in terms of that which can be analyzed but in terms of that which by act of faith has been laid hold on and in the symbol passed along to beneficiaries. We, too, know what the artist has had revealed to him, and, because we share his understanding, we are the more content to hope, to live, to labor.

Religion is an art, the most ancient of arts, the most general, the most revealing. The religionist denies the validity of neither science nor reason and uses them as best a man can; but, because he is an artist, he knows their limitations. In religion they who by science and reason cannot discover meaning make adventure of faith into that which lies beyond science, beyond reason. Here and there, now and then, a little they touch God who is the meaning, or are touched by Him.

In these contacts comes release from the pressures. Those who have known union with Him who makes sense are able with serenity and trust to concern themselves with a universe of matter-energy, still unable to digest the why of it but sure that, since it is of God's arranging, it is not to be feared. The first pressure is alleviated. They have apprehended what no man can comprehend. Again they touch God in extrascientific, superrational fashion and find One who is willing to take their love, their self-giving, accept it utterly; and when they have thus been accepted by Reality, they return to their hampered human loving with a tolerant understanding of their own limitations and the limitations of others. The second pressure is rendered endurable. Again, they apprehend Him who is perfection of Goodness and are thereafter enabled to look about them unshaken by man's fearsome sin, by their own abhorred sin, knowing well that even blundering fools, once they are humble enough to confess their need, can grow toward righteousness. The third pressure still exists, but now it can be borne. As they find themselves released from the crushing weight of their mental inability, their self-marred loving, their sin, they approach to peace and joy. Religion is a means of escape from incapacity, as all the arts are means of escape from incapacity, escape not from realities but escape into reality, into that reality which scientific method alone can never discover nor reason alone demonstrate.

Is all this beneath the interest and concern of men of learning? Not of those whose intelligence is high, those ready to follow logic to its honorable but unrevealing end. For them as for all other men there can be small venture into meaning unless they set forth upon the path of faith and adoration. Those who are humble as well as wise go the religious way. They proceed gladly, with gaiety, expectant that they, who have seen as in a glass darkly, will come at length to know as they are known. The scholar can be delivered from his limitations, but only when he has knowledge of what those limitations are and humility enough to admit them. God bring us to this wisdom!

EVANGELISM AND DECISION

# The Thirteenth Disciple

REVEREND ROY A. BURKHART, PH.D., D.D.
*Minister, First Community Church, Columbus, Ohio*

*Roy Burkhart puts a feeling of importance into his preaching—the importance of the kingdom of God. He was principal of the Mechanicsburg High School, field worker for the Pennsylvania State Sabbath School Association, and was national director of Young People's Work for the International Council of Religious Education for eight years. He has been minister of First Community Church, Columbus, Ohio, for twelve years.*

*He studied at Otterbein College and took his Ph.D. at the University of Chicago. Otterbein College conferred the honorary D.D. upon him in recognition of his outstanding work. He is the author of* Understanding Youth, From Friendship to Marriage, The Church and the Returning Soldier, How the Church Grows *and* Guiding Individual Growth. *He is active as a member of the board of trustees of the International Council of Religious Education and of Central Community House; a member of the Committee*

[ 126 ]

on Home and the Family of the Federal Council of Churches; and president of The National Council of Community Churches.

The First Community Church has a membership of over 3500 at the present time, and its seven-day program for adults and young people and children seeks to make religion vital in everyday living. It has been demonstrated here that thirty-two different denominations can work together in harmony.

Two preaching services are held each Sunday morning; nine youth groups meet on Sunday evening; and although everything is guided by Dr. Burkhart and the staff, they try to point everyone and everything to Christ as the spiritual center of life.

## Sermon Twenty=two

TEXT: A disciple . . . but secretly, for fear.   JOHN 19:38

ONE Sunday one of my men, while worshiping here with us, was inspired with this question: "Wasn't there someone who almost gave himself to the Way of Christ? Someone who might have been the thirteenth disciple?" When this idea was given to me, it excited my imagination. I recalled the verse in the nineteenth chapter of John: "A disciple . . . but secretly, for fear. . . ." The reference was to Joseph of Arimathea. Let us begin by learning all we can about him.

Joseph of Arimathea evidently was a young man of fine family connections. He had an earnest, cultivated mind and a charm of personality which in early life had exalted him to membership in the Sanhedrin, a body that interpreted and administered the Jewish law. We read that he was an honorable counselor, that is, that despite his youth he was a man of influence in the Council of Seventy. Moreover, he belonged to those who "waited for the kingdom of God." What an insight that gives us into his character! He may never have heard of Simeon who, when his dim eyes looked upon the child Jesus, said, "Now lettest thou thy servant depart in peace." Yet he was one in spirit with the older man who waited for the consolation of Israel; yet he belonged to the company of Anna of whom it is said, "She waited for the redemption of Israel."

These waiters for the morning, these wishers for the dawn, were not an organized group but those isolated individuals here and there, in high places and low, who kept the flame of faith burning on the altars of their hearts. Amid the spiritual sterility and lethargy of their time, they were divinely discontent, wistful, devout, expectant. Of this company were the pious Puritans of England, the persecuted Presbyterians of the Scotch highlands, the Waldensians of the Italian mountains, who, without program or organization, would draw together in barns or cottage kitchens or woodland glens and spend some hours in secret prayer and study of the Word. In all ages they have lived—those who scanned the stormy horizon watching for the dawn, those who in the darkest night confidently expected the daybreak. What a debt the world owes to them!

Joseph of Arimathea seems to have been the wealthy son of a godly household. He had, perhaps, studied in Jerusalem. Then, perhaps, he had gone back to his home in the quiet country town where he lived, later to be called back to the capital as a member of the Council. One may imagine the prayers that followed the brilliant young man as he went to his great task—how in the village home, morning and evening, his pious parents lifted up their voices and cried, "O Jehovah God, give unto our son wisdom and discretion. Save him from vanity and pride. Keep him from compromise, and give him courage to stand for all that is right." From such homes, whether in Arimathea or in America, prayers like these have followed sons and daughters wherever they have gone to find their careers.

This, then, was the background and spirit of the young rabbi who, soon after he became a member of the Council, began to hear of the strange young teacher from Nazareth. He heard his fellow officials speak with contempt and bitterness of this upstart Galilean who was talking of the kingdom of God in terms never heard before, and who told the heavy-laden and the laboring that he would give them rest. It was doubtless some words of Jesus he heard repeated contemptuously in this manner that sent him out to the country highways to see the Master. Perhaps during some quiet night when the stillness was broken only by the hoot of the owl and the cry of the jackal, he stole out of Bethany, like Nicodemus, and there on the flat roof of the cottage of Mary and Martha and Lazarus he talked to Jesus under the starlit sky and heard him say: "Ye must be born again. The wind bloweth where it listeth, and thou hearest the sound thereof, but canst not tell whence it cometh, and whither it goeth: so is every one that is born of the Spirit."

Then he saw his fellow members of the Sanhedrin become gravely alarmed. Perhaps there was called a special and secret meeting of the Council and they said: "What shall we do? The world is gone after him." And perhaps soon in his heart Joseph was saying, "This young carpenter is nearer the truth as it appeals to me than these Pharisees with all their endless debates and quibblings. Perhaps, after all, God reveals himself in that fresh young heart far more truly than in the old gray books."

Did Jesus in those last hectic days in Jerusalem sometimes see two young men standing on the outskirts of the crowd, men whose garb spoke of their wealth and authority? Did he see two upon whose lips there was no sneer, but whose silence was never broken by the cry of loyalty? And did Nicodemus and Joseph sometimes talk far into the night about the power and personality of the young Galilean and the radiant reality of his words? Did they ask themselves about their responsibility to him when he was endangered? Did they seek to save him from the impending cross? I think it must have been so. But all of which we can be sure is that after Jesus was crucified there burst forth the pent-up love of Joseph's heart. Flinging aside all discretion and indecision, he went to Pilate and begged for the body of Jesus that he might bury him in his own quiet garden tomb. Joseph was a disciple, but secretly. His was the example of a loyalty that went undeclared.

Let us consider the fact of secret discipleship. There are many who follow in the way of Joseph of Arimathea; many who hold in their hearts a deep conviction that in Jesus is the way, the truth and the life; many who would contemplate with horror a world in which his redemptive influence is not known. Yet they never have declared their loyalty to him. They live upon borrowed moral capital, yet never add to the principal. Some of us are fortunate in having as a guide the convictions and truths imparted to us from the lives and teachings of godly forbears. Whenever we are tempted to give ourselves to shallow or sinful living, we cannot do it without hearing the sobbing of our own souls. Like Joseph of Arimathea who failed to declare his loyalty, we come from homes that "wait for the kingdom of God," and all through life we know the lingering fragrance of a sincere and simple devotion. Somehow, even through the clouds, we always have a steadying star on the wide horizons of the world. Our hearts are grateful for this heritage, but none of us knows whence it comes; we do not look beyond our lives to the springs that rise in the higher hills. Ostensibly we are men and women with stronger wills, born with finer tastes, having some unexplainable touch of idealism. And yet, behind all these moral standards is a stream of morally consecrated lives—generations of men and women who were not afraid of great commitments and costly loyalties. Theirs was no easy faith. They paid for it in misunderstanding, in loss of worldly gain, in the dedication of their lives to the service of keeping the flame of religion burning in a dark and unfriendly world. With lives and with lips, they declared their faith and their fealty. You can trace that lineage back to a man climbing a hill and carrying a cross upon his shoulders. That is how the moral capital of society was accumulated; that is how were stored up the moral reserves upon which so many are living.

Today in all our communities there are half-hearted Christians and secret followers of Jesus. They mean to walk in his ways, they want his approval. In times of disappointment and sorrow they lean upon the great assurances that he gave. Their hearts believe in the God of love and mercy he revealed. They think life has the meaning which he defined for us. But never have they boldly and enthusiastically declared to the world: "I am on his side, I acknowledge my debt to him and I will do my share in making his spirit and his purpose regnant in human society."

If all the half loyalty and the secret discipleship and the lukewarm fealty that are accorded to Jesus were suddenly to flame into fiery, zealous devotion, this generation of Christians could save an imperiled civilization. Less and less place has the world of today for secret and divided loyalties. When a man is a Communist he sacrifices for its sake. He boasts his faith upon the street corners. Nazis everywhere display their convictions with symbols and salutes and uniforms and marching armies. Every anti-Christian movement is demanding a whole-hearted, one-directional devotion and a loyalty bravely and sincerely proclaimed. Least of all times in history can we today afford a Christian faith that is vague and undefined, a surreptitious lip service, a shrewd admixture of Christian idealism and worldly astuteness; a cautiousness that seeks to gain heaven without losing hold of earth. Never has there been greater need for those who believe in democracy to come out boldly and without reservation, to stand and work for it in all areas of life, to bridge the rifts between white and colored, and to work for equality of opportunity in a united consecration to the common good of all.

As I study the Gospel, I see an attitude in Jesus which I am almost afraid to declare. I see in him an understanding appreciation of the frank and wholehearted and complete sinner—the man who throws all aside and gives himself to the world with full measure of devotion—that he does not have for the careful, middle-of-the-road, respectable folk. Why else does he put the prodigal son in a more favorable light than the elder brother? Why does he speak with such withering contempt of scribes and pharisees; yes, why does he say to them, "Publicans and harlots go into the kingdom before you"? I think Jesus saw in sinners and outcasts the capacity at least for sheer devotion; he knew that once they were won to his way of life, they might stake all on their loyalty to him. And he knew that a careful, cautious, niggling religiosity might be nothing else than a product of fear and selfishness.

Vague loyalties . . . cautiousness . . . belief in Christ—yes, but not his passionate partisanship. Secret discipleship is a greater enemy of Christ than his fiercest antagonist. A half-hearted interest in our way of life with its democratic ideal is more dangerous than the most violent Nazi.

Think now of the tragedy of a loyalty that goes undeclared. Sometimes I wonder what would have been the result if Joseph and Nicodemus had come out strongly for Christ in the Council. No, it could not have saved him from the cross. That was inevitable for him in a world like this. But doubtless he would have lived some days longer. A divided Sanhedrin might have adjourned and sought to find unanimity. And it may be, it well may be, that in the calm before the storm Jesus would have uttered words even more searching than the Sermon on the Mount. Perhaps there would have been more discourse during the last days. Perhaps he would have said something even more reassuring than "In my Father's house are many mansions." It might be that some even more dramatic outgoing of his power would have been preserved in the pages of the New Testament, and some fuller revelation of God. Those last days were so crowded. John wrote of them from tradition nearly seventy years after Christ's death. But suppose those days of intense love and insight and power could have been lengthened —how much more keenly the world might have felt the redemptive impulse of his life! And what they might have meant to Joseph of Arimathea. Then, perhaps, having thrown all caution aside, he might have been in the upper room. Thus there might have been one disciple in Gethsemane who did not fall asleep, but watched with Jesus to the end. In the judgment hall there might have been one friend who stood by when all others fled. Aye, there might have been a gospel more human than Mark's, an evangel more scriptural than John's, an apostolate more fruitful than Paul's—that of the Arimathean.

An undeclared loyalty does not add much to the moral resources of the world. And the most alarming fact in our threatened world is that its moral reserves are depleted. You can see it in families. Those who are themselves living in half devotion and whose lives run by the moral momentum of a past generation cannot and are not communicating these moral ideals to their children. Neither family nor society can go upon its accumulated reserves. There must be new accessions of strength, strength which comes only through deep devotion and costly loyalties and high moral adventure upon the part of a people.

Now I say to you that the Church of Jesus Christ represents the moral hope of society. Clearly the lines are being drawn. The struggle in the world today is between the Church of the Living God and the revived paganisms of a yesteryear. You can be sure that the leadership in today's moral struggle must and will come only from an awakening Church. Can you not see that, wherever materialistic tyranny has arisen in the world, it has found its first necessity that of seeking to destroy the Church with its message of the dignity of life and the supreme value of human personality?

An English philosopher, speaking of imperiled democracy before the war, said this: "A detached, non-committal attitude is perhaps the greatest danger of democracy. For no fine living is possible in any sphere—whether we look to efficiency in business, poise in the home, or grandeur in politics— without some commanding standards, the acknowledgement of some un- qualified loyalty from which everything else derives its value and to which, at the test, all else must be sacrificed." And what calls to that loyalty save the Church? Where else save in Christ Jesus are those inner and independent standards that discipline life and cleanse society? Today the man who does not openly declare his loyalty to Christ is, I believe, no more than an onlooker, an inquiring neutral—in the face of Christianity's greatest test in all history and at a time of civilization's most dire danger. Surely it is time we give up our coldness of heart, our little excuses and defenses, and throw ourselves with the ardor of true discipleship into the Church which Christ loved, for which he gave himself, and on which he depends to keep

[131]

bright and aloft the torch of a living faith. And it is high time that we live these ideals in all relations of life. To delay will mean the loss of our chance to live them.

What are the reasons for undeclared loyalty? Why was Joseph of Arimathea a disciple, but secretly for fear? Always we come back to fear, the soul's most ancient enemy. For fear of failure, for fear that he might not have the courage to go through with it; for fear that he, the young aristocrat, might not find association with fishermen and converted publicans easy—aye, for fear of the world. . . . These were Joseph's reasons. "What will they say, the men I know, if I come out with a declaration of loyalty?" These must have been his thoughts.

There are those who are afraid of responsibility. It is so much easier to slip into church and worship and slip out again. To be a member would cost time and money. It ought to. If we all took the position of the secret disciple there would be no church anywhere. Someone must get beneath the load; someone must carry the burden of moral responsibility. What right have you or I to say, "Let other men do it and I will stand on the side lines to applaud or criticize"?

When it comes to living the teachings of Jesus in everyday life, living by unselfish love with others in the home, at work, in the school, in the market-place; living with others of different religions, colors and stations in life; when it comes to crusading for equality of opportunity for all persons; when it comes to taking definite steps to make brotherhood real; when it comes to being true to ideals for the richest personal, family and community life, then we shrink because of fear. Or we say, "I'm for it," but do little or nothing about it. We are against juvenile delinquency, but what do we do? We are for a more vital Church, but what do we do? We know that Jews and Gentiles, white and colored, must live in friendship, but what do we do? We are "for" these things but about all we do is to give a little money. Some of us may say, "The time isn't ripe . . . we must not hasten." Businessmen used to say to me, "You can't rush this business of paying employees more and improving their situation." They waited too long—they missed their opportunity. America needs a new spiritual birth of freedom, a new soul out of which courageous and daring action may be taken toward solving our problems and bringing our way of life to greater fulfilling. The time is now. We need the thirteenth disciple. We need to conquer our fears and become bold followers of the crucified one.

According to the record, Joseph did ultimately declare his loyalty. He moved beyond giving money; he came to the place where he openly declared himself and acted with all his soul for that purpose. It is a very old and lovely tradition that tells how Joseph came to a meeting of the disciples at their first communion after Jesus had gone. They invited him to join their company and he met Jesus in the breaking of bread. They showed him the cup out of which Jesus had drunk and had given them the wine of his high vision.

Joseph begged that the cup might be his, and in their gratitude to him for giving Jesus a tomb, they let him take it away. Joseph was the first evangelist ever to reach the shores of England. He spent his life there. And when he died they buried the cup with him beneath the hills of Glastonbury. But ere he died the glorified Christ came and walked with him, as friend with friend, through the green of England's pastures. Today you may see the ancient ruins of the Abbey of St. Joseph of Arimathea yonder at Glastonbury. William Blake's imagination, fired with that old tradition, moved him to write the Glastonbury hymn. And with the fine and stirring resolution of that hymn I close this appeal for your deeper consecration to live by the way of Christ. . . .

> And did those feet in ancient time
> Walk upon England's mountains green?
> And was the holy Lamb of God
> On England's pleasant pastures seen?
>
> And did the countenance Divine
> Shine forth upon our clouded hills?
> And was Jerusalem builded here
> Among these dark Satanic mills?
>
> Bring me my bow of burning gold!
> Bring me my arrows of desire!
> Bring me my spear! O clouds, unfold!
> Bring me my chariot of fire!
>
> I will not cease from mental fight,
> Nor shall my sword sleep in my hand,
> Till we have built Jerusalem
> In England's green and pleasant land.

## EVANGELISM AND DECISION

# Has It Your Vote?

REVEREND GERALD KENNEDY, Ph.D.
*Minister, St. Paul Methodist Church, Lincoln, Nebraska*

*Beginning his preaching as minister of First Congregational Church, Collins-ville, Connecticut, 1932-36, Dr. Kennedy was called to become minister of Calvary Methodist Church in San Jose, California, in 1936, and went to First Methodist Church, Palo Alto, in 1940, at the same time becoming director of the Wesley Foundation at Stanford University. During 1938 to 1942 he was acting professor of homiletics at the Pacific School of Religion, and was called to be minister of St. Paul Methodist Church, Lincoln, Nebraska, in 1942. The same year he was made lecturer in religion at Nebraska Wesleyan University.*

*He is a contributor to national religious magazines and is the author of* The Pause for Reflection (sermons) *and* His Word Through Preaching, *an excellent book on preaching and the Christian message. He is known as a radio preacher on* The Methodist Hour *and as the* Voice of St. Paul's, *and for his popular radio program,* Adventures Along the Book-Shelf *on Wednesday evenings. He was educated at the College of the Pacific, the Pacific School of Religion and Hartford Theological Seminary, where he took his Ph.D. degree in 1934.*

*This sermon has a persuasive, evangelistic note that appeals to the mind as well as to the heart. It is a fine type of modern preaching that does not "pull its punches," does not offend good taste, and effectively carries its message to listeners on the radio and at church.*

## Sermon Twenty=three

ROBERT BROWNING has a poem called "Bishop Bloughram's Apology" —one of his best, I think. In that poem the bishop is talking with a skeptic who is troubled because there are some things about religion that he cannot understand and some things with which he does not agree. Finally the bishop says to this man that he cannot live on the basis of doubt. When everything seems safe there is a flash of light, a belief that strikes in spite of doubt. And then he asks this question, "Like you this Christianity or not? Has it your vote to be so if it can?"

Perhaps we should begin by saying what this does not, or at least should not, mean to us. It does not mean for one moment that God Almighty is a sort of celestial politician who depends upon our vote in order to keep in office. It does not mean that the truth of Christianity will stand or fall according to whether or not a majority of people vote for it. Not at all! There is a sense in which it does not make the slightest difference whether I vote for Christianity or not. We who live in a democracy sometimes assume that everything is determined by a majority vote. If 51 per cent of the people decide that a policy is right, the other 49 per cent must go along, at least for a time. But let us not get the idea that because 51 per cent of the people vote for a thing that it necessarily makes it the right thing. It is possible for a whole nation, a whole world to go wrong, and truth is never dependent upon whether we vote for it or not. The Christian faith to the extent that it is true is utterly independent of you and of me.

I do not doubt democracy. I believe in it with all my heart. It is the best way because at the end of the day we will be nearer the truth if we follow what the majority of people want rather than listen to a tyrant or a party in power. But I think we should be very careful to escape if possible, that "Gallup Poll" psychology which seems to assume that you find truth when you find out what most people are thinking. Not always!

Sometimes this kind of philosophy affects our belief about morals and we come to the conclusion that morality is a matter of custom. It is a style—you put it on, you take it off the way you do your coat. Our fathers said this was right, but we will decide it is wrong and by that vote we think we make it wrong. Our fathers thought it was wrong to do this thing; but we say they were bigoted and narrow and we will change that. We think we can completely rearrange the moral order of the world, and so we talk about a new morality. Here was the morality of yesterday; here is the morality of today. That is nonsense. The moral law can no more be changed than the law of gravitation. We have no choice. We may go along our way blithely and say that we do not like it. Very well, but the moral law is not subject to a poll; it is in the ultimate nature of things and when we accept it, it holds us up, but if we deny it, we are destroyed.

One of the greatest series of books published in our generation is Arnold Toynbee's "A Study in History." Toynbee, going back to the beginning of civilizations, studying their rise and their fall, comes to the conclusion that there are certain fundamental spiritual laws in this universe. You can discover what they are and you can adjust to them and live, or you can refuse and die.

Now when you come to think of Christianity, that same false psychology sometimes influences us. A great many people think of the Christian faith as they think of the songs on the Hit Parade. As long as it is the first song it is the best because everybody is buying it, everybody is singing it, and everybody is playing it. But once it begins to slip down to the second or third place, or if it isn't even on the board, well that's the end of that. The preacher becomes a sort of insurance salesman, competing with other philosophies and other ways of life. He has to find customers. If he's a physician, he's on the search for patients. God depends upon us; we have to hold Him up. The Christian faith depends upon our vote and if we vote against it, automatically we have disposed of it.

I think Amos attacked this with the clearest reality. Coming into a generation somewhat like ours—a generation that was enjoying prosperity and had its main faith in materialism—he pronounced his woe upon it. He said, "You think you are going to come to the day of the Lord and it shall be light. Of course, you think that because you believe that God has to depend upon you. He has to have clients and it is His business to vindicate His own people. Therefore whatever your social system may be, when the day of the Lord dawns your enemies will be smashed. But no," he said. "You can't manipulate God to your own advantage. It is as if a man fled from a lion and a bear met him. As if he went into the house and put his hand on the wall and a serpent bit him." You see the picture. You try to use God as a means of escape but the evil is still there. You flee from the lion and suddenly you are face to face with the bear. You go into your house and your walls are strong. But you put your hand on the wall and the serpent bites you. "You can't escape God," he is saying, "the God whose will is justice. You who want the day of the Lord, why do you want it? It shall be darkness and not light." Amos was saying to his people that this is not the matter of a majority vote. God is God and His will shall be done whether you vote for Him or not.

There is, however, a real sense in which Christianity does depend upon my vote, and upon yours. It depends upon it because it is a religion and not a philosophy. A philosophy is a system of ideas on which you weigh, ponder and meditate. You begin with a premise and you follow through to ask if it makes sense. Perhaps it does and that is the end of the matter. But a religion comes to a man's heart and it says, "Choose ye this day." It demands a decision. You have to cast your vote—"Yes" or "No." It will not leave you alone. And the Christian faith comes to every man and it says, "Like you this faith or not? Does it have your vote or not?" What is involved in that?

In the first place, Christianity demands an action. If you are going to vote for it, you have to act. Read again your New Testament to see how Jesus nearly always came to those people with a demand for an action. The man who would not act was cast aside. There was that man who came one day and said he would like to follow Jesus after he buried his father. And with a kind of divine brutality, a violence that startled that man, Jesus said, "Leave the dead to bury their own dead." There was the rich young ruler who had been following the orthodox way of morality but who still felt something was lacking. He had the idea that this Galilean carpenter could tell him something that he could meditate on. So he went to talk to this new teacher. "What is your philosophy?" he asked. To his amazement Jesus, after asking some preliminary questions, answered, "Sell all you have and give it to the poor." And the young man went away sorrowful because it was not what he expected. He wanted contemplation but not action. It is almost as if Jesus came to that generation and to ours saying, "First venture an action, then we can walk together."

I was attending a meeting of a board of trustees some time ago. There was a fairly large endowment fund to administer. I was dreaming about next Sunday's sermon and was not listening to much of the business, when suddenly I heard the chairman of that board say, "Well, gentlemen, it seems to me that the Christian thing to do would be this." And I sprang awake and said, "What did you say?" He answered, "Doctor, I only said I thought that the Christian thing to do in this situation would be this." And I said to him, "If you knew how seldom I have heard any trustee of a church or any member of the board of a church make his decision on that basis, you would know why I was shocked." And perhaps the Church can make one of its greatest witnesses to the world if in its business life it should say, "But the Christian thing to do is this."

[ 136 ]

There are a great many things about Christianity that we do not understand. We are always in the realm of mystery in the Christian faith. It is like standing only on the shore. But I know that day by day there comes to me the demand to do something here and now. I am never doubtful about that. Every day I know that if I have ears to hear, I hear the voice of Christ saying to me, "Do you like this Christianity? If you do, here in this particular situation do that."

There was a man who came to a preacher one time, and said, "I don't know what's wrong with my life, but that first Christian joy I knew has passed by. I still live a moral life. I go to church. But how can I recover the lost radiance of my faith?" And that preacher said, "This is what you should do: go to the store and buy a big basketful of groceries and go to an address of a poor family I will give you. Then when you have given your gift, you sit down to find what they need. Let them know that you are interested in them and that you are their friend. Then you lead them in the Lord's Prayer before you leave, and the radiance will come back." I am convinced that as long as we keep our faith in the realm of the general, and as long as we try to make it only a matter of contemplation, the radiance cannot be recovered. But if there comes to us in this moment the decision that we shall act in his name whenever the chance comes to us, we shall find what we need. That is what it means, I think, to vote for Christ: to venture an act in his name.

In the second place, it means to risk something for Christ's sake. Let us look for a moment at the American home. One of the main troubles with it is that young people get married under a romantic, sentimental, false idea of what marriage and home are. It is partly the fault of Hollywood, our fiction, and all the muck of advertising. Read the advertisements in the month of June. First the bride has to be very small and dainty in spite of the fact that American girls are getting so big. They wear shoes two sizes larger than their mothers. The groom, of course, never has any thinning hair and his chin never recedes. The couple must have a car that costs about two thousand dollars and a home—providing they can get the material to build it—that costs, under these present prices, about twenty thousand dollars. And one must have expensive gifts. That is marriage. But worse than that, there is the idea that one just falls in love suddenly and that takes care of it. One boy meets one girl and the marriage is made in heaven; they get married and from there on life is a continuous honeymoon. When the moment comes that a little bickering begins to enter into the relationship, and somehow the boy discovers that it isn't as easy as he thought and there are some things about her that he had not counted on, he says, "I have the wrong girl. I must change and find happiness elsewhere." Or she says, "I have the wrong boy, obviously." The thing which neither has understood is that marriage is risky and perhaps the fundamental necessity for the success of it is the willingness to accept the risk with courage. Real love knows it will demand sacrifice on both sides, but as the years pass it will be worth doing.

That same romantic sentimental idea which affects the concept of marriage also affects religion. People come to the conclusion that one "falls" into religion very much as one "falls" in love. It comes like a bolt from the blue and suddenly one will never have any more worries and will receive that for which he prays. I had a letter from a lady who had listened to a sermon of mine over the radio. She said, "I do not understand why you make religion so much a divine demand. Religion to me is peace and quietness. As for me," she added, "I'm just waiting for the return of my Lord." In my judgment, that interpretation of religion is false. The Christian faith comes not to guarantee success as the world counts success, but as a mighty fascination. It is an irresistible call to risk something for Christ's sake.

I ask you as I ask myself: When was the last time we risked anything for the sake of Christ? really risked anything? When was the last time I dared speak a word that I knew some people would not like, but did it because I thought that was the thing I ought to say as a Christian? You businessmen: when was the last time you lost a customer or cut down a profit, because you thought you ought to take that chance since you were a Christian? As I look into my own life and you look into yours, do we discover that we have been playing it pretty safe? We go with him as long as he does not ask too much and we follow as long as it does not cost anything. But the moment it comes to us that if we like this Christianity it may demand that we risk something for it, how very prudent we become.

We have believed that somehow the great saints of the past were all miraculously carried to their goals and that our heritage has come to us from men and women who found the way easy. Dr. Luccock with his keen insight pointed it out very clearly when he talked about the "haze of distance." He quoted the psalmist who said, "He brought his people out with singing; his chosen with a song and shout, not a weary man among them." But Dr. Luccock says that when you go back to the book of Exodus which was more contemporary, you will find, "And the people thirsted there for water. And they murmured against Moses and said, Wherefore hast thou brought us up out of Egypt to kill us and our children and our cattle with thirst?" Ah, that's it. When you look back over the past it was not true that every man came out with singing and not wearied. They went into a land not knowing where they were going. Sometimes they thirsted and sometimes they were hungry. But the heritage of our faith comes down to us because it had the vote of men and women who risked their lives for God. In a day like ours, a very crucial time, a tragic moment, the time has come when we must say, "I will risk something of my own safety and my own comfort for it."

In the third place, to vote for Christianity means to take it as our standard. It is summed up completely by St. Paul when he said, "For me to live is Christ." How simple! How all-inclusive! "For me to live is Christ." In my thinking I will bring my thoughts in the light of the mind of Christ. So far as my success is concerned, I will take his standards. If it is to serve, very well; that is my success, too. "For me to live is Christ": I bring my life under his command.

Yet more and more as we go along our way we assume that Christ does not mean to be unreasonable in this thing. Surely he does not expect us to go too far. Therefore let us insist that he was talking about things as they might be. He was using his oriental imagery, not to be taken literally. Finally, we come to where our prayer, if we were honest, would be like the prayer in W. H. Auden's "Christmas Oratorio": "O God, put away justice and truth for we cannot understand them and do not want them. Eternity would bore us dreadfully. Leave thy heavens and come down to our earth of waterclocks and hedges. Become our uncle, look after Baby, amuse Grandfather, escort Madam to the Opera, help Willie with his homework, introduce Muriel to a handsome Naval officer. Be interesting and weak like us, and we will love you as we love ourselves." And if you think that is too bitter and too cynical, remember that we would not stand in this time uncertain about our future, if we Christians had been willing to take the mind of Christ for our standard.

Everyone thinks it is a good idea for everyone else. We want the other fellow to take the standard of Christ and take it literally. The labor union thinks it would be a very nice country if the National Association of Manufacturers would do it, and the employer is very sure that if the labor leaders and the labor union members would just take the mind of Christ as their standard, everything would be fine. The Republicans want the Democrats to do it. The Americans want the Russians to do it. I wish my neighbor would do it, and that fellow that I have a difficult time getting along with—if he'd do it, we would be all right. But that question comes to me and says, "Do you like this thing or not? Do you believe in it?" That means that whether anybody else does it or not I will dare to take the standard of Christ for my living. I will say with the Apostle Paul, "For me to live is Christ."

I do not believe these times come very often. I think we are deciding what the world of our children will be, or if there is going to be any world at all for them. I have never felt so certain that Christians have the answer to proclaim to the world. Literally, it is Christ or chaos for us. Because I feel that way I have to re-examine my own response to this thing. I have to ask again what it means to say "Yes" to Christianity. I would have to confess that I have not acted upon it, I have not risked anything for it, I have not agreed that for me to live is Christ. As we think together of what Christ means and has meant through the years, these are our questions: "Do we like this Christianity or not? Do we believe in it? Has it our vote to be so if it can?"

# Christ and Him Crucified

REVEREND CARL McINTIRE

*Pastor, Bible Presbyterian Church, Collingswood, New Jersey*

*The Rev. Carl McIntire is pastor of the Bible Presbyterian Church, Collingswood, New Jersey, a pastorate he has had for the past fourteen years. The congregation has a membership of more than fifteen hundred. Mr. McIntire is also president of the board of directors of Faith Theological Seminary, Wilmington, Delaware. He is a member of the Independent Board for Presbyterian Foreign Missions, director of the National Bible Institute, New York, and of the Harvey Cedars Bible Presbyterian Conference, Harvey Cedars, New Jersey.*

*He has edited the* Christian Beacon, *a weekly religious newspaper, since it was established in 1936. He served, too, as the first president of the American Council of Christian Churches, established in 1941. He was one of the leaders in establishing the Bible Presbyterian Synod. He received a teacher's diploma from the State College, Durant, Oklahoma, and the A.B. degree from Park College, Parkville, Missouri. His theological education was received in Princeton Theological Seminary, Princeton, New Jersey, and Westminster Theological Seminary, Philadelphia, Pennsylvania.*

*He is the author of* Twentieth Century Reformation, The Rise of the Tyrant, A Cloud of Witnesses, For Such a Time as This *and Author of* Liberty.

*In this sermon he discusses the need of preaching Christ and Him Crucified as a solution for man's personal problems and for the world's ills—as the true way of salvation.*

## Sermon Twenty=four

TEXT: I determined not to know any thing among you, save Jesus Christ, and him crucified. I CORINTHIANS 2:2

AMERICA needs the Bible as never before. She needs its message of salvation and the power from the living God which accompanies faith in His Word. America needs to read the Bible and to hear it preached. Only thus can she fulfill her destiny.

America is a land in which the Bible is an open book. He who runs may read. The liberties which we enjoy and for which we have so recently fought all came out of the Bible. Where tyranny has gone, the Bible has been crushed, and where the Word of God has been exalted tyranny has been banished. In a very real sense our armed forces fought to preserve a land in which men shall be free to believe and to proclaim and to obey the Scriptures. The future of our country, its prosperity and security, are inseparably connected with God's Word. When a people believe and follow its precepts, they are blessed. When they neglect and desert its message, they suffer.

The Bible gives us the eternal truth concerning God, man, sin, salvation, life and death, heaven and hell. The answers to the most pressing questions of man's existence are found in this Book of God, given to man to be his "only infallible rule of faith and practice."

But, we may ask, what is the central theme? What is the main emphasis of the Bible? We find this when our Saviour Jesus Christ declared, "The Son of man came not to be ministered unto, but to minister, and to give his life a ransom for many." Paul, the great apostle to the Gentiles, the brilliant Jew, the pioneer missionary, declared in the words of that famous text, "I determined not to know any thing among you, save Jesus Christ, and him crucified."

This text presents an important messenger and his message.

The messenger has made a personal, final decision concerning his life. Paul says, "I determined not to know any thing among you." He has just emphasized in the first verse of this chapter, "I, brethren, . . . came not with excellency of speech or of wisdom, declaring unto you the testimony of God." He did not desire to have God's testimony confused by the extravagances of speech or the obscurities of worldly folly. The issues involved were too great for trifling or show. But the Apostle emphasizes in the third verse, "I was with you in weakness, and in fear, and in much trembling." "My speech," he says, "and my preaching was not with enticing words of man's wisdom, but in demonstration of the Spirit and of power: that your faith"—and this is the matter which is the one thing the Apostle was concerned with, for he wanted men to have faith, true faith, a living faith, the faith that would work by love, and this faith, he says— "should not stand in the wisdom of men, but in the power of God." This is one reason he was so determined to know only Jesus Christ and him crucified.

This decision has in it the element of the deepest conviction. The word that the Apostle uses here in the original is the word for "judgment," and it suggests a scene, a courtroom. The great decision of a lifetime is to be made. How will the Apostle spend his life? How will he work among the people? Into this court comes every possible claim upon his time and his life. The Apostle reviews them all, and his only conclusion is that he shall have as his earthly course the keeping of the faith and preaching only Christ and him crucified. Paul summarizes this conviction and challenge of his life when he says in II Corinthians 4, "Therefore seeing we have this ministry, as we have received mercy, we faint not; but have renounced the hidden things of

[141]

dishonesty, not walking in craftiness, nor handling the word of God deceitfully; but by manifestation of the truth commending ourselves to every man's conscience in the sight of God. But if our gospel be hid, it is hid to them that are lost: in whom the god of this world hath blinded the minds of them which believe not, lest the light of the glorious gospel of Christ, who is the image of God, should shine unto them. For we preach not ourselves, but Christ Jesus the Lord." Paul, possessing great education, wide knowledge, high esteem among men, counts it all naught that he may know Christ and proclaim his gospel among men.

This brings us face to face with the second emphasis of the text, the message. This message in all its finality and glory is Christ and him crucified. There is none other that Paul would preach. He knew this Christ. He believed this Christ. On the road to Damascus Paul had seen Jesus Christ face to face. The glorified, risen, ascended Son of God appeared in person to Saul of Tarsus, and he became Paul the Apostle. What Paul once hated and was bent upon destroying he suddenly realized to be true, and he spent the rest of his days proclaiming Christ—Christ, the fulfillment of every Old Testament prophecy; Christ, the virgin-born Son of God; Christ, the coming King of glory.

Let us listen to Paul as he glories in this Christ by a marvelously compact and powerful passage in the first chapter of Colossians. Of Jesus Christ Paul says, "In whom we have redemption through his blood, even the forgiveness of sins: who is the image of the invisible God, the firstborn of every creature: for by him were all things created, that are in heaven, and that are in earth, visible and invisible, whether they be thrones, or dominions, or principalities, or powers: all things were created by him, and for him: and he is before all things, and by him all things consist. And he is the head of the body, the church: who is the beginning, the firstborn from the dead; that in all things he might have the preeminence." This Christ was not a philosophy. He was a living person. He came, he died, he arose, he lives, he ascended, he is coming back again. This is good news, the greatest news the world has ever had. This is the message of the historic Christian Church. Sin has been dealt with; death has been conquered. Eternal life is God's free gift to all who will receive it by faith.

But we must ask one question about this message of Paul's. Why does he not just say that he preached Christ? Is it not enough to say that we preach Jesus Christ? Why does Paul add, "And him crucified"? Paul did not know a Christ who was not crucified. Paul gives us this same emphasis when he declared, "God forbid that I should glory, save in the cross of our Lord Jesus Christ." And again, "The preaching of the cross is to them that perish foolishness; but unto us which are saved it is the power of God."

Why, why, we may ask, is there this emphasis upon the crucifixion? The answer is patent. On the cross of Calvary Jesus Christ, the Son of God, died for sin. He made a final, complete, and full atonement, bringing a lost race back to a holy God. On the cross of Calvary Christ died, the just for the unjust, that he might bring us to God. This is the ransom which Jesus Christ said he was giving. Sin is under judgment and condemnation from the holy and righteous God, and the only way that sinners can have their sins forgiven is to turn and accept the salvation which God has provided by His grace in the death of His Son Jesus Christ. This is the heart of the message. When men believe it they are saved; when they reject it they are lost. Instead of telling us that men, in view of the isotope, need a new message, we must declare the old, old story of Jesus and his love. The new man, the new nature, the new birth, which men so clearly see as the need of those who handle the atom, cannot come from collectivism, socialism, individualism, capitalism, or any other ideology of men, but from the preaching of the cross of Christ.

Death is no different in the atomic age than it was when Adam passed away. Sin has not changed with the twentieth century, and the remedy for both has not changed. Thus Paul emphasized with all the might of his soul, "I determined not to know any thing among you, save Jesus Christ, and him crucified."

So it is that the truly penitent sinner cries out:

> Just as I am, without one plea
> But that Thy blood was shed for me. . . .
> O Lamb of God, I come.

So the child of God sings:

> He died that we might be forgiven,
>   He died to make us good,
> That we might go at last to Heaven,
>   Saved by His precious blood.

The glorious thing about the message that Paul preached is that "whosoever shall call upon the name of the Lord shall be saved"—Jew or Greek, bond or free, no matter who the man, no matter how deep or dark his sin. This is the message of Christ and him crucified. May God use it to the salvation of souls today and for the blessing of His people. Amen.

# Doubt and Faith

REVEREND HERBERT H. FARMER, PH.D., D.D.

*Professor of Systematic Theology, Westminster College, Cambridge, England
and a Minister of the Presbyterian Church*

*Dr. Farmer's great preaching is well known in England and America, where the depth of his thought and feeling, based upon a sound scholarly background, have won him a wide hearing. He sees honest doubt as something to be faced, and answers found that faith may be radiant and true.*

*He was born in England in 1891, took his first degrees at Cambridge, studied theology at Westminster College, was ordained to the Presbyterian ministry in 1919 and became pastor of the Presbyterian Church at Stafford. In 1922 he was called to St. Augustine's Presbyterian Church, London, and remained there until invited to become professor of systematic theology at Hartford Theological Seminary in Connecticut. In 1935 he was called back to take the chair of systematic theology at Westminster College, Cambridge.*

*His preaching and writing have made a secure place for him both in England and America, where his reputation has steadily grown. Several books bring Dr. Farmer's mature thinking to his readers:* Things Not Seen, Experience of God, The World and God *(a great volume on the personal relationship of God and man, 1935),* The Healing Cross *(studies in the Christian interpretation of life; a collection of sermons; 1938).*

*The state of conflict in the human soul, the meaning of faith in the face of doubt, the influence of sin upon man's inner peace, and the way God speaks to trusting human hearts make this sermon a guide to deeper faith in Christ the Saviour. It is a message that should help to dispel "the fog of unbelief" that drifts across our lives.*

# Sermon Twenty=five

TEXT: Will the Lord cast off for ever? and will he be favourable no more? Is his mercy clean gone for ever? doth his promise fail for evermore? Hath God forgotten to be gracious? hath he in anger shut up his tender mercies? . . . Thou art the God that doest wonders: thou hast declared thy strength among the people.

PSALM 77:7-9, 14

THESE words are merely the starting point of what I have to say. I take them as the starting point because they reveal to us a man in what is a not uncommon state of mind, and it is of that state of mind I want to speak. The state of mind is this: that a man finds his thoughts about God in conflict with one another. There is one side of him which, when it is active, finds it an easy thing to affirm God, to believe that there is a high and holy purpose of righteousness and love, such as the Bible speaks of, behind our life and calling for the service of men. There is another side of him (usually, though not always, active at a different time and in different circumstances) which finds it just as easy to doubt and deny the goodness of God, and even to question whether there is, in any sense that really matters to anybody, a God at all. You have a picture of these two opposed moods in this psalm. In the first half the writer expresses a mood of doubt and questioning; in the second, he seems to recover himself, and to come through to a mood of affirmation and faith.

It is hardly necessary, I think, to give other illustration of this state of conflict in the soul, of doubt confronting faith, and faith doubt: of something within us that instantly says "Yes! a thousand times Yes!" to all that the New Testament bids us to believe about God, wrestling with something else within us which whispers, and indeed sometimes even bawls down the corridors of the mind, "No! it cannot be, it is a dream." For myself my mind often goes back to a quiet spring morning many years ago in an apple orchard. The trees were in blossom. There were daffodils under them. The scent of the trees, the soft air, the blue sky, the tender light—everything spoke of God. Then suddenly there hopped from behind a bush a thrush whose song I had heard a minute before. It was followed by a cat. The cat bit off its head at my feet. At that moment the Yes, which so much in life gives to God, met its own No face to face in my soul. Today for many people, because of the events of these times, this same conflict, in an even more poignant form, is their almost daily companion. To contemplate a bombed city, not to speak of other things, is at once to hear within the innermost recesses of one's soul the skeptic's question, the unbeliever's question, Where then is thy God? On the other hand, to see, as many of us have seen, the almost unbelievable courage and patience and self-sacrifice and humor of ordinary folk in that same bombed city is to hear again the answering Yes of faith: "Well, at any rate He is unmistakably here and here and here."

That being the state of affairs, what are we to do about it? I want to put to you this: that there is an extremely important question in regard to this conflict which we ought to ask and to answer, which we ought to settle with ourselves, once and for all, and perhaps the sooner we do it the better. It is this: to which of these two voices in the soul concerning God are we going to make up our minds deliberately and consciously always to give the greater weight? Are we going to adopt the policy of always putting our belief in God in the dock and making it justify itself before the magistrate of our doubts, and if it cannot do so, cast it out: or are we going to adopt the policy of always putting our doubt, our unbelief, in the dock and making it justify itself fully before the magistrate of our belief, and if it cannot do so, cast IT out? Are we going to say, my belief in God must prove itself up to the hilt in face of my doubt, before I will abide by it, or my doubt must prove itself up to the hilt before I will abide by it?

I have just said that we ought to ask and answer this extremely important question *deliberately and consciously.* I emphasize those words, for the position is this, that if we do not make ourselves answer it deliberately and consciously and thoughtfully, life itself will continually force us to answer it again and again undeliberately and unconsciously and unthoughtfully. The result will be that we shall continually oscillate between the two positions, sometimes answering it in one way without knowing it, and sometimes answering it in the other way without knowing it: this, to say the very least, is not a very dignified or effective position for an intelligent and responsible being, whom God has put in some measure in charge of his own destiny, to be in.

For my part I have settled it with myself, that without running away from doubts and questionings (for often through doubts and questionings we come to a deeper truth) I am always going to put the greater emphasis on faith. I am always going to put my doubts in the dock first. I am going to doubt doubt before I doubt faith. When it comes to an issue, I am going deliberately and consciously to trust my belief, my faith, that deep something within me which affirms God, which says yes to the God revealed in the New Testament, and to seek to direct my life accordingly. I have come to that conclusion for four main reasons, which I want to state to you very briefly. Perhaps I may be permitted to cast them in a personal form; it will help us to be a little more concrete and save us from a lot of roundabout phrases.

The first reason is this: I have noticed this quite unmistakable fact about myself, and I can only ask you to observe whether it is not true of you also, that my doubts and skepticisms about God tend to grow in frequency and force when my personal life for one reason or another has dropped to what can only be called a lower level. When in an even greater degree than is usual the spirit of slackness has crept in, when personal attitudes to others have not been what they ought to be, when, in the presence of the high requirements of righteousness and truth, I have prevaricated and compromised and indulged myself, then the positive affirmation of faith in God has seemed to grow more difficult, and the negative attitude of doubt and unbelief and fear more easy. The vision of God seems, in short, to vary with the order or disorder of my personal and moral life. This has happened far too often to be without significance. It suggests what I believe to be the fact, namely, that it is without whole personal being that we see God. Hence, if our personal life is not whole but, on the contrary, is disordered and undisciplined and disheveled, then the vision of God becomes, and must become, obscured and distorted—even as it is impossible to see the physical world properly if the physical eye is out of order. Perhaps this is what Jesus had in mind when he said *blessed are the pure in heart, for they shall see God.* Seeing God, on the one hand, and a certain sincerity of mind, a certain singleness of purpose in relation to what we know to be good and evil, or right and wrong, on the other hand, do undoubtedly go together. What, then, follows from this? Does it not plainly follow that the sensible thing to do, when it comes to a choice, is to trust, and to continue to trust, those things which I see most clearly when my life is at its best (even though it be admittedly a mighty poor best) and to distrust the doubts which arise, or at least gain strength when it is not at its best? to trust my vision of God as against my doubts of Him? It would seem to be the only honest and sensible thing to do.

The second reason is this. I have noticed that as people live in the light of belief in God, so many of those very things in life which help to create and nourish doubt and unbelief tend either to disappear or, if not to disappear, to lose their power to defeat and overwhelm the soul. Let me say a word on both these points.

First, then, belief in God tends to eliminate many of the evil things in life which suggest unbelief. Is there any question that a great many of such evil things are themselves, in the first instance, created by unbelief, by men's refusal to live as though there really is a divine purpose of righteousness and love at work in the world with which they have in the end to settle all accounts. They may cause unbelief, but they are themselves caused by unbelief and would disappear with the unbelief itself. I am not saying that this is true of every evil, but it is true of a great many, of far too many, for it to be ignored. Nor am I saying anything so pointless as that, if only everybody believed in God, everything in human life would be instantly what it ought to be. I am not talking vaguely about what might happen if only something else which has not happened and is not likely to happen did happen. I am talking about what *has* happened, and *does* happen, before our eyes; I am talking about evidence. I can stand here now and think of a half dozen evil situations I have personally observed, which are spreading a blight all around them, and which there is not the least hope of ever being put right until one or two persons involved can be brought to live a life of faith instead of a life of unbelief.

Second, it has been found again and again that if a man, when he is confronted with some evil which suggests unbelief and skepticism and doubt to his soul, ignores the suggestion and tackles the evil on the basis of faith in God, then, it begins to lose all its power even to make precisely that suggestion. It begins, indeed, to be no longer a source of questioning and doubt but, on the contrary, a source of light and increased certainty and knowledge of God. This has happened too often to be accidental and insignificant. The evidence is that some of life's richest gifts come, like registered parcels, in coverings which are tough and ugly and heavily sealed and tied with a multitude of entangling knots. Tackle the knots, remove the coverings, in the faith that the gift is there, and, behold, you find the gift and the wonder of an overshadowing presence.

This, then, is the second reason for making the decision to abide by one's faith and always to doubt one's doubts, namely, that the evidence is that the facts of life do, as it were, tend unmistakably to swing round in support of that belief in proportion as one lives by it. Evils do tend to disappear. Doors do open to those who knock—in faith. Enrichments are given to those who ask—in faith. Light does await those who seek it—in faith.

The third reason why I have decided always to trust my belief against my doubt is that I can see clearly why the God who speaks to my heart through all that is beautiful and good and true in human life and, above all, through Christ and the pages of the New Testament, should have left me to make precisely this choice; should have left room for doubts and questionings. If His aim is, as the New Testament says it is, to bring me to a mature personal life, in which I am a son to Him and not merely a slave or a puppet or a child, then He must leave room in my life for sheer adventurous faith and trust, for a readiness to affirm and commit myself to His goodness, even when I cannot for the life of me understand what He is at, and evil things happen which I would have preferred otherwise. It would be no use His "spoon-feeding" me. A truly personal relationship must have an element of adventurous confidence in it, without a continuous clamoring for full explanations and written guarantees. In other words, only from circumstances that strongly stimulate doubt can we learn courage and trust; and if God is the Father of my spirit, then courage and trust are two of the things I have simply got to learn. The point is: given the truth of my belief in God, I can see a reason why I am allowed to have doubts. But if I start from the supposition that my doubts are true and there is no God, I cannot see why something within me should speak so plainly and compellingly of Him.

The fourth reason is Jesus Christ. I look at Jesus and I see—well, what do I see? Not the somewhat meek and placid figure that looks down upon us from a stained-glass window, or from the pictures in a book of Bible stories for children. God forbid. I see a being of literally tremendous intellectual power. The more I study the Gospels the more I am impressed with the sheer mental force of Jesus. How he cuts right through all the subtle argumentation of his questioners to the one central issue! I see a being, too, of the intensest aesthetic sensitivity. The beauty of the world deeply stirred his soul. His sayings and parables are those of a poet. I see, above all, a being of intensest moral purity and strength, one so utterly released from himself that at one and the same time he has walked to the middle of the stage of history like a God, and yet has been forever afterwards the very pattern of humility. As I stand alongside him I know, without any affectation, that I am infinitely small and poor, and he infinitely great and rich, in personal life. And further, I find this: even as he is greater than I in every way, so he is the more certain than I am of God. The fog of unbelief and doubt which drifts at times across my spirit is absent from his. I cannot but believe that his spirit saw the reality of things more clearly than mine. I cannot but ask myself this question again and again: Which, after all, are more likely to be right, the doubts of H. H. Farmer or the magnificent certainties of Jesus Christ? The answer to that question is obvious. It seems to me to be the sincere thing, the intelligent thing, to trust his certainties and that voice in my own soul which, however falteringly at times, point the same way.

And if you say as you might well say: But was there not a time when Christ also doubted? did he not also in the weakness and agony of the cross cry, "My God, my God, why hast thou forsaken me"? the reply is that, when I come, as I must often come in this tragic world, to stake my life on Christ and on his vision of God rather than on my feeble thoughts and feelings, then I am more thankful than I can say that that cry of the Master is there recorded for us in the Gospels. For it shows that Christ himself at least once knew the fullest weight and pressure of those things which in our human life seem to hide the face of God, knew it as none of us can ever know it. Yes, and it shows too that even then he won the victory. For this is not a cry of defeat, not a cry of loss of faith: it is rather faith thrusting through to its final victory. It is faith asking a question, not unbelief asking it, for the question is addressed to *my* God, *my* God. And the answer was given to his cry, for shortly afterwards he said, "Into thy hands I commend my spirit." God succours our faith not less but more, because of that cry upon the cross.

Will you think about these things? Will you, especially those who are younger, make this decision, that if and when it comes to a conflict of two voices in your soul, you will always trust that voice that speaks of God rather than that one that is minded to deny him? You will doubt your doubts before you doubt that to which all that is best within you really points, namely, that Christ is the way and the truth and the life, and to him and to his vision of God you may, you must, come what may, commit your whole being and your whole life.

# Believing Too Little Too Much

REVEREND CLAYTON WILLIAMS, D.D.

*Minister, The American Church in Paris, France*

*The full French flavor of this sermon, preached in The American Church
in Paris, makes it fruitful for men who want to know what is being preached
by Americans in foreign lands today, for Clayton Williams is an American
at home in Paris. Since 1926 he has been helping Americans to find themselves in Paris and has had a brilliant part in keeping faith alive for diplomats
and G.I.'s, for artists and teachers, for students and people of wealth.*

*Born in 1894, the son of a Presbyterian minister, he graduated from Butler
College and then studied at the University of Pittsburgh. He went into war
service in France as a Y.M.C.A. secretary in 1917-18, and became an officer
in the air service of the United States in 1918-19. He studied at the
University of Paris in 1919, did social work at Château-Thierry in 1921, and
then later in that year came to the United States to act as minister of the
First Presbyterian Church in Indianapolis. From 1921 until 1925 he attended
Western Theological Seminary and had the highest standing in his class.
During 1925-26 he was assistant pastor at the First Presbyterian Church in
Poughkeepsie, New York.*

*Upon the termination of that year of service he was asked to go to Paris
to join Dr. Cochran at the famous American Church as the assistant minister
in charge of religious education and young people's work. This position he
held until 1933, when Dr. Cochran resigned and the full charge of the church
fell to Dr. Williams. The American Church in Paris was founded by
Americans and is largely supported by Americans in the United States and
in Paris. It is the oldest American church outside of the United States.*

*When World War II came and the evacuation of Paris by most Americans
took place, the church committee urged Dr. Williams to take his wife and
children to America, so that they would be out of the danger zone. This he
did, returning at once to France in the hope that he might continue the
work in Paris, if it proved possible. However, it did not. In France and
in the south of Spain and Portugal, he assisted in many ways with relief
and rescue work.*

*He finally had to return to the United States, where he served as pastor
of the Seventh Presbyterian Church, Cincinnati, Ohio, from December,
1941, to May, 1945. In June of 1945 it was possible for Dr. Williams to secure
transportation to France. He immediately resumed his pastorate in Paris.
The church was the one American church in the war zone which was able
to continue to hold services in English all through the conflict. In 1937*

the French government made him a Knight of the Legion of Honor for his work for Franco-American relations.

Clayton Williams makes faith a glowing and glorious matter as he brings the message of Jesus and the leper, of the man with a son to be cured, of pessimism and realism and cynicism. His use of history and his knowledge of man is a touch of genius.

## Sermon Twenty=six

TEXT: Jesus said unto him, If thou canst believe, all things are possible to him that believeth. And straightway the father of the child cried out, and said with tears, Lord, I believe; help thou mine unbelief.   MARK 9:23-24

THIS is the story of a man whose faith had about run out, suddenly realizing that he faced an opportunity that required more faith than he could muster! And in a way that was a blessing for it is an excellent thing for one to know when one's faith has reached its limits, to realize that one is thrown back upon the grace of God for the faith that one cannot supply oneself, and to say, as he did: "Lord, I believe; help thou mine unbelief"!

That kind of an experience is epochal in a man's spiritual life for, after all, the real source of all faith is God and our belief must be based on God's power and goodness rather than in the evidence presented by life's failures and frustrations!

That was the trouble with this man! Repeated disappointments, culminating in the unhappy experience when the disciples had failed to cure his son, had sapped his faith! He had sought everyone for help, he had tried every avenue of hope, without success. His son was still uncured. And at length the negative quality of his experience had overwhelmed his faith, hardly leaving room for hope! He was just about convinced that nothing could be done for his son as you can see from the way in which he approached Jesus: "If you really think that something can be done for my son, if thou canst do anything. . . ." And Jesus stops him, saying: "What do you mean, 'If thou canst do anything'? All things are possible if you have faith, if you believe in the right things."

The trouble with this man was that he had been convinced of the wrong things. He had given negative experience too much credence! It wasn't that he didn't believe. He believed too little too much! He had too much faith in the wrong evidence!

Have you ever thought how often that is the case with most of us? The real trouble with most of us is not that we have too little faith, but that we

[151]

have too much faith in the wrong things. If you think it through, that's really what lies behind most skepticism. The skeptic rather prides himself that he has no beliefs, and yet in reality skepticism is a creed itself, and skepticism can be very dogmatic. A man can say he doesn't believe anything so emphatically as to make a belief of his very denial.

Ernest Haeckel scornfully repudiated the opening clause of the Apostles' Creed: "I believe in God the Father Almighty, Creator of heaven and earth," as irrational and untenable! But the very basis of his denial was a creedal substitute which declared his belief "in a chemical substance of a viscous character having albuminous matter and water as its chief constituents."

A professor of medicine, quoted by Dr. Fosdick, has remarked that such a creed reduces all essential reality to mere "phosphorus and glue," and that means that when an Italian patriot cries, "The time for dying comes to all but the time for dishonoring oneself ought never to come to anyone," and when Edith Cavell faces a firing squad with the words, "Patriotism is not enough," Haeckel believed that nothing is involved but phosphorus and glue.

You see the trouble is that Haeckel believed too much in too little. He had never seen life in its larger setting, he had never given it an eternal perspective. He wanted to balance his books at sundown and draw his own conclusion from his own figures! He was convinced that the universe is a meaningless chaos and that man is merely an elaborate and complicated insect crawling over a pigmy planet revolving around a second-rate star. And yet, for all of life's meaninglessness, he insisted on giving it his own meaning! You see again the trouble is that he believed too little too much.

And that's the trouble with the pessimist. He also believes too little too much. He puts too much store by the evidence of the negative aspects of life! He is convinced of the wrong things because he is convinced by the wrong things.

There are two ways that one can appraise life, and the color of one's appraisal depends upon how one looks at life.

I remember that there were two students in our college class in English composition, both of whom were assigned the same subject: "The Backyard Side of City Life." Since both of them lived in the same district and came into the city by the same commuters' train, they made their observations from the same experience.

The one described how the irresistible urge in every human heart to bring beauty into life had showed itself, even in the city's slums, in the plants that lined the edges of the porch rails and fire escapes and windowsills: geraniums in tin cans, and morning glories trailing riotously over porch roofs, and corner plots aflame with calla lilies and flamboyant with elephant ears. There was no backyard so poor or so squalid that it was not brightened by a bit of floral color.

And the other wrote of the sordidness of the backyard scene with its

[152]

litter-strewn lots and its piles of refuse and its half-open garbage pails, of the backyard occupants lolling about in varying degrees of vulgar nudity, and dirty, ragged, half-naked children and malodorous cesspools.

The one saw the flowers and the other saw the filth!

And the same thing runs all through life. One can see the horror of war— and there is plenty of horror in it—or one can see its heroism and its courage and the fine spirit of dedication in those who must go through with it though they hate it.

It all depends on where you put the emphasis, on what you base your convictions!

Jesus was a realist! He never failed to look life full in the face. He saw the leper and the beggar and the fallen sparrow! But he also saw the lily and the swallow and the good Samaritan and the stars, and the unfailing providence of God in the rain and the sunshine and the grain. He saw the rocky ground and the thistle patch and the seed that was trodden under foot! But he also saw and rejoiced in the fertile soil that brought forth the harvest, some thirty, some sixty, some a hundredfold.

The trouble with the pessimist is that he bases his convictions on the wrong things. Convictions ought to be based on life in its highest terms, not its lowest. After all, who really represents man? The gangster and Hitler or Wilfred Grenfell and Louis Pasteur. And who represents woman? The woman of the street or Jane Addams and Helen Keller? What justifies God's handiwork? The one who conceived of the prison at Dachau or the creator of the Winged Victory.

You see the trouble with the pessimist is that he believes too little too much.

And that's the trouble with the cynic. You remember the impenitent thief on the cross. He was convinced that he knew life. He had been through it all. He had fought for liberty and look what it had got him—a cross! Talk about love and liberty. Life just wasn't like that! One can see the curl of his lips and hear the snarl in his voice: "Liberty!"

I remember how just before the fall of France, I overheard two French boys, about eighteen or nineteen, just about to be called up for service, talking together in the dusk of the evening in the city square of the Place de la Gare at Orleans. "*La liberté!*" said one. "*Qu'est-ce que c'est la liberté? Qu'est-ce que ça peut vous faire si vous avez la gueule cassée?*" ("Liberty! What's Liberty? What good will liberty do you if you get your face smashed in?")

There you have it! That's one of the reasons why France fell. That's why she let Petain take over! She believed too little too much. Faith in liberty had given way to cynicism!

Well, that's the way it was with the thief on the cross. He knew life and there was no room for God in it. And that is what some of us are saying today, isn't it? We know life! We know the kind of a world we live in. Our science has plumbed the universe, up to the nebulae, down to the meson.

[153]

Things are like this! They act like this, always! No place in this world for prayer, no place for miracle!

We're like Louis XV. When there was so much excitement about a few miracles which were supposed to have taken place in a certain cemetery in Paris, he locked up the gates of the cemetery and placed a sign on them which read, "By order of the King, God is hereby forbidden to work miracles in this place." No miracles by order of the king! No miracles by order of science! As though God were not Master of His own science! Believing in a little hamstrung God. Believing too little too much!

And it's no world for the ideals of Christ. We know about them too. We know what kind of a world we live in. It's a hard, competitive world, where might is always trying to dictate right, with Hitlers and Huey Longs and Hagues and Kellys, and others on both sides of the political fence, always trying to call the orders if we will let them. A world where every man's for himself and the devil of want and poverty and failure gets the hindmost! A world where hard struggle, not love, rules! Love is just an anachronism at this stage of things, and good will is a dangerous sentiment.

Life is like that, hard and real and not idealistic at all!

Now the trouble isn't that life is like that. Much of life is like that! This universe does run along lawful lines, and science is right in trying to discover how it runs. And Hitlers do use might as their right; and hatred and prejudice do have a say in things. The trouble isn't there! The trouble is in our accepting these things, in limiting life by these things, in orienting our thinking and our hopes by these things and then thinking that we are realists—closing in life and shutting out God's purposes and thinking we're on the right side of things, the real side!

Believing too much without believing enough!

And the tragedy, my friends, is that we may never see that we have believed the wrong things until it's too late. One can be trapped into death by an illusion!

Dudley Cavert tells a true story of a railway employee in Russia who accidentally locked himself in a refrigerator car! He was unable to escape and couldn't attract the attention of those outside, and so he resigned himself to his fate. As he felt his body becoming numb, he recorded the story of his approaching death in sentences scribbled on the wall of the car. "I'm becoming colder," he wrote. "Still colder, now. Nothing to do but to wait. . . . I am slowly freezing to death. . . . Half asleep now, I can hardly write. . . ." And finally, "These may be my last words."

And they were, for when at length the car was opened they found him dead. And yet the temperature of the car was only fifty-six degrees. The freezing apparatus was and had been out of order. There was no physical reason for his death. There was plenty of air; he hadn't suffocated. He was the victim of his own illusion. His conclusions were all wrong! He was so sure he knew!

[154]

That's a strange case and an unusual one! But the fact remains that it's possible for a man to be led astray by false convictions about life. Believing too little and missing out on life's opportunity!

So a man can convince himself that certain things are true: that Japanese are all treacherous! Or that Negroes are all shiftless and irresponsible. Or that a man is primarily of value for what one gets from him, as customer, laborer or technician! Or that you can't change human nature! Or that history always repeats itself or that there will always be wars!

A man can come to believe these things until his belief finally creates a world like that. Thus he destroys both his own soul and the world in which he lives by the folly of his beliefs, for our beliefs tend to confirm themselves just as our fears tend to confirm themselves, in our lives and in our world.

A Godless world will finally become a godless world! And a Godless life will finally become a godless life. "That's the Hell of it," for Hell is what happens to us when finally we shut ourselves off from the redeeming forces of life and are left to our own selfish devices and damning prejudices no longer haunted by the grace of God! And that means tragedy, the tragedy of believing too little too long, not having a faith that is in tune with destiny! Is your faith less than your destiny requires or have you a faith as large as your opportunity?

The greatness of the early Christians lay not in the success of their achievement, nor in the brilliance of the organization of the Church, but in the fact that the disciples had laid hold upon something vastly greater than themselves: "the on-going purposes of God." And they were lifted into significance by the greatness of their convictions, which gave their lives cosmic orientation, and bestowed upon them dignity and power and richness and meaning.

What a man believes shapes his life and destiny and there is no surer way to bring tragedy to one's spirit than by believing too little too much.

And it can happen right here in the sanctuary! There is nothing so devastating to one's spiritual life as to become confirmed in one's religious prejudices. There's nothing more damaging to one's spirit than to waste one's faith on petty things, marshaling all the spirit's resources for trivial purposes and making a travesty of religion, defeating the very intention of God by making us content and complacent with a little faith when it ought to be a great faith in great things!

One can make religion a matter of trivia: what one wears or eats or drinks, or the hour that one retires, or the way one kneels or genuflects, or celebrates the Lord's Supper! And a man can worship a little Christ, all of his own conceiving, putting in just what one wants and leaving out all of the best in him, never challenging one's faith with any great problems or any great spiritual adventure!

In his recent book for preachers, *For We Have This Treasure*, Paul Scherer says: "For your mind's sake, keep one book going that is just a bit

[155]

beyond you." That's a very suggestive idea and might we not add: "For your soul's sake, keep before you some word of Christ that is just a bit beyond you."

Stretch your soul! Enlarge your horizon and exercise the expansive powers of your spirit by including in your thought and practice something of the teaching of Jesus that seems impossible to you. There are some very challenging things in the Sermon on the Mount and the 13th of I Corinthians, and the 12th of Romans! Some things that may seem impossible! But how do you know they're impossible? Have you ever tried them? Or what's more to the point, have you ever tried them by relying on the grace of God to see you through them?

Have you ever been forced by the audacity of your Christian loyalty into saying: "Lord, I believe; help thou mine unbelief"? Have you ever had to fall back upon the grace of God to give meaning and power to your loyalty?

There are some things that we can believe only by the grace of God. There are some things that man's effort cannot generate in the human heart, that can take hold of our lives and hearts only after the grace of God has given them meaning! But it is the intent of the grace of God, the very meaning of the grace of God, to lift us out of our soul-damning complacency into soul-expanding experience. The mercy of God haunts us because it is God's purpose to make great souls of us, born of a great faith. For, my friends, if the cross of Christ means anything, it means that God will not let us go so long as His cross can wedge a bit of His redeeming love into our lives and challenge us, with a great faith in His eternal goodness and His eternal purposes, to become like Him through the grace of Christ!

FAITH

# The Audacity of Faith

REVEREND RALPH E. KNUDSEN, TH.D.
*Dean, Berkeley Baptist Divinity School, Berkeley, California
and a Baptist Minister*

*Dr. Knudsen's discussion of the great eleventh chapter of Hebrews brings new meaning to the old story of the achievement of faith. He shows what faith in God can do for a man and what a man of faith can do in the world. "History," he believes, "is made by men of faith."*

*A Baptist minister and an educator, Dr. Knudsen's work has taken him to Baptist pastorates in Montana, California and Washington. His last* church before his call to the faculty of the Berkeley Baptist Divinity School was as pastor of the University Baptist Church in Seattle, Washington. He was professor of Biblical introduction from 1943 to 1946 and has been dean and professor of New Testament since 1946.

He is active in the Church Council of Northern California, in denominational committees, as a speaker at youth assemblies, and is the author of various articles in several magazines. As he sees it,

"We are on the threshold of a world in the making . . ."


## Sermon Twenty=seven


THE eleventh chapter of Hebrews is one of the great treasures of Christian faith and experience. This chapter tells something of the meaning, the strength, the beauty and the achievement of faith. No one can read this chapter and say faith is credulity and men of faith are fools. The chapter begins with a declaration, "Now faith is," and then moves immediately to illustrate faith. The words "by faith" appear eighteen times in the chapter and then, eager to continue but knowing he cannot, the writer summarizes, "And what shall I more say? for the time will fail me if I tell of . . . who through faith. . . ." Verses 32-40 give in condensation what the writer desired to give in detail. These verses name some and leave unnamed many "who through faith" faced life on its hard side and overcame triumphantly.

These men and women of faith did the impossible because they believed in a God who knew no limitations. Men of faith stop at no cost and evade no dangers. It is proper to glory in these heroes of faith but it is also essential to be reminded that what God, through men of faith, has done once He can do again. Men of faith with God have given the world those values which are of enduring worth. Doubt and pessimism build nothing but empty structures of uselessness. Faith in God has been basic in the building of hospitals, schools, churches, homes and other constructive institutions for humanity. History is made by men of faith.

We are on the threshold of a world in the making. This is the atomic era. Many of us do not realize just what that means. The scientists tell us that it means new world understanding or destruction. A great American scientist said, "It is either Christ or the annihilation of the human race." There is something desperately lacking in our world. That which is lacking is not knowledge, nor skill, nor invention, nor materials; the lack is of character. Intelligent men may produce the atomic bomb but it takes men of character to use it. The quality of character needed is that which grows out of faith in God. The Church must thrust the positive faith of Christian men against world paganism moving toward catastrophe. Faith must match the hour or the world is lost. This is our day to add new names to the chapter of faith and only as we do that can we hope to perpetuate the triumph of our God in our generation, and bring about a new day of understanding.

A study of this eleventh chapter reveals certain qualities of faith which need a re-emphasis today. First, it was a positive faith. It was rooted in the God of the ages. He was a great God and one in whom absolute faith could be placed. He was always present and always interested in them. He revealed Himself to them but He also expected them to respond to Him. It was a "God-in-relation-to-man" experience which these men of faith knew. It was a God who said "Come" but who also said "Go." This relationship gave courage to faith because man not only knew God but he was certain he was known and loved by God. This "I-Thou" relationship is the primary factor in a positive and creative faith experience. These men of faith believed God and they believed Him all the time and in every experience. To them there was no experience which did not give them an assurance of God's purpose, and no time when they were not certain of His will. These were people who believed God and lived accordingly.

Modern faith has lost much of this positiveness. In fact much modern faith is so weak and anemic as to be ineffective and in essence negative in practice. Neutrality in faith means defeat in conflict. It is the inertia of good people which troubles a modern world. Good people of positive faith could bring a transformation to our world. Times of darkness are the times for faith. Those whose names appear in Hebrews eleven did not live in easy times or under fair weather conditions. In Acts twenty-seven, the story is told of Paul on his way to Rome. The little boat was in mid-Mediterranean in a terrible storm. Everything which human knowledge and skill could do had been tried. There was nothing to do but wait for the end. The only sounds to greet the paralyzed hearts of the sailors were the groanings of the ship and the howling of the wind. In the midst of these tense and frightful moments Paul appeared and said, "Sirs, be of good cheer, for I believe God." What mockery in the face of the raging storm, yet what calm and triumphant faith in God! When everything is lost, men of faith still have God and that is always more than enough.

There is no reason to question the possibility of creating a new era out of new men if men and women of faith believe God. When man is on the side of God, he discovers that God is all he needs for the accomplishment of the impossible. It is necessary to believe something if one is to be something and do something. One day at school Henry Ward Beecher was called upon to recite.[1] He had hardly begun when the teacher interrupted him with an emphatic "No." He started again but soon sat down when the

[1] Taken from *Take a Look at Yourself*, by John Homer Miller. Published by Abingdon-Cokesbury Press.

teacher again uttered a stern "No." The next pupil who recited heard from the teacher a resounding "No" but continued to the end of the lesson. "Very well," said the teacher. "I recited just as he did," complained young Beecher. The teacher replied, "It is not enough to know your lesson; you must be sure. When you allowed me to stop you, it meant that you were uncertain; if all the world says 'No,' it is your business to say 'Yes' and prove it." When our world says "No" it is the business of the Christian to say "Yes" and prove it. Faith must be positive if it becomes purposeful.

Second, it was a daring faith. The list of characters in chapter eleven with their accomplishments of faith reveals a rare and thrilling courage. Faith helped them face the sting of ridicule, the certainty of death, the mouth of lions, the threats of kings, and the might of the mighty. Their faith in God made them certain that one with God is never defeated. There is a strange stirring of spirit in reading the story of an Isaiah or a Jeremiah who dared to stand before kings and tell them their course of action was wrong and would only bring disaster to them and the people.

Christianity began as an adventure. In early Christian literature it was known as "The Way." It was a way which seemed new, impractical and irrational to many. The early Christians were called mad and treated with scorn by some leaders and many people. These of "The Way" would follow Jesus wherever he would lead them. They counted it a joy to go for him and to suffer for his work. Their faith was so daring that the threat of death could not stop them. These could have sung with meaning "Anywhere with Jesus I Can Safely Go" because they went with him anywhere and any time. Their faith sometimes meant death but their joy was unbounded even in that.

Faith today has lost much of this daring. The policy followed today is one of "safety first," which usually means no action and no power. The "safety first" faith is far removed from those of this chapter of heroes. Faith must dare to climb the mountains which are hindering progress on every front. There can be no stability of home life in America nor understanding among nations until some dare to believe in God and in one another. Before there can be much change in life and the world there must be faith in the possibility of a better world. Thomas Huxley said, "The most sacred act of a man's life is to say and feel, 'I believe.'" John Barrymore said of his brother Lionel, "What I envy in Lionel is not his mind but his ability to believe. If he never found love he would still believe there was such a thing." The history of the world is written by those who dare and persevere in their faith. Cyrus W. Field laid the first Atlantic Telegraph cable from Europe to America in 1866.[2] One day he was discussing the undertaking with Lord Clarendon, the one-time Prime Minister and Lord Chancellor of England. Lord Clarendon asked Field these questions, "But suppose you don't succeed? Suppose you make the attempt and fail and

[2] Ibid.

your cable is lost in the sea?" Then what will you do?" Mr. Field quickly responded, "Charge it to profit and loss and go to work and lay another." It takes daring faith to build for permanency. Faith must be daring if it is to be useful.

Third, it was a generous faith. The chapter gives the record of men who left home, country, fortunes and went out with God. The note of regret is never found in this catalogue of men of faith. Rather, these who gave all wanted always to give more. No miser or self-centered man ever got into faith's hall of fame. It has always been "he that loseth his life" who in reality findeth it.

After all it is only what one gives and shares which can be kept. It is wonderful to believe enough in God and in the possibility of man so that one gladly gives all to help others. A man who lost heavily in the depression had been a generous giver to his church. A friend one day said to him, "Aren't you sorry you gave so much to that church?" After a pause the churchman said, "All I've got is what I gave there." That is a glorious affirmation of faith.

Christian generosity is sacrificial generosity. Men and women give their lives for country in times of crisis. The crippled soldiers, sailors, marines and others seen on our streets give visible evidence of this sacrificial quality in life. The man of faith must have that same quality. Jesus Christ gave his all that he might have all of you and me. When we give our all for others, we are in line with the men and women of the ages whose heritage we enjoy and whose faith we perpetuate. So long as we express faith in Jesus Christ, we can do no less than give ourselves, which is the first step in giving all. Faith must be generous if it is helpful.

Fourth, it was a faith which did not wait to see the end before it acted. The writer said, "And these all, having had witness borne to them through their faith, received not the promise" (verse 39). These acted in their day, not demanding to know the end. Faith ought to act even though the outcome of faith cannot be seen.

Some say the age in which these men and women of faith lived was an impractical age. Our modern day wants to see results. The modern temper is to act only where ends are in view immediately. We say, "What is there in it?" That for which faith stands is greater than any immediate result. Faith must act today in confidence that results will come someday. A little over sixty years ago there appeared an editorial in a Boston newspaper about Alexander Graham Bell's invention:

Joshua Coppersmith, a man about forty-six years of age, has been arrested in New York for attempting to extort funds from innocent people by exhibiting a device which he says will convey the human voice over wires . . . even if it were possible, the thing would be of no practical value. . . . Authorities who apprehended this criminal are to be congratulated. It may serve as an example to other conscienceless schemers who may hope to enrich themselves at the expense of their fellow creatures.

Today we talk by telephone to San Francisco, Chicago, New York, London or any other desired place in the world. Generations yet to come are affected by the faith or lack of faith of the preceding generation. The church, the school, and the home of tomorrow will give evidence of the faith and life of the men and women today. It is necessary to develop this historic view whereby we believe and know that what we do now will mean something tomorrow. Faith must make us do our best today because of our interest and concern for those who are to come. Many of the blessings we enjoy today are ours because someone else had faith and lived as though it counted. Faith must be forward looking if it is permanent.

Our chapter has presented men and women with audacious faith. Will the next generation say of us that by faith we have left them a heritage of peace, good will and one world? God and the world are looking for new heroes of faith who through their faith do many mighty works now and leave a foundation for those who come. We are their successors. May we follow their faith.

> They climbed the steep ascent of heaven
> Through peril, toil, and pain:
> O God, to us may grace be given
> To follow in their train.

FAITH

# Babel

The Very Reverend Walter Robert Matthews,
K.C.V.O., D.D., D.Litt., S.T.D.
*Dean of St. Paul's Cathedral, London (Church of England)*

*Dean Matthews has preached for London and the people of England during two world wars and in the years of peace before and after the wars. His preaching is marked by independence of thinking, clear analysis of Biblical texts, and a fine application to the problems of the present. He stayed with his people through the blitz that destroyed much of London at the very doors of the Cathedral and all the buildings for nearly a half mile on one side of the great building. It is almost a miracle that the magnificent dome of St. Paul's was not destroyed.*

*He was educated at Wilson's Grammar School, Camberwell and King's College, London, and has been honored by the doctorate from the Universities of London, St. Andrews, Glasgow and Trinity College (Dublin), and Columbia University in New York in recognition of his long career in the Church. He has been dean of St. Paul's since 1934; fellow of King's*

College, London; member of senate, University of London; Honorary Bencher, Gray's Inn. He held curacies at St. Mary Abbots, Kensington, and St. Peter, Regent Square, was assistant chaplain at Magdalen Hospital. From 1908-18 he was lecturer in philosophy at King's College, and also in dogmatic theology, 1909-18. He became vicar of Christ Church, Crouch End,1916-18; and was dean and professor of the philosophy of religion in King's College, London, 1918-32. He was dean of Exeter from 1931-34, was canon theologian of Liverpool Cathedral, 1930. In 1920 he became chaplain to Gray's Inn and preacher to Gray's Inn in 1929. He was Boyle Lecturer, 1920-22; chaplain to the King, 1923-31; White Lecturer, 1927; Noble Lecturer, 1928; Wilde Lecturer, 1929; Warburton Lecturer, 1938.

Among his publications are Studies in Christian Philosophy, 1921; an edition of Butler's Ethical Writings in the Bohn Library; The Idea of Revelation, 1924; The Psychological Approach to Religion, The Gospel and the Modern Mind, 1925; God and Evolution, 1926; Editor, Dogma in History and Thought, 1929; God in Christian Thought and Experience, 1930; Seven Words, 1933; The Adventures of Gabriel in his Search for Mr. Shaw, 1933; Hope of Immortality; The Purpose of God, 1935; Our Faith in God, 1936; The Christian Faith, 1936; Signposts to God, 1938; Teaching of Christ, 1939; Following Christ; Moral Issues of the War, 1940; The Foundations of Peace, 1942; and many papers.

This sermon was preached in St. Paul's at Quinquagesima, 1946. In it the Dean has caught the dramatic qualities of the text in language that reminds one of the great sermons John Donne used to preach to the King and the people three hundred years ago in the same Cathedral. His discussion of the profound meaning of Scripture, of the limitations of language, and of the city of confusion and its causes will interest those who struggle to make the good life for man possible. His belief in the need of Christian public opinion in the affairs of nations is something to consider in view of present hopes for the success of the United Nations. Man-soul still needs Christ! How much trouble is caused because we do not understand men's feelings, thoughts, meanings.

# Sermon Twenty=eight

TEXT: Let us go down, and there confound their language, that
they may not understand one another's speech. GENESIS 11:7

THE story of the city of Babel is one of the best known in the Old
Testament. So familiar is it that it has given a word to the language, and
perhaps many people speak of a confusion and strife of tongues as a "Babel"
without knowing whence the expression comes.

It is a dramatic story: how the race of men were all of one speech and
formed a unity and were able to undertake great enterprises. They found
a plain in Shinar and there they built a great city of brick, bound together
with bitumen.

The men who first told this story evidently had Babylon in mind, for
that is how that ancient imperial capital was built and no doubt Babel is
simply the short way of saying Babylon.

In the center of the city the builders started to erect a great tower, "whose
top may reach unto heaven." The purpose of this enormous monument
seems to have been twofold—to perpetuate the memory of the builders,
"let us make us a name," and also to be a kind of symbol and a rallying
point of their unity, "lest we be scattered abroad upon the face of the whole
earth." Then, as you well remember, the story goes on to describe the
reaction of God to this ambitious human enterprise. The Lord "came down
to see the city and the tower." When He had surveyed it, He said, "Behold,
they are one people, and they have all one language; and this is what they
begin to do: and now nothing will be withholden from them which they
purpose to do. Come let us go down, and there confound their language,
that they may not understand one another's speech."

And so the tower failed, the unity was broken, and the human race was
scattered after all upon the face of the earth.

Of course, this fabulous city of Babel never really existed. The story
has come from the childlike imagination of people who brooded upon the
great urban civilization which they could not understand, and specially
upon its pride and self-confidence. Those who told the story had, one must
confess, an idea of God which to us is queer and even shocking. The Lord
is represented as fearing the rivalry of man. Measures had to be taken to
prevent the power of the human race from passing a point where it would
threaten the divine. There are signs too that the first narrators of the story
believed in many gods—"Let *us* go down," says Jahveh.

But most interesting of all the comments of the learned on this old

[163]

story is what they have to say about its motive. It is what they call an "etiological myth"—a story to explain something—a "just so" story. The mind of men, even of very simple men, cannot help being impressed by the strange fact that there are different languages. Why do the people of one valley speak unintelligible gibberish to the people of the next? This is a root fact of human life: and a very tiresome one. How did it come about, and for what reason? The story of Babel is the answer of men to whom science was utterly unknown and history no more than legends.

But you may say, While all this is no doubt interesting enough to students of early civilization, I do not see that it has any religious or moral value for us. What conceivable relevance can this old, and rather absurd myth have to our needs? Why include it in Holy Scripture? Why not let it rest in the realm of folklore, where it obviously belongs?

This is a very searching question which needs to be fairly faced and answered. It is also a wide question, because plainly it arises in connection with many other stories which are found in the Old Testament. The answer too would have to be deep and wide. I shall not attempt to give the whole of it now. I will concentrate upon one part of the answer—and that not the most important one.

There is, I suggest, one rather curious property of many of these old stories. When we cease to be bothered by the rather childish question, Did they really happen? and allow our minds to play freely upon them, they start us thinking on some very profound matters and hint at conclusions which have important bearings on our own problems. This, I suppose, is part of what we mean when we speak of the inspiration of Scripture.

The fact which is the basis of the Babel legend—the diversity of languages—is an important one for us. We have all experienced the strange and humiliating position of being in a foreign country where we understood little or nothing of the language. For a time we feel helpless and defenseless. We cannot say what we mean or grasp the meanings of others. We have become suddenly almost deaf and dumb.

This confusion of tongues has important social, moral and religious consequences. Is not some of the difficulty, which is only too obvious today, in getting understanding and agreement between nations and governments, and churches too, due to this language barrier? The laborious and imperfect process of interpretation holds up the exchange of ideas and mutual comprehension. Things might go very much better at U.N., if the representatives could talk freely with one another, if all round the table could quickly understand and respond.

The good people who recommend some universal language, Volapuk, Esperanto or Basic-English, are often regarded as hopeless cranks, but they have at least seen something which the men who told the Babel story long ago saw. The unity of the human race, and its effective co-operation, is destroyed, or at least gravely hampered, by the confusion of tongues. If there could be one language throughout the world, it might have real spiritual results. The great truth that we are brethren would be more easy to believe and to make effective. We might even come to believe in earnest what Jesus said, that all men are meant to be children of God and members of one family.

We live in the City of Babel—the city of confusion. But we should be wrong if we thought the confusion was only a matter of language. There are deeper causes. After all, we can contrive to co-operate with people who speak a different language, if we both want the same thing and want it badly enough. We get to the root of the modern confusion when we realize that this condition of co-operation does not exist. We don't want the same thing.

The most dangerous catastrophe which has occurred is not an event in the material world, but in the spiritual world—the collapse of a common scale of values. There is no generally-accepted idea of what we mean by good and the good life for man. I remember hearing an eminent statesman say, just before the war, that the most disquieting fact in the situation was that there was no Christian public opinion in Europe to which an appeal could be made. Was that not true? We made efforts, even dangerous efforts, to understand Nazi Germany, but it was in vain. We could not understand them or they us. We did not want the same things. We did not have the same idea of good and evil and, therefore, what to them was good and desirable was to us evil and detestable.

Would you say that the situation is better today? Not much, I fear. There is the same babel of opinions, the same conflicting ideas of value, the same diversity of aim. Do we not find it almost as difficult to understand the Russians now as we did the Germans in 1933?

There is talk now of the conversion of England and of the need to strengthen and support the Church in Europe, particularly in Germany. I fear that such enterprises are to many only the harmless fads of pious persons, which have no relevance to the world and its future. This is a profound error. The propagation of Christianity is, in these days, a desperate necessity. We cannot stay in Babel. If we don't find a way out, we shall destroy one another. We must get a common set of values; we must agree on the good. There is no other way of stopping the moral disintegration which will ruin us all. But is there a road out of Babel? Can we find the way? I know of no other than Christ, who said, "I am the way, the truth, and the life," and that he had come to draw all men unto himself.

In this vitally necessary propagation of the gospel it is of the utmost importance that we should concentrate upon the central and creative truth. So much of Christian propaganda seems to miss the point. It aims at persuading people to join the Church, or to accept certain dogmas. But adherence to a church or assent to dogmas may leave a man essentially just as he was before. The one thing needful was expressed in the simple creed of the Apostolic Church—"Jesus is Lord." The real acceptance of that means everything. If we can say that with sincerity, we have our values for life, we have our meaning of good, we have too the way out of Babel, for Jesus is not the Lord of one nation or race only, but of all—and his person and words have a universal claim.

Has this ancient tale of Babel any meaning for me as an individual? Does it awaken thoughts, not only about the plight of men, but about the plight of one man—of me? I think it does. Very many Christians have compared the soul of man to a city. Plato is one: and perhaps you remember that John Bunyan wrote an allegory of the spiritual life under the title of "the City of Man-soul." Well: my soul is perhaps rather like a city. What kind of city is it like? When I look into it, carefully and honestly, I am afraid, because it looks uncommonly like a little Babel. The confusion outside seems to be reflected in me. I am indeed sometimes tempted to wonder whether I really am one person. I seem to have so many selves, and sometimes one is uppermost and sometimes another. I am like a distracted city; like one divided into factions, which hardly understand one another. At times I am bitter and grudging; again I am generous and kind; but soon after, I am greedy and self-seeking; or lazy and self-indulgent; or diligent and hopeful; or again I sink into depression and lassitude. When I am in one mood I scarcely understand myself as I was in a different mood, though it may have been only yesterday. When I look at this bundle of contradictory selves which I call "me," I ask which is really myself? Is there a real "me" at all? I am Babel.

Perhaps you feel that you are not in so bad a case as this. You have attained some unity and stability. But I venture to think that, even the best of us, even the most unified, has some inkling of what I mean. Babel is not far away. It is just behind us. It is not abolished as a possibility. The city of confusion may still swallow me up.

St. Paul was one of those who sometimes thought of the soul as a city, and in one of his vivid phrases he suggests the picture of the Christian soul as a city occupied, defended and kept by a garrison. The city has surrendered. It has acknowledged its rightful Lord, and He has taken charge and given it serenity and peace. The way out of Babel is the surrender to Christ as Lord. That way may be long: the mortification of the self is not achieved in a moment. The great questions are, Has it begun, and is it going on? St. Paul has told us how it goes on: "Casting down imaginations, and every high thing that is exalted against the knowledge of God, and bringing every thought into captivity to the obedience of Christ" (II Cor. 10:5). So we pass from Babel to Zion—from the city of confusion and strife to the city of peace and love.

Through surrender of the self we find the true self, through submission we find freedom, through trust we find unity.

# The Self=Limitation of God

REVEREND HARRIS E. KIRK, D.D.

*Minister, The Franklin Street Presbyterian Church, Baltimore, Maryland*

*For forty-six years Dr. Kirk has been the minister of Franklin Street Church, Baltimore. His sermons and his circle of influence have grown with the years. Born in Tennessee, he graduated from Southwestern University at Memphis, and was ordained to the ministry of the Presbyterian Church in 1897. He was minister of Cottage Church, Nashville, 1897-99, First Presbyterian Church, Florence, Alabama, 1899-1901, and has been at the Franklin Street Church ever since.*

*He has held many lectureships, including the annual lectures on historical Christianity, Princeton University, 1923-29; Goucher College, 1925-28; professor of Biblical literature, Goucher, since 1928; Northfield Conferences, 1917-26; mission conferences in China in 1924; summer preacher, Westminster Chapel, London, 1922-40; Sprunt lecturer, Union Theological Seminary, Richmond, 1916; University preacher, Princeton, Yale, University of Virginia and other important institutions. He was moderator of the General Assembly of the Presbyterian Church in U.S., 1928.*

*His books include* The Religion of Power, The Consuming Fire, The Spirit of Protestantism, Stars, Atoms, and God, A Man of Property, A Design for Living.

*Dr. Kirk's interpretation of the passage from Jeremiah is stimulating in its characterization of God from a human point of view and lends greater power to his definition of the omnipotence of God. As pilgrims walk with God they learn new ways. The sermon was preached in Baltimore on October 20, 1946. Its philosophical, theological and devotional atmosphere make it a message to read with care.*

# Sermon Twenty=nine

TEXT: Howbeit I sent unto you all my servants the prophets, rising early and sending them, saying, Oh, do not this abominable thing I hate. But they hearkened not, nor inclined their ear to turn from their wickedness. . . . JEREMIAH 44:4

THIS striking phrase occurs several times in the Book of Jeremiah. It contains a characterization of God that from a human point of view is quite unexpected. For whatever be our conception, we usually think of Him as all powerful; as One whose will and desire cannot be gainsaid. Yet the prophet speaks of God's power as limited. Look at the details:

(1) God is represented as a hard worker, rising early and working late. He tries one plan after another to get His way with man.

(2) In so doing, He uses human helpers. He sends one after another of the prophets, with the same message.

(3) In spite of all this God's plans are checked, His will is disobeyed, and His aims are thwarted.

What, then, are we to think of this? Is God's will limited, His power subject to being checked by the will of man? This is not a natural conception of Deity, for the common way of thinking of the essence of Deity is of one who is all powerful, almighty. Yet when we become familiar with the Bible, we find a general agreement that within certain limits, God's power is capable of being set aside. In fact, the boldness and frankness of the Bible is a challenge to thought. In Isaiah the conception is set forth in the parable of the vineyard, wherein God is represented as having planted and cultivated a vineyard and naturally looked to it to bring forth grapes, and it brought forth wild grapes! When we turn to the New Testament we come upon the parable of the cruel vinedressers. One after another the master's servants were rejected, and when he sent in the last place his son, they slew him, and remained to the end disobedient and rebellious. And who can forget the lament of our Lord over Jerusalem? How often as a hen gathereth her chickens under her wings, would He have gathered His people together, but they would not!

Such bold teaching shows that in certain conditions God's power is limited; that under the economy of the world which He has ordained, it is possible to thwart His will, and render His beneficent purposes unavailing.

Of course, there are ways of thinking of this contrary to truth. One is to suggest that the evil of the world is more powerful than God; to represent Him as unable to stem the tide of wickedness on earth, which has ever been the source of a heart-chilling pessimism. Unhappily just now there are many who feel this way about the present world conditions; who cry out on all sides: Who will show us any good? Unless we have some notion of what is really involved we, too, may feel the paralyzing effect of this dreary skepticism.

Paint now, if you will, the present world situation in the darkest colors; look how sharply contrasted are the actual trends of the world, with the promises and hopes raised by faith in a good and all-powerful God, whose love has been declared to us in Christ and Christianity. A vague assertion of hope in face of this will hardly protect the spirit of man from depressing conclusions. We must certainly have some reasons for that hope, be able to justify it, and to understand the exceedingly slow progress of good in the history of man, and I believe we have one of the greatest principles of enlightenment in the conception of the self-limitation of God. And we must at once draw a sharp distinction between a pagan and a Christian conception of power in God. The pagan founded Deity upon unlimited power. The first sharp difference from this appears in the Old Testament conception, which founds Deity not on unlimited power, but character, and to this the Christian enlargement, power working through love. That is surely the one foundation of a durable hope, and on that foundation we must build our expectations for the future.

This helps us to define the word "omnipotence" as the power of God to do all possible things—where "possible" means the exercise of that power in harmony with God's character, and also in harmony with the purpose of God in creating the human family. God's power can never be exercised in contradiction of His holiness. God cannot do evil, or will evil. Neither must that power be exercised in the destruction of the essential element in man that makes him fit to become a child of God. In other words, it is of the first importance to make plain this truth, that the Divine power as revealed in the whole plan of creation contemplates the development in man of a free and spontaneous surrender of life to the will of God. Yet in this we find the explanation, yea, even the necessity of some kind of self-limitation in God. This becomes evident in this way:

(1) If God were to create a family of children in His own image, capable of learning how to trust, love and obey Him, then He had to allow for the possibility of the misuse of the power of choice, and run the risk of disobedience in the children He had created. If you were to build a fine house, well furnished according to your taste, all you need do is to give your orders. Everything will be done in accord with your will, and be in its place. But a well-furnished house is not a home. Put now a child in that house, and at once you will see how impossible it is to have your way. You know what a child will think and do with all your cherished possessions; and until you can educate him in your tastes, and purposes, you are going to have a very difficult task to perform. You cannot give orders to a child as you do to your workmen who build your house. Where no oxen are, the

crib is clean, yet without oxen where the need of cribs? So is it with the human family. And this analogy explains man's relation to God. Without freedom of will, which carries the risk of mistake, and willful disobedience, God could never have had a family at all. It was thus that sin entered the world, for sin is the disposition on the part of the child to disobey the father; and from this necessary limitation on His will, God saw His family pass into a state of lawlessness and rebellion. A world of human machines would never make a family, any more than mechanical robots would make up a human household. Man can and has disobeyed God, and from this has issued the evil of the world; and God has permitted it simply because without this risk, a family would have been impossible.

(2) We see this principle also in the great plan of redemption. Here is Jeremiah putting it into a heart-rending phrase: "Oh, do not this abominable thing I hate. But they hearkened not"! These are the saddest words in the Bible. Man's disobedience still haunts its pages, and when in the fullness of time God sent His Son, again we see Deity limiting itself to human nature, becoming like one of us, and pleading with man to return to his first allegiance. To think of Christianity as a system of moral laws, of commandments, of compulsions, and of prohibitions, is completely to mis-conceive it. There are no commandments in Christianity. It is throughout a religion of affirmations and invitations, and its great word is, "Come unto me, all ye that labour and are heavy laden, and I will give you rest." God's invitations are the appeals of love. And love from this point of view is the weakest thing in the world. Yet only by love offered and received can man find his right relation to God. Hence the only legitimate response to the love of God is just love: to love Him because He first loved us. For religion is not all giving on one side, but a matter of give and take. We always have our sins to confess and to receive forgiveness for them. But we have something far more important to give; ourselves—the loyalty of our highest aspirations, desires and purposes, and the more willingly we yield ourselves to the love of God the more thoroughly do we become aware of being united to His life. In this we rise above all mortal things, all defiling things, and find our perfect freedom in perfect obedience. I hold this the most rational and effective conception of life open to us. If by man's disobedience the world fell into sin, by man's obedience to the grace of God do we regain our high status as children of eternity.

Now this grave, this noble state of mind, which ought to be the normal mind of the Christian, becomes the fertile breeding ground of guiding principles of immense value to the stabilization of life, and equally of vast influence for good, even in the midst of an evil world.

(1) First of all, it reconciles us to the gradual growth of spiritual vitality within ourselves. How often do we lament our ignorance of God, ask why it should be so difficult to know Him or to apply His will to the affairs of our personal life. We must never forget that we live under the law of gradualness. It is first the blade, then the ear, then the full corn in the ear.

You can never go direct from the seedling to the full corn. The entire range of spiritual experience is governed by this law of gradualness. We fly a little, we run a little, but mostly we walk. The great enemy of our peace is the loss of heart because things move so slowly; yet we must learn to walk and not faint, and herein we gain a gradual understanding of the Divine principle of patience. Think of God's patience with the human family; of the years and years in which He has watched the slow growth of His earthly plans; of the many setbacks to His expectations, yet in it all a steadfast loyalty to all our human needs. Surely we are far from being mature Christians if we do not see that it is precisely in the later stages of our pilgrimage that we have need of patience. But patience is not a passive virtue, a mere attitude of acquiescence to things as they are, but an intensely active virtue which carries us immediately into full consciousness of participation with God in the fulfillment of a plan so vast that in this life we can never understand it. In this experience there is bound to be much pain, suffering and hardship. And there will certainly be times when we cannot possibly understand these unhappy experiences. But we should remember this: a life without mystery is a life without meaning. We do not yet see all things put under man's control, but we do see Jesus! Deep within the fabric of this universe we find pain and suffering. In this God himself is an active sharer. Surely in that life beyond the portals of this world we shall more intimately know its meaning. But here we must be content to run our race with patience, looking unto Jesus!

(2) If we can cultivate this sterling sort of faith we shall be the better able to be patient with the slow growth of goodness in the world at large. History shows again and again how great moral checks arise to stop its progress upward. In such times it is easy to lose heart; become hard, cynical and unbelieving. But it is just in times of darkness that the spiritual glow of a good life is seen to best advantage. It is here even when all around us it would seem as though men were shutting their ears to the Divine voice; it is here that we should stand firm in our place, speak with sureness of the things we do know, and believe that from each Christian personality there goes forth a radiance to light the path to peace for every man. For, after all, nothing is more true than that history shows that while checks may come, and the tides on the surface of the world recede again and again, the deep forces of good are working out their ultimate purposes toward some vast and glorious culmination. After the skeptics have said their sorrowful say; after the pessimists have fallen by the way, the steadfast believer in Christ is the one being on the pilgrim way that knows the way home. He keeps alight the torch on the way for the guidance of those that walk in darkness; and in this great service the Christian fulfills the purpose of his creation and redemption; and by uniting his life to the life of God he moves through the uncertainties of the future with authority, power and influence. Such a man has in his heart an understanding of the pilgrim ways, and can transform the valley of trouble into a place of springs.

# The Genealogy of Hope

Edwin Ewart Aubrey, Ph.D., D.D.

*President, Crozer Theological Seminary, Chester, Pennsylvania*

*Dr. Aubrey was born in Glasgow, Scotland, March 19, 1896. He came to the United States in 1913 and was naturalized in 1918 for service in the United States armed forces. During World War I he served as a corporal in the United States Army Ambulance Service. He graduated from Bucknell University in 1919 with highest honors, studied at Cambridge University and the University of Chicago, from which he received his Ph.D. in 1926. He received the honorary D.D. from Bucknell in 1939.*

*He has had a significant career in education and religious work. His teaching appointments have been at Union Theological College, Carleton College, Miami University and Vassar College. In 1929-44 he became professor of Christian theology and ethics, University of Chicago, chairman of the theological field, 1933-44, and president and professor of Christian social philosophy, Crozer Theological Seminary, since 1944. Cole lecturer, 1940; visiting lecturer in ethics, California Institute of Technology, 1942; visiting professor in philosophy of religion, Union Theological Seminary, 1942, 1943, 1945, 1946; Swander lecturer, 1946.*

*At the University of Chicago Dr. Aubrey played a significant part in building a new curriculum. He is a fellow of the National Council on Religion in Higher Education; member of the American Society of Church History.*

*He is well known as an outstanding theological writer. Among his contributions in this field are* Religion and the Next Generation, *1931;* Present Theological Tendencies, *1936;* Living the Christian Faith, *1939;* Man's Search for Himself, *1940. He is also co-author of several volumes including* Religion in Higher Education, *1931;* The Process of Religion, *1933;* Church and Community, *1938;* Environmental Factors in Christian History, *1939;* Approaches to World Peace, *1944; and* The Christian Answer, *1945.*

*Dr. Aubrey was president of the University of Chicago Settlement, 1941-1944, and a member of the executive committee of the Hyde Park Baptist Church, Chicago. Just as World War II broke Dr. Aubrey was scheduled to speak to various student groups in occupied and free China, and his tour had to be postponed. His activities in the wider aspects of the Christian movement have been many. He was a theological consultant at the Oxford Conference in 1937, and was founder and chairman of the Chicago Ecumenical Study Group, 1939-44. He was a founding member of the Conference on Science, Philosophy and Religion, and chairman of the Chicago* (*interfaith*) Institute for Religious Studies. He serves as a member of the National Y.M.C.A. Committee on Spiritual Emphasis. He has been a member of the important Federal Council Commissions on a Just and Durable Peace and on The Churches and the War. He is chairman of the Department of International Justice and Goodwill of the Federal Council of Churches, and a member of the Executive Committee of the Council. He is active in the work of the National Conference of Christians and Jews. During 1946 he was chairman of the Citizens' Sponsoring Committee for an intensive survey of race relations in Delaware County, Pennsylvania. Dr. Aubrey is the brother of the general secretary of the Baptist Union of Great Britain and Ireland.

In our day, when men are faced with enough problems on every side to defeat all our faith, here is a message of hope that will be a source of blessing. Recently Dr. Aubrey said, "We live in the present moment; but we live also between the ages, between a dying world and an order yet unborn."

"The Genealogy of Hope" was preached at Spelman College, Atlanta, Georgia, and is included here with the kind permission of President Florence M. Read.

## Sermon Thirty

THIS is a day when hope is hard. The voices of despair sound all about us; but the Christian must be a messenger of hope. Shall he "hope against hope," or shall he find ground for hope even in the midst of trouble? This is not merely a broad, social problem. It is an intense personal problem. It finds vigorous and touching poetic expression in Tennyson's "In Memoriam." It moves to a triumphant Christian solution in the apostle Paul. Such transcending hope as his has a personal history, and this is nowhere more clearly stated than in the opening section of the fifth chapter of his *Epistle to the Romans*: "We rejoice in hope of the glory of God. And not only so, but we also rejoice in our tribulations: knowing that the pressures of life develop staying power; and staying power develops competence; and competence develops hope." Here, in condensed form, is the genealogy of hope.

His hope arises not apart from the difficulties of life, but in them. Paul never lacked for trouble or anguish. In addition to that mysterious disease which he alludes to as a "thorn in the flesh" he suffered maltreatment and calumny, shipwreck and imprisonment, ingratitude and disappointment. The words, then, are not lightly spoken. To all of us, soon or late, such sufferings will come. Men will scorn our ideals, and often defeat them through the organized evil that is in the world. Our very eagerness to serve will threaten to distract us from our main aim by drawing us into activities that accomplish little. Scandal will impugn the leader's character; and the hostility of others bring out of him qualities that endanger his own spiritual integrity. He will be confronted with tasks that overwhelm his limited ability. He will face challenges from modern thought in science and philosophy to undermine his faith. As Phillips Brooks once put it, "Disappointment, mortification, misconception, enmity, pain, death—these may come to you, but if they come to you in doing your duty it is all right."

Why is it all right? Because they can develop staying power. They can help one to gain stamina. Stamina is the warp in the loom of life, as the Latin root of the word suggests. Across it are woven the trials and testings of experience, and both are needed if the pattern of life is to be completed. We are perfected through suffering. When pressure is put upon us it tests us. When the Grand Coulee Dam was being built engineers subjected the small concrete cylinders through which water was to pass to a pressure of as much as 200,000 pounds. If the mixture of concrete was not right, they flew apart. If they could stand the pressure they were ready to take their place in the great structure. "The pressures of life develop staying power."

Sometimes the tests of thinking are the hardest of all. When F. W. Robertson of Brighton, the great English preacher of the last century, entered the ministry he fought a desperate battle in his own study. Honest doubts grew within him till one after another the cardinal articles of his creed became for him incredible. Yet the measure of the man and the source of his tremendous later influence were shown in his determined preaching and thinking till he achieved the blessing of a larger and securer faith.

But only because he stayed with the fight. When I was a lad in an English public school we would set out each spring on long, cross-country runs starting at five miles and working up to fourteen. All the runners started with enthusiasm, but within the first mile or so came that grueling pain in the side called "the stitch"; and what agony it was! But the school wisely provided that some of the older and better runners should stay at the back of the pack for the first two miles as "whips." They kept us going through that acute pain till suddenly the pain was gone and we had our second wind. Then we could keep running as long as the muscles held out. Morale is the second wind of the spiritual life. When the initial pride and joy of the work give way to weariness and pain, we dare not stop. We must keep in the race that is set before us.

Boys who turned back in the short cross-country run never managed the longer runs. They never developed the lung power or the muscular strength for the job. But those who kept going found that they had developed new powers. Perpetual resistance strengthens the muscles. The European churches which stood up to the Nazis manifested this strength; and when the courageous documents issued during this struggle by German and

Dutch and Norwegian and other churches are published we shall find in them a steadily growing power to withstand the evil day. Our task in America is rather that of fighting against sheer inertia. It calls for perpetual exertion. A great chaplain of the first World War, Studdert-Kennedy, once wrote:

> When Jesus came to Birmingham, they simply passed him by.
> They never hurt a hair of him, they only let him die.

Intellectual leaders will grope in this pall of indifference. They must not turn away from it into the pleasanter company of their congenial colleagues. They must face it. Sometimes the leader lapses before it into apathy. Boswell once said to Dr. Johnson of a certain person's behavior, "That, Sir, was great fortitude of mind." To which Johnson promptly replied, "No, Sir; stark insensibility."

To face the tests of trouble is the way to stamina. The commando has his obstacle course, the jumper his ever-higher bar, the sailor his rough seas, all as part of his training in the power to stick it out.

If we can stay with it, then, says Paul, we develop competence, we pass the test, we achieve character. When a tree is transplanted in the autumn the gardener faces an anxious test during the winter. Will it survive the freezing weather, the heavy snow, the gale? If it does, the worst is over. In the next season it will show its vitality in new growth. It is so with a man. We ask of him, "Can he take it?" If so, then he can grow in the new job, the new testing time that will inevitably come. This is the truth in the doctrine of the survival of the fittest. Resilience, courage, adaptability to unexpected events, toughness of fiber: these are the marks of the man who has stayed with his difficult situations and carried out his decisions. Skills are born in the trial. We take on a job to find out if we can do it, and in taking it on we acquire the ability to do it. The weight of the loads we lift will determine the development of our strength. "Do not pray for tasks equal to your powers," said Phillips Brooks. "Pray for powers equal to your tasks. If the life which you have chosen to be your life is really worthy of you, it involves self-sacrifice and pain. If your Jerusalem really is your sacred city, there is certainly a cross in it." We shall never know our strength until we try it on a bigger task than we have attempted before.

This is the difference between the veteran and the raw recruit. The latter fears the battle largely because he does not know if he can "screw his courage to the sticking point," or if he has the skill that spells the chance of life against death. The veteran has been through it. He knows now that he can take it. He knows that in the din and terror of real warfare he can trust his training and his nerves. Little by little he has built up this competence. His life has learned the fine co-ordinations that spell proficiency. Because he stayed he became a seasoned soldier, ready for any assignment. In similar fashion any servant of society must grow, not by picking the easy assignments, but by facing the new and difficult tasks that tax his ingenuity, his vision, his ability to get on with all sorts of people, his faith in his cause, his love of men. He mellows, much as a violin or an organ mellows, by being played upon. He becomes a veteran in the spiritual war, like those saints who "climbed the steep ascent of heaven through peril, toil, and pain." In the feeble efforts of the child to walk come the balance and the strength necessary for the next stage, until the mature man walks easily and far, bending his body to the wind, picking his steps on a treacherous trail, knowing the quicksand from the firm earth, and climbing without effort to the summit. His strength was perfected in weakness. Stamina developed competence.

"Competence develops hope." Hope has been defined as "the expectation of good": but many hopes are part of the dangerous escape of daydreaming. "The hope of happy inexperience" to which Dickens referred, like the unfounded optimism that he personified in Micawber who was always hoping for "something to turn up," has brought the word into disrepute among the poets. They mostly take the cynical attitude toward it that Shakespeare put in the mouth of Lord Bardolph in *Henry IV* about young Hotspur who "lined himself with hope, eating the air on promise of supply." We need a more solid foundation of hope. Here is the answer: competence develops hope.

Achievement now becomes the firm foundation for hope. Surely this is realism. Why should we "rejoice in the hope of the glory of God" in life otherwise? Our hopes cannot be disconnected specters beyond the lethal stream. "Such stuff as dreams are made on" can achieve the status of a hope only when it is woven into the pattern of actual experience. "I *should like* to see him" is one thing; "I *hope* to see him" is very different. Hope here connotes some reasonable chance of fulfillment.

Hope grows out of the struggle in which good has triumphed. Religious thinkers talk much about the problem of evil. The real problem of evil is how to make good come out of a bad situation. Only the facing of evil and the winning of good can give confidence here. To believe in the goodness of God or of human nature without facing the dark and terrible evils of disease, disaster and sin is to flaunt a banner of faith that is only a flimsy rag.

The hard-won competence develops hope. Life lived in devotion to God's will begets its struggles, its tribulations. Out of the trials comes the power to stay in the fight. This trains the soul to competence; and hope is born. In our own day, the new power that the churches of the continent of Europe have found through stamina in suffering and persecution stands as the greatest hope of reconstruction in those tragic lands. The peoples know it, the military governors of the allies know it, the world ought to know it. The missionaries of China have won such confidence in the midst of the confusion that they are one of the great hopes of that vast land.

Just so the leader stands to other men as a harbinger of hope: in so far as he has shown them by his own life and in his leadership how to face life's moments of failure and disappointment, the staggering blows and the unfulfilled promises. Once the art of living has been learned, the future loses much of its terror, and we can hope legitimately for the best. Then we can dare to hope that every cloud can have a silver lining when we really turn it inside out; and every trial be productive of good if we are spiritually disciplined.

Hope here approaches confidence. Its expectation of good is justified.

So far I have spoken in psychological, perhaps in moralistic, terms. But here's the rub! How can we have confidence that the human venture to which we have set our hands has any hope of success? On what foundation is our expectation based? How can our human effort achieve success except by virtue of the powers that work in nature to sustain rather than to frustrate us? If the universe in which our lot is cast be totally indifferent or hostile, how shall the work of our hands be established? What ground have we for hope and confidence beyond the little span of our so recent human enterprise?

Listen to Paul again: "And hope does not disgrace us, because the love of God has been poured into our hearts through the Holy Spirit." We want to avoid being disgraced by our hopes. We could be disgraced in either of two ways: our hopes might be diabolical, and they might be foolish. If the Nazis had realized their hopes that would have been disgraceful. At the very moment of their triumph they would have been disgraced, because the things they sought were devilish. They had hoped to annihilate the Jews. They had expected to be the swollen leech of Europe, sucking the lifeblood of the other lands.

Have we examined our hopes for our own careers? Are they worthy? Are we hoping for honor and preferment rather than for maximum service to our fellow men? Are we looking forward to leisure and pleasant ease in some situation where the inertia of the group will allow it? Do we expect to solve the problems of humanity by talk and more talk? Then we shall be disgraced by our hopes.

We shall then have forsaken that love of God for us and other men which was meant to be a purifying and refreshing stream in our lives, running through it to cleanse and quicken the lives of those who look to us for help. Furthermore, we shall be trying to defeat that which is at the root of all life: that purpose and power of God which moves through the world bringing order out of chaos, peace out of dissension, good out of evil. We might as well say then in Milton's words:

> Farewell hope, and with hope, farewell fear,
> Farewell remorse; all good to me is lost.
> Evil, be thou my good.

Hope may be disgraced because it is diabolical.

Again, hope may be disgraced as folly. Baseless and futile, it may sing out without the slightest justification, foolishly. It is against such disgrace that Paul sets his fine declaration. "Hope does not disgrace us, because the love of God has been poured into our hearts through the Holy Spirit." The context makes it clear that it is God's love for us that is meant, for the death of Jesus Christ is the special manifestation which Paul cites. In the final analysis this is the foundation of our hope. The world means something. Man is not a cosmic orphan but a creature able to find power in his universe to realize his ideals if they be consistent with the character of the world. The trusting faith of the humanist that rational control can win a high destiny for the human race requires a solid grounding in the universe in which we have to carve out the utopia. Apart from some supporting tendency toward a better world we struggle without reasonable hope, and strive forward with no clear sense of direction. Why should goodness have a chance in an alien world? Why be confident of our reasoning itself if there be no order in the universe? To say that God is love is to say that deep in the cosmic order is a movement toward unity of spirit, sensitive mutual understanding, acute concern for our fellows, readiness to give ourselves up that another may profit. Nowhere is this more powerfully manifest than in the life and the death of Jesus Christ our Lord. It is this love of God, shown in Jesus Christ and flooding our lives, that vindicates our struggles and validates our hope. That love does not fail us in the end. In its light we have shaped our best thoughts and aspirations, borne our bitterest grief, endured our most heartbreaking disappointments, lifted up our heads to learn from our tribulations, and built up our expectation of greater good to come. The sense of God's love is our staying power. "He who believeth shall not be put to shame."

IMMORTALITY

## The Shores of Eternity

REVEREND HAROLD ELLIOTT NICELY, D.D.
*Pastor, Brick Presbyterian Church, Rochester, New York*

*Dr. Nicely's message on immortality will find lodgment in many hearts in these days when men are trying to find peace of mind and hope for tomorrow and for all eternity.*

*Born on Christmas Day, 1900, in Beirut, Syria, he studied at the University of Chicago, Princeton Theological Seminary, Princeton University, and did graduate work at Westminster College, Cambridge. Washington and Jefferson College, in 1941, conferred the honorary D.D. in recognition* of his work in his three parishes, Westminster Presbyterian Church, Wilmington, Delaware; Central-Brick Presbyterian Church, East Orange, New Jersey; and Brick Presbyterian Church, Rochester, New York.

He was given the Honorary Citation of the University of Chicago Alumni Association in 1946, is a trustee of Princeton Theological Seminary, and of the Rochester Chamber of Commerce; a director of the Rochester Council of Social Agencies, and of the Rochester School for the Deaf; president, Rochester Federation of Churches (1943-45); president, Rochester City Club (1945-46); a member of the Federal Council Commission on a Just and Durable Peace; a member of the Presbyterian Department of Church Co-operation and Union; author of What Religion Does to Men (a book of sermons). He is staff lecturer in homiletics at Colgate-Rochester Divinity School. His preaching is fresh, virile, challenging.

## Sermon Thirty=one

TEXT: When the fourteenth night was come, as we were driven up and down in Adria, about midnight the shipmen deemed that they drew near to some country.   ACTS 27:27

THERE was no way of knowing that they were near shore, but they began to believe that it was so. And there is no way of knowing that as we go farther on our earthly voyage we approach the shores of eternity, but as Christians we have some assurance that it is so. The reasons for our belief are not unlike the reasons that persuaded these storm-tossed sailors that a friendly haven was near at hand.

The first reason for the hope was the hope itself. They were sailors, to be sure, and they loved the sea, but it was meaningless without the land. Their voyage was incomplete until "Home is the sailor, home from the sea." Because they were looking, always looking into the darkness, it may be that they saw the faint outlines of distant hills. Because they were listening, it may be that they heard the rolling of the breakers on the shore.

Possibly under the spell of this longing they were only seeing things. Travelers lost in a desert, their lips parched and fever mounting, see in their delirium green trees and streams of cooling water. So the wayfarer on the journey of life, deprived of the things that he wants, unable to go forward, and unable to endure his present condition, may live in the never-never land of make-believe. There is a kind of wishful thinking that plays fast and loose with reality, and its findings can be very far from the truth.

But there is a kind of wishful or hopeful thinking which is consistent with our nature, which springs out of what we are and presses out into the unknown and unseen toward what we may yet become. If it be true that the first creatures of the earth came out of the waters, behind their transformation was a deep urge of their nature that was driving them, and they did not develop lungs and then decide to breathe. They had a yearning to breathe, and to satisfy this urge their lungs were developed. Wishful thinking is not to be despised, for when it springs out of our deepest necessities, and is consistent with truth, it is the forerunner of our most daring thoughts. A boy wishes to become a man because it is in him. It comes out of what he is, and points the way to what he will yet become.

This urge to live on is very old, according to the best opinion, deep and universal among the primitive races of mankind. It is as old as the pyramids quite literally, for the pyramids were a gigantic attempt to preserve the body which was thought to preserve the soul. They were a protest of the spirit hurled back at nature, defying the wind and the sun and the storm to destroy man if they could. Under their massive shelter was the man whose earthly toil had ended, his body preserved, with food and weapons for his continuing journey.

You may say all this is part of the primitive past. These are ancient superstitions, and now in the calm clear light of a more perfect wisdom we have abandoned such belief. But has life in any way become less precious? If, when the book of Job was written, it could be said, "Skin for skin, yea, all that a man hath will he give for his life," can it not be said with greater emphasis today? Is not truth more elevated, and beauty more refined, and honor more worthy, and love more noble and profound? These are the things that give life its worth. The value of life grows with our growth, and the desire for more life can never be separated from the conviction that life is good.

The spirit in man does not decline with the failing years. The strength of the body may be ebbing, but the impulses of the spirit are flowing strongly as though driven by mighty tides of the sea. At the end of the earthly journey the work of the body is finished, but the work of the spirit has just begun, its purposes unfinished, its aspirations unsatisfied, its questions unanswered, its hopes and loves and longing incomplete. If the true life of man is the life of the spirit, then the nature of his earthly life as a fragment cries out for its fulfillment in a further realm where the things that we now see dimly, we see face to face. Now we know in part, but then we shall know even as also we are known.

So there is something within us that cannot be reconciled to death. It is not that we shrink from physical pain, for what the uncounted multitudes who have gone before us have borne, we too can bear. It is not that we are afraid of some final and perpetual condemnation, for unworthy though we may be, if we can rely on God at all, we can rely on His mercy and forgiveness. It is not that we aspire to walk the golden streets or to see the procession of saints in long white robes. These are not the things of which a person thinks when he faces his own death, but his hand reaches out for the touch of little fingers, he looks long into a gentle face that he may carry it with him forever, he listens for the voices of his loved ones. For they are a part of his life and he is a part of theirs. By some mysterious and wonderful influence these bonds have been fashioned, and they are eternal and unchanging, and the moth and the rust cannot corrupt them, and no thief can break through and steal.

I do not know how it is with you. I can only speak for myself. There are friends of my youth, whom I have not seen for many years, and whom I do not expect to see on earth. But I should like to be with them again. And there are some who have been good to me, and I want some day to tell them of my gratitude. And there are some whose forgiveness I would seek. And there is much that I would like to understand and do. And when the midnight of my life draws near, I shall be standing on the forward deck, looking hopefully into the darkness, for a glimpse of loved ones on the shore.

If you tell me that we must all die and that is the end, speak for yourself. That is your world. It is not mine. I do not fit into that. I am a square peg in that kind of a hole, and to try to force myself into it is to fight against my own nature and, I think, against the truth of God. What was it Jesus said? Foxes have holes and birds of the air have nests, but the Son of Man hath nowhere to lay his head. It is true of man generally. There is no place among the things of sight and touch where he can lay his head and be at rest, for God hath set eternity in his heart. His earthly pillow is a pillow of stones, and his sleep is restless, and in his dreams he sees a ladder that reaches up to heaven, with angels going up and down.

So the hope that springs out of the deep and hidden things of our nature is the first reason for the persuasion that we approach eternal shores.

There was a further reason for their hope in bits of driftwood—here and there an object plainly seen in the foaming crest of the wave. Some inland river was forcing its current into the sea, carrying out these tokens, these assurances of land. The sea by itself could not produce this driftwood. It was plainly the indication of the shore.

So all about us, if we look carefully, we see from time to time the tokens and symbols of an eternal order. Beethoven sits down before his piano; he has lost his hearing completely, but into his soul there comes the impulse of a sweet melody. Where does it come from? Only God can answer that. He hears it and yet he does not hear it because he is deaf. But he knows it is music, and his hands on the keys obey the impulse in his soul. He takes his pencil and begins to write, curious little symbols, dots here and there in lines and spaces. He works over it patiently, lovingly, until it is finished at last. And over a hundred years later a person sits down at the piano. His fingers obey these symbols and find the keys. Little felt hammers are pounding on wires, and you hear the music of the Ninth Symphony, which the old master never heard—except in his soul—and what was there has entered now into your soul, the portals of another world swing open, you enter in and feel the joy and power of unseen beauty, and memory seals forever the loveliness of those moments in your heart.

Is that beauty real? It is not in the world of sight or touch, of time or space. You cannot weigh it or measure it, or see it under a microscope. It is of another order. The things that are seen are temporal. The things that are unseen are eternal. Is it real? Is anything else quite so real? Is it not a sign of eternity carried on the seas of time?

There is a nobleness in man that is also a sign of the spirit. Self-preservation may be the drive of the creatures of earth, but at some time in his history man began to feel and respond to something higher. There is a great truth in his keeping, a tradition that is his to preserve, freedom he has valued above his own life, and where duty has called he has not counted the cost. Among all that is sordid and cruel and shameful in war, the gallantry of men shines out, men who love honor more than life.

The law of the earth is self-preservation, but the law of God's kingdom is love, and greater love hath no man than this, that a man lay down his life for his friends. Is such love real? Is anything else quite so real? Eternal driftwood on the seas of time, if we have eyes to see, something to remind us that this sea on which our mortal lives are launched is bounded everywhere by eternal shores, and as we journey on, we draw near to some country.

And for some, at least, there was a final reason in the words of a man of God who sailed with them. A few days before when the storm was at its worst, and their condition was desperate, and they had given up hope, this man of God called them together and spoke to them. "In my prayers I have felt the promise of God to bring us all safely to land. Wherefore sirs be of good cheer, for I believe in God."

That was the word of promise, and for us a greater word was spoken by one greater than St. Paul. "Because I live, ye shall live also. In my Father's house are many mansions: if it were not so, I would have told you." He had held before their eyes the vision of the Holy City, kindled in their hearts the great loves and the great longings. And if it were a dream and nothing more, a way of life in this world only, he would have told them. Everything that they had learned seemed to point to something beyond. From their experience of God here and now there was a reasonable inference to be drawn. But how reasonable? Would he answer that? He would and did. If it were not so, I would have told you. I go to prepare a place for you, and if I go to prepare a place for you, I will come again and receive you unto myself, that where I am there ye may be also.

How much does God care for His children? When a coin is lost, a woman sweeps the house until she finds it. When a sheep is lost, a shepherd goes out into the wilderness at night and searches until he finds it. When a son is lost, a father waits day after day, night after night, and looks out the window and often walks down the road, and when he sees him coming, he runs to meet him. And the coin has no feeling, and the sheep knows little more, and the prodigal has put his father out of his mind, but the loss is felt in the heart of the woman, the shepherd, the father, in the heart of God. Let no one say: "I do not count for anything, it doesn't matter what becomes of me." You have no right to say it. Your life may not matter to you, but it matters to those who love you. They hold you in their hearts, and it matters to God, and His love will never let you go.

This may fall on deaf ears, and it will not be the first time. If it does, let me say what was once said to a younger person at a conference, who expressed some surprise that anyone who was intelligent could believe in immortality. This was said, "Live your life, your best life. Be true to your friends. Be just and patient and kind. When there is a good work to be done in your community, you be the first to help. And when you see a poor little child that needs a new dress or a doll for Christmas, you get it for her. And when your Aunt Mary is old and her eyes are dim, you go and read to her Sunday afternoons. And when someone is ill in your neighborhood, take him some flowers. And when sorrow comes to someone you know, you be the first to send a message of comfort. Do that all your life, and when it is all over, and you fall asleep for the last time, do not be surprised if you wake up in the kingdom of Heaven. You do your part, and God who loves you will do His."

There comes a time when the answer lies beyond our powers of thought, when what impresses us chiefly is what we do not know. Then it is that we turn to those who are supreme in their field. If I wanted the final word in astronomy, I would turn to the works of Eddington or Jeans. If I wanted the last word in mathematics, I would look to Einstein. But if I wanted to hear the greatest word on God and immortality, I would listen to Jesus. I have listened, and I know nothing truer than his words, "In my Father's house are many mansions: if it were not so, I would have told you."

The hope is very real and very dear, and the signs of the unseen world are all about us. And the great words of promise ring clear and true in the glory of the Resurrection morning.

# Immortality on Earth

REVEREND DAVID DE SOLA POOL, PH.D.[1]
*Rabbi, Spanish and Portuguese Synagogue, Shearith Israel, New York*

*Dr. Pool is the leader of the famous Spanish and Portuguese Synagogue, Shearith Israel, which was founded in 1655, when New York was a village and the western boundary of what is now the United States was east of the Delaware River. This great synagogue has had a distinguished history, and Dr. Pool has shown himself to be a capable leader of the Orthodox faith, a scholarly preacher, and a good pastor. He is active in interfaith work and has the respect of Catholics and Protestants.*

*He was born in London, England, in 1885, and was educated in universities of Europe, being graduated with honors from the University of London in 1905. Later he studied at the universities of Berlin and Heidelberg, receiving his Ph.D., summa cum laude, from Heidelberg.*

*Since 1907 he has been minister of the Spanish and Portuguese Synagogue. He is the representative of Jewish army and navy chaplains to the Chiefs of Chaplains.*

*In 1917 he was one of three Jewish representatives appointed to serve on Herbert Hoover's food conservation staff; in 1919 he was one of three American representatives on the Zionist Commission to Palestine; and from 1938-40, he was president of the Synagogue Council of America.*

*Dr. Pool has written numerous prayer books, pamphlets and reviews, and is the author of* The Kaddish, Hebrew Learning among the Puritans of New England, *and* Capital Punishment in Jewish Literature.

*This distinguished sermon asks several startling questions concerning the nature of human life in the time to come and whether the future will give us life triumphant. His positive belief in life in the hereafter will be helpful and so will his insistence upon the divine promise of the immortality of human goodness living on. "How each of us lives today determines the life of our children and all who will come after us tomorrow." The sermon was given on* The Church of the Air *of the Columbia Broadcasting System.*

[1] Sermons by members of the advisory committee were contributed at the special request of the editor and are included on his responsibility.

## Sermon Thirty=two

WHAT will be the nature of human life in the time to come? Will the future give us life triumphant? Or will it be life marked by increased technical mastery and also by increased confusion of purpose? Or will it be as some of our thinkers forecast, life driven underground because of fear of man's inordinately increased powers of destruction? Will it be life so beset by fears and by violence that the men of tomorrow will look back to our unhappy generation as to a golden age? Or will it be a fulfillment of the prophetic vision that looked to the latter days for messianic peace and universal human welfare? Must we look backwards to catch glimpses of greater happiness than we now know, or can we hope for a future in which "none shall hurt and none destroy in all God's holy mountain, for the earth shall be filled with the knowledge of the Lord as the waters cover the sea" (Isaiah 11:9)?

The answer to all these questions depends in a measure on you whoever you may be. It depends on every one of us, on every human being alive today, small as well as great. For what we do today determines the character of man's tomorrow.

Throughout the generations man has always groped for knowledge of life after death. But in one sense there is no death. After our physical death every one of us lives on in the conditions that we have helped bring about on earth. None of us leaves life the same as we found it. All of us influence life for better or for worse, or, perhaps I should say, both for better and for worse. The influence of our individual lives endures on earth after our death both for good and for evil. We all live on both in the good and in the evil that we do.

Our incredible ferocity and inhumanity will live on in the crushing burden of destruction and debt which our wars have bequeathed to the generations to come. Our ill-planned cities with their insufficient parks and playgrounds, their slums and their dark immoral tenements breeding stunted and thwarted lives, in them live the greed, the corruption and the stupidity of the dead of earlier generations. Think of some of the miserable social derelicts whom you know. In them there is living a drunkard, a criminal, a drug addict, or some other abnormal person, physically dead and buried, but still grimly living out his life in these unhappy descendants. Think of the physically stricken, the blind, the degenerate, the insane, who are living out the immorality of parents long since dead but who still live ruthlessly in these their wretched children.

Discussion is occasionally heard as to whether Adolf Hitler is really dead. Whether or not he and his mistress met their ignominious physical death under the Berlin which he had reduced to rubble, Hitler is living and will live on endlessly in human misery. His malignant life is still at work in hundreds of millions of stories of human sorrow, bereavement, frustration, hatred, homelessness, hopelessness and utter misery.

Truly the evil that men do lives after them. It cannot all be interred with their bones. Death sets no end to it. God does visit the iniquity of the fathers on the children to the third and the fourth generation.

But the good that men do also lives after them. That also cannot be interred with their bones. Generations long dead have given us a living heritage of their lives. We do not have to build society anew in each generation. Though our cities may often be ill-planned and inadequate, yet they have their parks, playgrounds, boulevards, libraries, museums, colleges and all the other gifts in which the dead of the past live endlessly in blessing. Though the evil of our forebears may have bequeathed to us many a human breakdown, yet the good that they did lives in hospitals, homes and noble institutions of human love.

James Watt and George Stephenson live every time steam gives us power. Gutenberg still lives in every printed word. Marconi lives in every radio. Lister, Pasteur and a vast gallery of deathless men and women of the past live in every life that is saved by modern science.

Just as our physical civilization breathes and lives through the good in the lives of the past, so also does our spiritual civilization breathe and live through spirit of past teachers and redeemers from Moses to Lincoln and Roosevelt. These men live, immortal in blessing. Their work is not finished and never can be finished.

When Socrates, the wisest of the ancient Greeks, was condemned to death and was about to drink the hemlock, his friend Crito asked him how he wished to be buried. Socrates replied that so far as the funeral formalities were concerned his friends could do whatever was conventionally called for; but, he said, "You cannot bury Socrates." Men might bury the body of a Socrates; they could never bury that vital spirit which we still acclaim as Socrates.

In the same spirit the rabbis call attention to the phrasing found in some Biblical verses. It is said of Jacob (Genesis 47:29), "the days of Israel drew near to die." And it is said of Moses (Deuteronomy 31:14), "And the Lord said unto Moses, behold thy days draw near to die." "Yes," says Rabbi Simeon son of Lakish, "it is the days of an Israel or the days of a Moses which can die. The good themselves never die." There is deep spiritual significance in the phrase used in the story of the death of Moses that "no man knows his sepulchre unto this day" (Deuteronomy 34:6). A Moses cannot be confined within a grave. He lives in the people to whom he gave a soul. He lives in every Jew, he lives in every Christian, he lives in every Moslem, for all of them have drawn and still draw on his spirit.

But, you may say, it is given to the fewest of us to be wise as Socrates or great as Moses. It is a rare individual who like Israel can be the founder of a people that will bear his name. Not everyone can leave behind him some great philanthropic foundation that will memorialize him in generations yet unborn. Nor can any but a chosen individual here and there live on as a great inventor, writer, scientist or other human benefactor bequeathing to the world an undying memory of deathless genius. But every one of us can in his life plant spiritual seed that shall give fruit, shade and loveliness to generations yet unborn.

The Talmud tells of a very old man who was seen planting a slow-growing tree. They said to him, "Do you expect to live to enjoy the fruit of that tree?" His answer was, "All my life I have been enjoying the fruit of trees planted by those now dead. Should not I in my turn plant for the benefit of those who will be here long after I am no more?" Every one of us will live in what we plant here on earth, whether it be a forest or only a lowly shrub.

In this sense, every one of us survives death in an earthly immortality. Every one of us helps build the future for we shall live into it long after our last breath on earth is drawn. If only men would be less concerned about the heavenly world to come and would give themselves more to beautifying and ennobling this earthly world, then how much the more compelling would be their claim on the happiness of an after life with God. And how much the better assured would be their faith in their own immortality.

Of old men believed that ultimate destruction took place. They saw wood pass through the flames and be destroyed. They saw a pond of water disappear under the summer's sun. Man now understands that in such phenomena there is no final destruction but only a chemical or a physical change. In the world of the spirit also there is no destruction, no end. Death, like some calendar marking up the 31st day of December, may seem to say, "this is the end." But neither death nor the calendar can annihilate the past or negate the future. There is an endless spiritual continuity in which we all share. We are all part of one great continuing eternal spiritual process. We all draw on it for the wealth poured into it by our parents, our ancestors and the untold myriads of the nameless dead. What in our turn shall we give to it? What shall be our contribution to the spiritual stream of human life?

In the inevitable course of the years every one of us will be gathered to his fathers. Then our loved ones will say of us, "gone but not forgotten." But as the years roll on we shall in due time be "gone and forgotten." Yet though our name be forgotten, we shall still be living. So let no one scoffingly say, "*après moi le déluge*—I should worry what should happen after I am dead." For every one of us will be living in our own children and in the lives of those, and the descendants of those, with whom our lives have been intertwined. Can we be selfish enough or conscienceless enough so to live that not only the lives of our loved ones now on earth but also our children's lives and the lives of innocent babes yet unborn shall be the darker, the harder, the unhappier, the crueler, because of what we have been? Or (and we have free choice) shall we achieve in this life within our own family, our own circle, our own community, and after our death in our children and in these to come after us, the glory of living in lives made the sweeter and the better because of our having lived?

To our ancestors there is nothing we can give; from our descendants there is nothing we can withhold. Whatever we are goes into making up the general record of the future. Do you want a blessed immortality? Even though in time it will not necessarily be associated with your name, it is yours as you give yourself now through friendliness, goodness, helpfulness, sweetness, light, truth, justice and love. That is a deathlessness in glory which you may command.

The rabbis of old had a saying that one need not erect a tombstone over the grave of the good. The good, they said, need no memorial of stone. Their goodness lives on. Their deathless lives are their immortal memorial in the lives of the generations to come. For though God visits the iniquity of the fathers upon the third and the fourth generation, He shows loving kindness to the thousandth generation of those who love Him and keep His commandments. This is the divine promise of the immortality of human goodness on earth. And this, I repeat, is the answer to the question, What will be the nature of life in the generations to come? That depends on every one of us. How each of us lives today determines the life of our children and all who will come after us tomorrow.

## NATIONAL AND INTERNATIONAL

# Sermon for the Confraternity of Christian Doctrine

His Eminence Francis Cardinal Spellman, D.D.
*Roman Catholic Archbishop of New York*

*Cardinal Spellman succeeded the late Cardinal Hayes in the great archdiocese of New York and has given brilliant guidance to his people in their churches, their hospitals, their homes, their schools, and their personal lives. Born in Whitman, Massachusetts, May 4, 1889, he took his A.B. at Fordham University, his S.T.D. at the University of the Propaganda, Rome, in 1916, and was ordained at St. John Lateran, Rome, May 14, 1916. He celebrated his first Mass at the tomb of St. Peter in the Basilica of St. Peter in Vatican City, May 15, 1916.*

*He returned to Boston, served on the editorial staff of the Boston Pilot and as Assistant Chancellor of the Archdiocese of Boston, then returned to*

Rome as Attache to the Secretary of State's Office at the Vatican from 1925-33. In September of 1932 he was consecrated Titular Bishop of Sila by His Eminence Eugenio Cardinal Pacelli and was Auxiliary Bishop of Boston from 1932-39. His Holiness, Pope Pius XII, appointed him as Archbishop of New York on April 15, 1939, and he was installed at St. Patrick's Cathedral on May 23. Sequere Deum ("Follow God") was the motto he chose then. On December 11 of that year he was appointed Military Vicar for the armed forces of the United States and made two journeys overseas to minister to the religious needs of the men in the army, navy and air corps. In 1945, he traveled around the world on a 32,000 mile journey to visit the men in service, the chaplains and the wounded in many hospitals. He frequently took an entire day to go from bed to bed to visit every one of the fifteen hundred wounded in a military or naval hospital. He was created a Cardinal by His Holiness, Pope Pius XII, at Christmas, 1945, in recognition of his world-wide service to the Catholics of the United States.

His books are making a place for themselves, especially those in blank verse. He is the author of The Word of God, In the Footsteps of the Master, The Road to Victory, Action This Day, The Risen Soldier and No Greater Love.

Cardinal Spellman is winning respect and appreciation from men of all denominations by his presentation of the Gospel message in verse. In this he is a worthy successor of Cardinal Newman. He ended his first statement after being made a Cardinal with these beautiful lines:

> This is the Godlike way, the Godlike life
> That each of us must live; and living, reap
> Rich harvest where no riches grew before.
> We who would gather in the autumn days
> Of life, must learn to sow, bravely to give.
> For only those who sow may hope to reap
> The fulsome harvest that alone they gain
> Who measure life in terms of give, and find
> Full payment in the Master's greater love,
> Reward beyond all measure; and their gifts
> Still theirs, beyond attrition of the year.
> Dear God, bless us with this, the spirit of
> Your Son. No nation from Your hand has drawn
> A greater largesse of the things of earth.
>
> No land has offered for her children's good
> So large a measure of those gifts that are
> Intangible—our liberties, our hopes.
> To be the friend of all, the foe of none,
> To win our victories upon the field
> Of peace, and seek this peace for all mankind,
> Not for ourselves alone, a place and right
> To live; as a Good Samaritan, patiently
> To heal the festered wounds that gall mankind;

To live God's plan at home, abroad, and humbly
Pray the guerdon of the Master's grace
Upon our hearths, our homes, our blessed land,
Upon our children's children, till the world's
Span of fleeting time shall come to end.
Bless us dear God, contrite, we kneel to Thee!

*This sermon of His Eminence was given at the Pontifical Mass of the Eighth Catechetical Congress of the Confraternity of Christian Doctrine at the Boston Garden on Sunday, October 27, 1946. The Cardinal's emphasis upon the mysticism of Christ is greatly needed in our world today.*

## Sermon Thirty=three

TEXT: Jesus spoke saying: "He who follows Me does not walk in darkness but will have the light of life." ST. JOHN 8:12

SHORTLY after the outbreak of World War II, Pope Pius XII addressed His first encyclical to the universal church. In that document the supreme teacher and shepherd of Christendom wrote of his apprehension that the hour of darkness had struck, and that midst storms of discord and violence, countless sorrows as from a chalice of blood would pour upon the earth.

After years of brutal and brutalizing battle victory was eventually achieved in a war of unequaled agonies and losses and all of us hoped that our triumph in arms would bring the dawning of the day-star of peace. But who now will say that the clouds of war have disappeared and that darkness does not shroud the earth? Who will say that enemies to peace no longer prowl in the shadows of the evils that beset us seeking whom and what they may devour? And who now, despite these portents, will see light shining through the mist of the torrents of tears of fellow human beings still tortured in slavery, still tormented by hunger and other sufferings and sorrows?

The answer is that we see this light of hope shining even in the blackest night. For, as we meet there in the presence of the distinguished Apostolic Delegate of our Holy Father and under the patronage of the zealous Archbishop of Boston, we publicly proclaim ourselves as apostles of light and renew the consecration of our lives and labors in the noble apostolate of faith, hope and charity. All of us belong to the army of Christ whose soldiers even in defeat find victory, even in death find life. And once again, we unfurl the standard of Christ and rally ourselves and our brethren to the joyful following of our Divine King and make known by our lives and labors the truth and glory of the saving Gospel of Christ.

Multitudes of our brothers and sisters have been blinded by error or charmed by passion away from Christ's teaching, and it is the vivid awareness of the dire need of Christ's doctrine, the need of more general and more faithful Christian living that brings us together in this great educational Conference of Boston. Our enthusiasm is enlivened and our zeal inflamed by the exhortation of our Holy Father that there is no duty more important or more urgent than making known to the world the unfathomable riches of Christ, diffusing the light that is Christ through the darkness of the world's long night. The clarion call of our vocations as Christians invites us to be successors of St. John the Baptist, precursors of Christ, shining on those who sit in darkness and in the shadow of death, guiding their footsteps on the pathway to peace.

Down through all eras education has been the most effective instrument of those who would build or destroy the temple of peace, and the conflict between Wisdom and Satan, between education and catastrophe, began with the fall of man and will continue until the last man has been summoned from life to judgment. In our own day we have observed the forces of evil furiously fashion forms of education wherein God has been both blasphemously ridiculed and ignominiously ignored, and we ourselves have been witnesses and heirs to the results produced by these devotees and dealers in a philosophy of death.

Often has it been said that America is the hope of the world, but if this hope is to be realized in the blessings of peace and prosperity, it will eventuate only through the leaven of education that is seeded and rooted in truth, that flowers and fruits in charity. It is the leaven which Christ, the Great Teacher, introduced into human life. And it is belief in the existence of a personal God and in the reality and the necessity of the observance of His moral law, that is the leaven of education. These beliefs were planted in the soul of America by the Founding Fathers of our Republic and of our Democracy. The Declaration of Independence speaks of the Creator, the Supreme Judge; and the signers of this immortal document pledged their lives, their fortunes and their sacred honor "with a firm reliance on the protection of Divine Providence." The heart of American tradition is faith in God and obedience to His law. Our National Congress opens with prayer, our National Motto is "In God We Trust," and these same words spiritualize our National Anthem. And even though at the opening of the General Assembly of the United Nations there was no prayer for divine guidance offered for the specious reason of the diversity of creeds that were represented, it was heartening to have President Truman brave the godless and confound the spineless by concluding his address to the delegates assembled from all parts of the world with this hope-reviving prayer: "May Almighty God, in His infinite wisdom and mercy, guide us and sustain us as we seek to bring peace everlasting to the world. With His help we shall succeed." And this morning, as I speak to you in Boston, men and women from at least thirty-one out of the fifty-two member-nations are in St. Patrick's Cathedral, New York, attending Mass offered to Almighty God praying for a blessing to the world of the priceless gift of peace.

It is both American tradition and Catholic practice publicly to proclaim faith in God, respect and obedience for His laws and our dependence on Him. And as Americans in peacetime, we have the same duties as our soldier sons and brothers had in wartime—to save America and the world from the doomsday of enslavement and death. As Catholics, we have the obligation to walk in the presence of God, to love Him and serve Him, to save our own souls and to help our fellow men to salvation.

And it is opportune that all Americans of good will, all lovers of American Democracy, realize that godless teaching and teaching godlessness may shrivel the very roots of our American way of life. To save America from such a catastrophe is surely the grave duty of us all, and we assembled here should reflect and resolve concerning ways and means to help a tottering world regain its rational and religious balance. But these reflections on some of the broader problems confronting the world today must not distract us and do not dispense us from personal soul-searching to enable us to fulfill with consuming devotion our vocation as apostles of light, and this light comes from the lamp of personal sanctification.

Calamitous facts in the world and in the life all about us grimly testify to the need of this light. The tragic arithmetic of juvenile delinquency appalls us as we consider that today more persons of the age of seventeen are arrested than in any other age group. Those under twenty-one years of age represent 15 per cent of all murders, 36 per cent of all robbers, 51 per cent of all burglars and 62 per cent of all car thieves. Since 1939, the last peacetime year, the arrest of girls under eighteen years of age has increased 198 per cent, while the arrest of boys under eighteen has increased 48 per cent for homicide and 72 per cent for assault.

Surely these sorrow-laden statistics should challenge each and every one of us to expend himself with a divine and apostolic prodigality to save American youth from the devouring demon of godlessness and sin. The problems are staggering and to solve them we must be ablaze with the light and ardor that compound zeal. Organization, technique and methods; congresses, resolutions and elaborate planning are helpful, but they will not suffice. They will not generate living apostles nor will cold intellectualism enlighten and liberate and save an unhappy world.

Our age is an age of mystical fires; the one, a spurious mysticism such as Nazism, Fascism, Communism and Nipponism; and the other the mysticism of Christ, diffusing a fire that is light, love, liberty and life. Ours is the mysticism that takes its light from the Light of the World. We receive and we give, and that is the epitome of the life of the Christian apostle of light who is a citizen of the "City of God, whose King is truth, whose law is charity, whose frontier is eternity." The flaming fire of a total and joyful love for Christ the Master will transform us into apostles of light who pray and labor that mankind may live in Him Who is life, in Whom and through Whom will come light and peace to the world.

# The Old Man and the New Man

REVEREND KARL BARTH, D.D., TH.D.

*Professor of Theology, the University of Basel, Switzerland
and a Minister of the Reformed Church*

*Karl Barth is probably the best known theologian of our time. In 1918 he startled Christian thinkers with his commentary on Paul's letter to the Romans. Through World War I the Swiss theologian was a pacifist; during World War II, he stated the view that those who did not oppose Hitler helped him and were dreaming over their news reports and the true meaning of their Bibles. He developed a theology, then added a theology of war and internationalism. He urged that Hitler must be resisted as a Christian act and that the Church must not give in to the modern state. He sees Christ over all history, over men and over the state and supports his thesis on the fact of the resurrection of Christ. The state serves as part of Christ's ministry in the world to oppose sin and wrong. World War II he saw as a restrictive or police war, to curb the evil of the Nazi regime against the kingdom of God. The war, as he proclaimed it, would not have been necessary if the Nazis had not tried to institute the supreme sovereignty and superiority of the German race and nation. Here he was in dead opposition to the philosophy of Nietzsche and the materialistic portions of Hegel's definition of man and the state.*

*In 1938, he wrote that the German church could not preach freely, was being restricted in its liberty; and in December, 1939, he wrote an understanding letter to the French Protestants, urging upon them the defeat of Hitler as a Christian act. In October, 1941, he wrote a second letter to the French Protestants and pointed out the false lure of the German realism of 1933, saying that the Germans traveled the road of the revolution of nihilism.*

*In 1941, Barth wrote* This Christian Cause, *an open letter to Great Britain from Switzerland, stating his belief that Great Britain would eventually win the war.*

*But Barth has insisted that the war was not a crusade, not the will of God and that nations cannot claim that their cause was the will of God in the war. Fight to the end, he urged, while the war lasted, but fight and even if nations were defeated, let them be humble toward God but not toward their oppressors. And if and when the German people are defeated, he urged tenderness in the treatment of them. The Germans, he said, are a sick people, have invented a mystical paganism that Christianity must help to overcome. Coming from a man who was one of the first to oppose Adolf Hitler, his plea for Christian tenderness has added weight.*

[193]

*Born in 1886, he was educated at Berne, Berlin, Tübingen, and Marburg. He has been urged to come to America, but feels that part of his work must be in Germany. To Barthians the logic of this sermon will have a real message; to those who disagree with Karl Barth it may be only a source of irritation. It is presented here as a typically Barthian sermon.*

## Sermon Thirty=four

TEXT: If so be that ye have heard him, and have been taught by him, as the truth is in Jesus: That ye put off concerning the former conversation the old man, which is corrupt according to the deceitful lusts; And be renewed in the spirit of your mind; And that ye put on the new man, which after God is created in righteousness and true holiness. Wherefore putting away lying, speak every man truth with his neighbour: for we are members one of another. Be ye angry, and sin not: let not the sun go down upon your wrath: Neither give place to the devil. Let him that stole steal no more: but rather let him labour, working with his hands the thing which is good, that he may have to give to him that needeth. Let no corrupt communication proceed out of your mouth, but that which is good to the use of edifying, that it may minister grace unto the hearers. And grieve not the holy Spirit of God, whereby ye are sealed unto the day of redemption. Let all bitterness, and wrath, and anger, and clamour, and evil speaking, be put away from you, with all malice: And be ye kind one to another, tenderhearted, forgiving one another, even as God for Christ's sake hath forgiven you. EPHESIANS 4:21-32

DEAR Congregation: The words we have just heard place a strong and powerful picture before our eyes. However, it is not just a picture but literally and actually the truth in Jesus, telling us that we should put off the old man and put on the new man.

Now if the old man is something that can be put off, he is apparently like a dress which has served its purpose and is of no further use. But the old man cannot be cleaned and mended. He cannot be put on again because he is worn out. He can only be put off once and for all. Three things are remarkable here.

First of all, the old man is only a dress. He is not your skin, not to mention your heart. He is not your very self. It is not true that clothes make the man; clothes can only cover and hide the man. You are not the old man. The old man and you are two different things. Of course he is your dress, but only your dress. Your carnival dress if you like, but nothing more.

This is really a remarkable statement when we think of all the characteristics of the old man which our text mentions. There is the lie: the conventional,

*[194]*

the social, the business, the political lie, the lies which dominate life. There is the vicious anger which we do not put aside at sundown but which we nurture within ourselves year after year, perhaps half a lifetime. There is the evil tongue—let us say it with more emphasis: the wickedly evil tongue of the people of Basel, which actually hides much sadness and fear of life as it is. All these characteristics are so familiar and so close to us. Now, is it really true that all that is not our real self, that we are just hidden in them as in a dress? Perhaps it comes to us sometimes like a sudden recollection: "Oh no, I am not really as I show myself here and act there. Please do not misunderstand me and think that I am like that." But it still is remarkable that this should really come to pass and be accepted that we are not liars, people that always lose their temper, and scandalmongers. Now remember, though it is odd it is nevertheless true. Indeed, you are in the old man up to your neck, but it is not true that you are the old man. That is not true at all.

The second thing that is remarkable is this, that the old man is a used, a ragged, a decaying—a useless dress. "Corrupt according to the deceitful lusts," we read. Therefore, he is one who wears himself out and destroys himself by the thing which drives him: just as a rocket dissolves and becomes dust and ashes by the same power which sent it into the sky and let it shine and sparkle. The old man can no longer accomplish his purpose of covering and hiding you. You need only to look at him to discover that he is full of holes and that the time has surely come to take leave of him.

It is of course an odd fact, when we stop to think about the essential characteristics of the old man mentioned here, i.e., his corrupt communication (Luther translates it as rotten gossip), which comes from our mouths. We need only to think of all the talk of busybodies and all the critical nonsense which we utter and with which we accomplish neither anything beautiful nor anything good or true. Just as we cannot carve or build or even start a good fire with rotten wood. And this characteristic of the old man is supposed to be worn out. He is supposed to be dead. But is this true, is this corrupt communication not inexhaustible, doesn't its rottenness stream from all our pores as if it would never stop?

We read about theft, of the man who grasps what does not belong to him. This includes also the man who lives by the labor of others and refuses to recognize that the abundance resulting from his work belongs according to the law of God to the needy and the poor. Is this characteristic of the old man exhausted and used up? Is not this theft the very solid, very healthy, very defensible system upon which our entire life is built? Sometimes we seem to hear a rumbling in the framework of this house. But how firm is its foundation! And if we finally speak of bitterness, wrath, anger, clamor and evil-speaking with all malice, do we not see powerful human spheres and realms before our eyes, which have no intention of passing away but which time and again prove to be extremely healthy, extremely powerful, extremely useful and do not give the least indication that they will ever outlive their usefulness? Is it true, then, that all this will perish because of the deceitful lusts from which it springs and so is truly no longer of any use? We shall not be too hasty to say that this is not true. Sometimes we see clearly how such a power, such a kingdom of evil-speaking, of theft and of bitterness, though only yesterday powerful and inflated and ready to devour everything, is today visibly shrunk like a tired balloon. And who knows if day after tomorrow it will not be said, "And the place thereof knoweth it no more." Of course, one does not always see this. And if one sees it, one sees it usually only in part. It remains a remarkable fact that all that, i.e., the old man, actually perishes. It is true: it is great, remarkable news, that he is in such poor shape. But it is true: it is so! Already he is no longer useful. We could hardly understand that, if we were not willing to accept it as truly remarkable news!

The third thing noteworthy here is that the old man *can* be put off. Quite clearly the suggestion is made here, so that we should realize it: he is only a dress, a ragged, faded, useless dress which we should take off and put away.

This is an amazing suggestion when we consider how close, how tight all that belongs to the characteristics of the old man fits our body! How deeply his roots are embedded in our very being! How often may this have been sung in this cathedral: "Lord, behold our chains, as we cry and pray with creation for salvation from the bondage of nature, from the service of vanity, which weighs upon us heavily even though our spirit at times strives for something better!" Indeed, we have sung this before and then we went outside, and even during our conversations on the Cathedral grounds and then on the homeward journey and especially on Sunday afternoon and on Monday morning we had to realize that all that was still there, the chains and the bondage of nature and the service of vanity. And the high vaulting and the stained-glass windows and lamps of the Cathedral were only a distant memory: "Even though our spirit at times strives for something better." However that may be, the demand that we should and can lay all this aside, this demand is made of us now. Please do not misunderstand me: it is not I who demand it. It is demanded of me also. I am merely showing you that according to the Word of God it is demanded of all of us and the demand is made to all of us. I do not know why you came to church today. Perhaps to hear this professor once again. Perhaps because you know very well: I must hear God's Word to be able to live! Be that as it may; you are here, and because you are here, Listen: This demand is made of you also, you can do nothing about it—you are meant. You shall and you can put off the old man. But it cannot be denied: it is a remarkable demand, just as this putting off of the old man is a remarkable thing in every respect.

And if the new man is something to put on, then clearly he too is something like a dress, that was made for us and laid out for us and offered us

[196]

and is only waiting to be put on by us. Remember, not a Sunday dress which we put on today only as something especially lovely, intending to take it off again tomorrow and change it for one of our ordinary, more practical dresses. No, the new man is a lovely dress fit not only for a special occasion and for Sunday (yes, truly, also for Sunday!) but also for every day. A dress definitely made to wear, wearable and usable for all time and for all eternity. And here again there are three things we want to consider.

First of all, the new man too is a dress. Therefore, no one can ever claim: I am a new man. You can and you shall put on the new man and you will then find that he protects you, that he warms you, yes, even that he adorns you, that he is exceedingly becoming. But you are not the new man. He and you are two different things. When the new man takes the place of the old, and begins and unfolds his life, you become, so to speak, merely his audience. He then carries on your business as a spokesman would carry on the business of his client, and you can and should let him take over.

For instance, we must consider this: If it should come true that instead of lying to one another we should speak the truth with our neighbor because we are members of one another, because we belong closely together and owe one another the truth which we ourselves hear; if it should further come to pass that we become kind toward one another instead of sharp, merciful instead of callous and suspicious; if the time should come that we forgive one another our sin instead of holding it against one another, and openly or secretly, directly or in a roundabout way, bring it up time after time; if thus we could come into fellowship with God who forgave us our sins in Christ, and if a miracle would happen, which is the opposite of theft: that we through our own life's work earn the good things for others, for those who are in need—don't you see if the new man comes into his own through such deeds then surely something entirely new has come into our lives! It might be like a strange artist, perhaps a musician, who has come to your home to give you the pleasure and do you the honor of playing for you, your guests and your neighbors. Surely you would not be conceited enough to think or to claim that this is you, that this is your music. You would not foolishly think that you had to keep time to his playing or even hum the melody. Instead, you would realize: I must let him do as he pleases and under no circumstances disturb him—that is the best I can do. So it is with the life of the new man. It is all to your advantage. You can be sure as your dress he will actually become your life. But don't forget that you are not this new man, that you must let him live his own life for you. You must not try to take credit for him, you must not butt in. Be glad that he is there to do what he does. And do not cease to be grateful.

The second point for our attention is this: Just as a dress that we are permitted to put on, this new man is useful and beautiful. For he was intended for you and cut to your measurement, and you will not regret accepting him and putting him on. You will live well and happily in him.

We should, for instance, consider this: If it should come true that we in our genuine and justified anger be constantly on guard so that the devil can gain no ground, if we no longer offend the Holy Spirit with the vile words that come from our mouths, if instead we are enabled to speak words that build rather than tear down, that help rather than hinder, that raise rather than destroy, if we are enabled to speak words that help those who hear them, words that—as it says literally in our text—communicate grace, if we should succeed in driving a real, even though a very small, wedge between ourselves and the world of bitterness, of harshness and evil-speaking, dear friends, be not deceived, something very real is then happening in our lives. The south wind which caused your recurrent headaches and asthma ceases to blow. Then you are no longer alone, and you must no longer feel alone, useless and empty. Then you can defy the forces of the enemy. It is the new man, your dress, in which you may quietly and safely live, and, what is even more important—quietly and safely die. And more yet: your life in the name of the new man will without doubt become radiant. This will be revealed on the day of salvation. But do not doubt; it will be noticed even here and now—not to your glory, but nevertheless as a radiance that will really emanate from you, and will surround you with happiness, light and well being; in short: you will then have a tangible reason to be grateful that this guest came to you, that you were permitted to put on and wear this dress of the new man. For he is truly the man "created in God's image in true righteousness and holiness." And so it is a great and radiant, fruitful, living and joyful event when this new man becomes your dress.

But there is yet a third item for our consideration: The new man can really be put on by us. All in all, there is nothing that belongs to this new man of which we could truthfully say: that I cannot do. Invent no excuses! Please do not think that you are the great exception, that you alone have the right to assume that you cannot do it. No, since you are here in church and can hear it, therefore, you must listen to it: Put on the new man! Let me tell you that it is precisely *you* who are meant. You may and you will probably wonder at the glory of this promise and the extent and strictness of this commandment. But remember: it concerns precisely you! This dress is made to be put on by you!

We have come to the conclusion. But we must consider two explanations in answer to certain questions which are raised here, and I ask you to listen attentively for everything depends upon our real understanding of what we have heard.

The first question: From whence comes this remarkable and important notice that we should put off the old and put on the new man? Why is it not just remarkable and important, why so immediate and so forceful, and why is it not just a notice but God's word and revelation to which we must bow?

Well, at the beginning of our text we read: It is truth in Jesus. Everything else follows this double point. That it is the truth in Jesus makes it powerful, makes it the Word of God. It is truth in Jesus, which means that in Jesus the taking off of the old man and the putting on of the new becomes necessary. In him no other way is possible. Since in him both were prepared for us, yes, in a certain sense, already accomplished for us, so that since we belong to him, since we are called through him and to him, baptized in his name—it cannot be otherwise than that now it shall come to pass in us.

When Jesus died he took upon himself all our sin and shame, that is, the old man took them with him into death and laid them in the grave, and at that moment our sin and shame ceased to be ours or alive. There our sin and shame became a mere dress, and it became apparent that it was rotten, henceforth a useless garment, so that it is possible and has become necessary to take it off at once.

And when Jesus rose from the dead he created and gave life to our righteousness and holiness, so that it is no longer his alone, but also ours and as such powerful, so that His righteousness and holiness have become the new dress intended for us and designated for our use. Now it has become possible and essential to put it on.

Dear Congregation, everything which we have heard has its reason in the fact that we were disrobed in Jesus' death and were again clothed at Jesus' Resurrection. It is the truth in Jesus that we should take off the old and put on the new man. Without Jesus one could not say that. In Jesus and in the mystery of our calling through him and to him, in the mystery of baptism in his name which we have all received because he is our Lord and our head, it is true, urgent and powerful as the Word of God and we cannot oppose it.

And the second question that you ask is: Well, who are we then, who am I, if I am neither the old nor the new man? Yes, that is a good question! The answer can be very short. You are he or she, you are the being who belongs to Jesus and to whom the truth in Jesus has once again been preached, to whom it has once again been said that we should take off the old man, put on the new. Do you need to know more about yourself? Of course, no sermon, be it long or short, can proclaim that you are really the one who heard this and then obediently became that which was told him as truth in Jesus. That is the work of God. For it says, with good reason, that our inner being is renewed through the Spirit. Amen.

# The Fate of Man—What Hope for the Future?

RABBI JOSHUA LOTH LIEBMAN

*Temple Israel, Boston, Massachusetts*

*Dr. Liebman, rabbi of Temple Israel, is considered one of the leading radio preachers in America. His sermons for the past six years over the NBC coast to coast hook-up and CBS are listened to by millions. On Sundays, Dr. Liebman preaches to the six New England States with an audience of between a million and two million worshipers.*

*He serves as university preacher at Harvard, Cornell, Vassar, Dartmouth, Wellesley and other leading universities. He has the distinction among American rabbis of serving as visiting professor on two important faculties; he is visiting professor of philosophy in the Graduate School of Boston University and visiting professor of Jewish philosophy and literature at Andover-Newton Theological Seminary.*

*Rabbi Liebman's special field of work is in Jewish philosophy, in which field he received his doctorate after studying at the Hebrew University in Jerusalem and the Hebrew Union College in Cincinnati. He is a leading Zionist and serves as a member of a number of Zionist boards and committees. Dr. Liebman has been for the last several years a member of the Governor's Committee on Racial and Religious Understanding, appointed by the Governor of Massachusetts, and is the chairman of the Governor's Committee of Clergymen.*

*He is the author of* Peace of Mind, *which in May, 1946, was the selection of the Religious Book Club and which has created a great deal of interest during recent months. Rabbi Liebman is a member of the National Hillel Commission of B'nai B'rith, a member of the Zionist Organization of America, and served during the war as a member of the Committee on Army and Navy Religious Activities directing the Jewish chaplaincy work for the United States government.*

*He studies the fate of man, sees hope in the wise use of the "resources now at our disposal" if we fulfill our moral responsibilities; we have a chance of laying the foundations of world peace and removing "the toothache in man's heart" if we will.*

# Sermon Thirty=five

TEXT:   But the word is very nigh unto thee, in thy mouth, and in thy heart, that thou mayest do it.   DEUTERONOMY 30:14

THIS morning I draw for you and for myself the portrait of the world today as one individual sees it with none of its dark shadows minimized and none of its rays of hope neglected. I want to discuss the dangers that confront us, and the hopes that we can realistically discover for human survival.

The words of the great German-Jewish poet Heinrich Heine, "My love, there is a toothache in my heart," express the feeling of sensitive human beings everywhere. There is a toothache in our heart as we read John Hersey's tragic story of Hiroshima—an ache for all of the burned flesh, the weakened bodies, the ruined families among the innocent in Japan. There is a toothache in our heart for many oppressed and hungry peoples, and above all for orphaned and betrayed Jewish people of Europe yearning for the justice of home and dignity in Palestine.

There is an ache in our heart as we confront the spectacle of bitterness and rivalry among the nations of the world and the haunting fear of a new war between great powers of the earth. "My love, there is a toothache in my heart"—the heart of man who has eaten of the fruit of the tree of knowledge and does not know how to transmute the poison of atomic insight into the healing medicine and the nourishing food of world-wide security and life.

Now the dangers confronting us are very real—dangers of physical destruction through war, and also of psychological panic driving us on to war. Recently I spoke at a conference of atomic scientists, and religious leaders; during the sessions I heard a world-famous physicist explain some basic truths about this new atomic age. He said in effect that there is no secret about the atomic bomb that can be kept for any real length of time, that the real secret was whether it could be created at all, but that now that the world knows it is possible, nations in the near future in other parts of the earth will definitely be able to create their own atomic weapon. Not only is there no real secret, but there is no real defense, for if, the Lord forbid, two thousand bombers ever would come to America with two hundred cities as their targets, enough of those planes could get through to destroy a vital part of our nation. Revenge forces we could have to retaliate, but that retaliation would be small consolation indeed to the millions of dead Americans. There must come true international control of atomic energy since there is no long time secret, no adequate defense, and no genuine security for any people save in the end of war itself.

The real dangers of atomic warfare, not to mention biological warfare, cannot be exaggerated, but what can be exaggerated is man's inability to control and master these dangers. Panic fear can sometimes paralyze us into doing nothing or hypnotize us into doing the wrong thing. This kind of group panic must be avoided now for the menace of war will never be solved by hysteria, but only by courage and maturity.

Can man avoid the supreme catastrophe of another war? Pessimists and cynics say "No," maintaining that human nature is primarily aggressive, brutal and evil, that man is just as attracted to war as the moth is attracted to the consuming flame. If this is the whole truth about man, then we ought to resign ourselves to the murder of the earth with titans draining one another's blood with the knives of atomic radiation and nations acting as leeches cupping the body of mankind, the red and white corpuscles of life. I do not believe that this is the whole story about man, and therefore I have hope, conditional hope, for the human future. I do not believe the pessimists because of what my religion, Judaism, teaches about man, and what the science of psychology verifies today about the correctness of the Jewish intuition.

Long centuries ago, Judaism proclaimed that human nature is a kind of undifferentiated raw material with two major impulses striving for supremacy —the self-assertive instinct wrestling with the social instinct; it depends upon the individual's personal decisions and his social environment as to whether the good and the social aspect of his potentialities will triumph over the destructive and aggressive drives of his character. Judaism thousands of years ago asserted the faith that man is not either simple evil nor simple goodness, but that he can become good through proper education, social law, spiritual inspiration—that he can come to adjust his selfish desires to the larger needs of the social welfare. Man is educable, malleable, transformable. "But the word is very nigh unto thee, in thy mouth, and in thy heart, that thou mayest do it."

Is this faith of Judaism in the potentialities of man naïve, Utopian, sublimely foolish? This is no academic question. This is the most important question before society today. If man is something more than a killer then we ought to learn under what circumstances and conditions he has been taught to master his antisocial instincts in the interests of law and love and life. If we turn to social scientists like Susan Isaacs in London, or the brilliant thinker, Ranyard West in his new work "Conscience and Society," we will find that the psychological laboratories and psychiatric clinics do give us a message of hope and verify not the total pessimism of the skeptic nor the naïve optimism of the dreamer, but the courageous realism of Judaism.

What is human nature? The brilliant child psychologist of London, Susan

Isaacs, gives us a scientific answer after years of experiment with young children. Normal little boys and girls living and playing together under all types of circumstances constitute a sample of human nature as universally true as a piece of matter in the physicists' laboratory reveals the truth about atoms and electrons applicable all over the world. These children displayed every kind of attitude, threatening and bullying and also loving and co-operating. A little war almost occurred in that nursery in a battle over the tricycle. Each one wanted it and refused to share it and there were hatred and selfishness there until the impartial authority above them all, Susan Isaacs, imposed rules for the use of the tricycle, and then since they all had shares in this great good, the little boys and girls ceased fighting, lost their enmity and began to co-operate. Under the impartial law and fair justice of the higher authority, the adult mother-figure, these normal children learned to control their selfishness and cruelty and to play, work and live together co-operatively. Human beings, as these children testify, are not only afraid of the violence of others, but of their own violence and can come to feel secure only under the impartial authority of some greater power. There is a tremendous aggressiveness and at the same time a tremendous co-operativeness in the human spirit, a deep need for social approval and friendship and love. Judaism is right. We are what those children are, both potentially cruel, and potentially co-operative; which potentiality will be realized depends upon the incentives of society and the safeguards of law.

What is true about children is likewise true about adults. The majority of normal men and women have learned to repress their aggressive and murderous instincts; if this were not true, we would not have occasional murders in families and violence in cities, but we would have a jungle everywhere. Within the national boundaries of such democracies as America or Switzerland or Britain, which phase of human nature predominates—the murderous or the constructive trend of psychic life? Within these national boundaries most men and women have learned to domesticate their aggressive and destructive impulses rather well, have achieved a sufficient degree of self control and mutual control within the small circle of the home, the school, the factory, the state and national government. The very existence of society at all is the proof that man can master his dark nature and build a co-operative existence. If man were what the pessimists say that he is, primarily a beast, and a destroyer, and only incidentally a builder, then we would have no law and no courts, no schools or roads, no music and no medicine, no science and no religion, all of which are the children of man's social rather than his antisocial impulses. The undeniable achievement of man's social nature and the many-dimensioned fear and shame of normal men and women about their self-assertive and aggressive impulses are two great witnesses to the truth that the human species is not hopeless. The sociability of man and his very guilt feelings about his inner aggressiveness are attorneys for the defense of man's potential goodness. Oh, it is true that from time to time the primitive in us

[203]

throws off its chains and growls in hate and anger at the world. Occasionally the bully in us wins a *coup d'état* against the established government of the mind and then violence and irrationality rule us. Occasionally the criminal and the tyrant overthrow society and the gangster comes to rule in the chancellery of power, but these tyrannies of the primitive have the seeds of their own destruction within them. Established decency does return from its exile to reassert its authority. Man within the limits of democracy has learned to subordinate his baser nature under the impact of law and the inspiration of conscience.

This is not just theory. We know today the thrilling story of how the majority of the Dutch people under the inspiration of conscience and law rose in defense of the Jews, fought many great battles against the Nazis and kept faith with human idealism even under all of the temptations of a barbaric climate. Man, as the Dutch have shown, can resist all of the seductions of savagery even while weaker peoples succumb to the lure of the jungle.

What then is the basic truth about human nature? It is that man has learned to control himself and his destructive instincts rather well in the circle of the family, the neighborhood, the city and the state. It is in the international realm where this is no effective law that man acts like a savage. Yet what has been done in past centuries by man in the small circle of the family, the city and the nation can and must be achieved in the international realm in the building of world law and world government. Why should we despair? If the task were absolutely new and no previous successes had been recorded we might be terrified, but the domestication of man has succeeded quite well in so many other areas and on so many smaller stages. The stage today is world-wide. Within democratic nations men have learned not to take the law into their own hands but to possess a law that transcends each individual—a law that would protect us not only against the violence of others but against our own inner temptations to violence, a law not to be vetoed by any of the parties to a dispute. Like the children in Susan Isaacs nursery—we are all of us in need of discipline and an impartial authority transcending our partial judgments and our insistent demands.

The supreme and greatest hope of the human race is a world government that will begin quite possibly out of the Baruch Atomic proposals and that will achieve more and more power to do for the world what the United States government does for all of the forty-eight states. We dare not be defeatist and fatalistic about this hope. A limited world government is no illusion and no impossibility. While some people will continue to think in old terms of their vested interests, their land, their money, their flag, their ideology, there are enough people among the leaders and the followers in every country to recognize that a new day is here and that there is no hiding place deep enough in the earth for a banker, an oil magnate, a millionaire, or a commissar to hide his children and himself, if the bombs begin falling or the germs begin choking the windpipe of life. The very biological instinct for self-preservation, the psychological drive of which Freud spoke many times toward larger and larger unity, the scientific and social necessity of "one world or none" will make it possible for man who has shown himself throughout history a creature gifted with the power to adjust to new reality to lay the foundations of a world government. Mothers and fathers will not long give their loyalty to a way of life that will not protect them and their children against destruction but they will give their loyalty to a world law and world power and world government just as they learned how to obey the smaller law of the city and the state. There is nothing difficult about such a transfer of loyalty. Millions of immigrants coming to America in the nineteenth century achieved miraculously speedy loyalty to their new homeland even before they could speak English because America represented the ideal of justice and opportunity and security. Today no national sovereignty can give either that justice or that security, and when the peoples of the world come to see this truth, the human urge for self-preservation and the psychological drive for life will combine to make possible a new loyalty to the Parliament of Man. Men will come to fear the loss of love and approval and security from the international world father—world government—and out of that fear of punishment and yearning for approval will be created a world-conscience.

There is no reason why man cannot extend the frontiers of his patriotism to the world under the flag of mankind guided by impartial rules of international justice and enforced by world power.

The dangers are real, the hopes are also real. We set before ourselves the one goal for mankind, the attainment of a world federation stronger than the United Nations that will give every human being security and freedom from war and want.

The resources are here—physical science, social science and a profound religion that can teach us the lessons of human personality and life as prior to all ideologies and human persuasion rather than force as the means and infinite patience as the technique whereby different systems of government and of economics can live side by side on the same street of destiny. America, Russia, Britain and China shall have to live on the same street of destiny or we shall all perish in the same dust.

Each one of us now bears the responsibility of decision—to think critically, to act liberally and courageously and to feel decently and nobly triumphing above all hate in our hearts and washing our emotions clean of any prejudice against any group, religion or nation.

If we shall wisely use the resources now at our disposal and fulfill the great moral responsibilities that now confront us we have a good chance of ending "the toothache in the heart" of mankind and of laying the foundations of a world which can yet become "the Tabernacle of Peace" for all mankind.

# The Neeö anö Task of the Church in Germany

REVEREND MARTIN NIEMÖLLER, D.D.
*Pastor, the Church at Dahlem-Berlin, Germany*
*(the German Confessional Church)*

*Even the infamous Dachau Concentration Camp did not dim the glory of the Gospel for Martin Niemöller. For eight years he was the special prisoner of Adolf Hitler, because he dared to oppose the excesses and oppressions of the Nazi regime. As pastor of the famous wealthy parish of Dahlem, a suburb of Berlin, he worked and preached between the two world wars. He was arrested in 1937 for his opposition to National Socialism and after his trial in 1938, he was taken to Sachsenhausen Concentration Camp. Three years later he was moved to Dachau, where nearly a quarter of a million people were exterminated by the Nazis in their upward rush for power. He could have been released at almost any time if he would have signed an agreement not to preach.*

*During World War I he had been a U-boat commander, but dared in the 1930's to oppose his own people when justice and liberty for Church and people were threatened. For the first four years at Dachau he was kept in solitary confinement and was not even permitted to have religious services until just a few months before the Nazi collapse, when monthly services were permitted for a small group of special prisoners. The sermons he preached on these monthly occasions have been printed under the title, Dachau Sermons. He was finally liberated by the American forces in May, 1945.*

*Since the war, he has worked to help his people rehabilitate themselves and to bring about international understanding; has spoken all over Germany, in Switzerland and the United States. He is one of the present leaders of the Evangelical Church in Germany, is its vice-president, is especially interested in ecumenical relations and is the representative of his church on the World Council of Churches. From December, 1946, to April, 1947, he toured the United States, speaking in the leading cities from coast to coast on themes similar to the sermon given here.*

*"The Need and Task of the Church in Germany" was given in the Cathedral in Zurich, Switzerland, on Sunday, March 7, 1946, and was also preached in Bern and Basel for thousands of people. It shows the thinking of a leading German clergyman on the position of the German church and the German people. His frank recognition of the shortcomings and the guilt of the Christian Church in Germany has done much to bring understanding to thousands of people in Germany, Switzerland and the United States.*

*Pastor Niemöller studied theology at the University of Münster (West-*

*falen), 1920-23. He received the honorary D.D. from Eden Theological Seminary in 1934, from Pine Hill Divinity School in 1946, and also from the German University of Göttingen in 1946. Before going to Dahlem in 1931, he spent seven years as executive secretary of home missions in Westfalen (Westphalia).*

## Sermon Thirty=six

The Grace of our Lord Jesus Christ, and the Love of God, and the Communion of the Holy Ghost be with you all.  Amen.

Let us listen to four Words of Holy Writ:

"Wherefore doth a living man complain, a man for the punishment of his sins?"  LAMENTATIONS 3:39

"If we confess our sins, he is faithful and just to forgive us our sins, and to cleanse us from all unrighteousness."  I JOHN 1:9

"Therefore being justified by faith, we have peace with God through our Lord Jesus Christ."  ROMANS 5:1

"Beloved, if God so loved us, we ought also to love one another."  I JOHN 4:11

I AM to speak about the need of the church in Germany. This need became apparent to me the very moment in June of last year when, having become a free man again after eight years' imprisonment, I stood on a street in Frankfort on the Main among the ruins of this old German city which had been a center of commerce, of intellectual life and of culture. And yet the ruins and the destruction are only outward characteristics of the real need, a need which, a year ago, one could not yet have estimated in its entire significance and one which even today cannot completely be surveyed. Millions and millions of people live in cellars and holes. This is an outward sign for the seeing and searching eye that there is nowhere evidence of real improvement in the past eight months. What the examining eye of the body notices, this the inspecting eye of the soul also notices. It is not only that in Germany a people now exists that has no further hope for its economic and physical future. This people that earns its living surrounded by ruins is also a people that does not know spiritually which way to turn. Time and again we Germans have become idealists and have turned everything into ideas and ideals. But whoever travels through Germany today will find instead of the ideas only empty concepts and in the place of the ideals of yesterday and the past only despondency if not utter despair.

Concerning the German spiritual attitude, people talk today, not without good reasons, about the threatening or actually present nihilism. There exist no values any more: Happen what may, it really does not matter at all! This is the present-day outward spiritual face of the German people, as

*[ 207 ]*

it presented itself to me during the last ten months. And these are the people with whom the Christian Church of Germany has to deal. One should think that such a catastrophe, which does not spare anything, in which all the concepts of property and economy, of future and hope, collapse completely, would out of the depth of his despair and his despondency make man reach with all his remaining strength for a message, which attributes to itself the title "Good Tidings"; that people will again open their ears to the message of the Christian Church, that it must result in a revival.

Up to this present hour the anticipated Christian revival in all Germany has not occurred. The Church still exists. The Church even seems to have escaped the chaos of the last twelve years almost untouched and undamaged. In the big cities, indeed, no church building is left standing but in the country the churches still remain, and in the big cities emergency measures are taken for the proclamation of the Gospel. Yet, the people who get together for worship are the same people who some two, three, four, five, six years ago went to church. Here and there, there is perhaps a new worshiper, but he stays away again after a short time. The need of the Church in Germany is revealed in the fact that even this tragic disturbance in the life of our people, which apparently could not have been any greater, has not been able to bring about the return of the Christian people to the Church. One can deplore this fact. One can remark: It is really a pity that this unique possibility which one could find for an inner regeneration is not used.

But, what is the cause of this? Has the Church not done her duty? Does she not offer to the searching and worrying people what she ought to offer to them? Certainly, it is not a lack of good will on the part of the Church in Germany.

For the external need, the Evangelical and Catholic churches in Germany are providing a most efficient help. In this respect, the German people under Hitler has passed through a preparatory school. The Church was forced to get accustomed to sacrifice substantial parts of her income. The "Winter-Emergency-Relief" which officially has now come to an end in Germany has been resumed again by the Christian Church. What the churches are collecting to alleviate all needs does not fall short of the *"Winterhilfswerk,"* but what is done today for the poor and worried people surpasses it by far. One needs only to remember that already many millions of people who have lost home, goods, belongings and property have come from the East of Germany, crowding into the western zones of occupation. Yet hardly any of them have to suffer more hunger than the people who are settled in these zones. All this is done and appears publicly as a charitable work of the Christian Church. Yet, in spite of all this help of the Christian Churches, there is no spiritual awakening or regeneration.

And if one asks: Does not then the Church do everything which is within her power also to get inwardly closer to these people? Then we can only answer: There is faithful preaching. The comfort of the Word of God and of the Gospel is conscientiously proclaimed according to the best of our knowledge. But with all this it seems as if it would not penetrate through the thick skin of the heart, as if it would not penetrate to the soul, as if the pastors were preaching to a wall. And the message comes back and one does not notice anything of the promise, "And shall not return in vain." This is the real need of the Church among us today in Germany: In spite of all efforts to help the neighbor in his need, to bring to him in his misery the comfort of the Word of God, in spite of all this nothing happens, nothing comes to pass. Everything remains as it was before. The people are sinking deeper and deeper into misery and despair. Misery and despair are not about to decrease, but they are at present on the increase at a rather frightening pace. Despair has already surpassed itself in the huge wave of suicide in the German East. We must reckon with the fact that such a new wave of suicide will break out amidst the cultivated West of the German zones of occupation.

Of all other worries and needs we have been liberated in Germany. This applies, for example, to the upkeep of the pastors. Formerly, it was a decisive problem: Can one venture to be the Church, to preach, if one does not know where to get the salary for the pastors? And note further that they work without salary and without food. These worries do not bear much weight.

But this is the real question: Does the Church still exist for the purpose which the Lord Jesus has appointed to her? Is she yet truly the preacher of the glad tidings? The worry about this can in the long run deprive one of sleep if one sees that without this message and without the effect of this message a whole people turn into men who not only die of hunger but who literally despair. Then this results, as it did actually result for us, in the question which God posed in our conscience: Well, tell me, you men of the Church and you pastors, is perhaps something the matter with you and your preaching, that this need, this great, great spiritual need can find no relief by that which you are preaching and proclaiming? Is this the reason that a ban rests upon the Church itself which as a matter of course sterilizes everything the Church attempts to do? Do you proclaim the Word of God impurely because of such a ban?

From thence Christian men and pastors in Germany were led to raise the question of guilt, that is, to ask if we could not be held guilty because the Word of God which we preach, that is, which we mean to preach to the people that sit in darkness, did actually bring no help, no deliverance, no salvation and no new life? "Wherefore doth a living man complain?"

Oh, one complains much in Germany even in the Evangelical Church. But we are beginning to understand that all our complaining is a sign that we think we could be discontented with God, but that in reality it is a sign that God is not content with us. "Wherefore doth a living man complain, a man for the punishment of his sins?"

And when we pastors want to proclaim the good tidings to people who are bogged down in misery, then we must face the question if we ourselves know these glad tidings, if we have heard the "glad tidings" which deal with guilt and grace, with sin and forgiveness.

In the course of the past summer it became clear to me that, first of all, I had to establish a relationship between myself and whatever misfortunes, catastrophes, afflictions and punishment happened amongst us. I saw that God has not only talked to my people and has given them a push but that God has wanted to push me too that I should regain consciousness; I realized anew how the 25th chapter of the Gospel of Matthew reveals something to me that did and would not let go of me. It is written there, and we hear it out of the mouth of the Lord Jesus Christ in regard to the way in which he will speak at the Last Day when he is going to judge the quick and the dead: "Inasmuch as ye did it not to one of the least of these, ye did it not to me" (Matthew 25:45). I did not kill anybody, and I have not delivered anybody to death; I feel in this sense as innocent of this horror as anybody else. But it became clear to me: For heaven's sake, I did not charge my sin of omission to my account. How can I once pass if Christ should also say to me: Inasmuch as ye did it not . . . "

This must also be applied to Communists who in 1933 were thrown into the concentration camps. I did not care about that and did not find it necessary to appear before the congregation and to testify by saying: Whatever is happening in this case is a big breach of law. It is a crime. Watch yourselves that you do not partake of the same guilt!—I did not say it and I did not do it, but I unconsciously acted according to the principle: "Am I my brother's keeper? Even if this brother is only a Communist?"

Here the question of guilt reveals for us Christians in Germany its horrible face. The Lord Jesus Christ asks his disciples, his Church, he asks you and me, whether we are really without guilt in regard to the horrors which came to pass in our midst. I cannot reply with a clear conscience: "Yea, Lord, I am without guilt. Thou wast in prison and I came unto Thee." Indeed, I have said: "I do not know this man."

It could be possible that Christendom in Germany carries a greater responsibility before God than the National Socialists, the Blackshirts and the Gestapo. We ought to have recognized the Lord Jesus Christ in the brother who suffered and was persecuted, regardless of whether he was a Communist or a Jew. And we did not recognize him!—Did the others know at all that they would have to see Christ in their fellow man? Are we Christians not more guilty? Am I not more guilty than some who have bathed their hands in blood?

This is the need of the Church, that in the face of these events and all this visible mountain of guilt and crime, piled up high in the midst of this world, she cannot say with a good conscience: We have done what we were obliged to do. We haven't done it. And when one becomes conscious of this fact then an immense horror comes over him, one becomes terribly shocked, so much so that sin and guilt are not merely pious phrases but definite reality, which absolutely signify to us the catastrophe, the end, and eternal death.

Consequently, we, Christians in Germany, came face to face with the question: What shall we really do?

"If we confess our sins, he is faithful and just to forgive us our sins" (I John 1:9).

If sin and guilt become so real that death, perdition and eternal damnation are at stake, then the "glad tidings" again turn actually into a joyful message on which death and life are depending. "Glad tidings" does not mean that a man is comforted for a little while, but it means salvation from death, eternal bliss for myself, the sinner, who can't hope any more so long as he doesn't know this message. Then one realizes at once: If the message of the Church can accomplish nothing among our exhausted and despondent people then this is because we have scarcely known and confessed the real "glad tidings" of the grace of God for the sinner who repents. This, in short, is the true task of the Church in Germany that we quite plainly and simply, and now also really quite clearly and impressively, bear witness before the congregation about the burden which rests upon our conscience, and about the Saviour who takes this burden away and who brings back to us peace with God. "Therefore being justified by faith, we have peace with God" (Romans 5:1). In the last ten months I have also complained against God, not only once but again and again. And when I look at my people I have asked: Lord God, are we Germans before all other people really such bad men, criminals, sadists, that this could have happened among us? Are we so much worse than the others?

Today I don't sigh like that any more. I praise and thank God that He has left to us still the "glad tidings." That he has positively sent it back to us, the grace of God presented to the sinner who knows of no salvation any more. Then all complaining ceases by itself. Then we do not ask any more if another people has the same amount of guilt and whatever reasons human self-righteousness may present. We become very grateful because God has given us His gracious creative Word of Life. And we live in peace with God. And finally our complaining ceases and there is another beginning:

"Beloved, if God so loved us, we ought also to love one another" (I John 4:11).

This means that I do not charge the other man with his sins, but that I help him with the gift God has given me. I try it at least so far as is in my power. Already one sees here and there where people suffer most they have gained a new understanding of the Word of the Redeeming Saviour. And then one sees today among us something that offers reason for hope: One sees Christian brotherly love.

At the end of October, 1945, I spent twelve days in my parish in Berlin —Dahlem, to which I had not been able to return until then. When in my parsonage, which is half shot to pieces, I came down to the kitchen for breakfast in the morning, I found a bombed out young girl occupied with preparing the breakfast. She held in her hands a loaf of bread which my wife and I had brought along from Brunswick and she began to slice the bread. She put aside the first slice. I said, "Give me that piece of bread. Don't worry I am not so spoiled that I could not eat this piece which is a little stale on one side." Thereupon she looked at me with surprise and said smilingly: "Pastor, you misunderstand me this time. The first slice of bread belongs to the refugees." I continued to ask and was informed that it has become a custom in my congregation that all households put aside the first slice of bread. The young girls then come around and gather these slices of bread and go with them out to the railway stations and highways and distribute these same slices of bread to the crowds of refugees which lie about in tens of thousands and for whose feeding no official provision has been made.

One can say: Well, is this something great? It is only a drop in the bucket. Yes, my dear friends! This congregation was once the wealthiest congregation in the German fatherland. Every year 800,000 RM were collected in church taxes. Their good taxpaying members included industrialists, business managers, presidents of banks, great artists, film actors, chemists and famous physicians. Nobody has any use for these people now. They are unemployed. Their fortunes have vanished. Their bank accounts have been frozen. Therefore, it might happen that when a pastor is visited by a millionaire his visitor might be very glad to receive a gift of 5 to 10 marks. But this is not yet the whole misery of all. These men are all unemployed people and because of that they receive the ration card of the fifth degree. At the end of October, 1945, this card was also called the "death card" because it only provided for one thousand calories a day. This card is given to the unemployed, the decrepit old folks, and to housewives. One thousand calories a day are not quite half of what a nonworking man needs to preserve his physical strength. Yet these people, who must live up to 90 per cent off the death card, each morning give away the first slice of bread to other people who, in the process of starvation, are but one step further than they themselves! People who two hours after their breakfast bend down on the street to pick up an orange peel which an American soldier has cast away. Dearly beloved! This is no "Winterhilfswerk" but this is something similar to the mite of the widow in the Gospel. This slice of bread indicates that the love of the Lord Jesus Christ, if it becomes effective in us, is stronger than death. It symbolizes that starving people do not start to devour one another as I happened to witness it in Dachau, but they share with their brother the last bit of their remaining provisions. Where this happens, I believe that one witnesses something of the power of God and of the effect of the love of Christ. In the midst of starvation and death one commences again to hope because one notices the existence of a power which does not capitulate before the death of starvation. If such a love spreads all over Evangelical Christianity in Germany then the Church in the midst of the dying people would have today a tremendous task, a beautiful task, which really finds its reward.

It will not stay at that alone. Christian love will and must also become effective otherwise. I talked about the despondent and despairing people. In my congregation two hundred people took their own lives on the day the Russians came. On that same day twenty Evangelical pastors took their own lives. I don't say this so that we might perhaps think: Well, it seems as if the Christian faith of these men has been of little value. Only the one could say it who might have successfully passed through the same trials without ever capitulating. And nobody among us has undergone such an ordeal. I say it in order to emphasize the wave of despair that is flooding everything. Why do people despair? Why do they venture to jump into the abyss? Not because they are afraid of starvation, but because they have gained the impression that life is not worth living any longer. The reason for this is not an outward ailment, but the utter despairing and desponding of mankind. The reason is most often the feeling of a man who, after he has lost everything, must pass through life far from home, a lonely refugee, who notices right and left nothing more than people, who in reality are not humans any longer; every one of these is loaded down with a heavy bag of worries and heavy blinkers before his very eyes. Everybody has only regard for his own way, and if anyone wants anything of him then the usual reply is: "Don't trouble me. Everyone has to carry his load. I have enough with my own!" People grow lonely, utterly lonely, because everyone is troubled more than enough with his own need. And this solitude is the source of despair and despondency. "If God so loved us, we ought also to love one another." If we could succeed so far (and here and there we are noticing something of that even among us) that Christian men in the midst of their own misery keep heart and eye open for the need of their neighbor; if we Christians would not repeat the mistake which we committed in 1933, that we simply did not recognize Christ when he passed by our side in the form of a needy brother-man; if the love of God opens our eyes that we meet our fellow men as we ought to meet the Saviour; then Christianity still has a task in all of Europe, which is worth while and which God can turn into a blessing for the whole continent, perhaps for the whole world, in which everything today points to the coming of the last and final catastrophe.

The whole world is desperately longing for peace. Big programs have been put before us. We have read about negotiations, plans, agreements, treaties, alliances; and the result of all this: The world today is trembling more than yesterday and yesterday more than the day before, before the fact that again and this time the last and worst catastrophe might descend upon us. Peace on earth! From where shall it come? This is part of the angel's message.

It is meant for men in whom God finds good will and who therefore can and must live together in peace.

God has given the Church a great task, a very big chance. What would it mean if in our days the world could again gain sight of the peace which rests among Christian people because love prevails among them? We have had the Ecumenical Conference in Geneva. I won't forget it as long as I live. In Geneva we met like brothers. This is a strange thing for a German who knows what Germany has meant to and for the world. It is a special thing when a German comes to Geneva and meets a Norwegian who embraces him and says: "Dear Brother! For months I have waited for this moment." If the world sees that, it should actually begin to listen and should notice that what it is looking for has become reality in a totally different corner. Peace exists. There is peace even in this world, yet only for men of good will whose hearts were opened by the Holy Spirit for the "glad tidings." There it is a tangible earthly reality! I could imagine that if Christianity so lives in Germany and elsewhere that it fulfills its tasks in the actual needs of this age to live an example of love and peace, a world peace might not actually break out, but the Lord Jesus Christ could once again in our days accomplish an enormous draught of fishes and that once more a really great revival could result.

I will never forget, and it will always remain as a promise with me, what happened among us in the prison cells of Dachau during Christmas, 1944. The non-Roman Catholic inmates were permitted to hold a divine service, the Roman Catholic Christians having their own. Altogether we were fifteen special prisoners, seven of us were non-Catholic, and among these seven I was the only pastor. I was expected to conduct a service in one of the cells. I was not merely the only pastor, but also the only German. They were an English colonel, a Dutch minister of war, two Norwegian ship owners, a Serbian diplomat and a Macedonian journalist.

It was on the 22nd of December that we received permission for the service. In my cell, I asked myself: How can I proclaim the Christmas message to these six men so that the fact that I am a German does not from the start invalidate its effect? They all belong to nations which are filled with a glowing hatred of anything that is German!

Turning this over in my mind, I sat in my cell on December 24, and did not know what I should do and how I should begin. Then there was a knock and in came the Dutch minister of war, accompanied by his S.S. guard, and said: "It will sound strange to you. I have come to speak to you in the name of tonight's congregation. We six have a big request for you. We would like to take Holy Communion with you after the sermon." And there, on Christmas, 1944, in the midst of war we celebrated Holy Communion together, Englishman, Norwegian, Dutchman, Serb, Bulgarian and one German. "Peace on earth to men of good will," to men, who through Jesus Christ the Saviour of sinners, have been given the Peace with God.

There we have all in one, dear friends, the need and task of the Church
in Germany. God grant that we recognize this task in the midst of all
need, that we take hold of it, and that we pray and work for its progress
in our midst. Amen.

# The War of Ideas

REVEREND J. BLANTON BELK, D.D.

*Minister, St. Giles' Presbyterian Church, Richmond, Virginia*

*Dr. Belk was born in Chatham, Virginia, in 1893, the son of a distin-
guished minister of the Southern Presbyterian Church. Two of Dr. Belk's
younger brothers also entered the Christian ministry and one sister is a
missionary in China. He attended Davidson College for two years, then
for twenty-six months he served in World War I as a lieutenant of artillery,
commanding the 8th Anti-Aircraft Battery with the A.E.F. in France.*

*After the war he entered the University of South Carolina and after
graduating there took his theological training at Columbia Theological
Seminary. In 1927 Rollins College conferred upon him the Doctor of Divinity
degree. He was pastor of First Presbyterian Church, Orlando, Florida, and
First Presbyterian Church, Huntington, West Virginia. He has been pastor
of the influential St. Giles' Presbyterian Church of Richmond, near the
campus of the University of Richmond, since 1937. He is in demand as a
speaker to college students and has participated in many successful preaching
missions.*

*As president of the Richmond Ministerial Union in 1946, he inaugurated
a movement to create a specialized court to deal exclusively with cases in-
volving divorce. He is now chairman of the Richmond Area Public Solicita-
tion Review Board. For twelve years he has served as chaplain in the Virginia State Legislature. His effort toward Christianizing American industry
has brought into his church leading labor leaders, as well as industrialists.
He has been a leader in efforts to improve conditions of minority groups.
He recently published a volume of sermons entitled* Our Fighting Faith.

*"The War of Ideas" sets forth the continual battle between the forces of
good and evil. The struggle against greed, lust and hate, against materialism
and communism and fascism. It shows the failures of the democracies and
of the divided churches. It shows how to fight for true freedom. Moral breakdown, confusion and division may turn our victory into defeat unless there is
a return to true religion on the part of every man, woman and child.*

[215]

# Sermon Thirty=seven

TEXT: Make me as one of thy hired servants.   LUKE 15:19

A BRILLIANT young WAVE, wearing the bars of a full lieutenant, came home recently from Pearl Harbor on terminal leave. "Postgraduate work and marriage will have to wait," she said. "I have some ideas this country needs." She is putting them down in black and white. "The real war is not over," she continued, "just because the big naval guns are now silent."

Ideas are powerful things. Two of them are battling now for world control. The forces of materialism are organized on a world front. The free spirit of man is under attack as never before in many centuries. That WAVE, like many other Americans, is seeing clearly this more important moral line of battle.

An aviator was shot down over London. His brother said he was fighting for the homes of the poor people of East Ham—he couldn't bear to see so many houses laid flat by the German blitz. But what of the homes in America laid waste by divorce? Bitter feelings and infidelity are more destructive than bombs. Starving children abroad present a tragic picture. But what of the emotionally starved and frustrated children who come from broken homes with two strikes against them when they are born! War criminals go to their death in Germany. But what of the Senate's investigation of graft and waste at home? High commands aimed their military might at industrial centers. But class hatred and selfishness have scuttled American production.

During the military struggle even our children had maps on which they could plot the positions of our advancing armies. It isn't so simple to plot the line of the moral battle. But the issue is more important. To lose our own national character while fighting for freedom! To become enslaved by lust and greed while winning the war of arms! To suffer defeat through division and hate while trying to unite the nations.

We have lived in a generation of world surprises. Unbelievable events have dulled our capacity to be startled. So we are not surprised that six million criminals are abroad in the United States, or that juvenile delinquency has reached an all-time high. Or that inflation is threatening our national credit. Or that sixty millions now are regularly using alcohol. No, such things do not surprise us. But the climactic surprise might well be for us suddenly to discover that having won a military victory abroad, we had lost the battle for the soul of our own country here at home.

Materialism does not fight always in the open. It infiltrates and uses fifth column tactics. It blinds and spreads confusion. It works in good people as well as in evil people. It permeates a country's educational system. It sneaks into the Church and divides. It masquerades behind "fronts." It discredits leadership. It raises false issues. It encourages the young to fling away discretion, to scorn discipline, and to look contemptuously at moral codes. It stirs up class hatred and racial prejudice. It inculcates in everyone a philosophy of "Gimme." It makes the palm itch, and tempts with easy money. It thrives on soft and indulgent living. It hates God and seeks to marshal the energies of a nation. Its aim is nation and world control. It has become rampant today, and is organized behind national ideologies—just when the most destructive power known to man has been put into our hands.

Of course it is an old struggle. It began in the Garden of Eden. It built a golden calf at Mt. Sinai. It plotted successfully at the trial of Jesus. It has emerged at a thousand points in history. But never before has it been able to organize the millions on such a world front. The breakdown of individual faith and character on a colossal scale has crystallized now into a war of ideas that is splitting the planet into two armed camps. The fighting may not be with guns. Bullets cannot destroy a wicked idea. The democracies must give the world an inspired ideology and a fighting faith or perish. But the war is on!

In 1917 there were two men in Europe with burning hatred in their hearts. One was a corporal in the German army. His hatred of the democracies was so intense that for a while he actually lost his sight. The other was being secretly guarded by the Gestapo in Switzerland. His name was Lenin. The military strategists of Germany had this man carried to the Russian border in a sealed car under heavy guard. They felt he could produce a revolution behind the czar's army. And they were right. Lenin changed the character of his country forevermore. He decided to replace the rule of one class by the rule of another. He loathed the wealth and pomp of the czars. He hated the luxury and indolence of the sated upper class. "He saw high society urging Christian ideals upon the masses and accepting the morals of the barnyard for themselves." He saw starvation and poverty against the background of selfish indifference. His dynamic energy has not often been equaled. His revolution swept the country and a cruel and godless dictatorship rose above the ruins of a decadent social order.

Communism sent a chill of horror throughout Europe. The peasants' weapons have often been pitchforks. The owning class was simply liquidated. The cultured intelligentsia were sent either to their graves or to Siberia. Fifteen million Russians were put to death. No wonder all Europe trembled! The idea of one man got legs—millions and millions of legs—and all the world began to be afraid.

Down in Italy an adventurer saw his opportunity. In the face of such a threat he offered the terrified bankers, industrialists, editors and government officials a program. "The answer to Communism," he said, "is Fascism." They had no other plan. They were like drowning men clutching at a straw.

Supported by these powerful factors, this adventurer began to inspire the multitudes. He had strong lungs. He soon became the most powerful man in Italy. He could even snap his fingers in the faces of men who gave him power. Even the king grovelled at his feet. The nation was enslaved. Led by this false alternative an old and beloved country started down the road to ruin.

But not before the German corporal saw how to implement his own idea. National Socialism was also born out of the womb of fear. The church in Germany was hopelessly divided. Bitter disputes in high ecclesiastical circles made a united front impossible. Unemployment had done its debilitating work. Promiscuity and homosexuality had ravaged the cities and universities. Bitter resentment against international injustice was fanned to white heat. The nation was bankrupt. The people were discouraged. For Hitler it was the moment of opportunity. He had a program to offer. With Lenin it was the rule of the masses. With Mussolini it was the dream of empire. But with Hitler it was the rule of the master race. Freedom was submerged and this nation too was enslaved. In a sense the people had asked for it. Dictatorship always moves into a nation on the waves of moral decadence.

The Western democracies might well thank God that for a season the Nazi-Fascist powers grappled with Russian Communism. Save for this fortunate circumstance the liberty of the world might have been destroyed for generations to come. What the average American is now beginning to see is that these dictatorships are the same thing under different masks. No wonder that for a while in 1939 they joined hands, for they are cousins under the skin. There is no liberty where they rule. Labor unions are reduced to slavery. Wealth is confiscated. No man owns himself. Life becomes a living death. The free spirit of man sinks beneath the deadening tyranny of materialism. True Americans despise them both. They cut across everything we hold dear.

The military war is over. Nazism lies bleeding. Communism may hide its full intention behind an iron curtain. But what we are sure of now is this: A bad idea cannot be stopped by armies or navies. Dictatorship is very much alive and on the march. Tanks and battleships, airplanes and bombs cannot defeat a wicked idea. Only a better idea can do that. Do we have one?

The answer is, Yes! It was born 1900 years ago. Then it gripped the hearts of a few. The Founder had said, "Ye shall know the truth and the truth shall make you free." He liberated men. He gave them a taste of freedom. It meant freedom within—freedom from fear, from hate, from greed, from the lusts of the flesh, and from the vanities of life. He freed men into glorious liberty. Even slaves found it. Women found it. Little children found it. One of the statesmen of that first century put it this way: "Stand fast therefore in the liberty wherewith Christ hath made you free." Christ's followers became the free men of the world. They gave to the word "freedom" its basic meaning.

"If the Son shall make you free, ye shall be free indeed!" they cried, as they took the message to the masses. People loved it. They stood ready to die for it. Even in an empire where, like Germany and Russia, the state became god, these followers of Christ were free. Their minds were free, their bodies were free, their souls were free. These liberated men and women dared to live in the very shadow of Nero's palace! Here was spiritual force! Here was a conquering philosophy that filled men with a passion and gave them a program. No wonder the Christian flag came to fly above the city of the Caesars! Here was the answer to every "ism."

For a thousand years this vital and revolutionary Christian idea was nursed within the bosom of the Church. At times even the Church itself became dictatorial but the idea always emerged triumphant. Through every form of tyranny it has fought its way back to the front. Today it offers the only alternative to materialism.

Shortly after the Bible was translated into the Elizabethan English of the seventeenth century, King Charles I came down to the British House of Commons with an armed guard. He came to arrest five members who had offended him. He strode in and demanded to know where these men were. No one spoke. Actually a lady had warned them, and they had paddled across the Thames a few minutes before. The angry king addressed the speaker, Mr. Lenthall, and ordered him to deliver his offending subjects. The speaker dropped to his knees, but refused to give any information, saying that he had "Neither eyes, nor ears, nor mouth, save with the permission of the House of Commons."

So at the very risk of life Parliament established the sovereignty of free people over kings and dictators. That was the last time a British king ever entered the House of Commons.

That was but part of the marching of the great idea. It crossed over to Jamestown. On June 20, 1610, a pastor stood among the ragged, half-starved pioneers and appropriated the words of God: "I will make of thee a great nation—and in thee shall all the families of the earth be blessed." The shell of an ancient Jamestown church still stands on the lonely little island down the river below Richmond. Ten years later in the hold of the *Mayflower* the torch bearers of freedom began to write: "In the name of God, Amen. We whose names are written—having undertaken for the glory of God and for the advancement of the Christian faith—do solemnly and mutually in the presence of God and one another covenant and combine ourselves together into a civil body—." That is the idea! That idea alone stands athwart the path of the tyrant and the dictator. America at its best has always echoed the burning words of Patrick Henry: "Give me liberty, or give me death." This is our heritage. This is why we despise the "isms." But do we see our danger? Have we grown soft and apathetic? Are we overfed and contented? Have we lost our passion for freedom? Is materialism working from underneath and from within? Is the very thing we hate growing more powerful in our very midst?

How do nations like ours lose their liberty? Is there a clew—some penetrating diagnosis that can arouse us to our peril? The national implication of the parable of the prodigal son is as fresh as though it were in yesterday's paper. That son was free—free to do anything he pleased. That is what freedom means. The father was willing for his son to experiment with freedom. The boy abused it. He became a waster. That is the meaning of "prodigal." He did as he pleased with what was his own. He wasted his money. He wasted his time. And he wasted something more precious than both—his character. Just so, a nation that wastes its resources comes at last to waste its very soul.

Most people coming from abroad are soon impressed with this terrible spirit of waste. Think of the man hours being wasted today. Think of the lives wasted on our highways. Think of the government's waste of our tax money. We may never know the extent of waste in war material. If ever there was a prodigal nation on the face of this earth, it is America. While most of the world is hungry, we waste enough food to feed the starving children of Europe. Character is cheap. Virtue is cheap. Human life is cheap. But strangely enough inflation has made the necessities of life increasingly dear. It is a strange commentary that in this land of plenty things are hard to get. We are not concerned greatly about it now, but at any moment something might happen to bring us to our senses. The prodigal son at last "came to himself." A terrible depression swept over the country and he was caught.

We have had frequent crises in America. Sometimes it has been a war. More often it has been a depression. Millions of Americans have been like this prodigal son, hungry and destitute—seeking a job as menial as "feeding swine."

At such a time men wake up! So does a nation. And people begin to wonder. They begin to blame the system, to complain of the government, to sit moodily and grow more and more resentful. They remember the times when they had food. They begin to doubt the value of freedom. Freedom got the prodigal son in such a fix! And he planned to say to his father: "Make me as one of thy hired servants"!

This is the cry of a man who had misused his freedom and who hesitated to take it back again. For what freedom had brought to him was want. Somehow it hadn't worked. There had been a joker in the pack. Something had tricked him. Freedom was to him then certainly not worth dying for. As a matter of fact, it wasn't even worth being hungry for. Most men today, morally defeated, would choose food before liberty. What we have seen in our generation is nation after nation doing it.

The prodigal son, having misused his freedom, wanted a superintendent, a manager, a guardian, someone to tell him what to do, and to give him what he needed. That is exactly what can happen to a prodigal nation in a crisis. For when a nation, having misused its freedom, starts the long road back and cries: "Make me as one of thy hired servants," some dictator will be listening around the corner of the house and will take it seriously.

Anyone appraising the moral crisis in America today would probably go back to 1918. Postwar America was getting under way. There was a general breakdown in our standards of conduct. It was the period of the "flapper" and the "lounge lizard." The old codes of ethics were tossed overboard. In all these twenty-eight years the downward moral drift has been steady and uninterrupted.

In one of the institutions of our city where young unmarried mothers go to have their babies, a social worker noticed a little girl in a pink summer dress: "She is thirteen," she said. And the matron's eyes were wet. "Her baby is due in two months. She was double-dating with her own mother." And then she added, "It is no longer an uncommon thing in Virginia." Why should we blind our eyes to the facts? We have had twenty-eight years of steady downward drift. What will stop it?

Gambling during the first World War broke the monotony and furnished a bit of excitement for the soldiers. Maybe that had something to do with it. Maybe it was the "get-rich-quick-Wallingford" stories. But suddenly after the war, the idea got around that if people were smart or lucky they wouldn't have to work. They began to give up the old ideas of thrift, hard work, and scrupulous honesty. They wanted a bonus. They prayed for a lucky break. The spiral of speculation started up. It lasted ten years. Then came the greatest financial tragedy in our history. Who will ever forget that Black Friday in October? Are we headed for another?

The prohibition experiment was a striking illustration of a free nation of self-governing citizens who could write a law which in their hearts they had no intention of obeying. Men high in government and in church had no qualms of conscience about breaking it. Disrespect of law spread rapidly. The constitution became a sort of shambles. It set the style of lawlessness. And today it is the same with traffic laws, interstate commerce laws, antitrust laws, ration laws, OPA laws, any laws. The standard of conduct seems to be: "Can I get by with it?"

Moral breakdown—laziness—disrespect for law! No wonder we were about to enter the worst depression this country ever saw. Twelve million men were idle. Grass grew in the streets of industrial cities. A prodigal nation suddenly came to itself! Democracy was put to a crucial test. Nothing short of a second World War could have united us, and given us another chance to work out our destiny. But let another depression like that one sweep our country—and we shall hear, not the cry of a disillusioned son, but the demand of a disillusioned nation for a dictator: "Make me as one of thy hired servants."

What we are asking now is just whether it is too late, or whether we can by some superhuman effort, save our freedom. Mr. David Lawrence of the United States News has stated that we have less than a fifty-fifty chance. If it can be saved we ought to do it. But how? No one surely can know all the answers. But the true answer must lie somewhere in this direction: We must rediscover the meaning of liberty.

What is liberty? The simplest definition is that it is the right to do as one pleases. Here in America we don't want any other kind. But there is a hitch in it somewhere. It is becoming increasingly clear that the right to do as one pleases depends upon one's pleasing to do what is right. The truly free people have always known that. More than any of our founding fathers, William Penn perhaps saw it clearly. Free people would never have but one choice. "Men must be governed by God or they will be ruled by tyrants!" There is no other choice. The multiplication of human laws is in direct proportion to our disregard of God's. We enjoy the right to do as we please only when we please to do what is right in the sight of God.

Once in the mountains of Virginia there was a traffic sign that would stop any motorist. It read: DANGER—FIVE DOWNHILL CURVES TO A ONE-WAY BRIDGE! The liberty a fool would demand at that point is the liberty to destroy himself and his family. A thoughtful driver would see in that sign the best possible defense of his freedom.

Think of that sign in terms of the second half of the decalogue. "Thou shalt do no murder"; "Thou shalt not commit adultery"; "Thou shalt not steal"; "Thou shalt not bear false witness"; "Thou shalt not covet."

And the words of Jesus: "Strait is the gate, and narrow is the way, which leadeth unto life, and few there be that find it."

Do we love our freedom enough to change?

There must be, too, a rediscovery of the true meaning of patriotism. For many it has meant the offering of one's life in battle and the purchase of government securities to prosecute the war. But patriotism is infinitely more than that. Dr. Frank Buchman has stated that "the true patriot today is the man who will give his life for the moral and spiritual resurrection of his country." No modern prophet has seen the issue more clearly. Every act of impurity, every act of dishonesty, every bit of covetousness weakens the sinews of our national life and makes us, even unwittingly, the allies of our enemies. Industrial strife and division, class warfare and hate are like traitors that stab our nation in the back. The issue is not political or economic. The issue is moral. Do we love America enough to change?

Religion is the only power that can change human nature. Religion can make a man see that he can be different. It can put him in touch with a superforce that can produce a miracle. Religion is as real as electricity. It can illumine the mind, warm the heart and empower the will. It is personal dealings between God and men. In the parable, the father's welcome of a sobered, humbled son made all the difference. He was not willing for his boy to live under a superintendent. He trusted him with his freedom again. He restored him to sonship.

Thinking along that line brings a person straight to Calvary. This experience of the cross changes a man. He sees everything differently. He hates what he used to love. Prodigal habits give way to disciplined living. The old philosophy of "gimme" yields to the new idea of "give." He sticks his neck out for the right kind of living. He risks the criticism of former friends. He takes a chance of losing some business. He enters the fight against materialism in all its forms. But he knows he's in a war. When he sings, "Onward, Christian Soldiers," he feels it and understands it.

No wonder Hitler sought to destroy Christianity. It stood squarely across his path to power. No wonder Stalin educated Russia with atheism for twenty-five years. The sickle had to hack the cross to pieces. Religion, true religion, is the force of the Holy Spirit remaking and uniting men and nations in a mighty crusade for liberty. Are you a part of it?

Up in Ottawa, Canada, is a baker. Some years ago he was very prosperous but he went under during the depression. As often happens, great distress turned him to God. He resolved to let God run his life and his business and told Him so. He began to get on his feet financially before the second World War started. Then some labor organizers became active in his plant. He hated labor. But he saw no connection between his bitter feeling and his religion. One day two employees whom he suspected as being labor leaders came to his office for an interview. When they left, they forgot their brief case. In a quick movement the baker rifled the contents, confirmed his suspicions, and two weeks later fired the two men as "unnecessary." They appealed to the Labor Board and the case became widely publicized. The baker stood his ground.

But one day, with his family, he confessed to a deep feeling of unhappiness and tension. In the stimulating Christian challenge of that home the truth came out. Not one member of the family tried to soften the situation. They held him to his own highest conviction. He recalled the two discharged men, confessed his dishonesty, restored them to their jobs and paid their back wages. He acknowledged his deception to the War Labor Board and the case was dropped. The plant was duly organized. A new respect and caring developed between the union and the management. Then Canada faced a crisis.

The war was on. The dark specter of inflation was hovering over the nation. The baking industry of Canada was asking for an increase of one cent a loaf. The price of wheat was rising. Labor matched this with a demand for an 11 per cent increase in pay. The vicious circle was beginning. What could be done? Some government officials remembered the simple honesty of one baker!

He was called to the capital and made Bread Administrator for the Dominion of Canada. So clear was his own mind, so free from greed and fear was his own spirit, so secure was his faith in the wisdom and power of God that he set forth on his task with a radiant heart. He appealed to management and labor both. "We all love Canada!" was his theme. They eliminated the slicing of bread and expensive wrapping. They served each other in deliveries all across the nation. Ingredients went up 27 per cent, but the price of bread in Canada stayed at prewar levels. Wages remained firm. The war was won. Inflation was arrested. An ordinary man, inspired by God, loved his country enough to change and listen to the guidance of the Holy Spirit. The result was that a whole nation's economy was kept healthy. That is religion. We must produce it quickly in America. It must start in you today—in your home tomorrow. It must get out into the nation and it must control the thinking of the world.

Someone put it this way:

> If Jesus Christ is God
> And the only God, I swear
> I will follow Him
> Through heaven and hell
> The earth, the sea and the air.

You can accept it. Or—you can skip it. But you can't avoid the battle. The war of ideas goes on. So if you refuse to fight for liberty, some day you'll find yourself on the other side—fighting against it.

## THE NEW YEAR

# A New Year and an Old World

REVEREND C. C. MARTINDALE, S.J.
*Farm Street Church (Roman Catholic), London, England*

*FATHER MARTINDALE is one of the great voices of the Catholic Church in the contemporary English-speaking world. His sermons, books and personal conferences have influenced thousands of people in England and America, yet he is still just as much interested in one individual as in a great crowd, for he realizes that even in a group the speaker must reach individual hearts and minds or his message fails of its personal and collective purpose. His plea for prayer for all men, Japanese, Jews, Russians, in the love of God is a good way to begin the New Year—any new year, or any new day.*

*Born in 1879, he entered the Jesuit novitiate, took highest classical honors at Oxford, and was ordained in 1911. He worked among soldiers during and after World War I, and has written almost without ceasing. Probably the most influential of his numerous books are Does God Matter to Me?, Essay on the Passion, Our Blessed Lady (Sermons), Poplar Leaves and Seaweed (Poems), The Faith of the Roman Church, and African Angelus. For five and one-half years he was interned in Denmark, where the events of the war had caught him.*

*Father Martindale talks knowingly of peace and justice, spirit and will, morals and motives, right and wrong, greed and guilt, of expediency and "interests," of heroism and sacrifice, of power and politics. He pleads for a peace that is a true peace, for men of conscience to live by faith. This sermon was preached in England in January, 1946. His sermons are widely accepted for their deeply spiritual messages.*

## Sermon Thirty=eight

Texts: The Spirit of God moved over the waters.   Genesis 1:2
Unless a man be born again of water and the Holy Spirit.
John 3:5

I PUT these two sentences together because Genesis is picturing the beginning of the world, and St. John, the beginning of a New World; and, because we are at the beginning of a New Year and at the ending of an Old World. That a "world" is ending, we cannot doubt. Is a New World, too, beginning?

"Chaos" is symbolized in Genesis by "water"—water without form or order, lifeless and unproductive. But then the Breath of God plunges upon it, broods upon it, divides it and puts order and life into it—life, which reaches its earthly maximum in Man. St. John, with Genesis so markedly in his mind, depicts the creation of a new world, a new Man, born in a new way, though even so, "of water and the Spirit."

Many are still asking: "What does this New Year hold? what will it bring to me?" The answer to that is: "Nothing!" We are not fatalists, passive like automata, just waiting for things to happen. The Year is a receptacle; and we approach it, having the duty to *put* something into it. Agreed—there comes along with us plenty of chaos—heaving, helpless water, with darkness upon its face. At least we must bring, we ourselves, our desire for Order; and, if we cannot create life, at least our hope to save and foster what remains and to bring it to something better.

I was always more anxious about the after-war than about the war itself. One could hear of, and anyone could foresee, a multitude of pacts, charters, conventions, promises, programs and even laws. Yet just to make those gets one no further than trying to draw a map upon the ever-shifting sea. The "spirit" must play its part, and by "spirit" I shall not mean merely the intelligence, because men certainly apply their minds to the making of such plans: I shall also mean, undoubtedly, the *will* to transfer them from paper into life; and, what is more, the general will, and a strong will; for, a weak will, or the will of a few only or even the wishes of the many, would not be enough: nor is just any kind of intelligence, however active, enough.

[ 225 ]

It has long been clear that fine ideas and noble words that correspond to them, are not enough. "Peace," "Freedom," "Unity" are on everybody's tongue: so are politico-social words that have been so cheapened, made so fluid, by misuse that they can mean almost anything, like Fascism, Democracy, Communism, and even the least educated talks of "ideologies." Have you ever tried to define what you mean by "peace"? Certainly not a mere negative—a mere nonshooting with guns! Even if we agree that "peace" is "freedom for orderly action," until the orderly action begins, "peace" thus defined is still but a "receptacle," like the New Year. And you would be hard put to it to define even "freedom"! No one claims that freedom should exclude all law. That would be anarchy. But what are the limits to lawmaking? None? Of course there are limits. In a true sense, the more laws a government makes, the worse it is, or the worse (in the sense of undisciplined, unable to govern themselves) the mass of the citizens are.

But here we have introduced the word "justice." We are evidently not speaking of what is only material, however good of its sort, like good houses or food or clothes or even of material health or comfort, and certainly not about mere money as such, but of something moral and therefore spiritual. And if I say that there is not the slightest chance of our human life being happy unless it is first and foremost moral, I am not reflecting only upon crude individual immoralities, like cruelties, frauds, adulteries, isolated acts of spite or of personal greed and grab and graft, but we must extend all that to the social and political domains. We must demand that what controls business methods must not be, primarily, the will to make the maximum profit, and that which settles political action of legislation must not be an affair of votes, or of prestige, or of power. If it be not principles of right and wrong, disaster lies ahead.

So long as we hear of group wars, class wars, cut-throat finance, cornering of commodities or forcing up of prices, of intrigue and ambition and bribery, disaster lies ahead: there is no morality there, no justice, no spirituality, and there is evidently no charity. But I have to insist on just that—on charity! When we pray that pests such as I have mentioned may be extirpated, and human society to some extent disinfected, even *that* we have to do without personal or party or nationalist spite or rancor which *always* make even the most righteous cause to become gangrened with that corruption which we deplore in what we deem unrighteous. Forgive a small reference to myself. During my five and a half years of internment, it was possible now and again to catch the echo of a voice speaking either from England or from some other country. This sometimes spoke of disputes, of strikes, of arguments pro and con. Well, in a flash you could catch alike the note of sincerity or kindliness, or, alas, that of partisan ill will, recrimination, and therefore lies. Believe me, when you are like that, homeless in mid-air, hanging between two worlds, able to believe neither the press nor placards nor conversation (when you were rash enough to embark on one), when even your friends hesitated as to what it might be prudent to say to you and would or could speak at best in terms of hints or guesswork, you really did become very sensitive to qualities of voice, to undertones unconsciously revealing states of mind—some fine and generous and honorable, others, utterly disheartening because sneering, malicious, hateful and therefore inflaming the passion of hate—clouding the intelligence, warping the will.

Ask yourselves honestly, when you look around at the dark chaotic countries of today, how often it is Right and Wrong which are asked to settle a question: how often the word "interests" crops up, instantly substituting expediency for justice: how often realism is being sacrificed to some doctrinaire system: how it is that "slogans" so rapidly succeed and contradict one another—are we not almost forced to conclude that their inventor finds them not so much helpful to me as remunerative to himself? Ask, when we insist that such or such a country must be free, if our politicians are primarily and tenderly concerned with the welfare of that country, and not rather afraid of someone else's influence there. Alas! We are today not only in the dark about half the relevant facts, but terribly unsure of motives—doubtful not only of what is being done, but of why it is being done. Does a fully and truthfully informed public mind exist? Is there a sensitive, honest and determinedly right conscience throughout each population? I cannot see it now.

Of course, this sort of thing is constantly being said, and we are no less regularly called fools for saying it, for, we are told, there is not the slightest chance of morality in the full strict and indivisible sense being applied to business at home, commerce abroad, or international politics. That will not prevent our demanding precisely that—demanding that our life, public no less than private, *shall* be "moralized," shall recognize and submit itself to a superior and eternal law—for it is not human lawyers, it is not human Parliaments that create Right and Wrong; it is not the State that may dare to define and decree what is good or evil. Righteousness has not its source in any human institution whatsoever. And where a world, or any department in it, is *not* governed by Righteousness, we revert very soon to "Power politics," as they say; to Machiavellianism; to the worship of the State; to Caesar Almighty, Lord of heaven and earth—or anyhow of earth, since he recognizes no heaven.

It is, of course, a joy to know of—and to know personally—so many men and women by no means from one nation only, who do not bow the knee to false gods: who do not worship the flesh and its cravings, nor money, nor yield to what corrupts a man quicker than almost anything else, the appetite for power: men who are not slothful nor take the easier path in act or intellectually, nor permit themselves to deceive themselves, but live according to their high ideal, relentlessly honest with themselves and their neighbor, unostentatiously generous, unselfish up to the point of self-sacrifice. Yes; in these two tragic wars we have seen how untrue was the suggestion that the mass of our people had somehow rotted, but to what utterly unsuspected and almost incredible heights of heroism they, with humble perseverance, both can and do arise. Yet there are two facts that cannot be disregarded.

The first is, that an immense amount of this heroism is evoked by a violent challenge or stimulus like the war, and weakens or disappears once that stimulus is withdrawn. This is, in many ways, quite natural, especially in the case of those who have been working too hard for too long, or have suffered and witnessed atrocious things that have blunted a man's power of reacting to anything else. One may indeed cry out that the needs of our human society are as great since the war as during it, if not greater because the issues are less clear: one might have hoped that all would put forth the maximum of unselfish co-operative zeal on behalf of the abominably suffering world, perhaps especially for the sake of countries other than their own—for if we haven't even learned national unselfishness and positive good will, what *have* we learned? And indeed we do see something of that—but relatively, how little! how horribly too little! And how much of that selfish playing for the interests of oneself, or one's party, or one's nation as though it were the sole supreme objective, to which we already alluded, and which exhibits all too cruelly the second fact, which is this:

Society as such, and too many of those who have power in their hands, and others, much younger, who in these recent five years have had no moral or mental discipline—nay, who in various countries have been positively trained to lie, to loot, to disregard all sexual control, and even to kill—have *not* been permeated by any moral impulse, are *not* proceeding from supreme spiritual principles, are *not* governing their activities by the rules of Right and Wrong—are "without God in the world."

At last, in this sermon, the Name of God has been spoken. And we see what happens when the divine Law is not attended to, nor the divine help asked. Every experiment has been tried save the conscious basing of morality, public as well as private, on the known fact of God, and of Him revealed in Jesus Christ. Certain prominent contemporaries, occupied with settling the destinies of nations, are, I know, personally Christian. (In a sermon like this, which is not, for example, a lecture, I do not mention names of men or countries, as I should unhesitatingly do elsewhere.) But in the powerful conferences to which we are growing, with ever greater despondency, accustomed, is the Name of God mentioned? Why—there are those who wish positively to exclude it, and for whose sake everyone else must exclude it. Well, neither one man, nor a nation, can continuously govern life with justice and in charity, without God's help, that is, without religion dominating everything else. No permanently righteous relationship of any sort can be come to unless the unchanging overlordship of God and His everlasting and absolute Law be recognized. Again and again men have tried to live ethically without religion: they have always failed. The best of pagans fails.

So I must return to the soul of each individual, a waste of tumultuous waters if it be, without the Wind of God; barren, without the vivifying Spirit. For what we cannot do on a world scale, please God we can, each of us, within our own soul. People often say to a broadcaster: "Isn't it wonderful, thrilling, even terrifying, to feel that you are speaking to tens of thousands of persons?" Well—but I would say that it should be all that, when you speak to even one person, precisely in proportion as you realize how amazing *is* any one person—alive, conscious, spiritual, immortal, the center of his whole world, his own world, so that as I face him my right is his left; what surrounds me is not what surrounds him nor anyone else in the whole universe: he is his own world center, as each of you is yours, and I, mine. You look forth at that world through *your* eyes, and through no one else's: no one else can think *your* thoughts—still less, make *your* choices. A French writer speaks of "the terrible loneliness of the human will." Yet there need be no such loneliness once you realize that God exists—exists *in you*—so that you can expand and issue forth from that unique and icebound self by prayer; and acts done for others, for the love of God, are prayer in the concrete. In prayer, you are at once "in touch with God"—what a mystery, that we can be *not* in touch with God, who Himself is always most intimately present in the very roots of our spirit! But if we are in vital touch with Him, we are in vital contact with all else that is in touch with Him, and that He is in touch with. You can fearlessly swim out into that heaving watery waste that so much of the world is, and, far from drowning, carry God's Spirit with you, and create order, and life. Far from flicking off, like Pilate, the drops that splash up against you as though they would contaminate you, you can turn that barren flood into a vast Font, and make it, as St. Paul says, a "Bath of New Birth": you can purify men's thoughts, and set a new life springing up within them and supernaturalize their very will.

Pray, and pray *in the very persons of those for whom you pray*. Why shouldn't you? God is in them, as in you. The same God: the Living God. Pray not only *for* those Japanese, those Indians, Jews, Russians—anyone between whom and yourselves there may seem to be no order, no unity, no charity—but *in their persons*: turn them, maybe unconsciously, into pray-ers. Yes, and extend your prayer beyond the confines of this earth, into Purgatory, the frontierland of that immortal world where souls are still being made ready for that perfect bliss toward which God ever designed them. As that old Syrian, John of Damascus, exclaimed twelve hundred years ago: "Yesterday, O Christ, I was with Thee buried: today am I co-risen in Thy Resurrection. Yesterday was I, with Thee, co-crucified: do Thou Thyself glorify me, together with Thyself, in Thy Kingdom." And thus may that Kingdom come even upon earth, as it is in heaven: thus may we, children too of Mary and brothers of Jesus Christ, achieve the New Man, the New World, and the eternal Peace of God.

# The Unknown Soldier of World War II Has His Say

REVEREND ALBERT JOSEPH McCARTNEY, D.D.

*A Presbyterian Minister and Director of the Chicago Sunday Evening Club*

*This distinguished sermon was delivered on Armistice Day, 1945, before the congregation of the Covenant-First Presbyterian Church of Washington, where Dr. McCartney was then minister. This church has just become the National Presbyterian Church. It has been Dr. McCartney's custom for years to go to Arlington an afternoon or two before Armistice Day, and musing there beside the Tomb of the Unknown Soldier he has woven his thoughts together upon the fortunes of our country.*

*He comes of a family of Presbyterian ministers, and has had parishes across the continent, beginning in a large country parish in Lawrence County, Pennsylvania, known as the Westfield Church; then Sharon, Pennsylvania; from there to the Kenwood Evangelical Church (interdenominational), Chicago, for sixteen years; next to the First Presbyterian Church of Santa Monica, California, for three years; and for the following sixteen years minister of the Church of the Covenant of Washington, D.C.; from which he took over the directorship of the Chicago Sunday Evening Club. This is an organization of trustees which provides a religious service of the highest order in Orchestra Hall, which seats 2600 people. The speakers are selected from all parts of the country and beyond the seas.*

*Dr. McCartney had two sons. The older one was killed in action as a bombardier over Italy; the other son, Albert N., is studying law in Harvard Law School.*

*The sermon carries a tremendous message. Since it speaks so eloquently for itself no explanation is necessary here. It should be read against the background of a former sermon delivered by Dr. McCartney on Armistice Day, 1932, entitled "The Unknown Soldier Wakes and Walks Again," available in the Congressional Library and the Congressional Record.*

*The substance and wording of the "Unknown Soldier" conversation is taken almost verbatim from a letter written by Lt. Benjamin McCartney five days before he was mortally wounded while on a bombing mission over Italy. The letter was addressed to his co-pilot who had been sent back to this country by the War Department to promote the publication of a play entitled* The Wings of the Morning *on which the two men had collaborated. The purpose of Lt. McCartney's letter, which unfortunately was never mailed, was to insist upon the above ideas being incorporated in the play. The quotation from Henry IV was selected by Lt. McCartney for his*

[230]

*"Dedication" to the graduating class of 1943 at the Air Training Station at Deming, New Mexico, of which he was a member.*

> O gentlemen, the time of life is short!
> To spend that shortness basely were too long
> If life did ride upon a dial's point,
> Still ending at the arrival of an hour.
> And if we live, we live to tread on kings;
> If die, brave death, when princes die with us!
> Now, for our consciences, the arms are fair,
> When the intent of bearing them is just.
>
> HENRY IV

*This sermon is included here with the kind permission of* The Christian Century.

## Sermon Thirty=nine

LATE one afternoon I made my annual pilgrimage to Arlington, to keep my usual rendezvous with my friend of many years' standing—the Unknown Soldier of World War I. As I mused there with the vagrant autumn winds sighing through the naked branches of the surrounding trees, and watched the beautiful Potomac creeping slowly along in the distance, like the river of man's life, and beyond it the capital city gray and partly obscured by the heavy autumn overcast, the Unknown Soldier, true to his tryst, emerged from his marble home, and stepping across the intervening pavement took his seat beside me against one of the pillars of the amphitheater.

As we conversed together I was telling him about World War II, and discussing the problems confronting the allied nations in their efforts at a constructive peace. Suddenly we were interrupted by the voice of a soldier whose presence had been obscured by our position, seated as we were against one of the pillars.

"Pardon me, sirs," he interrupted, "but I couldn't help overhearing your conversation. I happen to be an Unknown Soldier of the recent war, and I'm keenly interested in knowing how things are going and if the prospects for a world order are any better than they were after the last one."

"Sit down," I said, "and join us, won't you, please? And tell us something about yourself. This is our mutual comrade of World War I. What part of the country did you enlist from? And where did you see action?"

"Well," he drawled in unmistakable Virginia accent, "I haven't much to tell about myself. I was just a tail gunner in a bomber. I had one hundred hours to my credit as a pilot in training, but got washed out at the last.

We had a wonderful crew, for fortunately we had been kept together from our last training station. We learned to realize how each man's safety in that crew depended absolutely upon his concern for the safety of every other one in the crew. Our missions were around the Mediterranean, and off southern France. We went down on D-Day and the whole crew was lost. Some of us were washed ashore; and that's how I come to be here."

He seemed exceptionally keen and mature, and betrayed amazing understanding of what the war was all about, for he explained to me that after graduating he had spent two years in post-graduate work in Europe. I then told him about the progress of the war from D-Day on, the final capitulation of Germany, and the later surrender of Japan without an invasion. He was more interested, however, in what I had to tell him about the various peace conferences and the plan for the new world order. He wanted to know a great deal about the men who were sitting in on those conferences.

"My big regret," said he, "is that we who have not returned will have no say in the making of the peace; and I do wish that some way could be found by which our feelings and judgments and point of view might somehow get across to the people who are in the peacemaking." He spoke with great emotion and earnestness.

"Personally I have some very strong feelings about what ought to be done. I think many of our comrades whose lives have been fortunately spared ought to have more of a say than from what you tell me they seem to be having. Not many of those fellows who were so eagerly provided a seat in a foxhole, or in the cockpit of a plane, have been allowed to sit in the gilded chairs at the peace conference. Surely, if we can be trusted and directed to brain a Nazi private with the butt of a Garand, or do some pinpoint bombing around a great cathedral, we ought to be capable of knocking a few heads together with the butt of our logic—our moral logic!

"Some of us went over to fight for something we considered worth while, and because of our wide education we knew what we were fighting for. But we began to get a bit screwy when we found ourselves doing nothing but destroying. And now that the sands of war were running out, with little prospect of having anything to say about the constructive side of things, we felt shut out. We not only have fought, but we have thought, and we have felt, and now that our usefulness as destroyers is over, and our job of knocking things to pieces is done, we feel frustrated as we watch older men with portfolios grabbing all the seats at the table—men who have not actually sensed what war really means. It is we who have crouched with crawling stomachs in foxholes or cringed before plexiglass, as we watched the flak coming up at us, who can fully *know* what peace is. We feel an overwhelming sense of frustration, of being cut off, of never having a hand in what is to be done and decided."

[232]

At that I interrupted the soldier to say that I appreciated his point of view, and that to a certain extent he was right; but in the last analysis he and his comrades must trust the older men who will do the peacemaking, and who will have the future in their hands, with their fountain pens.

"I do not mean, of course," he said, "that the peace table should be crowded by boys in their early twenties; but there should be some provision for younger men, thinking young men, who have felt the danger side of war, and the great good society such as we have felt in the comradeship of a squadron."

At this point he began to speak as though he himself were one of the demobilized returning soldiers. "Certainly our voice ought to be heard in the peace recommendations and strategies. It's our generation of young men who have been decimated, and many of us went into this business voluntarily, with the vague idea that we would have a voice in what happened afterwards. I know that none of my comrades will have a chance to pound the table at some Versailles or San Francisco conference; but I certainly would like to have the satisfaction of knowing that our purposes, and ideals, and if I may say it humbly, our sacrifices, will not altogether be lost sight of in the snarling and quarreling confusion of the older peacemakers. We could tell them so much, for we who have come through this hell have learned so much more about what peace means, and many times have listed in our minds the elemental things that make for peace, as we have made a bomb run through the flak. But now we are voiceless . . ."

"Well," the soldier continued, after a silence, "we've done our bit, and we're through. It is up to you who survive us to remember us and what we wanted to accomplish. For God's sake, don't let us down at the peace conference; but pause with pen in hand, and take my comrades the world over into account before you put your names to any peace document. Remember us. That is all we can ask of you now. We belong to a great comradeship on the other side, and we would like to rest in the confidence that it is not broken on this side, and that we have kept the faith."

There was a long silence, and the three of us instinctively arose and without a word saluted, and the two Unknown Soldiers, arm in arm, vanished down the steps in the gathering dusk, and disappeared into the marble home from whence they had so recently emerged, leaving me to gaze thoughtfully upon the inscription—

*"Here rests in honored glory*
*An American Soldier*
*Known but to God."*

[233]

# The Havoc of War

REVEREND MICHEL RIQUET, S.J.
*Member of the Society of Jesus and Conferencier
of Notre Dame Cathedral, Paris, France*

*Père Riquet speaks as a* witness *in this sermon, which was delivered in the
Cathedral of Notre Dame in Paris on the First Sunday in Lent, March 10,
1946, the first of his series of messages preached as the "Conferences de
Notre Dame de Paris," after his return from captivity by the Nazis.*

*Father Riquet worked with the French Resistance until the Gestapo
arrested him on January 18, 1944. He was first imprisoned at Mauthausen,
then transferred to Dachau. He was kept a prisoner until the allied armies
released him in May, 1945. After his return, Cardinal Suhard asked him
to preach this series of sermons on "The Christian Confronts the Ruins"
("Le Chretien Face Aux Ruines").*

*The conference sermons were preached in the Cathedral, but were also
broadcast to all France by radio from Notre Dame and created quite a
sensation. Father R. F. Grady, S.J., a former chaplain in the U. S. Army,
now returned to Fordham University, made this translation, which is used
with his permission. The entire series of sermons will be published in America
by Sheed and Ward to bring Père Riquet's work more completely before
American readers; this first sermon is used with their permission. The message has also appeared in* Thought *magazine, national Catholic scholarly
quarterly, and acknowledgment of permission by* Thought *is gratefully made.
The original French edition Spes has the Nihil Obstat of the Reverend
Marcel Bith, S.J., Provincial of France, and the Imprimatur of His Eminence
Emmanuel Cardinal Suhard, Archbishop of Paris. The sermon is included
with the permission of Pere Riquet and with the sanction of Cardinal Suhard.*

*The conferences of Notre Dame were established in France in 1820 and
the greatest preachers of France were brought to Notre Dame for a course
of sermons. The Jesuit de Ravignow and the Dominican Lacordaire and the
great Montsabre made the conferences famous. The conferences have continued until now in spite of wars and difficulties.*

*Père Riquet was born in Paris in 1898, was a brilliant student, served in
the infantry in 1917-18, was cited for bravery, and was decorated with the
Legion of Honor in 1945 and recently was awarded the Medal of Freedom
with silver palm. He was also the 1947 Lenten preacher at Notre Dame.*

*He tells what he saw in this recent war, just as the apostles told what
they witnessed in the earlier days when Christ was on earth with them and
after his Resurrection. Battles, flying fortresses, terrifying defeat, dead*

*children, dying men, homeless women, hungry people—all these pass in
review as Père Riquet recounts the wreakage of land, man, morals, souls.
His final plea for the Christian attitude makes this a sermon to preserve
and read many times. It makes one wonder again when man will learn to
outlaw war as an outworn instrument of barbarian ages.*


# Sermon Forty


TEXTS: That which we have heard, what we have seen with our
eyes, that which we have looked upon and felt with our hands
of the Word of Life, that we declare unto you.   I JOHN 1:1, 3
We cannot but tell what we have seen and heard.
ACTS 4:20
We are ourselves eyewitnesses of all these things.
ACTS 2:32


YOUR Eminence: The great but weighty honor which falls to my lot
today—to speak in this Cathedral of Our Lady of Paris, and through
this microphone to all of France—is not due, I know, to any such talents
as have distinguished those who have spoken here before me. Quite the
contrary. Unlike them, I am no skilled orator; I am not an authority in
philosophical and theological science; I am not a literary figure; not a
technician. Nothing I possess can outweigh the regrets of those of my
listeners who esteemed the precise erudition, the clear line of argument,
the classic orderliness of my predecessor, as well as his conscientious effort
to reconcile, in those troublous days, the clash between a sinister censorship
and a heart truly Catholic and truly French. One title alone, I believe,
can possibly explain the surprising choice Your Eminence has made—a
choice which I dare only say was venturesome, but one which I hope you
never will have reason to regret. This unique title, the only one which
could attract, and the only one which I can rightly claim, is that I am—
*a witness.*

Interrupting the splendid succession of masterpieces of oratory, of dialectic,
of theology, of apologetic, by which my predecessors here made manifest the
vitality, the real-ness, the truth of Christianity, Your Eminence has wished
to make heard here the voice of a witness, the words of a man who tells
simply what he has seen, what he has heard, what he has lived.

And yet, the preaching of the Apostles had no other theme. "That which
we have heard, what we have seen with our eyes, that which we have looked
upon and felt with our hands of the Word of Life, that we declare unto
you." So spoke St. John. And Peter, to the Sanhedrin, when it wished to
silence him, replied without yielding: "We cannot but tell what we have
seen and heard." Like Paul, these first preachers of the Gospel had no

[235]

desire to win their point by superiority of language or by arts of human skill; but only to give testimony, to tell what they had seen and heard and looked upon. "We are, ourselves, eyewitnesses of all these things!" That was their final argument.

And was that not, besides, the very mission Christ had given them when he left them: "You will be witnesses for me in Jerusalem, in all Judea, and in Samaria, and even to the end of the earth"! And the history of the Church, across two thousand years—is it anything else but an unbroken succession of witnesses gathering up and passing on in their turn the first witness of the Apostles?

Witness! I have been, I am, I ought to be here witness to the truth, to the charity, to the vitality of Christ, of His Gospel, of His Church. Witness to the joy and power and freedom which Christ gives to souls who entrust themselves to Him. Witness under conditions, in circumstances, in trials the most varied: through all the diversity of a changing, busy life, from the peaceful, middle-class home where I was born—in the age of carriages and kerosene lamps, the fashions and manners of 1900—up to the concentration camps of Mauthausen and Dachau, where I had actual experience of the most thrilling and decisive proof of the solidity, the energy, the eternal reality of our Christian faith.

What one Christian has seen, heard, felt, smelled, suffered during this first half of our century, in peace, in war, in the Resistance, in the Deportation, shoulder to shoulder with the people of France—this it is, nothing but this, that he is going to tell here, as a witness who swears to speak without hate, and without fear; to tell the truth, the whole truth, and nothing but the truth.

He owes this much to the trust placed in him by Your Eminence—a trust he desires not to fail, for he cannot forget a day at Reims, and days thereafter throughout the perilous times from 1940 to 1944, at Saint-Séverin, at Saint-Léon, at the Invalides, it was your confidence in him that permitted him all the daring of a revolutionary patriot. This much he owes, too, to the attentive sympathy of those who listen to him this evening—to so many friends, childhood companions, comrades of the battles of 1918 and 1940; to those of the Resistance, and those of the Deportation, his comrades of Compiègne, Mauthausen, Dachau, whose joys and sufferings he shared; to all those whom he knows and knows not, who are now listening in! May his words bring to them, as he wishes with all his heart, enlightenment and joy, courage and resolution. May his words, above all else, sound a call to all men of good will, all whose hearts are for peace and justice, to build together brotherhood in France in a world that has made its peace.

May the Virgin who watches, in this sanctuary at the heart of our Paris, over the destinies of this ship which for so many centuries has braved the tides of fortune without ever being submerged by the flood—*fluctuat nec mergitur*—may Our Lady of Paris deign to bless my efforts and by the contagion of her smile make all those who hear me, hear me kindly. Ave Maria . . . pray for us poor sinners now, and at the hour of our death. Amen.

The testimony, the witness, which you are waiting for here is that of a Christian conscience that has been deeply involved in the various events through which we have been living since the beginning of this our century.

In the face of the unforeseen and unexpected unfolding of inventions and catastrophes, both alike without precedent, in the face of the ruins heaped up for six years by a curious use of the most ingenious discoveries made by the mind of man—what is, what ought to be the attitude of a Christian? Doltish fear? Discouragement? Doubt? Distress? Despair? Or, on the contrary, tranquil serenity in a faith, a hope, a love which would find in these facts, in these experiences through which we have just lived, a fresh vindication of what it believes, hopes and loves more firmly than ever before?

The whole course of these Conferences will strive to the utmost to give a solution to this problem: The Christian confronts the ruins! But first, we shall try to take the bearings of the situation, to draw up a balance sheet of these catastrophes before which the Christian conscience, taken aback for a little, a bit anxious even, examines itself and seeks to understand. . . .

At first our vision is dazed, our imaginations obsessed by the piling up everywhere on all sides of material ruin.

Like card-castles, houses by the millions have been thrown to the ground. Of cities once famous for the most modern planning and construction of all their buildings, there remain only ashes and dust. And those towns, which proudly boasted of having preserved intact the appearance of another age, have seen disappear, in a moment, as in the age of wizards, their belfries, their towers and turrets, their bastions and picturesque gables, in which the Middle Ages lived on alongside of motor highways and airports.

Look again, if you will, at the propaganda picture books glorifying the totalitarian regimes. They all vie with one another in presenting the same arguments, the same criteria of success and prosperity: stadia, swimming pools, sports palaces, motor highways; and workers' cities, lightsome, smart, comfortable, close to colossal factories. And what remains of all this? A little less, sometimes a great deal less, than remains of the aqueducts, the temples, the theaters and circuses by which, long ago, Rome made boast of the power and the glory of her empire. In a few years our civilization has created more ruins than did the barbarians in the course of many centuries. And these modern ruins have none of the majesty of the remains of the Forum or the Palatine, none of the charm of those fragments of Gothic arches which inspired the poems of Ossian and the romantic musings of Volney. The ivy and the bramble have not yet covered the blood and bits of human flesh that stain with tragic horror these segments of walls, these stubs of girders, these gutted roofs and floors, these housefronts breached and gaping like the face of a skull, without eyes, without nose, without lips, without life.

Like a blurred film there passes before my mind's eye the scene of the bombing—a commonplace now, but it was for me the first of this war—on May 12, 1940, in a village of the Ardennes, where for some months my battalion had been quietly encamped. All the people there had become as familiar to us as if we were in a new little country of our own. In one instant, in a hurricane crashing with thunders and fires, in the terror, the crushing, the murder of poor innocent folk, we saw uncovered the hideous face of total war, of *Blitzkrieg*. In the tangle of wires that strew the ground, every step I take breaking some fragment of glass, in the dust of plaster and mortar which settles slow, so slow, while smoke rises from fires smoldering under the debris, I stand confused, watching a soldier carrying in his arms the naked, bleeding corpse of a four-year-old child, while a man, just back from work, is searching despairingly for his wife and children, buried under the ruins of his home.

For six years, throughout all Europe and in Asia, this same scene was reproduced countless times, in countless forms. Millions of human lives, some hardly born, some already near to dying, have plunged into an abyss dug in an instant by the explosion of roaring meteors. Millions more have been thrown into the streets, to live henceforth without hearth or home, stripped of those humble treasures which made attractive, comfortable, even the commonest flat in a row of tenements.

Nothing has been spared, neither poor nor rich, neither castle nor hovel, neither the most ancient church nor up-to-the-minute factory, neither hospital nor school. Archives, libraries, laboratories, clinics, research centers, stocks of food and medicines—everything that could help to save humanity or to make it at least less miserable—all the tools of its progress, all the heights of its civilization, everything was laid bare to a fury of destruction which has no respect for art or beauty or science, or for children or the weak.

And to feed this torrent of destruction, the world has squandered its riches and reserves without counting the cost. It has impoverished itself, mortgaged itself the better to destroy the whole heritage of the past—all it has built, all it has accumulated, the creative work of generation on generation: roads, railways, dams, power stations, mines, factories, warehouses, docks, grain elevators—everything was put to work, used, exhausted, destroyed, with an unheard-of extravagance of inventions, of manufactures, of raw materials— of which only the most miserly use was made when there was question only of the health or welfare of the people.

Look at the wreckage of the flying fortress that has just crashed to earth in the course of a bombing raid. When it was soaring through the sky a moment ago, was it not a majestic symbol of man's most daring success in the conquest and mastery of the forces of the universe? How the dream of Icarus and the imaginative novels of Jules Verne were surpassed in this machine in which were assembled, as in some museum, all the latest discoveries, the most delicate technical achievements, with even refinements of comfort! No expense was spared. Complex alloys of steel and chrome and manganese, leathers, silver, platinum went into its making. And furs and silks were used for the dress of the simplest mechanic. For this frail masterpiece, so quickly destroyed, specialists had put to use the most precise gauges and clockwork, bombsights, radio receivers and transmitters. To our amazement, we even found in the calcined wreckage, an unlooked-for improvement, a television tube that permitted the pilot, in the black of night, to see unrolled before him on a luminous screen the countryside he was flying over.

And why all this accumulation of marvels? The better to destroy!

One day, those flying fortresses, fitted with the latest improvements in radio and radar were going to reduce to dust the famous Philipps works and laboratories at Eindhover, where there were made and tested most of the magic tubes thanks to which we are able today to hear and be heard, to see and be seen, from one end of the earth to the other.

We have been told, it is true, that in a short time these factories will be rebuilt bigger than before, more modern, more productive. That can never make up for the monstrous waste of the riches of earth squandered in a work of destruction and death.

Then, too, all this wreckage is not repaired so quickly as one rebuilds a house. A house can be rebuilt in a few months—when materials are at hand to work with. We need still more time to reconstruct the bridges that have been smashed, to re-establish railway and roadway networks that have been disrupted; to replace transport materiel, two-thirds of which has been destroyed; to transform back into seaports such shipwreckers' yards as are now Brest and Le Havre and Saint-Nazaire. It takes years and years for a forest to grow again. Above all, it takes years and more years to make a man.

In the shattered fuselage of the flying fortress, there is a relic more touching, more precious than the radar which sees through fog and dark. This relic, this fragment, which some good souls will presently gather up to carry in triumph and at peril of their lives, is the corpse of the pilot. It was he who gave a soul to this wrecked machine, it was he who conceived it, who mounted it, who steered it through the high heavens—he, a man. And he, too, the man, has been destroyed in this work of death.

Suppose that war should again shatter the windows and throw down the walls of our homes, our factories, our churches! So long as there are arms and hearts and heads, they can all be rebuilt, and rebuilt even more grand, more beautiful.

But war is a frightful slayer of men. The great slaughters that horrified antiquity, when the Medes, the Persians, the Greeks, the Egyptians confronted one another in battle array, or when Carthage made Rome quake with fear; our own Hundred Years' War, the countless victims of the wars of empire—we have exceeded them; far and far exceeded them. It is by the millions that the corpses heaped up by this war must be counted.

Yet it is a small thing to kill men. Far worse is it to corrupt and debase humanity, in body and in spirit. This war has not been wanting in that.

Those who survive are, in great part, marked, disfigured, thrown off balance, profoundly tainted. Darwin imagined that the Struggle for Existence selected in the species the best, the strongest, the most handsome for survival. We know too well that those who fell in May and June of 1940, after that in the Resistance, in the concentration camps, and in the last battle on the eve of liberation were, in large part, the most daring, the most courageous, the most resolute.

When one thinks on this wrong-way selection, on the formidable increase in the percentages of men who are lamed, armless, blind, unbalanced, crazy, unmanned, imbeciles—one cannot help recalling that the very ones who were mainly responsible for this disintegration of a race are the ones who had set out to renew the race, to make it better by a frenzy of eugenics and by the application to human beings of the most shameless, most brazen techniques of veterinarians.

A people of mutilated men, of stumbling cripples, of madmen and idiots—that is the unforeseen result of the eugenic craze. Add to that the moral corruption, the moral ruin the war bred and favored!

The lands laid waste are but a symbol of other wastelands, those of the mind and of the heart. The school emptied for the barracks, the home bereft of a father's authority—the education of the youth of the world has become haphazard, fatally superficial, quickly and easily undisciplined, to the detriment of the mind which is ill trained, of the character which is ill formed, of the will which is unsettled and distraught. From such slapdash studies, from such abortive education, we shall see, tomorrow even more than today, the repercussion on culture, on science, on manners. We cannot begrudge these young people too much who during the loveliest years of their youth have grown up without knowing the joys of a normal family, secure in a peaceful home; who have been distracted, their studies broken in on ceaselessly by air-raid alarms, by upheavals, evacuation; who have been deprived at the most critical age of their formation, of the food indispensable to their growth; deprived even more of the affection, the counsel, the guidance that springs from a truly fatherly heart.

What if war pulverize the stones of the hearthplace, scatter even the most precious family treasures in the ruin of other possessions—all *that* can be replaced. The blow dealt to the home that has been morally dislocated or broken is infinitely more grave.

Man is not a solitary being. He cannot of himself be born, nor flourish by himself, nor orient himself without the help of a community where his heart may be at ease and his need for compassion satisfied. The family—constituted of the enduring union of a man, a woman, and the children they beget in the voluntary sharing of their lives—is one of the basic elements of the welfare, of the stability and progress of mankind. Deprived of the mutual support they find therein, man, woman, children suffer profoundly in the very depths of their beings, in their growth, in their personality, from a disbalance it is difficult to set aright.

More than anything else, this war has broken up these basic human communities. For years, millions of men, the prisoners, the deportees, the mobilized soldiers, have been separated from their wives. And the wives have had to manage alone the education of the children, to preserve the family heritage, to make the most serious decisions, to go into exile at times—to care for everything. Separated from one another, men, women, children have grown up, matured, suffered, fought, each on his own, by himself. Inevitably, even the best no longer recognize one another, no longer find one another the same, not having developed, not having lived together for more than five years. As for the ordinary sort of people, to whom conjugal life was absolutely indispensable to keep the human way of things—they have become, during their life in the concentration camps or prisons, almost irremediably habituated to the morals of the herd, nay, of brute beasts. Excuse my language; it but says the truth.

Of all the ruins heaped up by this world war, the most disastrous, the most widespread, is without question the ruin of family life: shattered homes, hearts gone astray, childhood, adolescence thrown into confusion. It has gravely endangered the long struggle by which Christian civilization had, step by step, led man to win a mastery over and to restrain the brutality of sexual instincts; saved woman from the worst sort of slavery, that of her passions; and assured to childhood an atmosphere of tenderness, of respect, of purity in a home where one knew a happiness, without ecstasy perhaps, but without disaster, too.

How trite has become the story of the man, the prisoner or deportee, who comes back trembling with hope to the home of which he has been dreaming day and night for five long years. His wife, his children! Snapshots of them have never left him; how proudly he showed them to his comrades! From far off he lived this return, this tenderness recaptured. In the familiar surroundings of happy days, life would again be calm and infinitely sweet. But he comes up against the shock of the reality. His wife is dead, his children scattered, his home gutted. So, too, is the man, and for a long time. And yet more cruel is the unexpected return to a home dishonored, even occupied by an intruder!

More often, things are the same on the surface. But underneath, what disillusionment. They cannot find their bearings any more. "You are not the woman I left behind." "You are not the man I waited for." They will live, from necessity or from habit, side by side; but so far apart at heart. And the children will see, they will guess, they will suffer without saying anything; but they will be dreaming of escape, of far-off lands; too disillusioned, too disheartened to think of setting up a home that will end like this.

In the face of such defeat of true, simple, honest love—in the face of the collapse of long-hoped-for happiness, how resist the fascination of easy pleasure, the temptation to get drunk and to benumb one's self to the pain.

When you see so many fortunes ruined that seemed solidly based, so much success broken that you thought unbreakable, the obsession takes hold on you not to let pass a chance to be happy for at least an hour. Let us be merry today; tomorrow we die! Enjoy the little while that is left, the few moments you can snatch; don't be a dupe in a world where the rotters are always right.

And in this dizziness, the moral fabric of individuals and groups collapses. Every man for himself; every man takes his chance; every man makes his own morals, and they are nothing more than the code each one contrives to fit his temperament, his tastes, his appetite, his opportunities. Men cheat, deceive, traffic, and defraud without even a doubt any more that there is something wrong in doing so, without ever thinking that the sickness of society, of which the whole world complains, is the deadly end product in the social, economic, and political life, of this holiday from morality and honesty, even among those who are called and in their own opinion are honest people.

Later on, we shall speak of remedies, and, too, of some noble exceptions which happily brighten this picture so steeped in somber hues. For the instant, let us put it down on record that this flight from, this desertion of so many from probity, from loyalty, from fidelity in men's dealings with men, in business, in work, in public service, in civic responsibilities—is a heavy deficit in our accounting of the war; that it slows down and compromises the return of peace, of order and of happiness for all.

To that we have to add the collapse, the degradation even of mind, which is the inevitable result of the abuse made, during all these past years, of certain methods of propaganda and of the war of nerves. The trickery, the continuous faking of truth, the constant use of exaggeration, or, on the contrary, the cutting down of facts to fit the immediate interest of the war policy, the systematic abuse of the most sacred words: honor, justice, right, liberty, the dignity of the human person—all used without shame and even without purpose to hide or to justify the most shady combinations, the basest sort of deals, the most manifest injustice or the most dishonorable neglect. By that you can find justified, for example, Nietzsche's sarcastic comment on morality—a hypocritical defense of the weak against the strong. Certain politicians have the habit of appealing to Right and Respect for the Human Person whenever they do not feel up to cynically making the most of the right of their might.

The whole moral and spiritual vocabulary of humanity, everything that once signified some value, some grandeur, some nobility, has been shamelessly turned to account, worn threadbare, defiled. Men no longer know, no longer believe that words which once were sacred now retain any meaning worthy of respect. They see in them only some catchwords which everyone repeats without believing—slogans about the superiority of some *apéritif*, or the strength of a kitchen chair. The great ideals of humanism and of patriotism become, through the fault of such unscrupulous and unbridled propaganda, a cheap article for sale in the market of national and international controversy.

We have to add to that a whole lot of customs and tendencies and ways of action which have become widespread through the war and are particularly damaging to the peace which we are hoping to recapture.

Millions of men throughout the whole of Europe, the youth above all, have for five years under arms led a life which was not without its grandeur. Heroism at times blossomed out there all the day long. But men lost there too the habit, the taste for, nay even respect for the ordinary tasks of everyday life, of the regular routine in the prosaic setting of the workshop, the yards, the fields. The hankering for the epic life lived on planetary horizons spreads a drab, dull dreariness over the duties of an ordinary life of peace and toil. After a life of adventure and risks, which brought with it a freedom from worry, a certain ease, and some choice compensations, how painful it will seem to have to be confined by the restrictions of work that is monotonous, without glory, in order to earn a moderate wage and to win rewards less easy and less exciting than in the days when one was living off the country or on the enemy.

The military occupation of four fifths of Europe, the underground, the maquis, the resistance, all have habituated conquerors and conquered—and each was that in his turn—to methods and procedures and attitudes more or less revived from the days when the right of the fist, the *Faustrecht,* was without challenge.

Slow and difficult will be the return to the normal ways of civilized people, to respect for rights, for persons, for the institutions of peacetime.

Among these steps backward to barbarism that threaten to endure, how not evoke the unheard-of outburst of cruelty, of sadism, of terrorism which we saw shown at Mauthausen and at Dachau, as did so many others at Auschwitz, Buchenwald, Naetzweiler, Ravensbrueck, Bergen-Belsen, *und so weiter.*

It will be the indelible infamy of those responsible for the Third Reich that they restored to a place of honor, in a world which was believed to be civilized, all the processes of intimidation, of reprisal, of deportation, of enslavement, and torture and assassination, the origin and use of which history ascribed to Asiatic tyrants of the long ago, to the madness of a Nero or a Caligula, or to the cannibals of Central Africa. But, different from those historical precedents, the art of making men suffer, of killing slowly and hypocritically, became the object of a method, scientifically conceived and regularized: a *wissenschaftliche Methode.* The gas chamber, the quarries, the baths; the systematic undernourishment cleverly combined with exhausting labor; the constant employment of the scoundrel, the brute, the sadist, the hardened criminal to keep order in terror; the subtle blending of a ruthless severity with a seeming worry about the hygiene and comfort and entertainment of the prisoner; the music of a Strauss waltz accompanying the

[ 243 ]

death rattle of the hanged—all that is found everywhere methodically and systematically employed by a corps of specialists trained, as were the dogs of Mauthausen, to play innocently with the children of the *Lagerführer* as well as to tear to pieces the living man he threw to them for food.

The magnitude of this manifestation of evil, the number of victims counted by the hundreds of thousands, the no less considerable number of the executioners and their accomplices and helpers, forbids our treating this as an accidental, an exceptional fact; but as something tied in with a whole complex of tendencies, of doctrines, whose poison still runs strong in the heart of many a man, and not every one a German. The cessation of the war has not, alas, put an end to the hate, the selfishness, the conflict of warring interests which gave birth to the war. You see them smoldering, and bursting into flame, and throwing a light which shows us the ultimate prospect of a duel with atomic bombs.

And, finally, there is the immense wave of lassitude, of disillusionment, of pessimism which threatens to and at times does overwhelm souls of the finest temper, the very ones who in the day of danger had so cheerfully risked their life or resolutely affirmed their will to win. All the young people of today are confused and without hope. They no longer know why they live, they know not what to do, or what to dream about. A frightening, unfathomable emptiness harrows their hearts and upsets their thoughts. The philosophies of the absurd and of the void, of hopeless revolt and senseless existence now enjoy a disturbing popularity, while others are still awaiting from another war, from other massacres, the realization of a better world.

In the midst of these ruins, of these charnel pits, of these disorders, what is, what ought to be the attitude of a Christian, a true Christian?

Will he let himself be overwhelmed, too, by anguish and doubt?

Shall he take refuge in the desert, as of old did the anchorites, to find there liberty and consolation for his soul?

Will he utter an arrogant curse upon the faults of his fellow men, blaming *their* materialism, and *their* atheism for all the evils which are crushing mankind?

Rather than make a bitter indictment against *the others,* against all such as do not think as he does, the Christian wishes above all else to make heard a desperate and impassioned plea to the multitude of his brothers who have been separated and scattered, bruised and mutilated by this war. A fraternal and loyal plea to rebuild, together, a world freed from the mistakes and errors which have led it to this field of ruin, to these terrifying pyramids of corpses.

One could philosophize, discuss, reproach, condemn without end. That is not my task. Others will busy themselves with that. As a witness, I have to say simply what I have seen, lived through, experienced: the attitude of the Christian in the midst of this devastation. What this attitude is, how it is vindicated through the vision of the world which Christianity gives, what benefits it can produce in a man, as well in the depths of his own soul as in his social environment. By the simple presentation of an attitude, of facts in which it is embodied, of sacred texts which inspire it and explain it, I hope to convince you to adopt it, and having once adopted it, I hope you will find the power, the joy, the liberty, the happiness which so many Christians, of whom I wish to be here only a witness, have found in it.

Confronted by these ruins, confronted by collapse and catastrophe, the Christian attitude is essentially an attitude of faith, of hope, of love.

Here is what happened at Nantes, at a moment when a frightful bombing has just destroyed one whole section of the city. The hospital is completely demolished. The sick, the doctors, the nurses lie helpless under the debris. The rescue squads are mad at work. And look, in the beams of the floodlights, is an astonishing sight. From the powdery rubble emerges a hand, the fine white hand of a woman, its tapering fingers still moving, counting the beads of a large rosary, the rosary of the Daughters of Wisdom, nurses of this hospital. People call to her. The Sister replies: "Save the others first!" And quietly, peacefully, under the debris, she goes on telling off her Aves, "Hail Mary . . . Hail Mary . . . Hail Mary . . ."

The Christian attitude? There it is. Overwhelmed by ruins, the Christian goes on believing, hoping, loving. From that comes his power, his nobility, and his eternal joy.

PEACE AND WAR

# Los Alamos Sermon

CHAPLAIN (MAJOR) MATTHEW H. IMRIE
*Chaplains Corps, U. S. Army*

*This sermon was preached while Chaplain Imrie was Post Chaplain at the Los Alamos Atomic Research Center of the Manhattan District at Los Alamos, New Mexico. The fact that Chaplain Imrie, the first "atomic bomb chaplain," served with this unit for two years, provided him with unusual opportunities for insight into the problems involved.*

*Appointed to the Chaplains Corps in April, 1941, he was ordered to active duty in June of 1941. He served as Regimental Chaplain of the Fifth Infantry Regiment, on duty in Panama, until November of 1942. From November of 1942 to November of 1943 he was Combat Team Chaplain of the 158th Infantry Combat Team, the famous "Bushmasters," and saw action in New Guinea and the Bismarck Archipelago. He was hospitalized following injuries received when his plane burst into flames and crashed during troop movements on Kiriwina Island, and upon recovery was assigned* to temporary duty at the Chaplain School, Harvard University, Cambridge, Massachusetts. In July of 1944, Chaplain Imrie was assigned to the U. S. Engineer Office, Manhattan District, Los Alamos, New Mexico. In July of 1946, he was ordered to duty at the Office of the Chief of Chaplains, War Department, Washington, D. C. In addition to theater ribbons and battle stars, he has received the Army Commendation Award and the Legion of Merit.

Chaplain Imrie is a priest of the Episcopal Church, having been ordained in June of 1934 at St. Paul's Cathedral, Boston, Massachusetts. He has served on the staff of three parishes: Zion Episcopal Church, Rome, New York; St. Peter's Church, Port Chester, New York; and the Church of the Heavenly Rest, New York City. He received his B.A. from Columbia University, and completed graduate work at the General Theological Seminary and Teachers College, Columbia University; in 1939 he was awarded the honorary D.D. by the American Theological Seminary, Wilmington, Delaware.

## Sermon Forty=one

TEXT: Except ye repent, ye shall all likewise perish.   LUKE 13:3

DR. HAROLD C. UREY, professor of chemistry at the University of Chicago, has this to say in an article which appeared in *Colliers*, 5 January 1946:

> I write this to frighten you. I'm a frightened man, myself. All the scientists I know are frightened—frightened for their lives—and frightened for your life. For the past few weeks we have been in Washington giving our advice—when we are asked—concerning the potentialities of the atomic bomb. In so doing, we have naturally learned a good deal about the potentialities of politics. What we have learned has increased our fears. . . . Now, in Washington, we have learned a new fear: We are afraid of what the politicians and diplomats may do with the atomic bomb.

Dr. Urey and his frightened associates are both intelligent and courageous. Their academic achievements are sufficient testimony to their intelligence. Their dealing with the knowns and unknowns in the structure of matter has demonstrated their courage. Yet, they are frightened men; and they admit it.

Only fools are not afraid. Alexander Pope, in his *Essay on Criticism*, stated, "Fools rush in where angels fear to tread." Angelo Patri, noted American educator, informs us that "education consists of being afraid at the right time." Furthermore, it is common knowledge that courage is not the

[246]

absence of fear; courage is holding one's ground despite fear. What are these intelligent and courageous scientists afraid of? Is it atomic energy?

According to the article in *Colliers* already referred to, "We are afraid of what the politicians and diplomats may do with the atomic bomb." In short, these gentlemen of laboratory and classroom are frightened of men. And, on the basis of men's past performance, they have a right to be.

We have just ended a world-wide war which has smeared the globe with the blood of men, women and children and has brought death and destruction on a scale heretofore unknown. But twenty-one years after the signing of the armistice which terminated the hostilities of World War I, a war which resulted in 37½ million casualties, men again turned the world into a ghastly chamber of horrors. The approximate score of this second World War shows that man is becoming more expert in his slaughtering. World War II figures are these: 56 million casualties (22 million killed, 34 million wounded); at a cost of 1116 billions of dollars (694 billions, estimated Allied cost; 422 billions, estimated Axis cost). Man's history is enough to frighten anyone.

As these scientists point out, the fission of the atom is not the threat to society; the threat to human society is man himself. Man has demonstrated that he has within his heart and mind a demonic capacity, a spiritual insanity, that makes him, on occasions, a menace to himself and to all those associated with him. Because of this defect in his character, this "maggot in the apple," he constantly needs to be reconciled with his Maker and his brother. A plagiarist, he denies God's authorship of the world he abuses; egocentric, he worships either himself or his own image; a fratricide, his guilty conscience colors his reply, "Am I my brother's keeper?"

To subscribe to the scientists' fears "of what the politicians and diplomats may do with the atomic bomb" is pharisaically to place inaccurate limitations as to the quarters from which the threat to society emanates. Other groups in society—the scientists, the technologists, the academicians, the journalists, and other professional groups (including the ecclesiastics)—are also tainted with the curse of plagiarism, fratricide and inordinate pride. Hitler's almost successful attempt to blanket the world with a cloak of reactionism scheduled to last for at least a thousand years was not implemented by the aged, the infirm, the sick or the unschooled. Hitler's ideology, his diabolically successful diplomacy, his geopolitics, his industrial potential, his scientific research, his superlative war machine were all the work of educated men of science and letters who prostituted their skills, knowledge, intelligence and industry for a privileged position in his kingdom of blackmail and murder. Scientists at home might well be frightened—"afraid of politicians and diplomats" and men in other fields of human endeavor. Man's cruelty, refined and made gargantuan by science and technology, has put the beasts of the field to shame. In the words of the immortal Robert Burns, "Man's inhumanity to man makes countless thousands mourn."

[247]

What's the answer? First of all, the problem must be restated. The paramount issue of humanity in our time is a moral, and not a political and economic one. This does not mean that we should not concern ourselves with the discovery and the development of the most adequate political and economic structures. What it means is this: world order or disorder is the product of order or disorder in human character. It is one thing to build a house; it is another thing to create a happy family. The structure necessary for a peaceful world, like a house for a family, is important; but a peaceful world must not be thought of in terms of organizational structure alone. To put it bluntly, a better world order calls for better people. We must improve, transform ourselves. "Except ye repent, ye shall all likewise perish."

The organizational structure of society, with its laws and institutions, may be thought of as being analogous to an ordinary pump. The water that the laws and institutions of society pump is determined by the intellectual, moral and spiritual life of the people. The pump will draw from the people whatever is inside of them, no better, no worse. In short, if creative and spiritual forces are at work in the hearts and minds of men, the institutions of society will function. The foundation of world order must be laid in the hearts of men.

Will Rogers, with his pungent wit, understood this and gave expression to it a long time ago. During a discussion of general world conditions, a friend of his said, "Will, what's wrong with the world anyway?" Will moved his chewing gum to a speaking position and replied, "I don't know, friend; I guess it's people."

Some time ago Winston Churchill was credited with a statement similar to this:

> The League of Nations could have worked successfully. In it there was the possibility of a progressive world order that would have insured peace—if the intelligence and conscience of the world had really backed up its intent; if the spiritual quality had been in the world's people to demand of it what was inherent in it, to call from it, its effective operation. The League collapsed, not because its political structure, faulty though it was, was hopelessly wrong, but because the ethical and spiritual foundations underneath were not adequate.

In the words of an old Chinese proverb, "You cannot carve rotten wood."

Blaise Pascal's description of man fits in with our concern with what man might do with himself and his society:

> What a chimera, then, is man! What a novelty, what a monster, what a chaos, what a subject of contradiction, what a prodigy! A judge of all things, feeble worm of the earth, depository of the truth, cloaca of uncertainty and error, the glory and the shame of the universe!

What's wrong with the world? The answer is, "People." We need to repent ourselves of our mistakes; we need to be saved.

In our anxious quest for salvation we have turned to men of agile and

[248]

inventive brains, only to discover that agile and inventive brains, tainted with evil, cannot save us. We have turned with high hopes to education, only to discover that every gift that the pedagogue can bestow may go into crime. We have eagerly embraced science as saviour, only to become the victims of the tragic misuse of the discoveries of science. We have, in desperation, put our trust in the spiritual qualities of men, their unselfishness and loyalty, only to discover that these too may become perverted and harnessed to the wheels of a superstate. At last, at long last, we have learned that we need a saviour who can save us from our sins, that only he can save us who can reconcile us with God and man. Gradually, almost reluctantly, we realize with Paul, that "he is our peace, who hath made both one, and hath broken down the middle wall of partition between us."

The secular optimism that regards a political structure as the basic solution to the problems of the world is superficial self-deceit. The solution is rooted in the hearts of men. As Alexander Pope once said, "The proper study of mankind is man." Bigger and better political organization will not insure our survival; mutual good will, better understanding and reconciliation between God and man are fundamental.

Unless we can find something that will change men into good men, the immature into the socially minded, and the egotistic into the co-operative, the future of human society holds much evil. However, the search for such transforming power need not be in vain. In the words of St. Paul, "The gospel of Christ . . . is the power of God unto salvation to every one that believeth." To be saved by Christ means to enter into an imperishable fellowship with God in Christ. Saviourhood is the very essence of Christ. The angel proclaimed this truth to Joseph in the words, "Ye shall call his name Jesus, for he shall save his people from their sins."

Without the gospel of Christ, it is logical to resign oneself to a fearful "sea of troubles." If by his nature man's soul is irremediably warped and twisted, then we are without hope, for man cannot lift himself by his own bootstraps. However, such is not the case. Christ lived and died that man might know and believe that no man need stay the way he is, that miracles of rebirth and transformation are possible for all—for men, for families and for nations.

One of Martin Luther's magnificent hymns testifies to the gospel of Christ as the power of God in overwhelming the forces of evil:

> A Mighty fortress is our God,
> A Bulwark never failing;
> Our Helper He amid the flood
> Of mortal ills prevailing:
>
> Did we in our own strength confide,
> Our striving would be losing;
> Were not the right Man on our side,
> The Man of God's own choosing.

A necessary prelude to availing oneself of the power of God is repentance. The obstruction of sin must be cleared away; the misdirection of wickedness must be overcome. A man cannot take a single step in the right direction unless he first turns to his proper goal. This emphasis upon repentance is evident throughout the New Testament. St. Luke tells us that "Jesus came . . . preaching the gospel . . . saying . . . repent ye, and believe the gospel." Again, "Except ye repent, ye shall all likewise perish." In the Acts of the Apostles Peter teaches, "Repent, and be baptized every one of you in the name of Jesus Christ for the remission of sins, and ye shall receive the gift of the Holy Ghost."

Our attempts to solve the problems of life will fail if we do not begin with repentance for past misdeeds. It is recorded in the Gospel according to St. Luke that after Peter had denied Christ thrice, "the Lord turned, and looked at Peter. . . . And Peter went out, and wept bitterly." This moment of bitter regret is considered the turning point in Peter's career. We may not weep as Peter wept, but as we contemplate the harvest of our isolationism, the industrial conflicts which beset us, and our disturbed international relations, surely we must bitterly repent for the evil which accounts for the present turmoil and confusion. There can be no real progress in righteousness in any realm of life, there can be no genuine security, there can be no real freedom from fear, unless there is, first of all, a frank and fearless recognition and turning away from evil. We can be keenly aware of the need of this change within ourselves only when we see "the glory of God in the face of Jesus Christ." Then, and then only, can we overcome the absorption of ourselves in self and things and turn with all our hearts to "the gospel of Christ . . . which is the power of God unto salvation to everyone that believeth."

PRAYER

# Give Us This Day Our Daily Bread

REVEREND LUTHER ALLAN WEIGLE, PH.D., D.D., LITT.D.
*Dean of the Divinity School of Yale University, New Haven, Connecticut and a Minister of the Congregational Church*

*Dean Weigle's explanation and exposition of this much debated clause of our Lord's Prayer is especially timely with the present great interest in the recently published Revised Standard Version of the New Testament. He is Chairman of the Council of the World's Sunday School Association Committee, a member of the executive committee of the International Council of Religious Education, was president of the Federal Council of the Churches of Christ in America, and has been chairman of the American Standard Bible Commission since 1930.*

*He studied at Gettysburg College and the Lutheran Theological Seminary at Gettysburg, and took his Ph.D. at Yale in 1905. He was ordained a Lutheran minister in 1903 and held a parish in Bridgeport, Connecticut. Then he became an assistant on the Yale faculty, later taught at Carleton College, and became professor of Christian nurture at Yale in 1916. He has been Sterling professor of religious education since 1924 and dean of Yale Divinity School since 1928. In recognition of his long and successful career, Carleton, Gettysburg, Muhlenberg, Dickinson, Ohio, Boston and Queens have conferred the honorary Doctorate upon him.*

*Among his most important publications are* The Pupil and the Teacher, Talks to Sunday School Teachers, Training Children in the Christian Life, American Idealism *(vol. X in "The Pageant of America"),* Jesus and the Educational Method.

## Sermon Forty=two

TEXT: Give us this day our daily bread.   MATTHEW 6:11

THIS is a strange petition—some think—to stand in the middle of the prayer that our Lord taught His disciples! Before it are three petitions that are concerned with God—with reverence for His name, the coming of His kingdom, and the doing of His will. After it are three that are concerned with man's moral needs and duties—forgiveness for sin and failure, strength to meet temptation, and deliverance from evil. Between these it seems to stand oddly alone, a frank, natural, unashamed petition for food.

It is but natural that many should try to interpret this petition in more spiritual terms. Origen in the third century declared that the bread for which we are to pray is not material but heavenly—that when we repeat this petition, we pray for "the bread of life," "the spiritual bread which nourishes our spiritual being." In an eleventh century manuscript Jesus is made to say, "Give us this day for bread the word of God from heaven." The Bible of the Roman Catholics makes this petition read: "Give us this day our supersubstantial bread." Even the latest Roman Catholic version, by Father Ronald Knox, gives this reading in a footnote, and explains that it may refer to the Holy Eucharist.

The fact is that we do not know the exact meaning of the Greek adjective which is translated by the English word "daily." It appears only here, in the Lord's Prayer as recorded by Matthew and Luke. It is found nowhere else in any Greek writing that has come down to us. We are unable, therefore, to study it in different contexts. We must infer its meaning from its deriva-tion. And that, unfortunately, is uncertain. The adjective is derived either from the verb that means "to come" or from the word that means "being" or "essence."

From the beginning, both in the Greek churches and in the Latin, tradition has favored the derivation from the verb "to come." So bread for which we pray is our bread for the coming day; and in the old Latin translation of the Scripture this was expressed by the Latin adjective which means "daily."

But St. Jerome, when revising the Latin translation of the New Testament toward the end of the fourth century, did a strange thing. He changed the adjective in Matthew's account of the Lord's Prayer to *supersubstantialem*, while he left the word for "daily" remain unchanged in Luke's account. There is no good excuse that can be given for Jerome. His action only proves that even saints can make mistakes.

Jerome's mistake is responsible for the phrase "supersubstantial bread" in the Catholic version of Matthew, while this retains "daily bread" in Luke. There was an amusing controversy on the subject in the Middle Ages between two of the greatest men of their time, St. Bernard of Clairvaux and Peter Abelard. St. Bernard contended for the use of the phrase "daily bread"; but Abelard insisted that "supersubstantial bread" must be correct, since Matthew was an apostle and Luke was not. Matthew, he said, was himself present and heard our Lord utter the prayer; Luke got it only by hearsay. It never occurred to either of these medieval scholars to turn to the original Greek, where they would have found that Matthew and Luke had really used the same word.

That controversy is now well behind us. The standard Protestant versions of the New Testament have all used the phrase "daily bread." Moreover, the great liturgies of the Roman Catholic Church, from the beginning until now, have all used the phrase "daily bread," and have never adopted Jerome's innovation. The recent Catholic version of the New Testament, made under the auspices of the Confraternity of Christian Doctrine, and the new translation by Father Knox, likewise use the phrase "daily bread." There is general agreement among scholars that the traditional usage is correct, that the adjective is derived from the verb "to come," and that the phrase does not refer primarily to spiritual food, but to the material provision for the ongoing of life.

That conclusion led to a new debate, however, in the 1870's, when the King James Version was being revised by committees of British and American scholars. Since the phrase means literally "bread for the coming day," it was suggested that the petition ought to be translated "give us this day our bread for the morrow." This issue was thoroughly discussed, and in the end the proposal was rejected. Against it stands the fact that the Greek language has a definite word for the morrow which would doubtless have been used here if that meaning had been intended. Perhaps the decisive factor in the debate was that some of the protagonists of the suggested change went too far by proposing the translation, "give us tomorrow's bread today." That sounded so impatient and grasping as to seem ridiculous.

In the meetings of the committee which prepared the recently published Revised Standard Version of the New Testament, this issue was debated again. Professor James Moffatt had used "bread for the morrow" in his New Translation; but he voted against it for this authorized revision. In the end the decision was to retain the phrase that has been used through the centuries—"daily bread." We felt that it would be a mistake to try to date that bread too precisely. After all, the point to the petition is not that we are trying to set the hour when bread shall be delivered, or asking God to keep our pantries supplied a· day ahead of actual need; our prayer is that the regular provision for our physical needs may be maintained, and the material conditions of life be unfailing.

So understood, this petition surely belongs to the Lord's Prayer. And it stands properly where it does, at the point where we turn in thought from God's sovereignty to man's duty. If God's will is to be done on earth as it is in heaven, it must be done by men. And men must live, capable in body and mind, if they are to fulfill God's gracious purpose for them. The Christian faith is for this world as well as for heaven; it is concerned with men's bodies as well as their souls.

A bit later in the Sermon on the Mount Jesus tells us not to be anxious about food and drink and clothing. "Do not be anxious, saying 'What shall we eat?' or 'What shall we drink?' or 'What shall we wear?' For the Gentiles seek all these things; and your heavenly Father knows that you need them all. But seek first his kingdom and his righteousness, and all these things shall be yours as well."

There are some who think that Jesus' counsel on this point was based upon the idea that the end of the world was at hand, and that therefore its values and interests, even its necessities, were not worth bothering about. But they are mistaken. This passage has nothing to say about the end of the world; it sets forth considerations that are valid for life as we know it upon this earth. Jesus' counsel, "Do not be anxious," is based upon the fact that God is our Father, that His care is constant even for birds and flowers and grass, and that He is sure to provide for the human life that is of much more value than these. Jesus reminds us, moreover, that anxiety is useless and futile, and that it is but good sense to face life's problems and duties when and as they come.

These reasons are still sound. They were true when Jesus uttered them; they are true and cogent today. God is yet our Father; His gracious provision for human welfare is constant and abundant; anxiety is needless and futile; each day brings God's gift of strength to bear its burdens and courage to fulfill its duties. It is not God who has failed us in these difficult times. His bounty is available and sure. His good earth has not lost its productivity.

Sunshine and rain, seedtime and harvest, have not ceased. In spite of our wastefulness, the resources of nature are still ample to sustain human life in abundance and peace. There is no sign that God's love is waning or His grace tiring.

When we pray for daily bread, therefore, it is not because we are uncertain of God's disposition or feel that it is necessary to beg Him for His gifts. Our prayer is a simple recognition of His Fatherhood and of our dependence upon Him. "Your Father knows what you need before you ask him," said Jesus, as he began to teach this Prayer to his disciples. When we say, "Give us this day our daily bread," we declare our faith that life and its sustaining are God's gift, and we express our trust in His constancy.

Yet God's gifts are not to the idle; they must be sought, cultivated, produced and distributed by men. The development of the sciences and the arts, the practice of sound economics and effective politics, and the putting of these to the service of social justice and good will are essential to the fulfillment of this prayer. Only as men seek His kingdom and His righteousness can God's constancy be of full effect in human life. Millions of men and women and children are not receiving their daily bread today. Undernourishment, hunger, even starvation, are their lot.

We can sincerely pray the Prayer which our Lord taught us, only as we constantly remember that it deals with more than our individual need. It is not "*My* Father. . . . Give *me* this day *my* daily bread." It is "*Our* Father. . . . Give *us* this day *our* daily bread." We can offer this Prayer sincerely only as we identify ourselves with the needs of all mankind, and are willing to labor as well as to pray that all may have their fair share of God's good gifts. And these gifts provide for more than mere subsistence; they include all that is necessary for the development of individual persons in fulfillment of their birthright as children of God.

Shortly before his death, William Temple, Archbishop of Canterbury, formulated a brief statement of six objectives which Christians should set before themselves, and labor to secure, with such governmental aid as may be found necessary. I want to give you that statement. It sets forth what the prayer for daily bread includes, under the conditions of life today, in the thought of one of the greatest Christian ministers and statesmen of our time:

1. Every child should find itself a member of a family housed with decency and dignity, so that it may grow up as a member of that basic community in a happy fellowship unspoilt by underfeeding or overcrowding, by dirty and drab surroundings or by mechanical monotony of environment.

2. Every child should have the opportunity of an education till years of maturity, so planned as to allow for his peculiar aptitudes and make possible their full development. This education should throughout be inspired by faith in God and find its focus in worship.

3. Every citizen should be secure in possession of such income as will enable him to maintain a home and bring up children in such conditions as have been described.

4. Every citizen should have a voice in the conduct of the business or industry which is carried on by means of his labor, and the satisfaction of knowing that his labor is directed to the well-being of the community.

5. Every citizen should have sufficient daily leisure, with two days of rest in seven, and, if an employee, an annual holiday with pay, to enable him to enjoy a full personal life with such interests and activities as his tasks and talents may direct.

6. Every citizen should have assured liberty in the forms of freedom of worship, of speech, of assembly, and of association for special purposes.

Underlying this statement of six objectives Archbishop Temple insisted upon the principle which had been formulated earlier by the four religious leaders of Great Britain—Anglican, Free Church, Roman Catholic, and Jewish—in their *Foundations of Peace:*

The resources of the earth should be used as God's gifts to the whole human race, and used with due consideration for the needs of the present and future generations.

The Lord's Prayer is compact; but it means a great deal. And when we pray in these days for daily bread we ought to mean no less than the full range of necessities for the life of free persons that Archbishop Temple has outlined. Our use of that Prayer is not simply a petition; it is also a dedication of ourselves to live and to labor for its fulfillment. We cannot use any part of the Lord's Prayer without praying that God's will may be done on earth as in heaven. And that prayer is a pledge that we will ourselves seek sincerely to do His will, and that we will never be content simply to receive, but will labor to produce, and will give and share, in order that all may have their just portion of His good gifts.

**RELIGION**

# Frozen Doxologies

REVEREND HERBERT MORRISON GALE, PH.D.
*Lecturer, Department of Biblical History, Wellesley College
and a Methodist Minister*

*Dr. Gale's lectures at Wellesley College make the Bible a book of great depth and meaning for the students in his classes. His own study was done at Missouri Wesleyan College, the State University of Iowa, Boston University, Boston University School of Theology and the University of Berlin. He traveled and studied in Palestine, then took his Ph.D. (New Testament major) at Boston University in 1939.*

*He is an ordained minister of the Methodist church, and served as minister*

[255]

*of the Methodist Church at Carrollton, Missouri, 1933-35; the Congregational Church, Pelham, New Hampshire, 1935-38; and the Methodist Church, Westboro, Missouri, 1938-39. He was a teacher of Bible at the Northfield School for Girls, 1939-44 (head of the Bible department, 1940-44), and became lecturer in the department of Biblical history, Wellesley College, in 1944.*

*Among his publications are "A Suggestion Concerning Matthew 16" (an article in the* Journal of Biblical Literature), A Study of the Old Testament *and various sermons in* Zions Herald.

*This sermon shows the need for spiritual reality in our faith and practice today and Dr. Gale's style makes his thought and feeling easy to follow.*

## Sermon Forty=three

A MAGAZINE article describing some of the world's great cathedrals has referred to them as "frozen doxologies." The phrase is not inappropriate, for these architectural achievements are, indeed, the solidified or "frozen" expressions of man's praise to God. As a matter of fact, there are countless other kinds of frozen doxologies as well—the paintings of a Raphael, the sculpture of a Michelangelo, the musical compositions of a Bach. The Bible itself, from one point of view, represents man's attempt to preserve in frozen form his efforts to offer praise to the God whose Word has been revealed. The same may be said of the creeds which the Church has formulated down through the centuries.

One's first reaction to these innumerable frozen doxologies is that of tremendous gratitude. They preserve for us the products of the noblest thought and aspiration of the past, and they inspire us to deeper thought and higher aspiration. Yet, while these values are fully recognized, it needs to be emphasized again and again that these frozen doxologies may actually constitute a most serious threat to real religion and to vital, living religious experience. These *things*, after all, are *not* religion; they are simply some of the by-products of religion. That which creates is always more important than the thing created. Architectural vision and skill are more important than the cathedral produced. Artistic insight and talent are more wonderful than the painting or manuscript composed. The religious experience of Jesus' followers was far more comprehensive and meaningful than any gospel or creed which was intended to describe it. The frozen doxologies are, after all, those things which come *from* religion. They are not religion itself.

There are two figures of speech which together may prove to be helpful. In the Gospel according to St. John, Jesus is represented as saying to the woman of Samaria at the well: "Whosoever drinketh of this water shall thirst again; but whosoever drinketh of the water that I shall give him shall never thirst; but the water that I shall give him shall be in him a well of water springing up into everlasting life." Professor Emil Brunner, in his book, *The Divine-Human Encounter*, speaking of a long period in the history of Christianity, writes: "The age of Orthodoxy appears like a frozen waterfall—mighty shapes of movement, but no movement."[1]

The contrast suggested in these related figures of speech is highly significant. The message of the early Church constituted the proclamation of a "well of water springing up into everlasting life." Much of Christianity, on the other hand, "appears like a frozen waterfall—mighty shapes of movement, but no movement."

There seems to have been in the history of the Church the constantly recurring tendency to identify religion with its frozen products. At times religion has been identified with the acceptance of a body of scripture mechanically inspired—or with the giving of assent to a creed or to an ethical code. These *things* have variously been regarded as constituting the absolute and final authorities for religion. In so far as this has been true, religion has become, indeed, like the frozen waterfall, preserving evidence of past movement, but having no *living* movement of its own.

Among persons for whom education is important there is less danger that many will be content with any one of these fixed and static formulations, be it the Bible, or a body of doctrine, or an ethical code; for education, by its very nature, is a continued striving for nothing less than Truth itself. In so far as this is true, religion becomes identified, not with something frozen, but with something that has movement; it becomes identified with an ever-active seeking for Truth, for Knowledge, for Wisdom.

Here, then, it would appear, is a worthy concept of religion. And, of course, the Bible itself would seem to justify this conclusion. Perhaps the classic example is that which appears in the Fourth Gospel: "And ye shall know the truth, and the truth shall make you free." Truth is stressed repeatedly in the Fourth Gospel and also in the letters of Paul. Knowledge, likewise, is emphasized in the Bible. "My people are destroyed for lack of knowledge," writes Hosea. And as for wisdom, an entire body of Wisdom Literature arose, extolling knowledge, wisdom and understanding as the highest object of man's search.

All of this would seem to support the conviction that religion is essentially a moving, active search for, and an acquiring of, knowledge, or wisdom, or truth. But then comes a startling and perhaps dismaying discovery. What the most inspired writers of the Bible mean by knowledge, wisdom and truth is something rather different from what is generally meant by those terms today—different, at least, in the sense that much *more* is involved than in most contemporary usage. When Hosea and Jeremiah speak of "knowledge," for example, they employ a Hebrew word which connotes far more than mere acquaintance with the facts. It is a word which involves a sense of responsibility; and with Hosea it is identified with "loyalty." Certainly the

[1] Philadelphia: The Westminster Press, 1943, p. 31. Used by permission.

prophets presuppose that knowledge of God includes an apprehension of certain facts regarding the divine nature and will; but what concerns them most is not simply this knowledge *about* God; it is rather a knowledge which goes beyond the intellectual apprehension *about* God and involves man's giving of himself to that which he knows.

Or consider "truth," as that word is employed in the Bible. It is interesting to note how many times in the Psalms, especially, mercy and truth (according to the Authorized Version) are combined. But here the words might better be translated "love" and "loyalty" (as Moffatt has translated them). In other words, the emphasis is not upon something known, but rather upon something in a category with "love"—something active and living. Again, it is suggested by the term "loyalty."

And in the Fourth Gospel, where truth is mentioned more frequently than in any other New Testament book, truth is not that which is known intellectually, but rather that which *does* something: "Ye shall *know* the truth," it is said, to be sure; but note what is added: "the truth shall *make* you free." Or, as the gospel writer turns it the other way around, "he that *doeth* truth cometh to the light." Truth is not simply that which is comprehended by the mind; it is something to be *done* as well as something *doing*.

What I am attempting to say, of course, is that religion is something more than, and beyond, even a moving, active search for knowledge or truth, as these terms are popularly employed.

It was stated earlier that with our present-day educational interest there may be little danger that many will be content with a view which identifies religion simply with the possession of, or the acceptance of, a fixed and frozen formulation. Emphasis is placed rather upon something which seems to have movement—an active search after truth and after a knowledge of that truth. What I am attempting to suggest, however, is that even this, in a more subtle but nevertheless real way, lacks the essential movement and living quality which characterize real religion. It is true that we are *actively* engaged in a pursuit of knowledge and truth. And yet, whatever knowledge and truth we are able to apprehend become, like the specific formulations, something which we *possess*. The aim remains, still, that which pertains to the area of the frozen rather than the living water.

All of this needs to be said today, for there is a very real tendency to regard the acquiring of knowledge and truth as the highest attainment. To educate men and women is the panacea for the world's ills! To give them correct ideas concerning the nature of the world, concerning mankind, concerning man himself, concerning a code for behavior, and concerning God, will insure the establishing of the kingdom of God! It is no accident that in educational institutions everywhere some of the most popular Biblical readings are those found in the so-called "Wisdom Literature." The danger in this lies in the fact that usually no distinction is made between the wisdom which is related to religious truth and that other wisdom which is conceived in purely secular terms, as the two are joined so incongruously, for example, in the book of Proverbs. And where the distinction is not made, the impression may easily be created that religion is to be identified with the latter. The secular sages who produced this were expressing the view which Professor Robert H. Pfeiffer describes well in his *Introduction to the Old Testament*: "By acute observation of the human scene, witty or sarcastic remarks, vivid characterizations and descriptions, clear reasoning and deflation of humbug, and following the dictates of common sense, they inculcated the homely lesson that success is attained through diligence in work, knowledge, intelligence, and decent living."[2] But this type of wisdom originally had nothing to do with religion; it was even regarded as antagonistic to piety by such prophets as Isaiah and Jeremiah; and the apostle Paul certainly emphasized the limitations of what he calls the wisdom of men.

"To know" simply is not the equivalent of "to have religious faith." It is always *persons* who possess knowledge, who know truth. Persons ought "to know" more than they do know. But religion is concerned primarily, not with *what* persons know, but with the relationship between persons (who know) and God, for it is that relationship which determines the use to which they will apply their knowledge—or not apply it. And it is that relationship which gives meaning to their knowledge.

If the state in which the world finds itself teaches us anything, it ought to be that knowledge and wisdom and technical skill in and of themselves are wholly inadequate. The more we "know" the closer we are brought to the possibility of destruction and annihilation. In many ways it appears to be true that our wisdom is not unlike that of Solomon. It may be said that in a very real sense we are the sons of Solomon, using our wisdom, as did he, to build a kingdom destined for ruin. Or perhaps some would prefer to say that we are the sons of the Greeks, whose wisdom included the knowledge of lofty ideas and ideals. But here again it may be remarked that "to know" has not provided the answer. As someone once expressed it, "the sons of Athens will never build the new Jerusalem." One is reminded of a statement made by Will Durant in his *Life of Greece*: "The Greek might admit that honesty is the best policy, but he tries everything else first."[3] All of this ought to make it abundantly clear that knowledge itself cannot save us; what we know may either be used for our destruction, or it may become a part of an ideal which has little revelance for life as it is lived.

Perhaps the point that needs to be emphasized most strongly is that not even the acquiring and possessing of wisdom or knowledge concerning the nature and will of God constitute religion. Professor Nels F. S. Ferré, in his book, *The Christian Faith*,[4] states that "Christianity is threatened both by those who stress *what* God is at the expense of *that* He is, and by those who

2 New York: Harper & Brothers, 1941.
3 New York: Simon & Schuster, Inc. Copyright, 1939, by Will Durant.
4 New York: Harper & Brothers, 1942.

insist *that* He is and yet refuse to define *what* He is." He suggests that of the two groups the former is the more dangerous, for those within this group regard Christianity as an ideal rather than a "living reality whose source, standard, and dynamic is God." Ideas are necessary, of course. But as Professor Ferré adds, "God's truth must be more than an idea; for the idea to have truth must refer to the pre-eminently real."

It is the religion of the Hebrew-Christian tradition which finds in *faith* that which can transform human life. This is not a faith which is contrary to the knowing, but it is a faith which goes beyond the knowing to a personal commitment to the Source of all knowing. It is not a faith which stands opposed to the acquiring of truth or wisdom in any area whatever, but it is a faith which can make of the wisdom of this world what the apostle Paul might call an instrument of righteousness. It is a faith which means such surrender to God that the "living water" flows and a "new creature" is born. Man must still learn from the frozen doxologies of the past. Man must continue to learn and to know and to formulate in new frozen forms the knowledge which he acquires. But man's life consists not in the "abundance of the things which he possesseth," whether they be possessions of the body or of the mind. Life is found, rather, as man commits himself in faith, and the Spirit of God becomes the new life within him.

Professor Brunner, whom I do not follow at all points, states the situation here with clarity and insight:

> Knowing, thinking, possessing something is . . . first of all, something over which I have disposal; secondly, something that does not essentially change me; and, thirdly, something that leaves me solitary. But if the Word of God meets me in faith, this is all reversed. Then I do not have something like property that is at my disposal, but I myself become property; then I myself become disposable. This is what faith stammeringly says in the words, "My Lord." Faith says it, indeed, with the words denoting "having something," with the possessive pronoun "my"—for our speech is formed out of our everyday life, out of that life which we possess; and yet this "my" means exactly the opposite; not that God stands at my disposal, but I at His. Herewith, in the second place, a radical reversal occurs. Faith is no longer like that knowing which enriches, which leaves me unaltered in the core of my person; on the contrary, it . . . does change me in the very core of my person. Out of a lord faith converts me into a servant, and therefore transforms the whole meaning of my existence. The "content" of my person, indeed, is left how and where it is, but the ruling principle is changed. . . . And, thirdly, solitariness is now also past . . . now there is unconditional fellowship.[5]

Christianity has found in Jesus Christ the revelation of God which makes such faith possible. Without this faith religion involves only what Paul calls the "form" of knowledge, and it becomes something like a frozen waterfall—mighty shapes of movement, but without movement. Through this faith Christianity offers a "well of water springing up into everlasting life."

[5] *The Divine-Human Encounter*, by Emil Brunner. Philadelphia: The Westminster Press, 1943, pp. 87-89. Used by permission.

# The Nature of Religion

REVEREND JOHN J. DOUGHERTY
*Professor of Sacred Scripture*
*Immaculate Conception Seminary (Roman Catholic), Darlington, New Jersey*

*For the last ten years Father Dougherty has taught the Sacred Scriptures to seminarians of the Immaculate Conception Seminary at Darlington, New Jersey. He went to Darlington in 1937 after three years of graduate work at the Pontifical Biblical Institute in Rome and in Jerusalem. Prior to the years at the Biblical school there he spent four years studying theology at Gregorian University in Rome.*

*His seven years abroad were replete with the riches of books, travel and learned men. In those years he saw most of the countries of Europe and the Middle East. Before the schools abroad he laid a sound college background at Seton Hall. His very earliest schooling was in the parish school of St. Aloysius in Jersey City.*

*Pulpits and platforms are Father Dougherty's almost daily station. This message on the nature of religion was given on the Columbia Broadcasting System's Church of the Air, February 10, 1946. Father Dougherty is an associate editor of* The Catholic Biblical Quarterly, *a member of the Board of Revisers of the Old Testament in the current revision of the Bible, and many Catholic magazines carry his articles.*

*He sees our day as one in which the emphasis is on education—above all education for Christ, for only thus can true education and true religion bring man into right relationship with God. He sees true religion as an elemental hunger of the heart and mind. His discussion of the nature of religion makes it easy for any man to grasp the fundamental concept of the meaning of faith in God in our modern world. His definition of religion should make many men think.*

## Sermon Forty=four

BEFORE you can discuss what religion is you must take a position on what you yourself are and what God is, and you must take a precise position. Your idea of God and man will perforce color your idea of religion; it may happen that your viewpoint on yourself admits no place for God or religion. Before all I state the position I take on myself: I judge that I am composed of matter and spirit, that I have a soul as well as a body, and that the spirit part of me is immortal. My position on God is this: I judge God to be a living, thinking reality with the power of choice; in other words, I believe in a personal God. I do not mean that He is a person in the same sense that I am a person, but that this perfection in me is a reflection of the immense personal reality that He is. This is the position I take on these two most important realities, and I know that it is the position that most of my listeners take. I highly recommend to those who do not to do some serious thinking about it. We can now come to talk about religion.

Now there are many religions in the world, and if I am to tell what religion is my statement must be true of all of them; it must cover religions of the past as well as the present, false religions as well as true religions. I say then simply that religion is an expression of man's nature, or religion is the expression of man's reaction to the world in which he wakes up to find himself. It is first an inward expression, and then becomes external by some manifestation. He notices that he is something little in something big, a microcosm in a macrocosm; by comparison with its size he is small, and by comparison with its power he is powerless, and in regard to knowing it he is ignorant. Yet he lives in it and by it; its sun warms him, and its rains nurture the food he eats. To him it is a moving, changing, mighty, mysterious thing, and his mind inevitably moves beyond it to its maker. From the things experienced he interprets the thing behind them as vast, powerful and awesome, upon which he and the world depend. This reaction of his mind is taken up by his heart, and he desires, loves or fears the thing. This does not mean that his believing produced God, any more than his seeing produced his eyes. Religion did not make God; rather religion is nature's response to being made by God.

This inward reaction of man gives birth to an outward expression; the expression of worship or adoration, the religious act; he bows his head in an attitude of reverence, or raises his hands in an attitude of pleading. These acts are natural to him, as natural as breathing. His nature is expressing the awareness of its dependence; he is saying to his maker that he is a thing made. Religion, therefore, rises out of a relation, the relation of man to his maker. Man perceives the relation as real; he knows he is a subject and he expresses his subjection; he knows he is dependent and he expresses his dependency. Religion is then the nature of man reacting to his existence and expressing his reaction in conduct. It is at once an inward conviction and an outward behavior.

Man's awareness of himself as immortal leads him to see God as his destiny as well as his origin. His awareness of himself as free and responsible, the feeling that he ought to do certain things and ought not do others, the awareness of himself as a social being with duties toward his fellow men produce the system of attitudes and conduct we call religion.

What I have said thus far is quite general, and covers most religions. Now how did I arrive at this synthesis I have just given? I came to it by a study of man, or better, a study of myself. We acquire knowledge by experiment or we accept it on authority. There is an element of both in most of our knowledge. Now in this matter of defining religion we can experiment with men, with primitive men by interpreting their religious culture from scant remains, or we can experiment with aboriginal men in some dark forest, or with bankers, butchers and babies. But the limitations of such experiments are obvious, and if they are not, a look at the results will make them so. The variety of theories on the origin of religion is confusing, if I may be permitted an understatement. There is one thing, and only one in the whole universe, which we know more about than we could learn from external observation. That one thing is man. We don't merely observe men, we *are* men. Of course, this approach has its limitations too. I must strive to divest myself of inherited prejudice and bias, and then complete myself by an ideal perfecting to the full stature of man. Man as man is the measure of human nature, not man as prince, as landowner, or as male; the whole man; living, sensing, thinking man. Your greatest responsibility and sublimest task is to interpret yourself, to define your status in the universe, to determine whence *you* are, and whither *you* are going. That is of the utmost importance to *you*, and the surest way to get an answer is to experiment honestly upon yourself with your mind. It is not by aligning yourself with a school of thought or theory that you determine your own destiny. This is not merely an academic matter. It is your personal, primary and eminently practical problem.

There must be a set of checks and measurements of one's interpretation of himself and his status in the universe. Man must be sure that his reaction to God is a reaction of his whole nature, his mind as well as his emotions. He must correctly analyze his inward sense, and its expression must be complete and consistent. He must check his personal interpretation of himself with the experience of the race. If he does this he will find that there were religions that were twisted and distorted. He will find that there were religions that expressed only part of man's nature or expressed it wrongly. In one he expressed his sex, in another his emotions. There was some truth in them, but very little. It is true that man is male and female, but that is not all he is. Such religions could satisfy for a time, for they expressed some part of man's nature, but they were incomplete, and could not survive any more than incomplete infants can. Other religions worshiped the nature God made for the God that made it. This was an expression of their sense of dependence; it was a partial expression of their status. This was an easy step to realize that they were mistaken, and that thunder was just as dependent as they were. Some realizing He was spirit thought He must reside anywhere or everywhere; they saw Him in stones and trees and waters; they did not distinguish his power from his presence. Then there were the abnormalities of religion, superstition and magic. They do not discredit religion any more than monstrosities discredit procreation. These things are not the measurement of man's religion because they are not the measurement of man's nature. We must take care not to fall short in what they fall short. I do not mean in the same thing, but in the same kind of thing. The man that will not worship an idol may worship the dollar.

My next observation is this: In the investigation of man we can commit errors of judgment by reason of some subtle prejudice. Compare the investigation of art with religion. I have heard no one debunk art because of the primitive wall paintings of the caves of the Dordogne or the modern mystifying mazes of Salvadore Dali, but there is no lack of those who debunk religion on the evidence of a primitive cult or a modern aberration. Like art religion has its primitive expressions and its modern distortions, but like art it is the effort of man to express himself before the stupendous reality he perceives; his expression may be feeble or magnificent according to his genius, but no one can deny the reality he is expressing, truth and beauty. People can perpetrate any imbecility in art, devise any absurdity in social planning, plot a hoax in medicine, yet no one scoffs at art, planning or medicine as bunk. But let religion show one gap in its armor, and there is a concentration of hostile forces on that weakness, until many are led to believe that there is nothing to religion save the hole in its armor.

What I have said thus far comes down to this: Religion is the sum of customs, practices and beliefs by which man expresses his dependency on God as his origin and his destiny, and the moral behavior rising out of his mature reflection on God, himself and his fellow man. When his religion is a proper and full expression of his nature it will satisfy him and endure. It is man that needs religion, not God. Man needs right religion. It will appear then that the mind plays a large part in the whole affair as I have described it; in fact it must, because mind is the most important thing about man. I have anticipated the objection that many and perhaps most religions are affairs of emotion, fear, sex, or anything else found in man. I did this by interpreting these as incomplete or distorted reactions to the supreme problem of man's existence. My point is that they do not measure religion any more than pygmies measure men. Of course a pygmy who has seen only pygmies may think so, and a man who has experienced only distorted religions and twisted religionists may conclude that religion is a misshapen thing and useless. But the limitation then is in the experience of both, and both are unfortunate. But my example is unreal. It is minds that are limited more than experiences. Our minds are limited by our emotional loves and hates. If we clear these out the mist will rise from our minds, and we shall see things clearly.

Now reason has come a long way in religion since the primitive man, just as it has in science, art and philosophy. The great interpreters of the universe and man in terms of religion are household names to all of you. There is nothing old-fashioned in their interpretation any more than the Mona Lisa and the Parthenon are old-fashioned. Truth and beauty are eternal realities, and the minds of prophets, poets and artists catch glimpses of them. We enthrone these rare and fitful glimpses as the enduring achievements of mankind. But there is another possibility. Thus far we have spoken of the thinking creature, the mind of man. The term of his thinking and loving in religion is God. The effort of his mind is to discover *the* interpretation of the universe and himself, the one that squares with God's. Could he ever dream that the term of his thinking would speak, that the personal God he adores would give his expression of the meaning of man? Could he? He did. Socrates confessed that man's interpretation was a risk, only a second-best compared with "some word of God which would more surely and safely carry him." There is a religion that holds that the dream of Socrates has come true, that the word has come from God to carry us on more surely and safely. That is what St. Paul meant when he wrote with a throbbing heart, "God . . . last of all in these days has spoken to us in his Son" (Hebrews 1:1). That religion must answer man's needs, for he that made you knows your needs better than anyone including yourself.

NIHIL OBSTAT: Rt. Rev. Msgr. Cornelius J. Kane, *Censor Librorum*
IMPRIMATUR: ✠ Most Reverend Thomas J. Walsh, S.T.D., J.C.D.,
    *Archbishop of Newark*

# Religion in Silver Slippers

REVEREND FREDERICK M. ELIOT, D.D.
*President, the American Unitarian Association, Boston
and a Unitarian Minister*

*Born in Dorchester, Massachusetts, Dr. Eliot attended the Roxbury Latin School, Harvard College and the Harvard Divinity School, and was instructor in municipal goverment in Harvard College, 1912-13.*

*He was associate minister of the First Parish in Cambridge, Massachusetts 1915-17, minister of Unity Church, St. Paul, Minnesota, 1917-37, and president of the American Unitarian Association, 1937 to date.*

*In World War I he was chaplain, first lieutenant, assigned to duty with Base Hospital No. 7, Tours, France, 1918-19. He is a trustee of Mount Holyoke College and of Hackley School, Tarrytown, New York, has the honorary Doctor of Divinity from Carleton College, 1935, and Meadville Theological School, 1937, and the honorary Doctor of Laws from the University of Minnesota, 1937. He is a member of the Board of Preachers of Harvard University.*

*This sermon shows the way to stronger lessons in the life about us today,
and his use of John Bunyan's famous account of religion in silver slippers
demonstrates the value of using exactly the right illustration in sermons in
any age.*

## Sermon Forty=five

Text: . . . in the presence of mine enemies.   Psalm 23:5

THE commandment to love our enemies has been a serious stumbling block
for many Christians, not merely because it is an exceedingly difficult
thing to do but also because it runs counter to a deep and seemingly reasonable dislike of the very idea. Why in the world *should* we love our enemies?
Just because Jesus said we ought to? Or is there some reason inherent in
the nature of the moral law itself that reinforces the teaching of the Master?
If there is such a reason, most of us have been unable to find it; and we fall
back upon the authority of the clearest moral teacher the world has ever
known, "taking his word for it" and valiantly struggling to put his precept
into practice—a struggle that very few even devout and consecrated disciples
have successfully waged. Loving our enemies just doesn't seem to make sense.
It goes against the grain of our stubborn human nature.

Perhaps the trouble is that we try too hard. Perhaps we would do well
to begin with something less difficult, postponing for a little while the attempt to carry out the full commandment of Jesus, in the hope that if we
can achieve at least part of it the way may be opened for fuller understanding and obedience.

Suppose we start with the idea, not of loving our enemies but of learning
from them. Even that will not prove easy, but it may prove a profitable
preliminary effort. If we can transform our enemies into teachers, it is at
least conceivable that we can begin to see the possibility of loving them.

A good many years ago, when I was a young and very inexperienced
minister, I had a friend who used to come a considerable distance to hear
me preach and then, once in a while, give me a little slip of paper on which
he had written out a quotation that he thought I "might someday use in a
sermon." I accepted these suggestions with appreciation, but it took me some
time to realize that what my friend was really doing was not providing me
with 'homiletical material' but offering me very direct and personal help. He
wasn't concerned to improve my preaching, but to give me a chance to learn
certain things for myself.

One day he gave me a slip of paper with these lines from Walt Whitman.
You will find them in "Sands at Seventy":

Have you learn'd only of those who admired you, and were tender with you, and stood aside for you?

Have you not learn'd great lessons from those who reject you, and brace themselves against you? or who treat you with contempt, or dispute the passage with you?

The discovery that those who oppose us can teach us great lessons—that we can learn from our enemies, yes, even from those who hate us and revile us and say all manner of evil against us—marks an important advance in our spiritual development. It is a discovery that comes with the shock of surprise, but like many of the surprises that life provides for us on our earthly pilgrimage it is salutary. It opens new doors of opportunity in what had seemed to be a solid wall of unscalable height. It changes the whole picture and gives the world a new and fairer aspect. Some of the best things in life come to us only "in the presence of our enemies." Some of the greatest lessons can be taught to us only by those who "brace themselves against us."

That is indeed good news. It transforms our enemies into potential allies. It more than doubles our own resources. It makes many things seem possible that we used to think we could never do. It sets our shoulders back and our chins up and our blood tingling. Maybe we cannot love our enemies, but at any rate we can use them to good purpose, and that is a big step forward.

The first lesson we can learn from our enemies is to recognize our own weak points and set about the business of curing them. If our enemies have their wits about them, they will plan to attack us where we are most vulnerable; and that attack may be the first intimation we have had as to where our greatest weakness lies. That is useful information; and it is a good deal more trustworthy than our own private judgment, for the best of us cannot wholly escape the bias of natural self-esteem. We do not enjoy finding fault with ourselves, and we almost inevitably try to conceal from ourselves the presence of serious flaws in the defenses of our inner citadel. One shrewd thrust of an enemy's rapier can sometimes tell us more about our weak points than any amount of self-analysis. The thrust may hurt our feelings, and the first reaction may be an instinctive wave of resentment or anger, but unless we are foolishly sensitive, we shall acknowledge to ourselves (if not to our foe) that the blow was well aimed and the weakness is actually there.

Then we can get to work reinforcing the weak place. And the final result in many cases will be that what our enemy has done is to make us far stronger than we would have ever been without the help he had no intention of rendering. We have used him to good effect, and after a while we may even begin to feel a little gratitude to him!

This is the way of common sense. It is also the way of religion, for it presupposes the kind of faith that is the very essence of religion. If a man learns from his enemies, he is exhibiting a very definite faith—in himself, in his neighbor, and in the nature of the universe—that is the necessary preliminary to the fulfillment of the law that Jesus taught. He takes unpromising material and transforms it into good. He is positive, creative, successful, an exemplification of St. Paul's admonition, "Be not overcome of evil, but overcome evil with good."

A second great lesson we can learn from our enemies is the discovery of unexpected resources of strength within ourselves and the possibility of developing these inner resources not only to meet attacks but to achieve results of a positive kind. If an enemy "dispute the passage with you," the challenge summons into action latent strength that grows with its use and can then be turned to constructive purposes. The muscles called into play to withstand those who "brace themselves against you" will be available to labor for objectives more important than the immediate resistance of the foe. The self-control acquired in dealing with those who "treat you with contempt" will prove adequate to all sorts of other situations. Out of the conflict with stiff opposition comes the strength of character that will carry to completion great tasks of lasting significance.

There are many illustrations of this principle in the pages of the Bible, especially in the New Testament. If you will reread the book of Acts with this idea in mind, you will find abundant evidence that Paul grew in spiritual stature with every attack from his enemies. This truth lies behind his words, "I know both how to be abased, and I know how to abound." He had mastered the "stronger lessons" that only enemies can teach. "Everywhere and in all things I am instructed both to be full and to be hungry, both to abound and to suffer need." He had learned great lessons from those who rejected him, and he used the strength of character thus developed in the service of the Master to whom he had dedicated his life.

There is, however, a deeper lesson that is to be learned only from the element of conflict that destroys our sense of ease and comfort. This lesson has to do with the nature of life itself as we men and women experience it on this earth of ours, and it is of most urgent concern to those to whom religion is a matter of primary interest. Some of us imagine that religion ought to make life smooth and pleasant, relieving pain and teaching us how to avoid the tragic sufferings and disappointments that mark the lives of most people. We think of religion as an opiate, as a way of escape, as a short cut to happiness. Nothing could be further from the truth.

In *Pilgrim's Progress* there is a passage that sets forth in memorable fashion the contrast between the two ideas. Christian and Hopeful overtake "one that was going before them, whose name was By-ends," and in their talk together By-ends describes the people of the town of Fair-speech from which he had come. " 'Tis true, we somewhat differ in religion from those of the stricter sort, yet but in two small points: First we never strive against wind and tide. Secondly, we are always most zealous when Religion goes in his silver slippers; we love much to walk with him in the street, if the sun shines, and the people applaud him."

To which Christian replies, "If you will go with us, you must go against wind and tide. . . . You must also own Religion in his rags, as well as when in his silver slippers, and stand by him too, when bound in irons, as well as when he walketh the streets with applause."

Then By-ends makes his decision. "I shall never desert my old principles, since they are harmless and profitable." So Christian and Hopeful parted company with him, and he was joined by three other companions who rejoiced in the names of Mr. Hold-the-World, Mr. Money-love, and Mr. Save-all, all of whom were "for religion in what, and so far as, the times and my safety will bear it."

Religion in silver slippers! Yes, there are moments in all our lives when faith shines clear and bright, when the way before our feet is pleasant and gay, when the children in the market place pipe for us to dance. Religion has its days of happy festivals and celebrations. But it is not on those days that the "stronger lessons" are learned; and if we turn aside from the days when wind and tide are adverse, when faith is bound in irons, we shall reach the Celestial City. Religion is not a device by which we can escape conflict, but a trumpet call that sends us into the thick of battle for a great cause. Religion is not a short cut that enables us to by-pass the rough places, but a summons to use all our energies and all our brains in a determined effort to make the rough places smooth for those that shall come after us. To miss this understanding is to live in a dream world of our own devising and to miss the deeper and durable satisfactions of life.

These things, among others, we may learn from our enemies—if we will; and as we learn them, we shall find our attitude toward our enemies beginning to change. Not unmitigated hatred, but something more like respect, tempered with gratitude. And after a while, perhaps, gratitude touched with compassion and understanding, and a desire to serve. Then we shall find ourselves "not far" from the attitude toward at least some of our enemies that Jesus commanded us to feel and express; and we shall discover that some of life's greatest gifts are found only "in the presence of our enemies."

## Universal Charity

THE MOST REVEREND RICHARD J. CUSHING, D.D.
*Archbishop of Boston (Roman Catholic)*

*Archbishop Cushing was born in Boston on August 24, 1895 and was educated at Boston College and St. John's Seminary, Brighton, Massachusetts. He was ordained to the priesthood May 26, 1921, by the late William Cardinal O'Connell. He engaged in pastoral work in the Archdiocese of Boston from 1921-39. For many years he was the Diocesan Director of the Society for the Propagation of the Faith. During these years he acquired his famed reputation for knowledge of, and generosity to, missionary work throughout the world. He became the Auxiliary Bishop· of Boston in June, 1939, and Archbishop of Boston, succeeding the late Cardinal O'Connell, in September, 1944.*

*The Archbishop is a dynamic, forceful and celebrated preacher. His sermons are usually of a strictly devotional nature, but his public addresses on moral and social questions have attracted widespread attention among Catholics and non-Catholics alike. His sermons and addresses are characterized by forthrightness and uncompromising Catholic magnanimity.*

*His frank analysis of the state of chaos in the world and the need of Christ in education, politics and all of life make this a sermon to reach thoughtful minds everywhere.*

### Sermon Forty=six

THE world still hovers on the brink of chaos because Christ's Law of Universal Charity is not given its chance to shape the future of the world.

At the beginning of World War II our late President wrote these immortal words: "We shall win this war and in victory we shall seek not vengeance but the establishment of an international order in which the spirit of Christ shall rule the hearts of men and of nations." When a civil leader speaks in this outspoken fashion of the necessity that the spirit of Christ dominate the future, a religious leader, a teacher in the Church of Christ, need not apologize for availing himself of every possible opportunity to promulgate unto the public good that Law of Universal Love which gives concrete expression to the spirit of Christ. If it be true, and it is true, that the establishment of an international order and the preservation of national security both require the inspiration of Christ's Law of

Charity, then he who preaches that Law, in season and out, well serves his nation and best aids humanity.

The principal moral problem of life in society at this particular hour of the world's history is the problem of how to do precisely these two things: to serve one's nation worthily, and yet, at the same time, to aid in the building of an international order within which humanity can also be served. How can we cherish, as cherish we must, the heritage which became ours with our national independence, and yet share, as share we must, in the common good of the interdependent family of nations? How can we love, as love we must, America and everything for which she stands, and yet love, as love we also must, all humanity and all the human values which America, or any people, can only hold in common with the men of every land?

This is the Master Knot of human fate as men gather from their several nations in the effort to plan a better world in the face of a thousand political, economic and cultural forms which this problem takes. It is the stumbling block on every proposed path to peace. It is the foremost factor in every situation that leads to modern war.

Charters and constitutions may diagram an international order; they cannot create it, for they are purely legal instruments and legalism kills the spirit more often than it quickens. Trade agreements and commerce may develop from an international order, but they presuppose its existence; they cannot create it. In the absence of an international order they become exploitation at their best and piracy at their worst. Education, by itself, does not guarantee the peace; indeed, it is one of the most discouraging mysteries of our civilization that wars and the conditions which produce wars seem most to flourish among those peoples who, on the scientific level at least, are the most, rather than the least, educated nations. The Catholic hierarchy in the United States made an irrefutable analysis of the origins of World War II when they said: *"This war came largely from bad education. It was not brought on by primitives or unlettered peoples."*

Pervading all legal formulas, all economic arrangements, all educative programs there is needed the spirit of Christ and His Law of Universal Charity. Inspiring all efforts to write a new political law or to direct the laws of economics, there must be that Law of Love.

Let us apply this to the problem we stated for ourselves a little earlier. Christ blended in His personal life a perfect love for His own nation with an unparalleled love for humanity. Through all His life and even in the hour of His death, He fulfilled with scrupulous care the national observances of His people and the customs of His country. Reading His life, in the lines in which it is written and between those lines, we see and sense at every crisis of His career the tender preferential love of Christ for His own people and for their national way of life. He would have been less than human did not a perfect patriotism find its place in His moral personality. His parables provide so many precious pictures of the little details of daily life among the humble folk and in the out-of-the-way places where He spent His boyhood. The most sublime principles of His divine teaching come to us through the medium of figures of speech, comparisons and examples redolent of Nazareth and Galilee and of all the land and living of the Jewish people. With all His heart Christ loved this people to whom He belonged by bond of ancestry, of language, of common characteristics, of special friendships, of shared griefs, of mutually cherished traditions, land and hopes.

He loved His own people on the heroic level of their national greatness; He loved the history of His nation, the names of its great men and the glorious incidents of its immemorial struggles. The memory of the Patriarchs who had gathered and organized the Hebrews in Palestine, especially the memory of Abraham, father of his people, flashes constantly through the preaching of Christ. The authority of Moses, lawgiver of his people, is constantly invoked by Christ in His own moral legislation, and with Moses and Elias He chose to share the moment of His Transfiguration.

He loved His own people on the humble level of their popular traditions, and it is interesting to note how many times the Scripture recounts His intimate presence at the national feasts and popular festivals of His people. Countless homely phrases of His nation's simple folk find their way to His lips; He loved to speak of the naïve local manner in which they forecast the weather or planned their domestic economies or carried on their daily lives with one another. Little phrases, evocative of all these, illumine His most exalted doctrines, and even His most universal teachings are given lively form in local examples from the little province He best knew and loved.

Christ spent Himself so utterly for those who were close to Him, His friends, His people, His nation, that all His love might seem to have been not merely lavished, but exhausted on them. And yet, nothing could be further from the truth, for the truth is that He was the perfect type of the universal-minded man. Salvation, He taught, came from His people, the Jews, but He did not teach that it was destined for the people of any one nation. He sought to be the true light which illumines every man that comes into the world. He chose His Apostles from His own people but He gave them a world-wide mandate and fired them with a universal charity. He sent them to preach His Gospel to all men without distinction of race, or nation, or color or social rank.

Sometimes Christ called Himself and suffered others to call Him the Son of God but, strangely enough, He seems especially to have loved His other title: Son of Man. This phrase, indicative of His solidarity with, and love for, all the human race, was constantly used by Him to describe Himself, His work and His destiny.

Christ felt as a "Son" to all the human family, and His moral attitudes toward humanity are based, as a consequence, not on any cold sense of justice nor merely tender pity, but on an intense and reverent *filial* love for Man whose Son He was. His pride in the title "Son of Man" reflects the manner in which He loved every human being in the world and reverenced human nature wherever it was to be found, however degraded or guilty the persons in whom it abided.

I know of no greater lesson which our generation must learn from Christ than this lesson. They must learn it not merely for their personal sanctification but also for their political and social security, if not, indeed, survival! A time of war, and especially the period immediately following a victory, is apt to produce in men attitudes alien to Christ's Law of Universal Love. That, alas, is the reason why periods of peace are usually so brief and so precarious. No nation, however strong, can build a peace unless it be motivated by great love. Partisanship, nationalism, racism, any social particularisms and especially those tinged with hatred, can only be principles of destruction; only love can bring a positive inspiration to the building of a better world.

Universal Charity inspires the missionary to give his life in the service of people who put to death, perhaps, his elder brothers and sisters in the Faith. Universal Charity used to prompt even victorious princes in more humane days to seek their greater victories over the hearts and the intelligences of the conquered by means of clemency and forebearance. The world will belong to those who love it most and who win it by love; it can never belong to those who hate any part of it and strive to impose their will by violence upon their erstwhile enemies.

There is no lesson, I repeat, which we must more sincerely learn than this, and there is no more certain method of learning this lesson than by the development in our personal and collective lives of that spirit of Christ to which the late President pledged us. His spirit will require that we blend with our love for America a Universal Charity for all humanity; His example will teach us how to do so.

Historical circumstances may set one group of men against another for a time, and occasionally all society must act against even one man who has tried to be a law unto himself. Sometimes retributive justice or even simple prudence will require measures of sternness against a group or an individual, but the substance of Christ's Law of Universal Charity still holds, and so long as our society is Christian, so long as it is humane, there can be no place in its vocabulary for *hatred* against any group or any nation, no matter what that nation may have done. The spirit of Christ is no longer abroad in a land whose leaders of public opinion can speak unchallenged of the possibility of *hating* their enemies. That nation has acquired a thoroughly pagan soul, whatever its outward religious rites, which speaks of hatred as the due of its enemies and adopts measures based on hatred as the policy of its peacemaking.

[ 273 ]

There are grave indications in certain popular books, periodicals, radio "columns" and public speeches that many influential leaders of opinion about peace planning are victims of that pagan spirit. But their attitudes are condemned by the spirit of Christ: "You have heard it said," Christ told His followers, "that thou shalt love thy neighbor and hate thine enemy, but I tell you, love your enemies and pray for them that persecute you!" That is Christ's Law of Universal Charity.

No one can promise that if tomorrow all men begin the effort to keep this precept of Christ the peace of the world will be assured the day after tomorrow. No one can promise that the imitation of Christ will renew the face of the earth in this or that predictable period of time. The Kingdom of God cometh not with observation, and the building of a perfect society out of members still imperfect must be a long and patient task. No one can predict that the acceptance of Christ's Law of Love will immediately result, even among the devout, in the resolution of the ancient conflict between loyalty to our national independence and love for the international community.

But we can be sure that if we reject the example of Christ, then we may as well despair of ever solving any of these problems now or later. And I do confidently make my own the implied warning of the departed President under whom this nation went forth to war: the war will be lost and the victory in vain if we become ourselves victims of the spirit of vengeance and if we fail to establish an international order in which the spirit of Christ shall rule the hearts of men and of nations.

Let us pray that Christ's Law of Universal Charity will enlighten the minds and unite the hearts of men and nations. Thus will the best beginning be made toward the peace that all men crave.

# George Washington Carver: A Scientist Who Knew God

REVEREND DANIEL G. HILL, TH.D.

*Acting Dean of the Chapel, Howard University, Washington, D.C.*
*and a Minister of the A.M.E. Church*

*Born in Annapolis, Maryland, Dr. Hill was the son of a minister of the local annual conference of the A.M.E. Church, studied at Lincoln University, Iliff School of Theology, the University of Oregon, Pacific School of Religion, and took his Th.D. at Iliff School of Theology.*

*In World War I, he was a second lieutenant in the infantry, U. S. Army. On his return, he became probation officer, Court of Domestic Relations of Multnomah County, Oregon, 1930-33; case worker and supervisor, State Relief Administration, Oakland, California, 1936-40. He has had twenty-five years pastoral experience with the A.M.E. Church in Missouri, Colorado, Oregon and California, was a member of the board of directors, Oakland Y.M.C.A., 1938-43, member of the Mayor's Defense and Recreation Committee, Oakland and Berkeley, California, 1942-43, co-chairman Race Relations Commission, Denver Council of Churches 1944-45; chairman, Denver, Colorado, F.E.P.C. Committee, 1945.*

*He is resource leader for race relations conferences and activities among student groups and for the application of social work techniques in pastoral programs. At present he is acting dean of the Andrew Rankin Memorial Chapel and associate professor of practical theology, the School of Religion, Howard University. This biographical sermon brings the life and work and faith of a great Negro into clear perspective.*

## Sermon Forty=seven

TEXT: He hath put a new song in my mouth, even praise unto our God. PSALM 40:3

A FEW years ago, over the chartered lanes of the air, and through myriad releases of the Associated Press, the United Press and in countless independent newssheets throughout America and the world, flashed the news of the death of a great man—the passing of one whom the wise men of the world shall, in the days to come, call "One of the saintly men of God." Doctor George Washington Carver, agricultural chemist of Tuskegee, Alabama, had answered the call of his Creator. For him the sweet chariot had swung very low; he stepped on board and he was at rest with his God. Believe me when I tell you that I speak reverently of this man, for there was something about the mind and heart and spirit of the eminent scientist of Tuskegee which makes us know that he had been with God and had learned of His ways—his life, his achievements inspire one to seek and find the hidden source of power—that it was his to know, to drink deep of the celestial spring of life whence he daily quenched his thirst, and to walk and talk with God in the quiet cool of the morning! Surely the praises of the psalmist were in his heart: "I waited patiently for the Lord; and he inclined unto me, and heard my cry. He brought me up also out of an horrible pit, out of the miry clay, and set my feet upon a rock, and established my goings. And he hath put a new song in my mouth, even praise unto our God" (Psalm 40:1-3).

George Washington Carver overcame apparently insurmountable difficulties. He was born a slave, about 1864 at Dimond Grove, Missouri, the property of a German-born slave master who bore the name of Carver. The exact date of his birth has really never been established. In his early and impressionable childhood his mother and he were kidnaped by slave traders and, although Carver's owner succeeded in finding him and ransomed him for the sum of three hundred dollars (which sum was obtained by the sale of a race horse), the boy's mother was never found. At the age of ten this precocious lad found a country school located eight miles from his home and attended it! He was a frail and sickly child, but possessed of an unquenchable desire for knowledge. He finally found his way to Simpson College, Iowa, which he attended for three years, working the meanwhile at the common, everyday tasks to pay his tuition and to support himself. From Simpson College and the office of its president, Dr. Edwin E. Voight, came this touching tribute upon the passing of Dr. Carver:

> Dr. George W. Carver was Simpson's most illustrious son and his services to mankind were a constant inspiration to the generations of students who succeeded him here. The entire Simpson family enters with you in the fellowship of sorrow as he enters his eternal reward and leaves us to carry on from where he left off.

George W. Carver entered Iowa State College where he was given a seat at the servants' table: when he graduated with distinction, and wrote the class poem, he was accorded a place at the table with the faculty and remained at the institution two years to teach as a member of the staff in charge of systematic botany, and the bacteriological laboratories. He earned the bachelor and master of science degrees, and became a doctor of philosophy in the field of agricultural chemistry. It was at Iowa State College that he was discovered by the eminent Booker T. Washington, and persuaded to go to Tuskegee Institute, Alabama, the great school which was to become the scene of his greatest services and scientific triumphs. Here, at Tuskegee, he taught the farmers of the South, white and black men who were expending their energies upon an exhausted soil, to experiment with crop rotation. Federal and state agencies assisted him in this project: *thus he helped to save and to rebuild the agricultural economy of the South*. He took the common crops, such as the sweet potato, cotton, the lowly peanut, persimmons and common weeds, and brought forth, as though by magic, hundreds of new and useful products. From the peanut alone he developed more than three hundred products, including milk, butter, cheese, vinegar, salad oil, face powder, flour, instant coffee, Worcestershire sauce, pickles, complexion cream, shampoo, axle grease, ink, a breakfast food, and an ointment for the treatment of infantile paralysis; nineteen shades of dyes and stains and face powder from the sweet potato; paving blocks from cotton and numerous products from the dandelion, tomatoes and trees. Throughout the southland he sent hundreds of thousands of bulletins demonstrating how to make salads or boiled greens of dandelions, clover, poke weed and white potato tops. England, in an extremity for food one year, requested Dr. Carver to send his bulletins to her.

"The Wizard of Tuskegee," as he was frequently called, was invited to speak before the Ways and Means Committee of the Congress, to explain his work among the rural farmers of the South and to tell of his plans for the reconstruction of the agricultural economy of the South. He was allotted ten minutes to tell of his work: but so fascinated did his hearers become with his message, that he spoke, at their insistence, for one hour and forty-five minutes!

Fabulous offers came to this lowly man of genius, which he refused in order to work with his fellow men of the South. In 1938, Ripley, of "Believe It Or Not" fame, reported that Dr. Carver had refused an offer of two hundred thousand dollars a year to work in the Edison Laboratories: the Russian government sought his services and, although Mr. Carver refused again to leave his laboratories in Tuskegee, he did send a pupil, Mr. John Sutton, who has been working in the Soviet Republic for about nine years. Henry Ford invited him to the Dearborn Laboratories, but Carver steadfastly remained at his work in Alabama. He returned to the region of his early childhood and slavery to liberate his fellow men from the bondage of poverty and ignorance, from suspicion and prejudice and hate. *And in his own workshop in the heart of the deep South, the recognition of the world was accorded him.* In 1928, the Crown Prince of Sweden visited him. Here came, also, the Duke of Windsor and the president of the United States of America. He was made a Fellow of the Royal Society of Arts of London. The Spingarn Medal was awarded him in 1923; the Roosevelt Medal was given to him in 1939 for "distinguished services in the field of sciences." This award read: "TO A SCIENTIST HUMBLY SEEKING THE GUIDANCE OF GOD—AND A LIBERATOR TO MEN OF THE WHITE RACE AS WELL AS THE BLACK." In 1940, the International Federation of Architects, Engineers, Chemists and

Technicians presented him with a bronze plaque for his great contributions to his fellow men. Eleven hundred persons cheered him for five minutes in Atlantic City a few years ago, when the Variety Clubs of America gave him the one thousand dollars Humanitarian Award as the "Greatest Living Scientist in America."

Nevertheless, this man of great scientific accomplishments was so retiring, so utterly self-effacing in his own way, so humble and commonplace, that he was often mistaken for a tramp or ordinary man of the streets. When he visited a Philadelphia chemical laboratory some years ago where work had begun on his tonic made from the peanut, he was so shabbily dressed that members of the staff thought he was a decrepit old man looking for a handout; he was arrested in Chicago because he gave the appearance of being a bootlegger as he carried an old carpet bag; a New York hotel clerk refused him accommodations because his suit was unpressed, torn and patched; a delegation sent to meet the great chemist at a certain station in Kentucky returned home without him because "no one got off the train except an old Negro farmer."

There are those who would ask: How account for the greatness of one who was born a slave? What was the secret of his success? Where and how did he summon the energy and the mental alertness to bring to pass these great discoveries. This, I believe is the answer: George Washington Carver was a scientist who knew God. A spiritual kinship with the Man of Galilee was the basis of his greatness. He would arise daily at four o'clock in the morning and walk out into the woods to commune with his Creator; to talk with the flowers and the trees, and to listen to the liquid music of yonder rivulet as it sang and danced on its way down to the river—and there, in the presence of God, the mysteries of life would yield their secrets to him; there the rocks would unlock their treasures, and the common clay became his servant and was molded by his hands; every bird recognized him to be a friend and serenaded him with its call. The petals of the wild rose and the perfume of the shrinking violet were but the outward revelation of secrets awaiting to be born. As Tennyson said:

> Flower in the crannied wall,
> I pluck you out of the crannies;
> Hold you here, root and all,
> In my hand, little flower—
> But if I could understand what you are,
> Root and all, and all in all,
> I should know what God and man is.

And this was Dr. Carver's explanation: *"Alone in the woods each morning, I best hear and understand God's plan for me."*

Yes, it was this great spiritual influence that made him a servant and worker with God and a friend to man.

The Honorable Henry A. Wallace, former vice-president of our nation, has predicated the life of Tuskegee's great scientist upon the foundation of his faith in Jehovah. Recently, Mr. Wallace said:

> When Doctor Carver died the United States lost one of its finest Christian gentlemen. He was a good friend of my father and mother, and I had known him for forty-seven years. To the world he was known as a scientist. Those who knew him best, however, realized that his outstanding characteristic was a strong feeling of the eminence of God. Everything he was and did found its origin in that strong and continuous feeling.

Here surely was a saint of God and a servant of men who now rests from his labors.

J. H. Shelton, chairman of the nonsectarian, Anti-Nazi League, said of Carver:

> America has lost one of her greatest minds, and in the example of his life, the world has gained a powerful weapon against the abhorrent doctrines of Hitlerism. Dr. Carver was one of the least Aryan of all the earth's inhabitants, and yet he was the acknowledged leader of one of the most complex of all the fields of Twentieth Century science.

George Washington Carver, real age unknown, born in obscurity and poverty of slave parents, is today one of America's immortals. In the unfolding and development of his soulful personality, delicately and sensitively attuned as it was to the Divine in his numerous, constructive benefactions to America and to the world, in his tireless and unselfish service to his countrymen, is seen the miracle that is AMERICA—and the witness that "God moves in a mysterious way his wonders to perform." And today, as we work for world brotherhood and better race relations and think in terms of world peace, we are a step nearer the goal of our dream of the centuries—for the orphaned slave of Dimond Grove, Missouri, this waif of the Missouri prairies who was ransomed with money obtained by the sale of a race horse, this servant of the black and white farmers of the South, this teacher of the hopeful youth of Tuskegee's famed Institute, inspires us with the unprecedented accomplishments of his life: "He hath put a new song in my mouth, even praise unto our God."

# It's the Plus That Counts

REVEREND FRANKLIN CLARK FRY, D.D., LL.D., L.H.D., LITT.D

*President of the United Lutheran Church in America
and a Minister of the Lutheran Church*

*Late in 1945, Dr. Fry spent six weeks in Europe, visiting England, Denmark, France, Holland, Germany and Switzerland as a member of two special commissions—one representing the American Section of the Lutheran World Convention, the other, the Federal Council of the Churches of Christ in America, in the interest of postwar relief and reconstruction among the churches abroad, with findings reported to President Truman. He is president of Lutheran World Relief, one of the eleven bodies licensed by the President's War Relief Control Board to collect and distribute relief in Germany under the Council for Relief Agencies Licensed for Operation in Germany (CRALOG).*

*As president of the United Lutheran Church in America, with an adult membership of more than 1,250,000, Dr. Fry heads the largest Lutheran body in the United States, and is also prominent in interdenominational activities. He is the third American member of the World Council of Churches' Department of Reconstruction and Inter-Church Aid, serves as a director of Church World Service, and is a member of the North American Administrative Committee of the World's Sunday School Association.*

*Born in Bethlehem, Pennsylvania, August 30, 1900, he spent his early life in Rochester, New York, graduated from Hamilton College in 1921 and studied at the American School for Classical Students in Athens, Greece. He took his theological training at the Lutheran Theological Seminary in Philadelphia, and was ordained by the Lutheran Synod of New York and New England at Ithaca, New York, on June 10, 1925. During the next four years he was pastor of the Lutheran Church of the Redeemer at Yonkers, New York, then served as pastor of Trinity Lutheran Church, Akron, Ohio, from 1929-44 when he was named president of the United Lutheran Church in America. Muhlenberg College, Roanoke College, Wittenberg College, Thiel College Gettysburg College, Wagner College, Hartwick College and Hamilton College have conferred the honorary doctorate upon him.*

*This sermon was given on The National Radio Pulpit, Sunday, February 10, 1946, when Dr. Fry was guest preacher in the absence of Dr. Ralph W. Sockman. The distinguished leader of the United Lutheran Church raises an important question: What is the outstanding mark of a Christian? On the answer to this may hinge the conversion of some of the seventy million people who never attend any church in America; it is an important matter for each individual. Dr. Fry proves himself a preacher of power, a man of perception, judgment and heart.*

# Sermon Forty=eight

WHAT do you say is the outstanding mark of a Christian? In asking it, mind you, I am not thinking at all of what you might call merely the external signs of our religion, things like Bible reading and church attendance and prayer. They are indispensable, of course. In modern mechanical terms, they are the generators of religious life. The testimony of Dr. Hans Asmussen, the chancellor of the newly awakened German Evangelical Church, still rings in my ears as he sent it through me recently. "When people stop going to church," he warned, "then comes a movement like Naziism. Tell America." Yet after all, these outward means are only intended to be stimuli of the spirit. What is inside? And in what order?

One popular view will focus immediately upon a Christian's imagined optimism. There, surprisingly many seem to think, is the quality which is always most typical of a follower of Jesus. A Christian, you hear them say, and even arch their eyebrows in saying it, invariably expects the best. It makes no difference what calamities threaten, how bleak the prospects are; even if he has to do it blindly, it is his nature to look for a happy outcome. The flaw in that picture, of course, is that it is sadly overdrawn. It is not so much a portrait as a caricature. It is the strange way in which those who have never possessed it, misinterpret our faith. We who believe in God, admitted, do have a sturdy confidence that He will triumph in the end. We glory in it. Yet that does not indicate by any means that we are unprepared for jolts along the way. A Christian couldn't be, in a religion with a cross at its heart! No, begging your pardon, an indiscriminating optimism is not our plainest badge.

Or some might venture that charity is. Without too much boasting, truthfully a strong case might be made for that. There can be no doubt that a vigorous and sincere Christian discipleship does make a man generous. If any of us hasn't had that happen in our own characters, we had better ask ourselves some searching questions. Do we genuinely have the Spirit of the Lord? There *is* a liberality that flows from love. Almost every charitable organization in the country has been strengthened by it. If you were to ask these organizations where they get their main support, practically without exception they would answer in a chorus that they find it in Americans who have learned the grace of giving at the feet of Jesus Christ. Yet even charity regrettably is not distinctive enough.

Dearly as I would love to do so, this is the last false lead that I will start you on, we cannot claim it even for patience. I am most loath of all to admit this but even it is not an infallible mark of every Christian. Emphatically it ought to be, for there is no virtue in all the galaxy of goodness that is more Godlike. Think how marvelously, inexhaustibly willing the Master has been to wait for us, year after weary year. Certainly we, his followers, should be equally ready to be patient with him and with one another. We should be but, alas, we aren't!

From all such human speculations, it is a relief to turn to Jesus' own Sermon on the Mount, in Matthew 5:47, and learn from the lips of the Saviour himself what the outstanding mark of a Christian must be. You will be surprised if you are not very familiar with the Bible. In expressing his standard for us, Jesus casts it in the form of a curt, piercing question. Looking us squarely in the eye, he asks bluntly, "What do ye more than others?"

Christ's query to you and me has two distinct facets and both repay tarrying over them. In the first, the verb has the accent, "What *do* ye more than others?" That is enough by itself to make this text popular today, for the modern mood powerfully stresses action. The principal reason, I verily believe, why for many Christianity has lost its glamour, if that word ever rightly fits religion, is because almost everywhere a disastrous notion has spread that it is negative. All the colors have been bleached out of it. If you ask the traditional man-in-the-street what you must do to be a Christian, the overwhelming chances are that he will fling back that you must not do this and not that and not the third. From the irritation in his voice you can tell he feels that Christianity is a killjoy. All that is left is a drab and repellent gray.

That is a slander. It is a false and stunted estimate of our religion and is absolutely not true. The rub is that we have carelessly allowed crowds of people to believe it. Actually many have even been incited to it by Christians who ought to know better. No one alive can measure the sapping weakness that has resulted in our common spiritual life. You just can't hold the allegiance of warm-blooded people to a vacuum and it is high time that we awakened to it. Our guilt is that we have permitted a whole generation to forget, and ironically we have chosen this generation which can least afford to do so, that a striding after Christ means daring and adventure and life.

But if the accent naturally lingers on the verb, on "do," there is another word in our text on which it should fall most hauntingly and persuasively of all. That is the word "more." Let me read it again with that altered inflection, "What do ye *more* than others?" In a brilliant flash, *there*, I verily believe, is revealed what we have been seeking for, the hidden essential quality of the Christian life. It is as if the Master says to us, Christians, it is the plus that counts. Others may be moral. Millions of them are. We must be more—righteous. Others may be kind. All honor to them. Life would be intolerable without it. We must be more—compassionate! Others may be honest. We must be more—generous! Others may mete out exact justice. We must do more. We must pervade that justice with love! "So shall men know that ye are my disciples." The test of Christianity dazzlingly, all-inclusively the more we think of it, shines in that "more."

If a vague memory serves me right, it was Kirby Page who remarked what seemed to him an anomaly. This may appear an odd place to begin but it is where I shall. He said that people with deep religious convictions even fight more tenaciously than the average. The justification, of course, is obvious. The explanation is simply that although Christians are regularly the slowest to be aroused, as they ought to be, once principles are involved then they are the most grimly unwilling to compromise. They won't give over the right at any cost. Christians fight on. Dramatically that has been proved in the late war. All who have been in Europe within the past few months, as I have, have learned of many magnificent examples of it. They are enough to make us rejoice and take courage.

Everyone is acquainted without any doubt with the gallant resistance of the Church in Holland. Under all the terror and the oppression of the Nazis it was its unbending, Christlike determination and its unconquerable hope that put an inflexible iron into the soul of that heroic nation. Equal in worthy renown is also the name of Eivind Berggrav, the primate of Norway, who so charmed even his guards with the Gospel that they connived with him to let him slip away by night in disguise into the heart of the enemy-occupied city of Oslo. There he kept the flame of a faith in liberation burning fiercely until the day of victory.

But how many know about Denmark? Let me tell you about it. While I was in Copenhagen, I met a Pastor Fabritius, who is now a member of Parliament, who did the most daring things during the war I think I have ever heard of. He became a focus of the Danish espionage. No one will ever know the number of the lives of allied fliers which he saved by smuggling out forbidden photographs of antiaircraft batteries to Sweden. His very parsonage became an armory. By May, 1945, amazing as it sounds, he had two thousand hand grenades under his roof. There was not a man in his congregation, he told me with a wry smile, who expected him to come out of the war alive. Many valiant spirits were in the underground but it was the mark of the Christians that they resisted even more.

Turning to the land of our erstwhile enemies, it is heartening to find that it is Christians who repent more as well. In case you are ready to despair of the regeneration of Germany, there is our single and substantial hope. Again, anomalously, it is the true souls who never consented in the barbarities of the godless leaders of their nation who are the most smitten in conscience. You will be interested to hear that there isn't one man in the Council of Twelve which is at the head of the Evangelical Church in Germany today, who has not been either under arrest or in detention at some time, most of them repeatedly, since 1933. It takes a special brand of moral courage and of tenacity to principle to contribute to the overthrow

[283]

of your own government in a war to the finish—and they did. Yet these are the men, in their Stuttgart declaration of October, who confessed:

> With great pain do we say: through us has endless suffering been brought to many people and countries. True, we have struggled for many years in the name of Jesus Christ against a spirit which has found its terrible expression in the National Socialist regime of violence, but we accuse ourselves for not witnessing more courageously, for not praying more faithfully, for not believing more joyously and for not loving more ardently.

Never will I forget the almost transfigured expression on the face of Pastor Maahs of Heidelberg when he exclaimed to my colleagues and me, "My guilt is that I am alive. We must all have died in this time." The fact was that he had been roughly seized time and again and his execution was already set for the very day on which the American troops burst in to set him free.

It is a rare thing for any non-Christian to repent. Christians repent more.

As for us in America, the criterion, the gauge of our Christianity will be if we give more. We must—if we are to relieve distress, actually even to preserve life—and certainly if we are to kindle a new faith in friend or former foe alike. And what else is our hope? Mustn't it be to win men to a nobler ideal, especially to win those who have been in love with hell? It is trite to say that America ought to do it out of gratitude for its unravaged cities, but no one who has not seen the shambles that Europe is today can conceivably appreciate the awful, pulverized desolation; how ruinously a whole continent has been smashed. In my eyes our motive is all-eclipsing.

America is humanitarian. Let those who would scorn, hiss that we are "soft" if they will. We are humanitarian. That is our glory. But this time we must be Christian—and that is more. One of the most sterling of our fellow citizens whispered his secret fear to me abroad, and the echo of it still disquiets my heart. His dread, he confided, was not that we Americans will be wicked in these desperate days but that we shall be small. Hearers, it is only Christ who can enlarge. Listen to him. His voice says probingly, winsomely, "What do you more?"

My last "more"—it caps it all—is the "more" that we Christians must add to the shape of things to come, not only to a durable but to an endurable peace. And I pray more earnestly that we shall. The seal of God has been placed uniquely in our hands and we alone can press it upon the wax of this world. The figure of a French theological student rises before me as the last in this picture gallery. He was as shabby and threadbare as poverty could make him that evening. There was an apologetic look in his eyes because he was scarcely presentable in the comfortable hotel where we Americans awaited him. But to me, almost above everyone else whom I have met in the last few months, he was a true prophet. He had served in his country's army, he informed us in self-introduction, and when France had collapsed, oh, what a bottomless abyss had been in his soul! An added wrench had come immediately because, being an Alsatian, he was drafted straight out of the prisoner-of-war camp into a German division and sent to the eastern front.

But his worst despondency by far—and now the wistfulness on his face deepened into melancholy and his tones became oppressive—had descended on him only after he had returned home. What had almost crushed him, stifled his spirit, was the sight of the land that he loved, on which he had set his dreams, building again merely on the old cracked foundations, the ones that had crumbled before, and nothing stronger. There were only the old shibboleths and the same worldly, grasping rivalries. If they had been too honeycombed and weak to bear the weight of a nation earlier in a far more placid epoch, what hope could there be now? What hope?—the echo must have rung around and around in his soul. Oh how I admired him! Under the impact of his own doubt, you could see him visibly squaring his shoulders. He was a man, a Christian man, and he supplied his own answer. The hope could only be one. No sentiment now, it was clear-eyed realism. The single prospect for a better, sounder postwar world was in the vigor, the cleanness, the unbending standards, the creative magnetism of Jesus Christ. He was convinced of it. And consequently, he told us in ringing tones, he himself had enlisted, was offering his all. It made no difference that he was likely to be sent into an obscure village. He expected that. Since he was only a single recruit, it was by no means sure that his act would be enough. It would take thousands like him. But as for him, he had given his life to humanity and to God.

Christians, what the new age waits for in its birth pangs is for more, both in the pulpit and in the pew, to make that commitment. The key man for a decent future is you, all of us. "What *do* ye more?" Awake now—and to action! "What do ye *more?*" In the turmoil of these years it is the plus that counts.

# Now Thank We All Our God

BLISS FORBUSH

*Headmaster, Friends School, Baltimore, Maryland
and Chairman, Friends General Conference*

*Thanksgiving is one of the great American religious holidays born out of the suffering of men and women at Plymouth. Mr. Forbush interprets the spiritual meaning of the occasion for people today. It is a message of significance to Americans everywhere.*

*Bliss Forbush was born in Yarmouth, Nova Scotia, attended Oberlin College, Johns Hopkins University, and graduated from the Divinity School of the University of Chicago. In 1939 he was awarded the Geneva Travel Fellowship for study in Europe. He became the executive secretary of the Baltimore Meeting of Friends in 1921, and was made a recorded minister in 1925. Three years later he became responsible for assisting the Friends meetings in Maryland, Virginia and Western Pennsylvania. Through the years he served as instructor in Bible and religion in Friends School, Baltimore, and became headmaster of the School in 1943.*

*After serving the Friends in the fields of young people's activities, leadership training and religious education, he was named chairman of Friends General Conference in June, 1941, an office he still holds. He is a member of the board of directors of the Maryland-Delaware Council of Churches, and the American Committee of the World Council of Churches; he is a trustee of several schools and a Regent of Morgan State College. His book,* Towards Understanding Jesus, *is widely used in courses in Bible and religion in independent secondary schools, and a later book,* With Cymbals and Harp, *has found an appreciative audience.*

## Sermon Forty=nine

THANKSGIVING is distinctly an American holiday; there is nothing like it elsewhere in the world. It celebrates neither a savage battle nor the fall of a great city. It does not mark the anniversary of a great conqueror or the birthday of a famous statesman. It does not commemorate the writing of a historic public document or the launching of a new constitution. The American Thanksgiving Day is the expression of a deep feeling of gratitude by our people for the rich productivity of the land, a memorial of the dangers and hardships through which we have safely passed, and a fitting recognition of all that God in His goodness has bestowed upon us.

It is the custom of members of some religious fellowships to use a rosary as an aid in fixing in the mind those things of which St. Paul spoke as true, just, pure, lovely and of good report. Dr. Henry N. Wieman has suggested that each individual should make a mental rosary of his most precious memories, including the beauty he has seen, the fellowship he has enjoyed, and the good gifts that life has brought him. Then he suggests that each person frequently count the beads of his rosary and give thanks to God for each separate favor.

Another writer has suggested an alphabet of God's bounty. Such a summary of gifts, great and small, personal or universal, might read as follows:

A. America.
B. Beauty, books, brotherhood, birds, brooks, bonfires.
C. Children, churches, camps, crops, cranberries.
D. Democracy, dawns, duties, doughnuts.
E. Eyes, education.
F. Faith, friends, fun, flowers, freedom.
G. God.
H. Hope, happiness, home.
I. Ideals, institutions, independence, immortality.
J. Jesus.
K. Knowledge, keepsakes.
L. Love, loyalties, longings, laughter.
M. Mother, music.
N. Nights, nature.
O. Oceans, opportunities.
P. Prayer, pictures, peace, pumpkin pie.
Q. Quests, quoits.
R. Right, reasons, rest.
S. Strength, strangers, ships, sunsets.
T. Truth, tomorrow, turkey.
U. Universe, universities.
V. Victories.
W. Worship, work.
X. Xmas!
Y. Youth, years, yesterdays.
Z. Zoos, zest, zippers.

In early New England it was the custom at Thanksgiving time to place five grains of corn at every plate as a reminder of those stern days in the first winter when the food of the Pilgrims was so depleted that only five grains of corn were rationed to each individual at a time. The Pilgrim Fathers wanted their children to remember the sacrifice, suffering and hardship which made possible the settlement of a free people in a free land. They wanted to keep alive the memory of that long sixty-three-day trip taken in the tiny *Mayflower*. They desired to keep alive the thought of that "stern and rock bound coast," its inhospitable welcome, and the first terrible winter which took such a toll of lives. They did not want their descendants to forget that on the day in which their ration was reduced to five grains of corn only seven healthy colonists remained to nurse the sick, and nearly half their numbers lay in the "windswept graveyard" on the hill. They did not want to forget that when the *Mayflower* sailed back to England in the spring only the sailors were aboard.

The use of five grains of corn placed by each plate was a fitting reminder of a heroic past. Symbolically it may still serve as a useful means of recalling those great gifts for which we are grateful to God. The first grain of corn might stand for that wonderful beauty of nature which is all about us. We can say it in the words of Georgia Harkness:

> For these, O God, I give Thee thanks:
> For autumn hills all tapestried in gold,
> For sleeping valleys nestling near Thy heart,
> For gleams of burnished silver on a stream,
> For jewels flashing in the night-time skies,
> For flaming sunlit clouds,
> For soft horizon haze,
> For bare brown earth and rugged wind-swept trees,
> For rain,
> For dew,
> For frost,
> For nature's sleep,
> And for glad resurgent life of Easter time,
> For these, O God, I thank thee.[1]

Some years ago an Englishman had the happy notion of asking children the simple question: "What are the loveliest things you know, persons not counted?" Here is the list a boy made:

A swallow flying.
Looking into deep clear water.
Water being cut at the bow of a boat.
An express train rushing.
A builder's crane lifting something heavy.
My dog's eyes.

An English girl made this list:

A thrush singing.
Street lights on the river.
Red roofs in the trees.
Smoke rising.
Red velvet.
The moon in the clouds.

[1] "I Give Thee Thanks" from *Holy Flame* by Georgia Harkness (Boston: Bruce Humphries, Inc.). Used with permission.

Thus we can say: Now Thank We All Our God for the beauties of nature which are all about us.

Our second grain of symbolic corn reminds us of the great men and women of the past. They have lived in every age and in every country. In our own land great men have stepped forward to lead the people through difficulties and to inspire others by their vision. In colonial days there were Brewster and Bradford, William Penn and Lord Baltimore. In the stormy period of the revolution there were Washington, Franklin, Jefferson, Adams and a dozen more. In the restless period when our country was passing through its growing pains there were Andrew Jackson, John Calhoun and Daniel Webster; and through the dark days of the Civil War Abraham Lincoln walked the floors of the White House through the lonely nights as he strove to preserve the union; and in the days of expansion there were Grover Cleveland and Theodore Roosevelt. The dream of Woodrow Wilson of a united world has not yet come true but his vision beckons men forward and we can trust that in the future his hope for a brotherhood of man will be a reality.

The words of the wise men of our land still inspire us. Said Washington, "Let us set up a standard to which the wise and the good may repair; the event is in the hands of God." Lincoln gave us words of matchless council for the months directly ahead, "With malice toward none; with charity for all . . . let us strive on to finish the work we are in . . . to do all which may achieve and cherish a just and lasting peace among ourselves and with all nations." We are moved by the words of a great man, half Englishman and half American, who announced the fall of France to the British Cabinet in June of 1940 with these words, "That means, gentlemen, that we are left alone to face the enemy," and after a pause he added, "Rather bracing that, isn't it?"

Now Thank We All Our God for the great men and women of the past!

Our third grain of corn might stand for the work of the world that must be done, some portion of which will fall to each one of us. At times we all indulge in wishful thinking and dream that the good things of life may be ours without any real effort. But it is only in Castles in Spain that the plumbing never leaks!

Years ago I knew a farmer in New Hampshire named Ed McCollister who was a wonderful planner, but not much of a doer. In the winter Ed McCollister would plan to cut a stand of lumber and sell it to a neighboring lumber mill; but when the snows began to fall and the drifts filled the forest Ed always felt that it would be a dangerous thing to take his team into the woods. He would end by cutting barely enough for his own woodshed. In the spring Ed McCollister would plan to tap all the trees in his large sugar bush, but when the time came he always found there were many sap buckets that needed mending, and so he would never tap more than enough maple sugar trees to provide for his own table syrup. In the spring Ed might plan for acres of potatoes but in June the acreage had shrunk to the size of a good family garden plot. Ed McCollister never learned the lesson so well expressed by Will Rogers when he said, "We won't have roses at our door unless we plant them there." Nor do any values and goods of life come to us without hard, conscientious work.

Work seems to be a squirrel cage for some who are forced to spend their days in hard, monotonous tasks which crush the human spirit. An English child who saw the miners of the Rhonda Valley during the last depression exclaimed, "Their eyes look like vacant windows." Our work does not need to be a squirrel cage. It may be a doorway through which we may go to serve and to bless those about us. The nurse may use her skill to help the sufferer in his hour of desperate need. The traveling salesman may use his work to move goods sorely needed by his fellow men. The teacher may use his subject as a start in reaching boys and girls who need advice and direction. The engineer may leave behind him good roads, well-constructed bridges, newly developed oil fields, and a multitude of machines which will take the drudgery out of the lives of others. If we choose our work wisely we shall be able to say as did Thomas Edison, "I never worked a day in my life, it was all fun."

Principal Jacks of Manchester College tells of finding an ancient mathematical instrument made by a Moslem in India a thousand years ago. On the edge of the fine brass work was carved in delicate Arabic characters these words, "This is the work of Hussein Ali, mechanic, mathematician, servant of the Most High God."

Now Thank We All Our God for the work of the world that waits for our hands to do.

Our fourth grain of symbolic corn may stand for our friends and loved ones. We do not wear our hearts on our sleeves, nor do we talk much about our friends and those at home. But within ourselves we know what joy we take in our friends, and we understand why Guy Fukes asked that these words be carved on his tomb, "Here lies Sir Guy Fukes, author, servant of Queen Elizabeth, and friend of Sir Philip Sidney."

Our friends teach us to learn the meaning of that ancient Greek motto, "Know Thyself!" Sometimes they are frank and brutal, pointing out our mistakes in no mincing words. They may speak of trivial things such as the slant of a hat or the color of a tie; but they also warn us of imperfections in our ideal and our attitudes. To them we are grateful for the frequent renewal and glorification of life. By their sympathy and understanding they help us in our day of defeat and discouragement. By sharing our small victories they double our pleasures. On those dark days when bitter sorrow has been our lot they have transmuted the bitterness and blunted the arrow which otherwise might have pierced our strongest armor. Emerson wrote, "Friends are not only for vacation times, but for days of shipwreck; not only to be with us on our pleasant rambles, but to be with us as we travel over the rough roads of life."

Thus we can say, "Now Thank We All Our God," for our friends and loved ones.

Only one symbolic grain of corn remains. Can we do better than to dedicate it to God? It is not hard to see why the ancient writer of the Law of Israel cried, "The Lord, our God, is the great God, the mighty and the terrible, who regardeth not persons, nor taketh rewards. He doth execute justice for the fatherless and widow. . . . The Lord is merciful and gracious, slow to anger, and abundant in loving kindness and truth." It is not difficult for us to recognize the power of God. Every crack of thunder, every earthquake which stirs the earth to its depths, every comet's tail that streams across the sky, all testify to the power of God.

It is not difficult to appreciate the aesthetic quality in God when He has made so much of beauty all about us. It is not difficult to see that only a rational power could create the universe with all its wonders revealed by microscope and telescope. Power, beauty, intellect all are revelations of God. But these qualities do not satisfy the hungering heart of man. The glory of God in the eyes of man is Creative Love. Much of what God is must always remain a mystery to us since our minds are finite; but this we know, the quality in the personality of God is Creative Love. We all know something about human love, we have seen it, we have experienced it, it is the most wonderful thing in the world. But God is greater than man; in Him love is raised to the nth degree, it is the dominant factor in the reality of God, the ruling principle.

St. Paul wrote to the Colossians: "Christ who is the image of the invisible God." We can see God in beauty, power and mind. We can see God dimly in men and women at their best; but in Jesus Christ we see something more. His life is the expression of complete service and love. In Jesus we see revealed as nowhere else that same Quality which is the chief characteristic of God—Creative Love.

And if the core of the universe is Creative Love, God's kingdom will yet come; a kingdom of peace, harmony, good will and abundant life. Thus with grateful hearts, mindful of the beauty of nature all about us and the greatness of the leaders of the past; thankful for the work of the world that must be done and conscious of what we owe our friends and loved ones, we can but add our voices to all those who sing "Now thank we all our God!"

# They Prophesied but They Did So No More

RABBI BERYL D. COHON
*Temple Sinai, Brookline, Massachusetts*

*Temple Sinai was founded by a small group of men and women in the summer of 1939. Rabbi Cohon has been the first and only rabbi. His preaching has built the attendance and membership of the Temple month by month.*

*He studied at the University of Illinois. Debating a profession, and thinking of the ministry, he was influenced by his brother, Professor Samuel S. Cohon of Hebrew Union College, and also by a former Congregational minister, Professor Edward Chauncey Baldwin, to enter the rabbinate. He took extra courses in geology to find reality. Teaching, journalism, the ministry bothered him; he got tired of the Hamletlike argument and registered at Hebrew Union College, took his rabbinic degree, and was ordained in 1925.*

*His first rabbinate was in Pensacola, Florida, then for three years in industrial Cumberland, Maryland, and later with the late Rabbi Harry Levi to serve as associate at Temple Israel, Boston. He was very much interested in adult education and spent nine happy years there.*

*Temple Sinai is a free pulpit and a free pew; he preaches with a liberal interpretation of Judaism, emphasizes the poetic and the prophetic. Boston University invited him to teach courses in the Bible and Judaism in 1933. Needing a book for his class in the Hebrew prophets and not finding anything suitable, he wrote his own. His Introduction to Judaism, a textbook for Jewish children, is used widely in the English-speaking world. Tufts College invited him to teach Bible and Jewish literature, which he does now as an avocation.*

## Sermon Fifty

MOSES had his troubles with the children of Israel. They were not the easiest people to get along with. The Bible condemns them roundly and repeatedly. Our remote Biblical ancestors, the Bible reports, "fell alusting." At every obstacle in their path—and there were many obstacles on a path in the desert forty years long—they rebelled against Moses, demanding impossible things of him. Lacking water, parched with thirst on the burning sands, they demanded a miracle of their leader. Lacking food they demanded a miracle. Tired of the same old manna day after day and year after year, they demanded a miracle. Always they attacked their leader; it never dawned on them to attack the problem! "We remember the fish we were wont to eat in Egypt for nought; the cucumbers, and the melons, and the leeks, and the onions, and the garlic; but now our soul is dried away; there is nothing at all; we have nought save this manna to look to."

They did not understand their leader. Fortunately for them, and for all of us who value the Mosaic tradition in history, they did not elect their leaders. Moses did not have to stand election. The people were not ready for that. Moses would never have been elected; his brother Aaron was much more popular. He gave them a golden calf, you recall. Moses was facing the crucial problem of his career: how to win the understanding and the support of his people. He decided, under the impact of inspiration, to organize a body of seventy men to serve as an inner council. He would inspire this small group, win them, transmit his own spirit to them. They would serve as agents of his will and vision. He convoked these seventy elders. And they proved to be a promising group. They did catch his spirit, but could not hold it. For a while they would prophesy, but for only a brief moment. A flickering light; flickers and goes out! flickers and goes out! It's like striking your lighter out-of-doors on a windy day. Or, like pushing the electric button: the light flashes, and goes out. The bulb is burned out. The Bible narrator reports: ". . . and it came to pass, that, when the spirit rested upon them, they prophesied, but they did so no more."

A significant incident is reported as a further detail in this story. Two of the seventy—Eldad and Medad, forever honored in our tradition—did hold the spirit. They continued to prophesy after their colleagues had stopped. They were roundly berated for arrogance, for presumption, even accused of treachery. It was a young bigot, (And who is as bigoted as a young bigot?) who started the hue and cry against them. They were disloyal! As a matter of fact, the two were the only ones who were loyal; all the rest were duds. Moses, however, took another position; they were not disloyal. "Would that all the Lord's people were prophets," he said. That is because he was of magnificent stature!

"They prophesied, but they did so no more." The tragedy of life is here; the tragedy of mankind and the tragedy of every man and woman may be here. Inconstancy of vision; incapacity to maintain an ideal; smug, arid middle age; embittered old age; smoke when there should be creative fire; barracks where there should be homes; among nations, suspicion, fear, hatred, war, instead of understanding co-operation, peace. How much of our sorrows may be traced to this ineptitude! "They prophesied, but they did so no more."

Back in 1918 a bleeding humanity raised its weeping eyes thrilled with a new vision. The President of the United States had spoken magic words. Men everywhere breathed anew, their backs straightened, their eyes on far horizons. They heard mighty words. Trumpets sounded in their souls. A war to end war! Self-determination of peoples! Open covenants openly arrived

[ 293 ]

at! The world must be made safe for democracy! A league of nations! Justice, law, order in the world! Men went into battle like crusaders. They killed and were killed. Then men met in conference to implement their vision. The crowds cheered. The crowds always cheer or jeer, and do not understand. Like the children of Israel in our Bible story they attacked not the problems but their leaders. And not all the leaders had the sustained prophetic fire of Moses. Rather, they were more like the sixty-eight of the seventy. "They prophesied, but they did so no more." The few lone prophetic voices, the world over, were howled down, as were Eldad and Medad. Young nationalist bigots led in the shouting. And the war that was to have been the end of all wars was only the prelude to the second World War. The lights flickered, and the lights went out.

We are emerging from the second World War. Will it be said of us—from this pulpit perhaps, by another rabbi speaking to our children or grand-children—that we too prophesied, "but they did so no more"?

That is what is being said in many quarters by observing men. Our own sons, a victorious army of occupation, are hated and despised as plundering hordes. They came as liberators; they turned into hoodlums. We talked of freedom, of democracy, of liberation. The pitiful remnant of some million and a half Jews are still in camps—stateless, homeless, not a spot on the face of God's earth to give them refuge. Our statesmen spoke of freedom from fear, freedom from want, freedom of conscience, freedom of speech. Again humanity was thrilled. The magic of vision was in the air; words rang with the power of prophecy. What will happen to our vision? God knows. Iron curtains are imprisoning the intelligence of men not only in Russia but everywhere in the world. There is an iron curtain in front of, behind, all around every country in the world. In our country the Ku Klux Klan is riding again; isolationism is climbing into the saddle again; white mobs lynch again.

National state sovereignty—the deadly curse consuming the minds and visions of men and nations—holds its ugly head high and hisses. Today national sovereignty is the primary obstacle to international understanding and international co-operation. Not even the atomic bomb will compel it to down its head. Mr. Bernard Baruch submitted a plan, in the name of the Atomic Energy Control Commission to control internationally atomic power. Russia opposed it. Why? Because according to his plan—the only plan offered us, the only plan to save us from a repetition of the vicious old race in armaments, this time with atomic bombs—Russia is afraid her national sovereignty may be compromised. National sovereignty! The Secretary General of the United Nations, Mr. Trygve Lie, put the matter clearly some time ago: "The United Nations started out fine, but national pride is one of the biggest problems it has to cope with." One writer adds, "For 'national pride' substitute its diplomatic equivalent, 'national sovereignty,' and the impasse on the question of atomic power emerges clearly. At Bikini, in New York, and in Moscow the one factor present in all equations of atomic difficulty is national sovereignty."

We prophesied. We saw a world beyond isolationist nationalism. We said: Cities embraced larger sovereignty and surrendered their local sovereignty; states embraced federal sovereignty and surrendered their state sovereignty. They thrived in their progress. Nations, we spoke in the hour of vision, must embrace the sovereignty of an international system—international law! international sovereignty! We prophesied. And then we prophesied no more. On the brain of every statesman and politician, in Washington, London, Paris, Moscow, beats the demon: national sovereignty! Which is nothing more than "My country, right or wrong."

I am not saying that the vision has gone out finally. I am not a fatalist. The bulb is not burned out. The switch is stuck. I do believe we have made much gain in keeping the lights burning. We do have an even chance of succeeding this time; but we also face the probability of re-enacting the tragic story.

The task before us is not to recall the Bible incident and all it symbolized in our weary history so that we might be confirmed in our pessimism; the reverse is what we want: we want to be roused to our duty, so that, like those two dissenters in the Bible story, we remain constant to our vision, even in the teeth of intolerance and bigotry. Let the young fanatics and the old cynics fulminate. We stand by the few who will not allow prophecy to die in Israel, nor in the life of humanity.

I wish to speak now of the same malady as it afflicts us in our personal lives.

Some of us are in the professions—doctors, lawyers, teachers, preachers, writers, musicians, artists; some of us are in business. We had hours of vision, back in our youth. We prophesied in one form or another. We are mighty poor stuff if we cannot look back to a period of idealistic youth and high enthusiasm. We were going to be real doctors, not mere humdrum mediocrities; we were going to be real lawyers—following in the footsteps of men such as Marshall, Holmes, Brandeis, not mere routinized mediocrities, interested in nothing but fees. We were going to fight causes, champion the rights of men. We caught glimpses of beauty and greatness in the writings, in the music, in the paintings of the masters; we were not going to be mere conventional drudges, grinding out stuff because it paid. We prophesied. Then, somehow, the years kept slipping by. Most of us, in middle age, came on arid stretches, "the middle span," as it has been called.

A colleague of mine, in "the midlle span," speaking of his early days in the pulpit, when he ministered to a comparatively modest congregation, in contrast to the enormous and wealthy one he has today, said, "I was young then; then I carried a torch!" What happened to his torch? and to yours and mine? As young doctors, as young lawyers, as young businessmen, as young husbands or wives or parents, we carried torches. What has happened to them? Perhaps we have enough of the idealism of youth left in us to recall with nostalgia those charmed days when we held torches. Then, you remember, we had the least money and the largest measure of happiness. Those were our finest hours.

Young people stand before me and take the vows of marriage. They are young, daring, enthusiastic, preoccupied with plans and dreams. Careers and homes and children are before them. Yes, they prophesy. Theirs would be happy, creative homes, homes in which love and loveliness abide. Some do continue. Their visions and ideals are constant. They even enlarge with the years. Of course, they have their hours of disillusionment; of course, they turn weary and long for change; but they carry on, year after year, and gray hair does not find them cynical. Many of them are more youthful and more idealistic than their grandchildren. Happy and blessed of the Lord are they.

But, there are the others. They too prophesied; but they do so no more. The divorce rate is ominous in our day. No wonder people drink so much, rush from one movie to another, afraid to be at home with themselves a single evening.

"Where there is no vision the people perish," says the Bible sage. Where the vision fails, nations perish; where the vision fails, doctors, lawyers, writers, merchants, teachers fail. They may become rich and popular but they are only successful failures. Where the vision fails parents, husbands, wives, friends fail, and life turns to ashes in our mouths.

How shall we guard ourselves against the arid stretches of middle age, avoid growing fat of mind and spirit as well as of body?

I suggest two preventives: (1) Be alert, be ever conscious of the danger. If we are aware of the rocks and are intelligent we shall set our sails so as to avoid the danger. Eternal vigilance is the price of integrity as well as of liberty. (2) Be in close touch with the sources of inspiration. Books, good books; magazines, good magazines, not mere comics; friends that stimulate and inspire rather than deaden us; forums that deal with great causes. A thousand worthy causes are clamoring for help. That is the great gift that enlightened, spiritually sensitive synagogues can give to their members: stimulation, encouragement, challenge, in all matters pertaining to ethics, idealism, duty. That is the great gift I covet for you from your synagogue. Association with our congregation, sharing in its program of worship, of activity, and education, should keep you stimulated, roused to the struggling visions of the world, keep the spirit of prophecy alive.

Moses never entered the Promised Land. He died on the heights—not only on the heights of Mount Nebo, but on the heights of his spiritual aspirations. He saw the Promised Land from afar, but into it he was denied entrance. He died young in spirit, though old in years. At least he saw the Promised Land. "His eyes were not dim, nor his natural force abated." That was far more than physical resilience. He prophesied; and he continued to prophesy, whatever burdens he had to carry, whatever the discouragements he knew.

On my desk, under the glass top, I have a copy of a letter written by Justice Oliver Wendell Holmes. It is entitled, "Flag at the Peak." I keep it on my desk where I see it constantly. This is the letter, and its preface written by an editor:

In February, 1931, Justice Oliver Wendell Holmes of the United States Supreme Court, had a letter from President E. O. Holland of the State College of Washington. The boys out there wanted, it seemed, to celebrate the Justice's approaching ninetieth birthday. Would the Justice be kind enough to write a word of greeting for the occasion?

The Justice would. . . .

SUPREME COURT OF THE UNITED STATES
Washington, D. C.

February 24, 1931

MY DEAR SIR:

On the eighth of March, 1862, sixty-nine years ago, the sloop Cumberland was sunk by the Merrimac, off Newport News. The vessel went down with her flag flying—and when a little later my regiment arrived to begin the campaign on the Peninsula I saw the flag still flying above the waters beneath which the Cumberland lay. It was a life long text for a young man. Fight to the end and go down with your flag at the peak. I hope that I shall be able to do it—and that your students may live and die by the same text.

Very sincerely yours,
O. W. HOLMES

Which shall it be for you and for me:

"They prophesied, and they did so no more"

*or*

"Fight to the end and go down with your flag at the peak"?

VISION

# Where Realism and Faith Meet

REVEREND SAMUEL SHOEMAKER
*Rector, Calvary Protestant Episcopal Church, New York*

*Samuel Shoemaker is interested in making the spiritual life keep pace with the material world. This sermon reflects that interest.*

*A graduate of Princeton University, he became a Y.M.C.A. secretary in Peking, China, 1917-19, was ordained a deacon in 1920, and priest in 1921. He was called to be rector of Calvary Protestant Episcopal Church, New York City, in 1925, and has brought new life to this old church.*

*Among his books and pamphlets* Realizing Religion, A Young Man's View of the Ministry, Children of the Second Birth, Religion That Works *and* National Awakening *have won him recognition as an author.* Christ and

This Crisis, How You Can Help Other People, *and* How You Can Find Happiness, *his latest books, are Religious Book Club selections.*

*From March to June of 1945, Mr. Shoemaker broadcast weekly on the program* Your Life Today *over station WJZ, New York, and independent affiliated stations, in co-operation with the Radio Department of the Federal Council of the Churches of Christ in America; and from October, 1945, through April, 1946, he gave two weekly addresses over the American Broadcasting Company, station WJZ. In September, 1946, he returned to the air for three Sunday broadcasts over WOR's Radio Chapel, and now continues to broadcast twice a week on the program* Gems for Thought, *a presentation of the American Broadcasting Company, over station WJZ and independent affiliated stations.*

*His sermons preached at Calvary are mimeographed each week, are subscribed to by a large number of people across the country, and one appears in each issue of* The Evangel, *Calvary's monthly magazine. Mr. Shoemaker spends many hours in personal counseling with individuals and does as much guest preaching in other churches as his busy schedule permits.*

*His deep interest in the more adequate preparation of young men for a career in the ministry led to the establishment in the fall of 1945 of the Calvary Clergy School, to help develop "the high order of leadership needed by the Church to meet today's new challenges. . . ." Since the beginning of his ministry, the outstanding aspects of his work have been leading young men into the ministry and working with individuals to deepen their religious convictions and training lay people to become spiritual leaders.*

## Sermon Fifty=one

TEXT: And I saw a new heaven and a new earth . . .
REVELATION 21:1

EVERY God-inspired prophet and seer looks straight at the conditions of his own time, and then looks straight through them to the coming of a better day. Even when that day is seen through the dimness of human tragedy—or even when its fulfillment must be in another world than this— there it gleams before him just the same. Hope does not spring eternally only in the wishful human breast; but hope springs also eternally in the inspired spiritual consciousness. You just cannot believe in the Christian God without the inevitable corollary of believing that one day, and under some unpredictable circumstances, our best hopes shall be our surest realities, and all that man has striven for shall somewhere be achieved.

But how shall this process be effected? How shall these dreams and hopes which so often lie before us as if they were tantalizing mirages ever be made actual in the real world? Look at the words of St. John the Divine, "I saw a new heaven and a new earth," and see whether you find in them a truth I am seeing there. If you look at heaven and earth at the same time, you must look at that juncture of heaven and earth which we call the horizon.

A physical horizon is the place where the material earth is met by the immaterial sky. It looks almost as if there were a right angle formed at the place where the wide plane of sky touches the wide plane of earth. I believe that there is a correspondence here between the outward world and the inward. For there is a spiritual horizon which closely corresponds to the visible horizon—a place where the ideal meets the actual, where they impinge one upon the other. I believe that if we are to have "a new heaven and a new earth," it must be because we see both heaven and earth in a new way, and see them at the same time.

For I take "heaven" in this sense to mean all that world of ideals, of hopes, of aspirations, of true dreams—in a word, of faith—which beckons us on all the while, and which we lose sight of at our peril. And the word "earth" in this sense I take to mean all that world of actualities, of duty, of responsibility, of materiality which we know and with which we are concerned most of our lives.

It is a world which descends into mere materiality unless it is somehow lifted and sanctified by that other world of vision and of faith: but it is the world where we live, and from which we can only flee by death. It is the world which continually challenges and tests the worth, the courage of our dreams.

Now my theme is that effective, healthy, progressive living—living which satisfies because it is real—is living very close in to that angle where realism and faith meet. The closer people are to the realities of the situation, and to the power of faith to affect it, and both at the same time, the more effective are their lives. And the further out on either leg of that angle they get, away from the junction of the two planes, whether in the direction of facts unmodified by faith, or of faith unmodified by facts, the less effective are their lives.

Safe living, wise living, effective living means never moving very far from the place where heaven and earth meet, where the energies of heaven go to work on the problems of earth, where the ideals of heaven provide the direction for earth, where the twin dangers of humanism and idealism find their corrective at the same time.

Take the matter of sickness. Purely material science tells you that all the trouble lies in the body, and must be corrected through the body. A germ is loose and multiplying, and the progress of the germ must be stopped. Or a foreign and hostile growth has begun, which must be eliminated by chemistry or by surgery. The body is a material thing, and its aches and ailments are material, too. But out on the other leg of the angle are those who say that the trouble lies in the mind, and must be corrected through the mind.

Fear thoughts, guilt thoughts, negative and despairing thoughts, have been pouring down into the subconscious from a disturbed, uncontrolled and faithless mind; and the physical ailments of the body are but expressions of this.

Whole systems and movements arise which are based on this belief. Are not both positions extreme? Do we not need the truth that is found in both? Is it not plain to all of us who look the thing in the face that there are times when an avenue to cure lies along the path of medicine or surgery or physical rest, and also times when an avenue to cure lies primarily along the path of a new attitude toward life, the surrender of some possessive relationship, or perhaps the immensely releasing experience of Divine Forgiveness?

Have we not seen great harm done where either the body or the mind was overemphasized, to the exclusion of the other? Science must watch out for materialism: and faith must watch out for foolishness. But science and faith, meeting at the right angle where heaven meets earth, can join hands and work together.

Or take the meeting of those daily situations which vary from ordinary occurrences to crises. Most people make their decisions without a moment of spiritual consideration: previous experience and personal bent combine to bring about a decision. We look at the facts and think what it is best to do and then do it. And it is thus that God and faith are unconsciously and often unintentionally dropped from our lives as a vital force. But on the other side, there is the type of person who has a tender conscience and is very eager to do the right thing: so there is more searching of heart than looking at concrete facts.

Such people often so much fear to leave God out that they come to believe that all practical considerations are a kind of working unbelief, as if God did not want us to use our minds or consider actualities of a material kind. How many times have we seen these two things, not in a balanced and well-ordered equilibrium, but in some exaggerated form, each without the corrective of the other! How often does the "practical" person become so realistic that only the bare present realities touch his mind.

Yet also how often does the "spiritual" person remain maddeningly impractical, saying he is "trusting God" when really he is simply letting things slide in irresponsible fashion, or making of prayer itself a kind of wishful self-willed daydreaming, in order to evade facing an unpaid bill, a neglected duty, or a tough situation. Oh, if only we could just move these two dear people nearer to each other, and get them down off one leg of the angle to the point of it instead! Both need to move in from where they are—the so-called "practical" person must remember that, while faith does not alter facts, it does most enormously alter what we do with facts, how we take them, and therefore their ultimate outcome and effect upon us—and the so-called "spiritual" person must remember that in the Christian religion "the Word was made flesh"—and that wherever there is true Christianity today the "word" of faith, of ideals, of religion, is always "made flesh" by its incarnation in lives and situations. Without this, religion trails off into a rarefied form of daydreaming, evading the world because it does not know how to challenge and to change it.

Or consider the way in which we seek to help people meet their problems. Hardly a day passes, I'll wager, that someone does not open to you some situation in his life or touching it, upon which he would like to draw you out; and which, if you understand God and life, you can help him to solve. If we are to be of any help whatever, we must take care we do not fall into the cheapness of merely saying something we think the person would like to hear: this is, alas, the commonest way in which we seek to ease one another's burdens. For those who refuse this sop to their own consciences and insult to their friends, and seek to grapple seriously with their problems, there will be two ways of doing it, or rather two things that need to be done.

We must help them to face and understand their situation, and often the total facts look very different when spread out before another. Much clarifies as they talk with freedom because we are sympathetic, and as they answer pertinent questions we ask. The situation may appear graver to them after we have helped them to consider it realistically, and yet easier to face, just because they now see what they are up against, and are looking straight at it, instead of looking away into some make-believe account of it they have given themselves. That first. But then a second thing. We must help them away from cheap answers, which by ignoring the moral law somewhere create further difficulties. We must help them to see that Christ's way is not only ideal, but practical—the only practical way. We must help them to find faith, and then to set it actually at work on the problems they face. We must help them take account of God in their situation.

Or again, think of how we shall deal with this vast, suffering, complex, agonized world of which we are a part. Never did men need to be so realistic about the world, and never did they need so much to look at it with faith! But it must be a true realism. A man said to me recently, "I am a realist!" and he went on to tell me how he had come up the hard way, was tough on himself and tough on other people; and very soon we were seeing that he carried over his so-called "realism" into his own home and was creating tensions there that could easily be disastrous. He is typical of those who think themselves so "practical" that they become very impractical indeed.

People like this are so exclusively occupied with the facts, that they never hear the "higher harmonies," they know no springs of renewal in life from which to drink, only the old stale well of profits and power. There is so much of earth, and so little of heaven, in such people's philosophy that they help to bring us to the brink of hell. When we have faced facts, there still remains the question what we shall do about them: and there faith must have its say. Yet we all know others who view life from within an ivory tower. Many who write long books about the world's condition, who talk in big generalizations, who believe in some solution for our problems, like many columnists and commentators and most preachers, are in danger of creating a little ideal world of their own. They see the thing from within their own theory, and are half-blinded by their own neat but theoretical ideas. They need more exposure to the realities, they need to come down out of the sweet, clean emptiness of their ivory towers, and rub their noses in the mud and filth of the pigsty of the actual. A man need not give up his ideals to be a realist, but he will need to test them on the actual, and get them down out of the ether to solid ground.

How does a man look up and say, "I saw a new heaven and a new earth"? He says it because heaven and earth are both in his heart. Realism is right when it says that human nature belongs to the kingdom of the animals; it is wrong when it says it belongs only to that kingdom. Idealism is right when it says human nature belongs to the realm of the angels; it is wrong when it says it belongs only to that realm.

If we are to be Christians in our world, and lift it nearer Christ's will for it, we must stay close by the place where heaven and earth meet, being wise as serpents about conditions, facts and actualities, and being people of such faith and prayer and assurance about God as can interpret these facts and actualities and transform them through faith.

Let us, then, move in from too great emphasis on conditions so that we leave out faith, and too great emphasis on faith so that we leave out honest appraisal of situations. Let us take our stand right where realism and faith meet, that belonging truly to both worlds, we may be used of God to create "a new heaven and a new earth."


## THE END OF THE WAY

# The Desire of All Nations

REVEREND JAMES A. STEWART, D.D.
*Professor of New Testament, New College, Edinburgh
and formerly Minister, North Morningside Church (Church of Scotland)
Edinburgh, Scotland*

*James Stewart's great preaching gift is one of the spiritual treasures of Scotland today. Men and women find faith in Christ at the altar when Stewart preaches! "Stewart of Morningside" is able to preach and also to teach other ministers how to preach with more effectiveness.*

*In his church in Edinburgh he was so successful that men thronged to church even on Sunday nights. It was worth a pilgrimage to his city to hear* him. As he enlarges his work at New College to impart his preaching secrets and plans to others, he will join a long line of great men who have made the College and New College trained men world famous.

His books have enriched our contemporary religious literature: A Man in Christ (the vital elements of St. Paul's religion), The Life and Teaching of Jesus Christ, The Gates of New Life, The Strong Name. His latest book, Heralds of God, is a study of preaching and practical advice to preachers. Those who read the book will find part of the secret of his great success in preaching.

There is something of the profound, a deep spiritual insight, and a persuasiveness in all his sermons. The sermon given here was chosen to end this volume because of its three conversations that bring the Gospel message near to all our hearts and that show, not man's self-sufficiency, but God's redemptive love and Christ the hope of all the earth.

## Sermon Fifty=two

TEXT: All the ends of the earth shall see the salvation of our God.
ISAIAH 52:10

## PROLOGUE

THE hope of the world lies in the Christmas message: Immanuel, God with us. Today some are looking to political machinery to fashion a new earth, some to social security, some to humanitarian sentiment and ethical endeavor. We need these things indeed; but unless there is a surer foundation we shall be heading straight for disillusionment. Not man's self-sufficiency but God's redemptive action, not mere human planning on the horizontal level but the inrush of a new power from the beyond—this is our supreme need now. In short, Christ is (albeit often unrecognized) the Desire of all nations, the Hope of the ends of the earth.

Now will you make an act of imagination? Imagine it is the year 1 B.C. We are going on a journey. We are about to visit three great cities: Rome, Athens, Jerusalem. We shall overhear three conversations—three groups of typical men discussing their hopes and fears for the world, just before the birth of Christ. Perhaps we shall find our own hopes and fears mirrored there.

## I

The City of Rome. A room in an Officers' Club. Three junior Officers of Caesar's Army—Gaius, Cassius, Octavius—are discussing new postings for overseas which have just been announced.

GAIUS:

So you are going off, Cassius, with the next draft to Asia; and you, Octavius, to the forgotten legion in the wilds of Britain. I'm luckier than either of you! I'm for Carthage and North Africa. The gods only know when we three shall meet again. Do you like this overseas service, Cassius?

CASSIUS:

Like it? I hate it! But what can you do? It is the penalty of belonging to so great an Empire. It is the price of being a citizen of the master race. That's what we owe to Caesar. Have you heard the terms of Caesar's latest edict? "There has gone forth a decree from Caesar Augustus that all the world should be taxed." Those were the very words. All the world—*that's* our Empire! That's why you have to go to Africa, Gaius, and you, Octavius, to Britain, and myself to Asia. Do you know what they are calling Caesar now? I heard them shouting it as he drove to the Colosseum yesterday. The air was ringing with it. They cried— "Caesar! Hail, Caesar Augustus, Saviour of the world!" Wasn't it fine?

OCTAVIUS:

Fine? I wonder. Saviour of the world Caesar? Oh, no doubt he has given us the Pax Romana: but what is that, when all is said and done? A subtle manipulation of the balance of power, and the legions massed on the frontiers. The thing looks secure, built to last a thousand years—but don't you trust it. The foundations are creaking. I tell you, the glittering civilization we are so proud of is disintegrating, and it will take more than Caesar to stop the rot. The recent revolt of the slaves, for instance—that was a symptom. Oh, I know they crucified the lot, and silenced them: but it showed what is coming. And I ask you, Cassius and Gaius, is it right that there should be a million slaves? Is it right that with all the resources of civilization at our disposal, there should still be those subhuman conditions? Is it right that life should be so cheap? There was Quirinus the other day. They wanted a son in the family, and when that baby was born it was a girl; and they threw the child out to die. Is *that* right? Surely you must see it—this shining civilization of ours has in itself the seeds of its own corruption and death. What do you say, Gaius?

GAIUS:

I say, Octavius, you're mad to talk like that! Don't you know that if Rome relaxed its hold, the world would fall to pieces? Don't you know that if you liberate the slaves, you wreck the State? Am I not right, Cassius?

CASSIUS:

Of course you are, Gaius. Don't you get playing with these revolutionary ideas, Octavius! In any case, you won't find any support—unless it is from some of those meddling Jews. Pompey was a fool ever to bring them here to Rome, but Caesar will look after them. Caesar knows what he is about. He has this cosmopolitan crowd under his thumb. Bread and circuses—that is all they want. As long as they have bread to eat, and circuses to amuse them, they ask no more. Can't you see that, Octavius?

OCTAVIUS:

No, Cassius, I can't. Bread and circuses! Do you think man can live by that? He wants more. He wants life. He wants freedom. I tell you, Cassius, he wants God!

CASSIUS:

Hark, Gaius, to our very religious Captain! He tells us we need God. Well—that, too, Caesar has given. Has not Caesar himself been raised to the rank of divinity? You and I, of course, don't believe it. We know it is just political expediency. But the man-in-the-street does believe it—and it hoaxes him all right. This Emperor-worship keeps men quiet: and what else is religion for? Do you agree, Gaius?

GAIUS:

Yes, heartily. That crowd at the Colosseum was right. Caesar *is* the Saviour of the world. And if you want peace on earth, good will among men, power politics will give it—nothing else!

OCTAVIUS:

You're wrong, Gaius! I know you're wrong. I had a dream one night. It was when I was away last year with the Fifteenth Legion building the great new military road across Macedonia to the East. One night I dreamt another army was using the road we had made—an army coming out of the East to match its power with Caesar. A strange army it was—peasants and artisans and fisherfolk and slaves. And on their banners they had—what do you think? A gallows-tree! A cross! And they spoke of another Emperor, both God and man in one, both dead and alive forever. And nothing could stop them. I saw them reaching Rome. I saw them casting down the throne of Caesar. I saw their strange new Emperor taking his place. Then I awoke, and it was a dream. But—Gaius, Cassius—I think God sent it. I think it meant that power politics has had its day. I think the strange new Emperor will be the Saviour of the world.

## II

*Now we leave Rome, and pass on to Athens. Three dons of the University of Athens, members of the Hellenic Academy of philosophy and the sciences, are having a walk together on the Areopagus, conversing as they go. Their names are Aristo, Leonidas and Dionysius. It is still the year* 1 B.C.

ARISTO:

I hear you had a famous triumph in the debate last night, Leonidas. What was it all about?

LEONIDAS:

It was about the ideal society—the new order we have all been talking about for the last four hundred years, ever since Plato wrote his *Republic*.

The actual title of the debate was "Can Culture Save the World?" I led for the affirmative.

ARISTO:

And who took the negative?

LEONIDAS:

It was Thrasymachus. You know him. He's a melancholy dog. His argument amounted to this—that if Culture could have saved the world, then why didn't Plato and Pericles save it, four hundred years ago? A fallacy, of course.

ARISTO:

Indeed, Leonidas, a glaring fallacy. And what did you say?

LEONIDAS:

Oh, I took the line that Plato and Aristotle laid the foundation, but the new knowledge has to permeate the general mind—which means universal education. I pointed out that we are moving in that direction: witness the fact that we have a universal language now—the Greek tongue will carry you anywhere in the world today. What a chance, by the way, for the missionaries of a new religion, if one should ever appear! I pointed out that little by little we are banishing ignorance, that we are translating knowledge into practical resources for living, that indeed there is no limit to what scientific enlightenment and intellectual energy may achieve. And with the last words of my peroration, I quite brought down the house!

ARISTO:

I'm sure you did, Leonidas. What were your last words?

LEONIDAS:

They were these: "The mind of man the only Saviour of the world!" Oh yes, it was a good debate; and when they took the vote, a splendid triumph —one hundred and seventy votes to forty-five—no doubt about it! You should have been there, Aristo; and you too, Dionysius. You're very quiet today, Dionysius. You don't challenge my argument, do you?

DIONYSIUS:

Yes, Leonidas, I do. You say knowledge—Culture—can save the world. I say it can't—not ever! You say knowledge is power. Yes, but power for what? Suppose a man is dominated by self-interest, what is to prevent him using his power for selfish instead of benevolent ends? Nothing. What is to prevent him making intelligence, Culture, truth itself the accomplice of evil? Nothing. All your argument in the debate last night, Leonidas, goes to pieces on one rock—the fact of evil, which not all your logic can rationalize away. You're a philosopher. You must see that!

LEONIDAS:

Yes, I think I do. But what is the alternative? If you rule out Culture and enlightenment as the Saviour of the world, what are you to put in their place? Force—like those imperial masters of ours at Rome?

DIONYSIUS:

No, Leonidas, certainly not force!

LEONIDAS:

Well, then, if salvation can come neither from the war lords at Rome nor from the Academy at Athens, where is it to come from? You are not suggesting we should look to Olympus, are you? We have a whole Pantheon of gods there to choose from—Zeus, Athene, Artemis, Apollo, and all the bickering hierarchy of heaven. Why, our very Acropolis is stuffed full of their statues: I hear that the latest—in case any deity should have been inadvertently over-looked—is inscribed "To the Unknown God"! This multiplicity of gods is the satire of every cheap comedian. You are not suggesting we should be credulous enough to make our prayer to them? Are you, Dionysius?

DIONYSIUS:

No, Leonidas, I don't mean that. But listen. You have read your Homer. You have heard Homer tell of gods like Apollo coming down to earth in human form. That's myth, of course. There is no salvation there. But just think, Leonidas—think, Aristo—what if the Great Spirit Himself, the First Cause and Creator of the universe, took flesh and came amongst us, and shared with us His being, His infinite power, His eternal life? Would *that* not be salvation?

LEONIDAS:

Oh, Dionysius, if only it could be! The great God . . . walking this very earth . . . the Healer and the Saviour of the world!

### III

*Once again we move on. From Rome and Athens we pass to Jerusalem. Let us enter one of the porches of the Temple. There three men are talking: a priest, a scribe, a Rabbi. They are Abner, Baruch and Joseph. The time is still 1 B.C.*

BARUCH:

I love that psalm we had at morning prayers—the longest and the greatest of them all. Its words keep ringing in my heart: "O how I love Thy law! It is my meditation all the day." If men would only keep the law, and practice its precepts of brotherhood and good will and mutual kindliness, all our troubles would be solved. Salvation is such a simple thing: keep the law, and earn God's favor—do good works, and merit heaven. And if you fail, there is all the ritual of the sacrifices to put you right again. That's your part, Abner. You're a priest.

ABNER:

Yes, Baruch, if your lifework is the law, mine is the sacrificial system. Our fathers gave us everything when they gave us these. The law and the sacri-fices—the salvation of the world! Why are you frowning, Rabbi Joseph? Don't you agree?

JOSEPH:

Listen, Abner—and you, Baruch. You've got the law and the sacrifices: are you content with the result? I certainly am not. Here am I, a Rabbi, a religious man: but I know my life, my character, are far short of what they ought to be. And you? Are you never disappointed? Never frustrated? Is the good always victorious—in you? Can you say that honestly? Oh, why are we all so impotent? Tell me that, Abner, priest of God!

ABNER:

Speak for yourself, Rabbi Joseph. I don't admit the impeachment. I am a righteous man. I thank God I am. I fast twice in the week. I give tithes of all I possess. I am quite satisfied with my record.

JOSEPH:

Are you really, Abner? Are you sure you are not running away from the truth about yourself? Have you ever faced yourself with all pretenses down? You're so proud of your good works. That's precisely the trouble: good works and pride—always hand in hand. And pride is the cardinal sin. Sö that our very good works, our very obediences to the law, are our undoing. That's the vicious circle, Abner; and neither your sacrifices nor Baruch's law can break it. Don't you see that's true?

BARUCH:

I see, Joseph, that you are becoming much too subtle. Besides, you're forgetting something. What about the Messiah? You don't imagine that Messiah, when He comes, is going to trouble about your bits of sins—or mine, or Abner's? He will have more to do than that! He is coming to deal with those Roman usurpers of our liberties, coming to consign the whole hateful crew to Gehenna. Down with Rome and up with Jewry! That's what I say. That's the kind of Saviour Israel needs. Rabbi Joseph, face the facts!

JOSEPH:

But I do! And the more I face them the more I see that your kind of Saviour will never save the world. Not through that sort of Messiah will man's inward spiritual nature find renewal. Above everything else man needs forgiveness. He needs cleansing. He needs the power of a new nature. And I tell you, Abner, all your religious observance can't do it. Baruch, all your moral effort is hopeless. If the human predicament is ever to be resolved, God alone must do it. But just think, Abner, when you talk about sacrifice—what if God should make the sacrifice? Remember, Baruch, when you quote your psalms about the law, what another psalmist says: "If I make my bed in Hell, behold, Thou art there!" If God were in very truth to come and meet us there, the great eternal Maker of us all humbling Himself for our sakes to the lowest depths, nothing could stand against that! It would be the routing of the darkness and the ending of the night. All things would be made new. O come, Redeemer of the race! Come now, O Saviour of the world!

# EPILOGUE

Our journey is over. We have visited Rome, Athens, Jerusalem in the year I B.C. The hopes and fears we have encountered there—are they not just our own hopes and fears today? For still some look to power and government for the saving of the world; and some to knowledge and enlightenment; and some to the self-sufficiency of the morally religious man. But through it all, the human heart, unhealed, stands crying for a better deliverance. And at this holy Christmas season Jesus comes again. He comes—the Desire of all nations. He comes—your everlasting Hope.

> Our glad hosannas, Prince of Peace,
> Thy welcome shall proclaim;
> And heaven's exalted arches ring
> With Thy most honoured Name.

# INDEX

[ 313 ]

[ 314 ]

Loyalty, 21, 50, 52, 87, 129
Loyola, 12
Lucey, Robert E., 108
Lukewarmness, 74
Lust, 25
Luther, Martin, 12, 69, 249

Machiavelli, 227
Machine, 4
Machine Age, 49
Magna Carta, 68
Man, 2, 5, 7, 11, 14, 17, 21, 110, 200,
    240, 248, 261
Marriage, 25, 86, 137
Martindale, C. C., 224
Mary, 94
Mary Magdalene, 93
Marx, Karl, 4, 9, 50
Masefield, John, 94
Master, 23, 93, 94, 95, 128, 149
Master race, 304
Materialism, 10, 25, 110, 113, 216
Material wants, 74
Matthews, Walter Robert, 161
Maturity, 105
Mauthausen, 244
*Mayflower*, 96
McCartney, Albert Joseph, 230
McCracken, Robert James, 19
McDaniel, George, 64
McIntire, Carl, 140
Meaning, 122
Mental health, 67
Mercy, 180
Messiah, 117
Michelangelo, 45, 256
Miller, John Homer, 158
Minds, 116
Minister, 24
Miracle, 293
Misery, 70, 210
Misfortune, 118
Missionary, 176, 273
Modern age, 9
Moffatt, James, 2, 253
Monasticism, 10
Morals, 7, 221, 248
Moral corruption, 11
Moral right, 68
Moral standards, 25
Moral values, 10
Moses, 77, 138, 186, 272, 292
Mother, 55
Motivation, 112
Music, 4, 6
Mussolini, 7
Mystery, 7, 11
Mysticism, 45

Napoleon, 100
National, 200, 206, 215, 294
Nationalism, 7, 12
Nations, 2, 102
Natural law, 114
Nature, 75, 110, 262
Nature, laws of, 52
Nazareth, 9, 11, 75, 128, 271
Negroes, 70, 120
Neighbor, 17
New England, 287
New man, 196
New Orleans, 58
New Testament, 2, 59, 90, 130, 148, 168,
    250, 252, 258
Newton, 45
Nicely, Harold Elliott, 178
Nicodemus, 24, 128
Niemoeller, Martin, 43, 106, 206
Nietzsche, 10, 21
Nightingale, Florence, 3
Nomads, 49
Nominalism, 12
Nuremberg trials, 7

Offense, 23
Old man, 194
Old Testament, 11, 58, 61, 82, 142, 163
One World, 2, 161
Oppression, 22, 90
Oppressors, 52
Optimism, 281
Our Father, 253

Pacifism, 25
Paganism, 169
Pain, 119
Palestine, 23, 47, 80, 81, 201
Parents, 57
Paris, 154
Parliament, 5, 219, 283
Parliament of man, 205
Pascal, Blaise, 40, 248
Passivity, 21
Past, 180
Pasteur, 3, 153
Patience, 21
Paul, St., 7, 21, 35, 48, 62, 84, 88, 117,
    138, 139, 141, 143, 175, 177
Peace, 11, 13, 68, 70, 71, 83, 89, 190, 205,
    213, 226, 230, 232, 233, 234, 274
Péan, Charles, 32
Penn, William, 222
Person of God, 76
Personality, 4, 5, 171
Pessimism, 3, 153, 168, 202
Pestilence, 39
Peter, 71, 72, 76, 95, 100, 107

[ 317 ]